SAP Security and Authorizations

SAP PRESS

SAP PRESS is a joint initiative of SAP and Galileo Press. The know-how offered by SAP specialists combined with the expertise of the publishing house Galileo Press offers the reader expert books in the field. SAP PRESS features first-hand information and expert advice, and provides useful skills for professional decision-making.

SAP PRESS offers a variety of books on technical and business related topics for the SAP user. For further information, please visit our website: *www.sap-press.com*.

S. Karch, L. Heilig, C. Bernhardt, A. Hardt, F. Heidfeld, R. Pfennig
SAP NetWeaver Roadmap
2005, 312 pp., ISBN 1-59229-041-8

A. Koesegi, R. Nerding
SAP Change and Transport Management
2nd edition 2006, 744 pp., ISBN 1-59229-059-0

J. Stumpe, J. Orb
SAP Exchange Infrastructure
2005, 270 pp., ISBN 1-59229-037-X

M. Missbach, P. Gibbels, J. Karnstädt, J. Stelzel, T. Wagenblast
Adaptive Hardware Infrastructures for SAP
2005, 534 pp., ISBN 1-59229-035-3

Mario Linkies, Frank Off

SAP® Security and Authorizations

Galileo Press

Bonn • Boston

ISBN 978-1-59229-062-8
1st edition 2006, 2nd reprint 2008

Contents

4   Requirements   67

5   Security Standards   83

6   Basic Principles of Technical Security   101

Part 2 Security in SAP NetWeaver and Application Security

7 SAP Applications and Technology   123

8 SAP Web Application Server   135

9   SAP ERP Central Component   181

10   mySAP ERP Human Capital Management   223

11   SAP Industry Solutions   237

20 SAP Exchange Infrastructure 375

21 SAP Partner Connectivity Kit 405

29   Mobile Devices   491

The Authors   499

Index   501

Foreword by Prof. Wolfgang Lassmann

The increasing global networking of computers, reach of national and international business processes over the Internet, and complexity of information systems magnify the risk potential of negligent actions or intentional attacks on information systems. Unauthorized, anonymous attackers with an Internet connection can enter remote systems from any location and cause significant material or economic damage.

SAP, Microsoft, and other well-known companies have recently begun initiatives to improve overall IT security, such as "Deutschland sicher im Netz" in Germany and the "SAP Global Security Alliance." These initiatives help both customers and solution providers collaborate on the design and implementation of the simplest possible solutions for the complex world of IT security.

It is the task of academic and research institutions related to IT to highlight the complicated relationships and risks of attacks on system security and to suggest effective solutions for defense against them.

Mario Linkies and Frank Off have skillfully dedicated themselves to this task in this book. As experienced specialists in the area of IT security at the SAP consulting organization, they possess not only valuable and up-to-date practical knowledge, but also the required theoretical background to understand the essential context.

This book provides a manageable introduction to the broad topic of IT security. The authors have succeeded very well in joining externally oriented technological security management (security reporting) with internally oriented business risk management (risk reporting). Integrated solutions, attention to risks, and a holistic approach are all important aspects of IT security.

This book encourages a critical review of the security solutions that companies have used to date and an examination of them in light of new requirements. Step by step, readers move from risk analysis to effective methods of control and, ultimately, to IT security that meets legal requirements.

This book illustrates the relationships among SAP solutions and other IT components with the required communications and security solutions, the overall theme being the global security positioning system (GSPS). The GSPS points out the options available for using a simulation tool to optimize an IT landscape comprised of SAP and other industry solutions.

I am sure that this book makes a significant contribution to important work in the area of security and risk management in the IT industry. The authors are to be thanked for their efforts.

April 2006
Prof. Wolfgang Lassmann
Professor of Business IT and Operations Research
at Martin Luther University, Halle-Wittenberg, Germany

Foreword by Dr. Sachar Paulus

From the vantage point of security management, the central observation of the past few months is that security and compliance are increasingly converging. Until recently, the fulfillment of legal requirements in IT (except in a few industries) was a topic that primarily interested boards of directors, because compliance was limited to supervisory authorities in stock markets and correct accounting. IT security experts paid more attention to infrastructure topics.

Until 2002, the interest groups were split, with accountants and internal auditors on one side, and IT security experts on the other side. The latter dealt with the network security, email systems with firewalls, anti-virus management, and password management; the former dealt with authorization in business applications.

Although both groups have the same objective (everything should take place correctly), each uses a different language. Security experts speak of activities and threats; auditors speak of controls and risks.

The convergence of both areas is due to two factors:

▶ The collapse of Enron and the resulting legal initiative of the Sarbanes-Oxley Act (SOX) have significantly increased the liability for controls in IT systems and specified procedures for dealing with risk. IT security has often taken many of the required steps, but not when necessary to comply with auditors.

▶ The opening of business systems to customers and partners over the Internet became an urgent necessity. All of a sudden, personnel in IT security and auditors had to speak to each other. Such conversations weren't necessary in the past, because auditors looked at the inner workings of a company and IT security experts were responsible for the surroundings. But today there is no more inside and outside. Now, each individual process must be protected properly, and that requires collaboration between those responsible for the infrastructure and those responsible for applications.

At SAP, a global organization with more than 33,000 employees in 60 locations, we now find ourselves at such a juncture. We have a global security organization and a global risk management organization; local units often give both roles to one employee. We have risk reporting, and we have security reporting. Security risks show up in risk reporting, while legal guidelines for security requirements show up in security reporting. Cooperation between both methods and their subsequent integration are always being driven ahead at the technical and process levels. It is only a matter of time before cooperation and integration are implemented organizationally.

Many SAP customers have already taken this step and set up central departments called Security & Controls or Chief Information Security Office. These departments are responsible for the implementation of legal guidelines like SOX, the German data protection law, FDA CFR Part 11, and California Civil Act SB 1386, and for technical, organizational, and personnel activities and controls. The separation of risk management and security solutions is no longer visible in these companies.

Yet despite all the competency on the market, finding concentrated success factors is still rare: practical knowledge about controls for specific technologies, a uniform language, and best practices. Specialists at the interfaces of business and technology are required to bundle this knowledge and then format and spread it methodologically so that proper controls can be effectively implemented throughout the industry. SAP has a special role to play here. SAP is active at the crossroads of business processes and technology more than any other software company. Its objective is to make the most of technological advances in innovative business processes. That's why SAP also has a special responsibility for modeling controls for these new types of business processes:

▶ The solutions offered by SAP must support integrated control options up front and include them as part of the processes. The use of new technology, like service-oriented architecture (SOA) will probably not work with traditional methods and requires integrative solutions and methods.

▶ SAP, its partners, and specialists close to SAP are best able to develop and spread the knowledge required to define proper controls, to establish it at national and international levels in companies, and thus use trustworthy business processes productively.

This book is an important step toward recognizing compliance and security requirements in future architectures and illustrating the required solutions. For the first time, the security aspects of SAP software are examined with regard to compliance and risk; the necessity of such aspects is also evaluated. Above all, the book looks at new SAP solutions that already show the first characteristics of SOA. As the director of the Risk Management & IT Security global focus group of the SAP consulting organizations, to which Dr. Frank Off also belongs, Mario Linkies has the practical experience of bringing SAP solutions to clients around the world—in a manner that conforms to legal requirements—and a sufficient familiarity with new concepts to influence the design of new products based on his experience. Mario Linkies and Frank Off are therefore the ideal authors for this broad subject area.

I hope that this book offers you a good introduction to the topics of risk and control management, compliance, and IT security. I hope it simplifies your work in operating SAP solutions securely and in conformity with legal requirements. Moreover, I hope that you obtain food for thought and ideas from this book, and that you make the right investments in IT security to be able to lower operating costs.

April 2006
Dr. Sachar Paulus
Chief Security Officer
SAP AG

1 Introduction

We live in an insecure world. Markets, finances, company assets, people, work, health, culture, and values: everything seems threatened. Some of these threats are real; others influence many developments in our lives. Security is a basic human need. And that's true in one's personal and professional life. Risks are a part of life. They offer opportunities, but they must remain calculable. That's why transparency is required. There are various ways to minimize risks and reach your required level of security.

The control and reduction of risks will be a primary focus of IT in the coming years. Growing functionality, changing technology, the opening of internal IT systems, and increasing national and international regulations like Sarbanes-Oxley (SOX) and Basel II necessarily produce new requirements for secure processes, systems, and users. Globalization links national and international business partners via B2B, I2I, and B2G scenarios. Employees are equipped to use new and more effective means of communications and applications. Customers and consumers increasingly use the Internet and mobile devices to access information, make reservations, or place orders. Dramatic economic and technological changes are reflected in business and market processes. But these changes are accompanied by new risks that affect, greatly influence, and disturb markets, processes, systems, organizations, employees, partners, and customers. These developments and the interaction of business partners, employees, and customers can be protected only with appropriate security strategies and measures. This book highlights the essential elements of security measures and controls.

1.1 Background

In the last few years, SAP has made a quantum leap. Its offerings of functionality have been expanded, along with its implementation of new technologies, applications, and systems. An essential step in this leap is the move from the previously delimited architecture based on the ABAP/4 programming language to the new SAP NetWeaver architecture with components like SAP Enterprise Portal, SAP Exchange Infrastructure, J2EE, and a mobile infrastructure. On the one hand, the new technologies and enhanced functionalities improve options for integrating partner companies and customers. On the other hand, they require attention to and reduction of the risks that the new developments pose.

The financial collapse of large companies like Enron and the activities of managers and auditing companies at the beginning of the new millennium have profoundly shaken investors' and shareholders' trust in publicly traded companies in particular. These developments led to new laws and the expansion of national controlling standards like the Sarbanes-Oxley Act in the United States for publicly traded companies, and Basel II for the financial industry. The objective of such laws is to establish stronger controls and improved security measures within companies and organizations to protect investors, companies, employees, and consumers. One way to implement the laws for national control, which include fines for the managers responsible, is the use of consistent security of IT-supported processes, business transactions, and financial data extracted from IT security measures.

Furthermore, many of the existing organizations that have implemented SAP products have a large backlog of measures needed to establish effective authorizations and secure, optimized administrative processes. Because practically no methodological standards for authorizations and role structures exist, companies use an almost endless variety of solutions related to technical IT security. Authorization administrators are somewhat overwhelmed, and processes often don't meet actual requirements for secure user administration and management.

This book is based on the international consulting and teaching experience of the authors and their close collaboration with SAP and partner companies in the area of risk and security. It provides an overview of SAP NetWeaver security, in general, and an introduction to the components of a secure implementation of SAP products. The authors do not profess to have written everything about security that you need to know, but they do follow a consulting methodology when describing concepts, problems, procedures, and examples. The information in this book will be beneficial to company management, financial auditors and internal accountants, Sarbanes-Oxley teams, information owners, data protection officers, authorization administrators, leaders of SAP implementation projects, security officers, as well as employees, service providers, and consultants who are interested in security. Readers will get a beginner's guide to evaluating risks, creating control options, security measure design, and the appropriate procedure to set up supporting practices and processes.

The objectives of the book are to contribute to the improved security of existing SAP systems and processes, to help companies include new technologies and enhanced functionality in the consideration of security measures, and to provide assistance in working through legal requirements in the areas of risk and control management. Individual IT security topics may no longer be looked at in isolation. They must be understood as part of a comprehensive, strategic, and continuous whole to establish security throughout a company and thus for business partners and shareholders.

This book is intended to help, provide support, offer new ideas, indicate best-practice solutions, and offer a view into the complex but important world of IT security so that companies are able to meet growing requirements with efficient methods, solutions, and strategies.

1.2 Contents

The following overview highlights the content of each chapter of this book.

Part 1

Chapter 2 gives an overview of risk and control management. It explains terms like company assets, risk and control types, and potential risks, and covers methods like risk analysis and control consulting.

Chapter 3 provides basics on security strategy, proven procedures, implementation project and system audit experiences, new methods and principles, SAP security solutions, solutions from security companies, and examples of best practices.

Chapter 4 covers some important legal regulations and requirements that influence IT security and its characteristics.

Chapter 5 describes the country-specific and international security standards that can serve as guidelines for security projects.

Chapter 6 describes the technical and conceptual basics of security solutions for active inclusion in companywide control measures.

Part 2

Chapter 7 provides a basic introduction to the topic of SAP NetWeaver security. It also provides a map of the *global security positioning system* (GSPS) and helps you navigate through it, explains the basic principles of SAP NetWeaver technology, and discusses proven and new security methods and technologies.

Chapters 8–29 cover the essential components of SAP NetWeaver along with risks and control measures. These chapters explain potential risks based on examples and the concepts of application and system security tailored for individual examples. This section provides an overview based on expert knowledge, without becoming enmeshed in technical details.

1.3 How to Read This Book

This book has a modular structure, which should provide value to experienced and inexperienced readers, project leaders and decision-makers in organizations, internal and external employees, and consultants. This book offers an introduction to IT security and aims to provide a comprehensive overview of the complex world of securing IT-supported processes and connected systems. The chapters build on each other, and most of them follow the same structure.

Explanatory sections and content on the basics, examples, and best-practice methods supplement that material. Best-practice methods are solutions that were used very successfully in the past or that reflect the newest developments in security consulting. They indicate the places where security strategies can be optimized with little effort and quick success.

1.4 Acknowledgements

The authors wrote this book in their free time, that is, in addition to their many responsibilities in national and international consulting and teaching. Therefore, this book would not have been possible without the support they received from their SAP group colleagues, subject-matter experts, security consultants, collaboration with well-known consulting and auditing firms, and the help and encouragement they got from family, friends, and professionals in Germany, South Africa, and Canada. Freda Li (Toronto) created the GSPS map. The authors would like to sincerely thank all of these people for their support.

Part 1
Basic Principles of Risk Management and IT Security

2 Risk and Control Management

Risk and control management is the central means of long-term protection of company assets and establishing the control and security solutions required for it. This chapter covers the components of comprehensive risk and control management.

Risk and control management is a comprehensive set of procedures used to determine company assets, potential risks, and the required control and security solutions. It protects assets and processes in the short and long term and ensures effective and optimal use of funds and resources.

2.1 Security Objectives

Over the past two decades, companies and organizations have standardized their business operations with enterprise resource planning (ERP) software like SAP R/2, SAP R/3, and mySAP ERP. The development from mainframe systems to client/server architecture led to the increasing networking of business processes and systems. Doing business electronically enabled business partners to execute their transactions with new forms of communication like electronic data interchange (EDI).

The invention of the Internet opened new possibilities and requirements. Today, companies no longer have the luxury of executing their business transactions based on traditional forms of commerce and communications. The Internet and the increasingly networked business worlds of intranets and extranets are ever-more rapidly becoming the most important channels for information, sales, procurement, distribution, management, and marketing. And the next new architectures are already being developed: net-centric multi-tier and service-oriented architectures. The opening of company activities and information to transactions and communications over the Internet, networked systems, and point-to-point or multi-point connections, along with the increasing collaboration among organizations, should lead to faster data exchange, increased efficiency, expanded sales opportunities, and capital expansion because of IT-supported systems.

The advantages of networking and collaboration are obvious: aggregated purchasing, lowered labor costs, higher revenues, transparent prices, increased visibility, more rapid market penetration and global expansion, strategic competitive advantages, and increased shareholder value. But these strategic and operating advantages cannot be attained without the required protection of the systems and persons involved.

The new technologies and the rather high level of networking that exists today also bring risk potentials. "New" often means immature, unproven, and insecure. It also means a challenge—the challenge of potential attackers who exploit existing vulnerabilities within companies and the challenge of external attackers who are imminent threats for business processes and technical systems. The potential risks associated with such attackers for the companies involved are multifaceted and primarily financial. The requirements for trouble-free business processes entail general security objectives. These objectives serve as a guideline when determining concrete needs for security, analyzing criteria for implementing security measures, and the measurability of such criteria.

"Security" means a condition of relative rest, not only in terms of the parameters relevant to IT. The adjective "secure" is derived from the Latin "securus" and means "without worry." Security is an apparent constant that must be reached. Mathematically, complete security cannot exist except as a subset of an achievable, imaginary quantity. All the components that contribute to security are therefore incomplete subsets of an unachievable condition of security. That means that although security can be defined as a concrete objective, it can never be completely reached in actual practice.

But how can the existing needs for protection and security among participating business partners be converted into a high level of security in the IT environment? The answer to this question leads to the definition of the term "IT security." IT security describes the need for data, processes, systems, networks, business partners, and employees to be secure. It means that no significant break-ins, interruptions, or losses are occurring or are foreseen. The primary concern here is the protection of company assets and adherence to legal guidelines on regulatory control. The development of objectives relevant to security helps to determine the required influencing variables required to reach IT security.

Important IT security objectives include the following:

▶ The reliability of systems and networks
▶ The availability of business information and data
▶ The confidentiality of commercial actions and data related to specific persons
▶ The integrity of business processes, flows, information, and persons
▶ The binding character of the business activities of partners involved
▶ The adherence to legal and internal company requirements and influencing factors (their legally binding nature)
▶ The accountability of business transactions
▶ The controllability of systems, users, and business actions

- The authenticity of application data and user actions
- The ability to manage IT systems, users, and communications partners
- The flexibility of applications, communications channels, and users

Additional security needs can enhance these core objectives of IT security (see Figure 2.1). Depending on the type of company, IT security objectives can be variously defined and evaluated to enable the company to respond to specific risks and to invest calculably in appropriate measures.

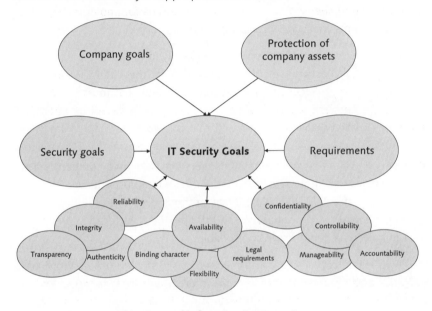

Figure 2.1 IT Security Objectives and Influencing Components

Best-Practice Method: Analysis of Objectives

An analysis of objectives examines company objectives, the relevant information, and the processes most important to a company's success. The analysis determines and then documents general IT security objectives as control objectives for the company or a given organization in a strategy document. The IT security objectives are generally binding guidelines or directives to establish and support a company-specific IT strategy.

2.2 Company Assets

IT security must be established throughout a company to create the necessary trust for all those who participate in processes supported by IT. The protection of company assets and of processes used dynamically within an organization helps ensure the continuity of flows within a company. The measures taken to develop IT security thus lead to providing the supporting IT systems, applications, and employees involved with total protection from active and passive threats.

Table 2.1 lists the components that should be protected in a company environment.

No.	Component
1	Buildings and facilities
2	IT infrastructure with systems, applications, and networks
3	Business and administrative processes
4	Organization and employees
5	Information and data

Table 2.1 Components to Be Protected

Recognizing and evaluating the potential dangers and risks for a company's business process chains that should be protected is one of the most effective means of establishing successful defensive and control methods as security solutions. These actions limit the existing, potential risks and the related risks for the company as a whole can be reduced and made controllable.

Potential risks exist because the components to be protected noted above have vulnerabilities and because of threats from internal and external attackers (see Figure 2.2).

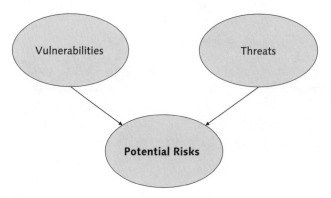

Figure 2.2 Vulnerabilities and Threats

Various types of dangers exist and are a variable risk to the company depending on the individual case. The establishment of countermeasures requires a targeted analysis of a company's technical, organizational, or process-related vulnerabilities and an evaluation of scenarios that simulate an attack by potential attackers. Company assets are the focus of the examination.

2.2.1 Types of Company Assets

Company assets that are affected by IT and are thus threatened and need to be protected can be grouped into physical and informational assets. *Physical assets* like technical servers, networks, lines of communication, mobile end-devices, or computers are concrete assets in a company; they are procured and are investments, and they represent a company's inventory. Influencing factors like procurement price, depreciation, and so on define the loss of these assets. The characteristics of informational assets, on the other hand, often make it more difficult to set an actual value when evaluating the need to protect such assets. In the worst case, the total value of the company is threatened. *Informational assets* include personal data, development and product information, price calculations, a company's reputation, brands, experience, and the knowledge of employees. Company assets are determined, categorized, and evaluated based on the definition of value categories and their assignment to factors like costs, sales volume, and profit margins. Subdividing company assets into types and determining the values of those types are important tasks of establishing the required security solutions in an IT environment. The relevant company assets and parameters must be known in order to determine the potential for risks related to the company assets. Figure 2.3 illustrates this relationship.

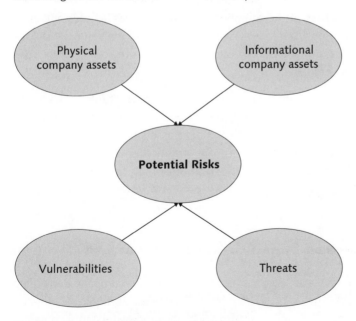

Figure 2.3 Company Assets and Potential Risks

2.2.2 Classification of Company Assets

The protection of company assets is the objective of every IT security solution in use. An organization's need to protect itself from potential threats is called its *protection need*. A protection analysis determines the protection need. The following classification values for company assets apply during the analysis:

▶ The availability of business information, personal data, and systems

▶ The confidentiality of commercial actions and data

▶ The integrity of business processes, flows, information, and persons

Additional classification criteria include:

▶ The binding character of the business activities of the partners involved

▶ The legally binding nature of business processes and adherence to legal requirements

▶ The accountability, controllability, and manageability of IT systems and users

The company assets to be protected are determined based on these and other classification parameters. In IT, the analysis of the protection needs primarily includes the information and data to be protected; the technical infrastructure and other company assets can also be included.

Information is classified according to various levels of confidentiality, such as "secret" or "top secret." In individual cases, the value results from where the information originates from in the company, how the information adds or creates value to the company, how the information is examined in the event of damage (loss, criminal falsification, and so on), and how the information will be used going forward in the company.

In addition, legal considerations play an increasingly important role in the evaluation of company parameters and categories to be protected. The classification parameters given above help classify the company assets that define the protection need. Accordingly, company assets can be classified as *worth protecting* and *not worth protecting*. The company assets worth protecting can be further subdivided into the following levels of protection need: low, normal (medium), high, and extremely high.

Best-Practice Method: Protection Requirements Analysis

The analysis of the protection need evaluates and classifies the various types of company assets. The evaluation primarily depends on a consideration of information worth protecting and its systematic storage, processing, and communication in IT systems, networks, and processes. The analysis sets, classifies, and documents a special value for the company or the related organization in a strategy document. The evaluation of company assets and the resulting protection need is the precondition for a targeted risk analysis that determines the potential dangers and the resulting risk for the company assets.

2.3 Risks

Once the company assets and their parameters have been determined, an analysis of the risks can begin. The determination of risks requires concentrating on the necessary company assets that were identified by the protection requirements analysis to optimize investments in IT security. The risk depends on the potential dangers to the applications involved, the IT systems, the communications channels, the processes and their users, and parameters like the probability of occurrence and the affects of damage. Because appropriate measures can minimize risk, the security solutions for reducing risk are themselves a relevant influencing parameter (see Figure 2.4). The IT security solutions, the potential risks, and the size of the potential risks all influence each other.

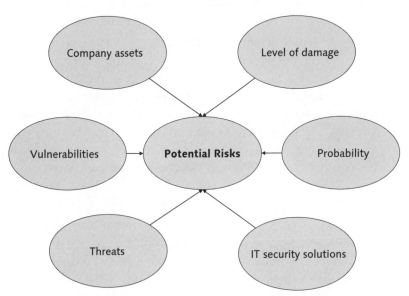

Figure 2.4 Influencing Parameters for Potential Risks

Best-Practice Method: Risk Analysis

Risk analysis summarizes the results of danger and effects analyses. The result is a detailed list of company assets and their protection need; the list serves as preparation for the control analysis. The analysis assigns the risks to areas like IT systems, processes, organization, and so on. The risk analysis examines the data, the information to be processed, process flows, individual process steps, applications, IT systems, and user authorizations for possible risks.

2.3.1 Types of Risks

In IT, risks result from the components of company assets that are worth protecting. Because analyses primarily consider data, IT systems, processes, and employees, risks are subdivided into the following types:

▶ **Risk of loss**
The risk of loss involves a consideration of the potential risks arising from the loss of important information (caused by an operating or application error), personal data ending up with an unauthorized third party (caused by unauthorized user rights in an application in mySAP ERP Human Capital Management), or simply theft of technical devices. Depending on the influencing parameter, risks from loss can involve significant effects such as the loss of reputation, the loss of investments, or unfavorable judicial decisions.

▶ **Process risk**
Process risks result from a potential risk that destroys, interrupts, or causes undesirable changes to internal business processes, administrative processes, or external business transactions. Examples include data changed by unauthorized third parties during its transmission, the failure of administrative processes and supporting technologies to meet the requirements of internal management processes, and the granting of too many user rights without any control. In the worst case, these risks lead to a loss of business partners, interrupted production, and multifaceted reductions of company assets.

▶ **Technical risk**
Technical risks are usually symptoms of vulnerabilities in IT systems. Nonetheless, individual components of the IT architecture can be considered secure. If an analysis of vulnerabilities reveals significant defects, the overall system cannot be seen as secure. Technical risks can occur in individual system components and in transport equipment, storage media, communications channels, or output devices. These risks affect secure data storage, the loss of information, or the continuity of process flows.

▶ **Legal risk**

New legal requirements, especially those involving data protection, financial reporting, accounting practices, or stronger involvement of managers in control processes can result in significant legal risks to companies. Legal obligations and requirements have existed for some time, but some of the new laws involve not only financial, but also personal consequences like imprisonment and liability in serious cases. These legal risks primarily affect the management level of companies, and they are real and therefore pose a great potential risk to the shareholder value of a company and its employees.

▶ **Organizational risk**

Because of their direct effect on employees, partners, and the users of IT applications, organizational risks are extremely important when determining overall risk. Erroneous use of SAP applications due to human error belongs to this type of risk category, as does incorrect maintenance of authorization components like roles or user-specific values. For example, risks include the negative influence exerted on a company's culture or organizational processes, and serious problems like the uncontrolled expansion of authorization in various SAP systems and the use of such authorization by unauthorized users.

All types of risk almost always result in financial losses. A large number of risks clearly indicates the need for an urgent evaluation of necessary IT security and control measures. Because the interaction of technical IT components, processes, and users as a whole can lead to risks, only a comprehensive examination of these risks enables fulfillment of security objectives (see Figure 2.5).

Too many companies trust their instincts and experience, or simply cannot imagine the risk that IT systems and their applications represent—a risk that grows daily. Operating in the dark, however, is no protection from loss and aggressive attackers. In many cases, proper execution of a risk examination saves a company from unnecessary IT security expenses and allows it to focus its investments on the necessary measures required to control and reduce risks.

Best-Practice Method: Danger Analysis

A danger analysis examines the vulnerabilities of and threats to IT systems and architectures, the information worth protecting, and the processes and applications important to the success of the company. The results of the analysis show the vulnerabilities of technical systems, processes, and applications. An examination of the threats posed by internal employees, partner companies, and external attakkers completes the analysis of potential dangers. It also estimates the likelihood of occurrence for individual risks to determine the threat potential.

Figure 2.5 Influencing Factors for Risks

2.3.2 Classification of Risks

As a general rule, the evaluation and classification of a risk results from an examination of the potential level of damage (effect) and the expected likelihood of the occurrence of an attack that causes damage. Risks can be grouped as follows: low risk, normal risk, high risk, and extremely high risk.

The evaluation of risks is critical to determining the protective measures a company must take. The insights gained during the danger analysis are classified according to the influencing factors of probability and effect in the next step. As the amount to be invested in IT control and security measures typically depends on the expected amount of damage, information on the effects of vulnerabilities of and threats to IT is an important source for estimating and making decisions about relevant security measures.

Best-Practice Method: Impact Analysis

The impact analysis details the consequences of an attack, a failure of IT systems, or human error. An examination of the potential risks and the company assets worth protecting leads to a determination of the effects in various areas like technical systems, processes, or applications. The effects that can result from vulnerabilities, threats, or mutual influences are the foundation for the control measures to be defined in the subsequent step. The documentation of the impact analysis becomes part of a risk control matrix.

2.4 Controls

The term "controls" is defined as all measures that protect company assets. This includes the consideration of protection needs, the associated risks, and possible methods of minimizing risk. In IT, control measures are therefore just as important as all the necessary items that result from threats to company assets as a whole. The task of controls is to recognize vulnerabilities early, to inspect the identified vulnerabilities, and to prevent passive and active attacks. Controls also help monitor existing company assets. In the event of damage, controls are used to investigate and explain the matter. The objective of control measures is to lower the probability of damage occurring, minimize the effects, and control the risks that remain.

Because the various analyses described above have defined the necessity for IT security measures, the following sections identify and describe general and concrete controls.

2.4.1 Types of Controls

The determination of controls can be quite comprehensive. Depending on the area of IT security and its relevance to the objective, measures can have a controlling character—the required critical activities, for example—or can have an active influence on existing IT systems and their components, processes, applications, and users. Controls are therefore subdivided into various types:

▶ **Upstream controls**
  Upstream controls help a company avoid and reduce risks. Examples include measures like strong authentication, the separation of user rights in applications, the installation of release steps in business flows, and the encryption of communication channels for the transfer of business data. The objective of this type of control is to capture a potential threat, to remove a weakness, to reduce the potential of risks drastically, and thus to minimize the existing risks.

► Downstream controls

Downstream controls help uncover damage to avoid having the situation become even worse and to avoid further harm to the company. As a rule, this type of control is used to improve existing processes and for an ongoing control of company assets and their protective mechanisms.

Depending on the objectives for specific company assets, controls can be established as technical measures, authorization solutions, or administrative process solutions.

In the SAP environment, controls are subdivided into internal IT security solutions and external solutions from partner or security companies. The solutions of other security companies can complete the security solutions from SAP in various applications and systems.

Best-Practice Method: Control Analysis

A control analysis helps identify possible solutions to define upstream, downstream, and investigative control measures. This procedure lists the possible control options as internal SAP solutions and solutions from other suppliers as part of a risk control matrix, without, however, evaluating specific solutions. The control analysis can contain concrete measures to reduce risks, such as the separation of authorizations and the implementation of release steps in the order process. Various options can be included, which would then require evaluation later.

2.4.2 Classification of Controls

An evaluation of the various solutions is to be performed based on the results of the risk control analysis. Above all, companies should note the evaluation criteria given in Table 2.2.

No.	Evaluation Criterion
1	Functionality
2	Reduction of existing risks
3	Strategic principles
4	Best-practice solution for existing problems
5	Fields of use

Table 2.2 Evaluation Criteria

No.	Evaluation Criterion
6	Adoptability
7	Support from solution suppliers
8	Experience
9	Effort needed to implement
10	Ongoing costs
11	General benefits for the company

Table 2.2 Evaluation Criteria (cont.)

Based on the results of the risk analysis and the prioritization of the existing need for protection, the control list then ranks the recommended controls and IT solutions. The results are entered into the risk control matrix. The matrix is the recommendation for the use of IT security solutions. The following classification can be used to prioritize the recommended control measures: low priority, normal (medium) priority, high priority, and extremely high priority.

The individual analyses are part of the overall risk control analysis (see Figure 2.6) and are summarized in the risk control matrix.

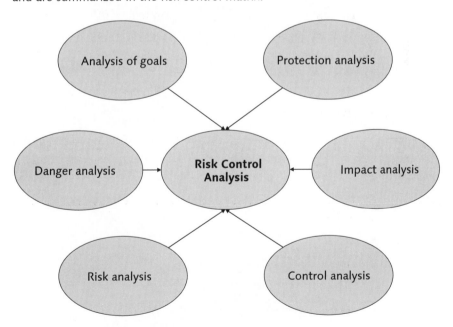

Figure 2.6 Components of the Risk Control Analysis

Best-Practice Method: Risk Control Analysis

The risk control analysis is the superordinate concept for the required individual analyses that are summarized in a risk control matrix as part of the evaluation of company assets, the protection need, and controls. A risk control analysis is performed for various areas and components. It produces a list of the required protective and control measures. The measures are then transferred to a catalog of countermeasures that helps prepare an activity plan and a work plan.

3   Security Strategy

The security strategy is the framework for evaluating a company's need for protection and for determining the controls required to guarantee the required level of security. This chapter describes the components needed to successfully establish a security strategy.

3.1   Status Quo

The mounting globalization and international orientation of business processes have led to a stronger networking of IT landscapes and applications. The portion of work performed with computers is escalating continuously. The degree of networking is rising with the growing integration of business processes and the use of IT. The increased rate of criminal activities in these areas is growing globally at a threatening rate. More and more complex IT structures make it increasingly difficult to determine risk and put into place appropriate security measures. Greater competition among companies, organizations, and countries also puts added pressure on employees and therefore on users of IT applications. The result is users are making a larger number of errors.

Traditional business life must adapt to new developments that are emerging in the age of e-business. In a traditional view, the decision-making criteria includes *return on investment* (ROI), *return on equity* (ROE), *return on assets* (ROA), and *mergers and acquisitions*. Electronic business life includes criteria that reach further, such as market capitalization, productivity, turnover times, alliances, shared markets and customers, customer management, retention, and profitability. No one sleeps on the Internet; online orders can be triggered around the clock. The following trends express the rapid developments in electronic business:

▶ The Internet revolutionizes sales and product management.

▶ Economic models change constantly. Firms experience a transformation into enterprises with a global reach.

▶ The speed of economic developments and business activities increases.

▶ The customer is once again the focus of business activities and information flows.

▶ Companies reevaluate their role in the value chain.

▶ Competition becomes more intense.

▶ Knowledge and experience become evermore important as strategic components.

▶ Threats to company assets grow.

Based on these insights, IT security as a strategic control measure for long-term protection of company assets becomes increasingly important. Accordingly, the topic of IT security has experienced a renaissance in the last few years. IT security was long considered a necessary evil, but the situation has changed in many ways since the mid-1990s. Companies and organizations are increasingly anxious to protect their investments with appropriate security measures. This development established important elements of IT security. In the course of this development, SAP contributed to IT security by equipping the components of its systems and applications with control options and the required IT security and by providing corresponding interfaces for external solutions.

But many of these solutions are insular and are not considered within the overall landscape of systems, applications, networks, user rights, and legal requirements. Although companies pay attention to technical security measures by using firewalls, encryption mechanisms, or authentication solutions, they are guilty of ignoring things like authorization systems. Although some companies have made significant investments to develop an orderly authorization concept for their SAP systems, they lack or do not follow the administrative processes needed to remain at that level. Because many companies try to establish individual security measures without examining their own risks, a great deal of catch-up is needed for the level of security that has been reached and for the use of investments in this area—despite the progress that has been made.

The interaction of individual areas in a company and its employees is another critical area. IT security requires the involvement of most, if not all business areas, and a large number of decision-makers, managers, providers of information, and others who must contribute to the successful implementation of a security strategy. The coordination of these areas and this information is truly a difficult task. Accordingly, it must be planned, executed, and controlled as much as possible with clear and standardized procedures.

In addition, ignorance and bad advice only make the road to a comprehensive security strategy with objective-oriented solutions more difficult.

However, SAP, suppliers of security solutions, and consulting firms have increased their efforts to develop comprehensive security solutions for individual problems and strategic security consulting. Comprehensive experience improves the security solutions and the related consulting services for SAP customers.

IT security has now reached a point where companies and organizations actively seek solutions. Individual solutions have been preferred so far, but the trend in security is moving toward the much-needed overall solutions.

3.2   Components

The IT security strategy includes all the activities and solutions that lead to an improved security situation in the company and to establishing trustworthy business connections. Particularly in the SAP environment, the multiplicity of systems, applications, and users and the related emphasis require you to regard these tasks as important criteria for a company's long-term success. Security is not only a means to reduce risks, but also a way to build a foundation of trust for business partners. Without appropriate control measures, no business can succeed in the long term. Because security without a strategic concept leads only to insufficient results, a methodical procedure is needed. A transparent security strategy captures all areas worth protecting, including SAP systems and networks, data and applications, organizational structure and users, external business partners, and administrative and business processes. Only a comprehensive examination of risks and control options in all areas touched by IT helps companies to establish an IT security strategy that truly offers them the required standard of security.

The IT or SAP security strategy described here is part of the company's overall security strategy, which is discussed below.

Figure 3.1 shows the general components that lead to the building of an SAP security strategy: general framework, strategy, methods, and best practices.

Figure 3.1 Security Strategy—Components and Objectives

3.2.1 General Framework

The general framework must be known before a security strategy can be set up. The general framework includes requirements that affect the security strategy. Such requirements include internal and legal requirements, the number and types of IT systems and applications, the functional scope for authorizations, the number of users in individual systems, the technical architecture with communication channels, the type of information to be processed, and other indicators. The identification of the general framework is important for targeted planning of individual security components. Such identification primarily uses technical architecture, documentation of business processes, legal determinations, and general instructions from internal security guidelines, inspection reports, and similar items.

Best-Practice Method: Requirements Analysis

All requirements are mapped out in a requirements analysis and summarized in a requirements catalog. The requirements catalog is a component of the strategy document for SAP risk management and IT security, which should be the written foundation for the company's security strategy. This includes, for example, requirements that result from the *Sarbanes-Oxley Act* (SOX: see Section 4.1.1), data protection, internal auditing, the IT department, or the employee representatives.

Example

▶ Legal determinations: data protection law, Basel II, and SOX

▶ Internal requirements: internal auditing reports

▶ Guidelines: internal security guidelines

▶ Processes: documentation on existing processes for authorization and user management

3.2.2 Strategy

The strategy is a central component of the (overall) security strategy and covers all the required characteristics needed to build a strategy document. The strategy helps describe the scope and reach of the studies and planned activities, the general concepts to be considered, the required documentation, and administrative processes. The strategy is part of the overall document that describes the security strategy and serves as a template for planned activities, documentation, the description of administrative processes, and a decision-making aid when planning the use of security and control measures in IT, in general, and in the SAP environment in particular.

Best-Practice Method: Strategy Concept

The strategy concept is part of the security strategy and is also described in a strategy document for risk management and IT security in the SAP environment.

Example

▶ Scope and reach: functional scope, technical scope, geographical scope, and timing

▶ Concepts: SAP authorization concept and standard SAP solutions in the area of technical security

▶ Documentation: strategy document for risk management and IT security; risk control matrix

▶ Processes: documentation on authorization and user management

3.2.3   Methods

Methods describe the procedures, required activities and individual steps, suggestions for possible solutions, and examples for working out and implementing a security strategy in an enterprise environment. The required components result from the general requirements described in the requirements catalog. A methodological procedure should be a basic condition for the use of security measures, to make investments optimal and to attain the highest possible levels of use and therefore benefit.

Best-Practice Method: Method Concept

The method concept is an important component of the security strategy and is also described in the strategy document for risk management and IT security. It introduces the procedure models, the advantages and disadvantages of options for strategic solutions, and plans.

Example

▶ Procedure: phases like planning, design, and implementation

▶ Staffing: identification of project team members

▶ Options for solutions: SAP solution for single sign-on (SSO); other security solutions for SSO

▶ Planning: work plan with individual activities and milestones

3.2.4 Best Practices

Best practices involve a company's requirement to establish the best solutions in the area of security. Best practices are proven solutions that have been tested and used successfully in other locations and companies—nationally and internationally. They are also new technologies, innovative principles, or improvements for individual solutions. The introduction of these solutions as part of the security strategy and their evaluation by the participating project members, directors, and decision-makers is important for making long-term, correct decisions when selecting IT security solutions and for their strategic consequences. Appropriate advice from experienced consultants covers the introduction of best practices.

Best-Practice Method: Best-Practice Analysis

As a necessary component of the IT security strategy, the best-practice analysis helps determine the evaluation benchmarks for solutions in the area of IT security. The analysis addresses concepts and solutions, describes functionalities and benefits, and shows advantages and disadvantages—it thus helps those responsible to evaluate the items and make a decision.

Example

▶ Principles: phased procedures, the principle of information ownership, and change management

▶ Trustworthy transactions: PKI

▶ Communications security: SSL

▶ Authentication: digital certificates

▶ Methods: BSI manual on basic protection

3.2.5   Documentation

Two basic rules are advisable for a simple documentation of the security strategy and its components:

▶ The number of documents should be minimized.

▶ The documents should contain all the necessary information.

The necessary information includes the requirements and an explanation of the requirements, the protection needed for company assets, a consideration of the risks and the control objectives and control measures, the design of the security components, and a description of the administrative security and monitoring processes. The documentation should include the security policy of the entire company, general and specific guidelines, laws and internal rules to be followed, forms, and technical descriptions that are important for decision-makers, information owners, the IT department, the security team, and all users.

3.3   Best Practices of an SAP Security Strategy

The necessity of security measures and continuous monitoring and improvement of the processes and measures arises from the requirements that exist in every company and organization. Individual measures, as a rule, lead only to temporary or limited security. Therefore, the topic of IT security should always be looked at as a whole. All dimensions of security—technology, applications, processes, organizational structure, users, and partners—must be examined and protected accordingly.

The following sections describe best practices that are important for an SAP security strategy.

3.3.1   Procedure

The procedure or methodology used in establishing a security strategy in the SAP environment is one of the first strategic decisions that a company must make when determining its security risks. The company must see what previous documentation is available, when security solutions must be established, if it needs to perform a risk control analysis, and so on. The estimated degree of overall protection needed and a focus on a security area affect the components of the security strategy. The correct procedure is of vital importance for the success of security measures and for the protection of such investments.

Targeted and comprehensive development of a security strategy requires the components illustrated in Figure 3.2, which are described in more detail below.

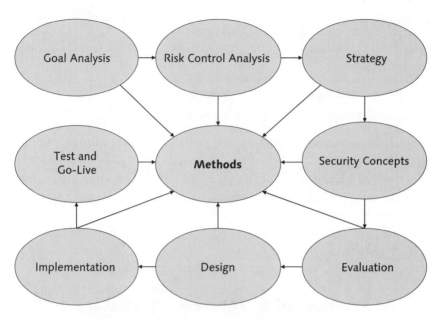

Figure 3.2 Methodology to Implement a Security Strategy

Objective Analysis in the SAP Environment

A objective analysis defines important control objectives and general rules. In the SAP environment, the technical security of the SAP systems involved, authorization in individual applications, and adherence to legal requirements play a special role in this context. Control objectives—such as reliable SAP systems and related networks, the guaranteed availability of information and systems, and improved confidentiality of transactions and data—are important indicators and must be taken into account when you define security objectives and the procedures necessary for attaining these objectives. The sources of information include the requirements catalog and the protection requirements analysis.

> **Example**
>
> ▶ The requirements catalog contains important information on legal requirements like SOX and its relevance to the company.
>
> ▶ Protection requirements analysis (see Figure 3.3)

Goal Analysis				Protection Needs Analysis					
No.	Description	Type	SAP System/ Application	Confidentiality*	Integrity*	Availability*	Evaluation*	Estimated percentage share in overall revenues	Approximate quantitative financial equivalent
1	Confidential product information containing formula details	Corporate knowledge	SAP BI	H	H	H	H	20%	238,000.00 USD
2	Compliance with SOX requirements	Legal Regulations	all	H	H	H	H	90%	1,100,000.00 USD

* (L = low, N = normal, H = high, E = extremely high)

Figure 3.3 Protection Requirements Analysis

Risk Control Analysis in the SAP Environment

The risk control analysis helps identify risks in the areas of SAP technology, applications, organization, and legal requirements. For example, it classifies transactions according to their risk evaluation. Risky transactions and combinations of transactions with a high or extremely high risk factor are labeled as such and given control measures. The risk control analysis is one of the basic components of a successful security strategy. It examines risks in terms of data and information, business processes, applications and functionalities in the SAP applications, SAP systems, organizational structures, and authorizations (see Figure 3.4).

Figure 3.4 Scope of a Risk Control Analysis

A risk control analysis is performed in four steps: danger analysis, impact analysis, risk analysis, and control analysis. The evaluation of the risks leads to concrete control and security measures (see Figure 3.5).

Goal Analysis Area			Danger Analysis		Impact Analysis	Risk Analysis				Control Analysis	Recommended Evaluations							Recomm. Priority		Activity Planning
No.	Area	Subarea	Vulnerability	Threat	Effect	Potential damage *	Probability **	Overall risk factor	Qualitative financial equivalent according to probability	Control measure	Implementation costs	Financial equivalent implementation costs	Implementation speed	Simplicity of administration	Efficiency of the solution	User-friendliness	Degree of compliance with business priorities	Priority calculation	Priority of security recommendation	Planning steps
1	Technology	Web server	No encrypted SSL connection is established.	Information can be viewed and modified without authorization.	The production process can be viewed and adopted by a competitor. A decisive competitive advantage would be lost.	H	H	H	X	SSL encryption of communication channels	L	X	H	L	H	H	H	H	H	Development of the solution, evaluation, pilot test
2	Processes	HCM	Each user has authorizations to display tables using Transaction SE16. Tables are not restricted in any way.	Personal data can be viewed.	Violation of the data protection law. Loss of reputation. Damage for the affected person. Legal consequences for the company due to action by injured party.	H	H	H	X	Revision of authorizations for tables in the role concept.	L	X	L	H	L	H	H	H	H	Development of authorization solution, evaluation, decision and role design

* (L = low, N = normal, H = high, E = extremely high)   ** (L = 2%, N = 15%, H = 25%, E = 40%, Basis: 24h)

Figure 3.5 Risk Control Analysis

Strategy

The strategy determines the components of the security strategy. In the SAP environment, it's best to avoid using many different documents in your security strategy. One document can contain all the strategic descriptions, important remarks on protection needs and options for solutions, and so on. This strategy document can then be consulted as needed. It serves as the basis for all conceptual statements, such as security and control objectives, requirements, and naming of security components to guarantee a uniform procedure in the entire company. Various departments that handle different tasks within the overall security process can use the strategy document as a template for developments, processes, and activities. The following section provides a sample strategy document.

Example: Contents of a Strategy Document

- ▶ Background and Objectives
- ▶ Scope and Reach
  - ▷ Functional scope for application security
  - ▷ Functional scope for IT security
  - ▷ Technical scope for IT security
  - ▷ Geographical scope
  - ▷ Organizational scope
  - ▷ Scope of risk examination
  - ▷ Timing
- ▶ Requirements and Protection Needs
  - ▷ Legal requirements (SOX, Basel II, GoBS, and KontrAG)
  - ▷ Data protection regulations
  - ▷ Industry-specific requirements
  - ▷ Internal requirements
- ▶ Risk control matrix
- ▶ General SAP concepts
  - ▷ Identity management
  - ▷ IT security for SAP systems
  - ▷ Authorizations in SAP applications
  - ▷ Corporate governance

- ▶ Best Practices
  - ▷ Technology solutions with functional description, advantages and disadvantages, and recommendations
  - ▷ Principles
- ▶ Evaluation Criteria and Evaluations
- ▶ Decision Sheet
- ▶ Design
  - ▷ Technical design
  - ▷ Authorization design
- ▶ Targets for Conversion and Implementation
- ▶ Administrative Processes
  - ▷ Identity management
  - ▷ Authorization management
  - ▷ Security management
  - ▷ Monitoring and reporting
  - ▷ Internal auditing
- ▶ Appendix
  - ▷ Work planning with short-, medium-, and long-term tasks
  - ▷ Example for evaluations
  - ▷ Role and authorization documentation
  - ▷ Technical representation of SAP systems (architecture)

Security Concepts

Security concepts can be derived from the security solutions taken from the risk control matrix, as described in the following steps. The description helps companies prepare for and make decisions.

Examples of security concepts in the SAP environment include authorization concepts for SAP applications, remarks on various options regarding SSO, and the presentation of best-practice methods and principles to follow legal regulations in IT. Security concepts are later enhanced with technical guidelines and instructions to guarantee comprehensive and correct administration.

In all security phases (see Figure 3.6), security concepts must be known to all responsible parties: information owners, those responsible for IT, security managers, administrators, and so on. The security phases described here or similar phases can also be seen as best-practice methods.

- ▶ **Planning phase**
  Planning activities to establish comprehensive security measures in a company

- ▶ **Analysis phase**
  Recording the requirements and evaluating the security needs in a company

- ▶ **Design phase**
  Designing security and control measures

- ▶ **Implementation phase**
  Implementing security and control measures

- ▶ **Production phase**
  Using the security and control measures in the company in a productive environment

- ▶ **Continuity phase**
  Ensuring a smooth flow of control measures and monitoring the measures

- ▶ **Improvement phase**
  Continuously checking the relevance of control measures, improving the measures, and adjusting the measures as needed

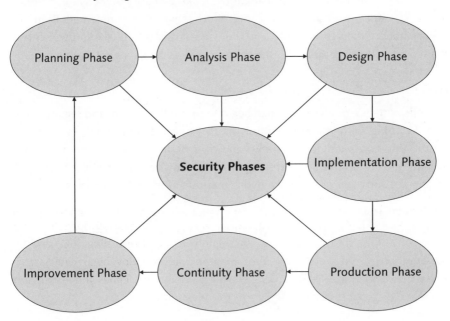

Figure 3.6 Security Phases

Evaluation

Security measures must be evaluated to guarantee long-term and correct decisions on the protection of company assets. Decisions are made easier when the security concept clearly works out the advantages and disadvantages of individual solutions. Evaluation is important work. It's not reserved for technical consultants and experts from the IT department. It must be performed and guaranteed by the information owners in the individual departments, data protection managers, internal auditors, members of the SOX compliance team, and SAP project managers.

The topic of security, with all its influencing factors, pertains to almost every area of a company. That's why an evaluation requires the inclusion of these areas in decision-making. The advantage here is that many departments can participate in the decision-making process. However, it can often make the decision-making process itself tedious and less efficient, which in the end leads to compromised solutions.

That's why from the very beginning an SAP security team should be formed— a team that unites people from all important areas and lets them participate in strategic discussions under the direction of subject-matter experts and corporate consultants. Ultimately, the company must make a decision by paying attention to the efficiency, the functionality, the effort required for implementation and administration, the sustainability, and the benefits and potential improvements of the security solution along with the support offered by its manufacturer.

Design

The following design phase can then begin to set up the control and security measures. Starting with the risk control matrix, authorization concepts, technical security solutions, and administrative and control processes are worked out and included in the SAP security strategy. Apart from the risk control analysis, the design demands one of the most involved efforts in the whole process.

The design must also be accepted and released by the information owners involved. Implementation of the security design can begin afterwards.

Implementation

During implementation, it is very important that the individual departments are involved to ensure that the principle of information ownership is carried out consistently throughout the company.

A thorough test phase in the context of the implementation of authorizations is required. Authorization components like roles, user groups, functionality, and business processes should be examined in the context of positive and negative authorization tests and integration tests in terms of their ability to function and for errors. Positive authorization tests involve comprehensive tests of all the transactions associated with a role. Negative authorization tests help spot-check functional assignments and their positive mapping in authorization components. The objective of authorization tests is the exclusive testing of the ability of authorization components to work. They are the basis for further use of authorization components in integration tests and user rights. Integration tests, however, test functions and business flows within and among SAP applications. The byproduct of integration tests is a check of the ability of the authorization components to function. However, the disadvantage of these tests is that they don't test all authorizations. Individual tests are needed when special functions are to be tested or after normal administrative authorization changes for individual authorizations.

For technical security solutions like SSO, encryption mechanisms, the use of digital certificates, or biometric authentication, pilot tests are usually performed—usually for acceptance of the solution. Pilot tests also involve positive, negative, and integration tests (see Figure 3.7).

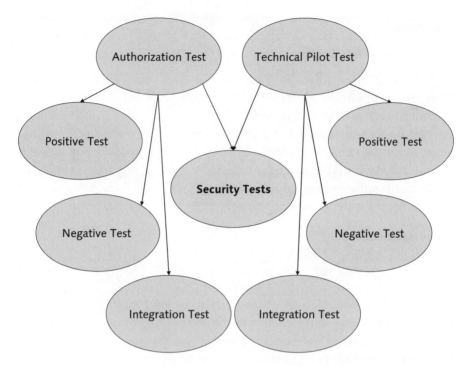

Figure 3.7 Security Tests

Note that concrete test scenarios are worked out for each security test so that the success of concrete tests is repeatable and measurable.

3.3.2 Principle of Information Ownership

Over the years, in the area of authorizations, SAP has created a number of solutions that implement authorization components and general requirements flexibly. Consider the *SAP Profile Generator*. It helps users work with roles according to groups of transactions and the related menu structures in any form. mySAP ERP HCM uses structural profiles. Users of SAP BW define their own authorization objects. The use of only a few transactions in SAP industry offerings must be limited.

Because of the high level of flexibility of these tools, their design is rather technical and complex. Therefore, after an initial and often complex design and implementation phase, only the IT department can manage these authorizations. The department has the technical knowledge to do so, but is often overwhelmed when it comes to evaluating the risks and the authorizations being requested. Authorization checks on transactions are simply taken as is, without asking those responsible if it is really necessary to accept them because of the risks involved, the organizational structure, or internal or legal requirements. A consideration of risk for business processes and technical components is often avoided or the quality does not deal with the reality.

For many companies, a lack of knowledge creates several problems with the design of authorizations and administration. The number of authorization concepts and solutions is almost infinite. Consequently, a variety of strategies and concepts—even within an industry or within the company itself—can be produced. Either too many or too few authorizations are granted. The level of security and the administrative processes linked to it are designed unsatisfactorily or less than optimally in many companies. Transparency into the assignment of authorizations, the design, and the administration and the ability for control are often lacking.

Why is there such a lack of transparency into the assignment of authorizations? One reason is not understanding or recognizing the real risks inherent in designing and granting authorizations. Many authorization systems are just too complex: the types and number of roles and authorization components, the inner structure, and the naming conventions often make sense to technical administrators, but not to those responsible for the specific areas. Comprehensive, standard authorizations are created because SAP must handle a number of optional requirements that are reflected in functionality and the scope of activity. The number of authorization checks often creates very comprehensive authorization systems; administration of the systems provides only little transparency and serves only limited security needs. Authorization administrators must only rely on expert input from those responsible for roles or processes in user departments—and these people do not speak the technical language of IT administrators. Important decisions are only rarely handled as such, because it's impossible to go into the details of comprehensive checks. Integrated solutions that handle the authorization side along with risk and control options are lacking. No reproducible and meticulous rules process exists. Vulnerabilities are often discovered only later on. The cost of ineffective management is very high in the long run. A lack of control leads to less security, significant risks, mounting frustration among participants due to many errors being made, the result of which can be a company's failure to comply with legal requirements and auditors' demands. Figure 3.8 illustrates this vicious circle of vulnerabilities.

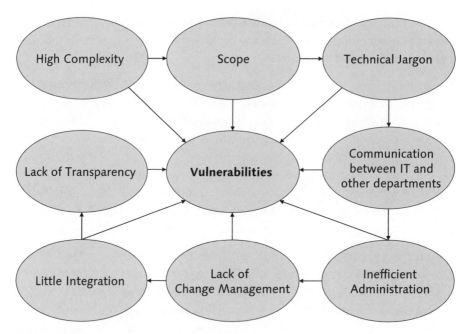

Figure 3.8 Vulnerabilities of Authorization Solutions

The protection of intellectual and material property is becoming more and more important. Continuous provision of business processes and efficient administration are basic elements of secure economic life. These elements affect the profitability of companies and organizations at a fundamental level. That's why a proactive limitation of damage is becoming increasingly important. With legal frameworks like SOX and Basel II (see Sections 4.1.1 and 4.1.2), legislatures have forced companies to take topics like application security, reporting, change management, and internal controls seriously and dedicate themselves to this task of self-protection. That's why there's an urgent need for standardized simplifications, for the establishment of transparency in authorization processes, and for a consideration of the potential risks as an integrated component of the authorization and control structure.

Authorization components must be created simply and transparently based on the required functionality, the existing risks, and the control objectives. Administrative processes need a general overhaul.

Security is related to responsibility. In normal cases, authorization administrators understand one or two specialized applications—if they have enough experience. But it often happens that specific requirements simply cannot be implemented. No check is usually performed, but if it is, it is performed later on by auditors. This situation leads to permanent procrastination with problems and risks. In a serious case, it can lead to significant losses. Figure 3.9 shows the required, but often disordered, communication channels between individual owners of information and the areas responsible.

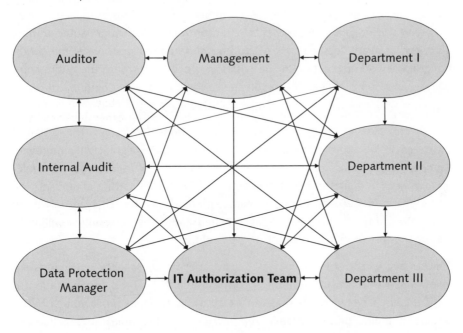

Figure 3.9 Traditional Structure Without Clear Information Ownership

The components of application security must be considered as a whole. And this approach requires a new qualitative and conceptual leap that supports these requirements.

The assignment of authorization in SAP systems directs access to functionalities, transactions, and information for the users of SAP applications. Expert business and organizational decisions are needed to materialize user rights to SAP systems, applications, information, transactions, activities, and reports. IT can support this process, but it cannot initiate it or assume full responsibility for it. That responsibility must remain with the owners of information in the individual departments: those responsible for processes and areas, owners of roles, and those responsible for functions. Only they are in a position to make expert judgments in their areas, to estimate and evaluate risks, to identify the required control options, to define the controls, and to exhibit responsibility for these decisions. That responsibility must flow into the departments, where it is needed and where the experience and knowledge lie. Fundamental and efficient decisions are crucial to the ongoing success of a company.

The responsibility—with or without legal effects—can and must be taken. An increased number of complex structures, the growing functionality of SAP applications, and increased legal requirements for the minimization of risks, for a greater transparency, and for the control of business decisions produce the need to involve the individual departments in the control of information, authorization, and users relevant to security. SAP authorization administrators set the conditional framework and establish the basics of process control in the entire company. Each responsible person creates the content.

With the right information, processes, and authorizations, users can now manage and control access to their own business applications themselves. The design of the processes becomes more secure and data protection is significantly improved. Comprehensive transparency, integrated control, and efficiency can be implemented with this method. But the aspect of corporate culture should not be underestimated. Security and best-practice methods can be achieved only if the corporate culture is oriented in that direction and if the company is willing to accept and provide active support for new solutions.

The novelty in this approach is that tasks relevant to security and consistent involvement of risk evaluation and controls move from IT-led administration to the company's departments that can execute the activities much, much better because of their expert knowledge. A transparent and plausible authorization system supports the tasks of internal and external auditing, which lowers the effort involved for all participants. Management must understand this fundamental change to authorization management, accept it, and support its implementation and daily use. Only then can profound success and a stable level of security be achieved. The overview in Figure 3.10 shows the distribution of responsibility to information owners in a uniform and communicative control system.

The principle of information ownership is a best-practice method and can be initiated and implemented successfully in a company only as an integrated strategy with the required support of management and technology. The ownership of information and authorizations can be established only with a combination of SAP software (for example SAP MIC, SAP AIS, the authorization information system, and check-ID) and external authorization solutions like SecurInfo for SAP.

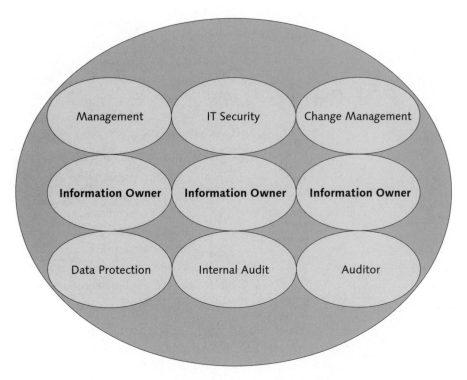

Figure 3.10 Distribution of Responsibilities and Integrative Management Based on Information Ownership

3.3.3 Identity Management

Starting Point

As users of applications, the beneficiaries of data, and employees, users of SAP systems play a central role in internal company processes. They hold responsibilities, maintain operations, and control the security of the established procedures. Employees secure the protection of company assets. Accordingly, employees themselves become an object worth protecting within the process of IT security. In this context, one speaks of *identities*.

These days, the design of administrative processes for identity and authorization management is still too complex, involves too much effort, and is inefficient. The processes are thus a considerable cost factor that do not really guarantee security and cannot reduce the existing risks as required. The results include inconsistencies, a small amount of transparency, and users with inappropriate, incorrect, or too much authorization (see Figure 3.11).

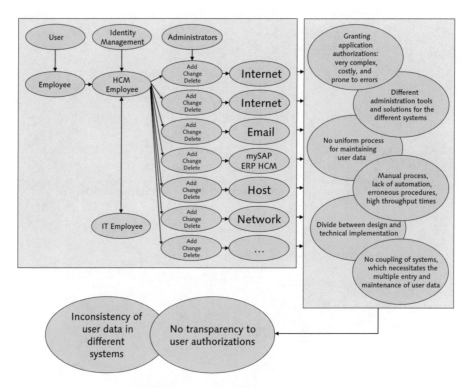

Figure 3.11 Starting Point for Identity Management

In many cases, increased complexity and costs result from the drastic increase in the number of identities and authorizations. Users have too many authorizations because identity management does not permit real-time processing. Employees who have long since left the company still have access to various systems within the organization. The security requirements lead to the need to establish a uniform solution for the management of identities. Control helps improve internal administrative processes related to employees and users of systems. It also helps protect against external attacks by inimical identities that can destabilize internal company processes. If identities and system access are unprotected, even the best authorization systems can't provide help; all company assets are in danger.

Objectives and Influencing Factors

The main problem is the decentralized management of identities and their related rights for all types of systems and applications. A central identity management system used throughout the entire organization exists only in the most unusual cases. The objective can only be a holistic consideration of the weaknesses, the individuals coming into question as identities, and the systems being managed along with the related processes (see Figure 3.12).

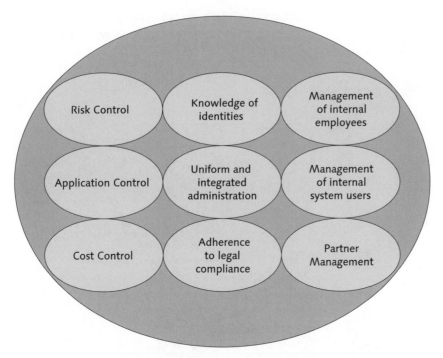

Figure 3.12 Requirements and Objectives of an Integrated, Central Identity Management

That comprehensive objective includes the following preliminary objectives:

▶ A reduction of risks and increase in security in the company

▶ Uniform knowledge, transparency, and management of identities throughout the entire company (avoiding multiple identities for an employee, for example)

▶ A reduction of effort and administrative costs

▶ Effective management of external partners with and without access to systems and applications

▶ Adherence to legal requirements like SOX, Basel II, or data protection laws by controlled management of all identities, assigned rights to data, and functional access. Examples include personal data such as an employee's medical information, which might be stored centrally or in a distributed manner.

The most important factors that affect identity management (see also Figure 3.13) include:

▶ The technology that tackles authentication. It creates control options for authorization and must therefore take over the management of identities.

▶ The accompanying processes that regulate administration, operation, monitoring, and exceptions.

▶ The organization. Its structure must map identities as positions, jobs, and external partners. It must also manage the required assignments and authorizations and distribute responsibilities.

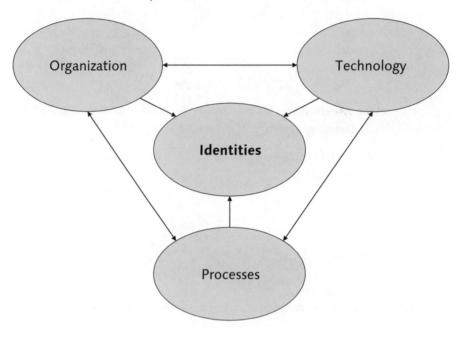

Figure 3.13 Determining Factors for Identity Management

Solution

Companies must decide on a leading identity management system (*User Persistence Store*, UPS) for a more centralized design of management, building upon standards and rules, clearing out the sources of errors, and using best-practice solutions. Several alternatives exist and, like the processes to be managed, they seek to distribute tasks in the future according to organizational, functional, legal, and internal company requirements. Technology supports the various solutions at different levels and therefore directly affects the selection of an identity management solution.

User and employee data must be stored, managed, distributed, controlled, called, and archived. Users need authorizations for applications, email, Internet access, or their own desktop computers. These activities must be coordinated uniformly to meet the growing requirements. Section 8.3 concretely names some cases for user management.

The roles of the administrative units like human resources, the IT help desk, the heads of departments, the IT department, and other responsible persons must be unambiguously defined and assigned. They must also be mapped consistently by the system and technologically. Who should be responsible for creating new users? How are passwords changed and by whom? Who releases user rights? What supporting technology and which security solution have been selected? These questions must be answered ahead of time to secure the required investments in the correct identity management methods and the sustainability of the investments in these control measures.

Best-Practice Method: Involving the Organizational Structure and Identifying a Leading Identity Management System

Take a look at the following two scenarios (see Figures 3.14 and 3.15): each provides an alternate solution.

The solution in Figure 3.14 provides decentralized management and involves various CUA (central user administration) systems, an LDAP directory service, and the HCM organizational structure. It manages various types of identities like internal employees, internal and external users, users with an internal status, and additional types of users. The participating identity management systems manage various groups of identities. Synchronization and process control make the solution up to date, even if it is not the optimum alternative for many companies.

The second alternative (see Figure 3.15) provides a simpler and more manageable solution. Identities are completely managed in a metadirectory (directory service) and distributed to the various systems. However, this efficient and objective-oriented solution assumes cleansed datasets, uniform rules on procedures or naming conventions, clarity with regard to the technical implementation, and distribution of the tasks involved in identity management. To use this solution, a company must overcome existing sovereign rights for functional claims and historical areas of responsibility—without affecting harmonious operations and creating new potentials for risks.

Identity management by itself won't help much, but as part of a general IT security strategy, it can contribute to the overall success of establishing efficient and comprehensive control measures for IT security.

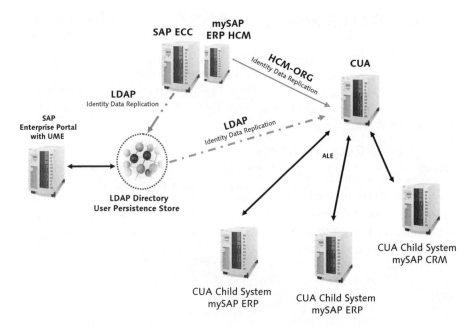

Figure 3.14 Identity Management with HCM-ORG and LDAP

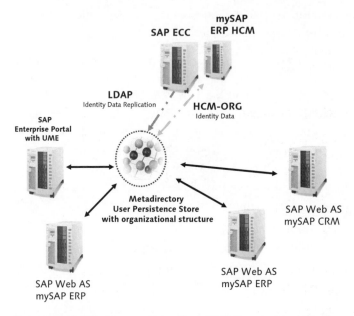

Figure 3.15 Identity Management with an HCM Organizational Structure and Metadirectory Service

4 Requirements

An efficient internal control system can be set up only on the basis of concrete requirements. This chapter explains the various requirements with examples.

4.1 Legal Requirements

Investments in secure and efficient control and security solutions result from the required needs for protection in an organization and from those of partner companies, shareholders, and other private and corporate individuals. Persons, information, transactions, and systems are the objects of protective activities. Regulatory institutions and associations recognize the needs and support them with legal instruments like laws, directives, and guidelines. The support of SAP and Microsoft for initiatives like "Deutschland sicher im Netz" ("Secure Germany on the web") in Germany and the foundation of the "Global Security Alliance" by SAP Consulting help many companies and foster awareness of the topic of security.

However, legal requirements demand that corporations respond and take action to improve the security of business transactions and investments, and this action is worthwhile for a variety of reasons. The rules established by directives or laws involve industry-specific, national, and international regulations.

> **Best-Practice Method: Requirements Analysis**
>
> The requirements analysis outlines all the important requirements for the correct choice of methods and solutions to protect company assets and the choice of investments for IT security. It summarizes the requirements in a requirements catalog. The requirements catalog is also a component of a strategy document for SAP risk management and IT security; it is supplemented by a compliance analysis for legal requirements.

This chapter cannot treat all national and international laws—such a treatment is too broad for its scope. The following sections describe some important laws to provide an introduction to the current legal situation with examples.

4.1.1 Sarbanes-Oxley Act

One of the most important laws affecting IT security is the *Sarbanes-Oxley Act* (SOX). SOX is a legal set of rules primarily directed toward companies traded on the New York Stock Exchange or NASDAQ in the United States. The law affects both American and foreign companies. Because it is a national law, SOX has direct and indirect international effects. SOX regulations affect both publicly traded organizations and auditing firms.

SOX arose in the United States as a result of stock-market financial scandals in 2002. The law was written by Paul S. Sarbanes (a senator from the Democratic Party) and Michael Oxley (a representative from the Republican Party). The objective of the law is to improve corporate reporting and to reestablish shareholder trust in the correctness of financial data published by companies. The central topic of the law is the successful establishment of organizational structures within companies to guarantee the correctness and reliability of annual reports and to contribute to greater transparency in financial processes.

A positive effect of SOX is that organizations must deal with the topic and establish solutions for appropriate control measures in their companies according to the relevant requirements. This situation finally gives IT security some long-overdue attention. Overall, SOX helps companies develop a uniform consideration of processes, IT solutions, and control measures to create fundamental and continuous improvement of accounting methods, organizational management, and internal control systems. IT security plays a central role in this task. The implementation of improved standards in financial processes alone is insufficient to achieve the required process security.

In the past, missing internal controls and immature leadership qualities on the part of management have led to a series of spectacular scandals (i.e., Enron) ultimately caused by insufficient control processes in the company involved. The consequences were dire: Although many stockholders were left alone with the damages, the managers responsible were made accountable.

For many companies and organizations, SOX is one of the most important legal directives—and rightly so. Although companies like Enron, Anderson, or Parmalat shook their industries and financial markets, there is now a legal foundation of direct consequences for managers, including several years in prison. The most recent example is the CEO of MCI WorldCom, who was sentenced to several years in prison for corruption and abusing his position. The effects on business and capital markets are much more important. The intertwining of companies, the increasingly international economy, investors, and company employees experience this kind of shock at a global level. SOX helps protect a company's own needs and those of participating partners.

The American *Securities and Exchange Commission* (SEC) and the *Public Company Accounting Oversight Board* (PCAOB) handle enforcement of SOX. The SEC can investigate and issue sanctions. The role of auditors becomes more important; they are monitored by the PCAOB. Audits of publicly traded companies are the responsibility of the PCAOB. SOX went into effect on July 30, 2002. Most auditing and IT consulting firms have already developed a great deal of expert knowledge surrounding SOX and work actively with SAP clients on individual solutions.

Contents of SOX

SOX regulations require the members of a company's board of directors and financial board to explicitly confirm the correctness of annual reports and the ability of *publicity control systems* to function. That means that processes relevant to finances, and all other processes that affect finances and operations, along with their utilities (like IT) are to be controlled and designed transparently and securely. Evaluating accounting activities and their controlled involvement in business flows is an important component of the compliance process. Another equally important aspect of SOX is the total protection of data, processes, IT, and applications, because they have a direct or indirect influence on the financial success or failure of a company.

SOX includes the following:

▶ Rules regarding transparent and proper *corporate governance* and liability for insider trading

▶ Expanded requirements for the disclosure of closing statements, such as annual reports, and the related upper management confirmation requirement (with the use of Form 20F)

▶ Regulations regarding the creation of a supervisory agency for auditors (PCAOB)

▶ Introduction of a notification requirement for when companies become aware of internal damage like embezzlement or comparable crimes

▶ A notification requirement for when the financial or operative situation of a company changes

▶ New regulations on the responsibilities of managers of publicly traded companies and the introduction of auditing committees at the level of the board of directors

- ▶ The threat of significant penalties for not fulfilling the notification requirements noted above for the persons responsible and for attempted deception and obstruction, such as the destruction of electronic data as evidence (Section 802/1102 of SOX)
- ▶ The related duty to set up an internal control system and monitor the system continuously to guarantee compliance by company management to eliminate recognized risks and vulnerabilities in the long term (Section 404 of SOX)
- ▶ Rules for the independence of auditors and increased penalties for them
- ▶ A requirement regarding a company's regular disclosure of risks and vulnerabilities
- ▶ Real-time implications (Section 409 of SOX)

Section 404 of SOX requires the definition, documentation, and creation of appropriate control procedures for company transactions to minimize the risk of erroneous information, misinterpretations, incorrect balances, and so on. Because these control measures have comprehensive effects on corporate governance, concrete requirements result, especially for IT security.

Effects of SOX on IT Security

Sections 302, 404, and 409 of SOX are particularly important in regards to IT security.

The requirements of Section 302 of SOX regulate a company's responsibilities. This section makes the chair of the board of directors and the director of the finance department responsible for the correctness of quarterly and annual reports. Their signatures confirm that the documents contain no untrue statements and that they faithfully represent the financial situation and the net operating profit. The signatories declare that they are responsible for the setup and maintenance of internal control systems, and that conclusions about the effectiveness of control measures have been derived from the most recent evaluation. The chair of the board of directors and the director of the finance department further confirm that they have informed the auditors and auditing committee about any important deficits and irregularities ahead of time. If the report nonetheless contains something other than the truth, fines can be assigned and the CEO and CFO can be made personally liable.

Section 404 requires management to create an appropriate, internal control structure and to set up transparent processes for creating financial reports. The effectiveness of the internal controls and measures must be assessed at the end of every fiscal year. The auditors confirm the correctness of the report.

Section 409 regulates the necessity of continuous control measures that the company must monitor without limits and in real time.

Violations of the requirements of SOX are met with severe consequences that can include a delisting of the once publicly listed company and serious prison sentences. The expanded responsibilities of company management consistently lead to required measures in the area of IT security:

▶ Acceptance of the requirements of SOX

▶ Translating the requirements into a catalog of countermeasures that's based on concrete national conditions and conditions in the company

▶ Identification of risks in the company that can lead to violations of SOX requirements

▶ Establishment of control measures including monitoring processes, evaluation criteria, information rules, and protection of the ongoing performance of all measures as a whole

Because responsibility lies at the level of company management, it can be exercised only by a distribution of the control processes throughout the entire company. It's not simply a matter of identifying and presenting risks, but of establishing efficient protective measures and controls that will significantly contribute to the elimination, minimization and monitoring of those identified risks. To secure the protection of information, transactions, and financial data, a strategy that covers all operations must be established. This generally involves the setup of an SOX team that includes employees from the financial department and the auditing department, and persons with responsibilities in the areas of data protection, IT security, authorization administration, and process operations. Because the requirements of SOX demand significant investments in the company, experienced auditors, risk consultants, and SAP security experts should have a role in the development of the solution.

Most problems occur because of everyday use of systems by company employees. Accordingly, IT security measures become a necessity. Some common problems are:

▶ The *relevance of critical data* or the risk group to which the data belongs is often unknown. That's why data remains unprotected. And this applies to business transactions, financial data, and personal data.

▶ *Functional separations of tasks* have been implemented insufficiently in the SAP systems. This situation results in users with authorizations that reach far beyond their normal activities. It often happens that the most comprehensive

SAP_ALL and SAP_NEW profile authorizations are given to administrators. In many cases, even the administrators are not subject to further monitoring.

▶ The *documentation of processes, risks, and controls* is either missing or only partially available, has omissions and errors, and is no longer up to date. As a result, the documentation does not correspond to the SAP system configuration and procedures. Verifiabilty therefore does not exist.

▶ Risks are not identified or are *inadequately identified*. Internal controls are hardly ever tuned and are often the task of overwhelmed IT departments.

▶ Authorization systems do not meet the *necessary requirements*. Changes to user authorizations are frequently carried out by simply adding more information to the profiles. Development employees often have complete authorizations (SAP_ALL).

▶ *Management of users* is incomplete. Experience shows that at least 20% of user master records are no longer up to date (problems arise with temporary, external, and former employees and consultants).

▶ There is no integrated system with risk, control, and change management dedicated to the *management of users and authorizations*.

Although the problems listed represent only a sample, it's easy to see how comprehensive the changes in most companies must be to reach full compliance with SOX requirements. The measures developed for SOX in the area of IT security include the following activities:

▶ Recognition and analysis of vulnerabilities and their relevance to SOX

▶ Internal company analysis of internal controls

▶ Evaluation of data, processes, and systems relevant to SOX and their need for protection

▶ Evaluation of risks relevant to SOX within SAP applications

▶ Assignment of internal control objectives to SOX requirements

▶ Addressing the relevant differences between the actual state and the target objectives for SOX compliance

▶ Definition of a process to implement SOX requirements on schedule

▶ Definition of user authorizations for data, transactions, and systems with segregation of responsibilities

▶ Selection of methods and tools for IT security that provide conceptual, methodological, and technological support

- Introduction of principles for the integration of decision-makers to distribute responsibilities better—according to the principle of information ownership, for example
- Reallocation of administrative processes like authorization management and user management
- The use of SOX as a driver for additional critical IT security measures that directly or indirectly affect the ability to comply with SOX
- Setup of an effective change management system—to provide controlled management of users and authorizations, for example
- Definition of monitoring and quality assurance processes to ensure the continuity and integrity of internal and business flows

SOX therefore supports the general demand for more transparency and security of financial and commercial transactions and business processes. Responsibilities now lie within the direct responsibilities of upper management. Internal control structures and procedures that maintain these responsibilities must be continuously analyzed in terms of their efficiency and usability to recognize vulnerabilities up front and remove them before damage results.

SOX also directly affects user authorizations and identity management. Given SOX, whistle-blowing measures are no longer sufficient. For example, the assignment of authorizations gives users of SAP applications access rights to critical data, business transactions, confidential data, and personal information. Since wrongdoing can come from a lack of knowledge or a deliberate act, the assignment of correct authorizations protects users and the company itself and helps a company comply with SOX requirements. SAP systems and applications are needed to perform all types of activities related to business processes. Every day, SAP users execute thousands of transactions and combinations of transactions. As a logical consequence, risks that result from executing functions and function calls in SAP applications should be determined and avoided ahead of time.

The measures must generally conform to the establishment of comprehensive change management to guarantee the maintenance and continuity of the defined and implemented measures. Effective change management improves the ability to control and the security of processes and systems.

The control measures must also lead to more transparency in all business areas. Accordingly, consistent implementation of the principle of information ownership is an important element. In most cases, the IT department still handles the concerns of and controls users: Central security administrators traditionally handle the administration of authorizations and users. This approach records the requirements of the various business units and processes them according to the administrators' best knowledge and intentions. But central management of security and control systems is usually not transparent for those responsible for processes. In the past, oftentimes risks were not considered or were considered inadequately. The result is decisions based on estimates, and this type of situation leaves too much leeway. The administrating processes thus develop in such a way that the administrators simply record and execute requirements of the individual departments. When push comes to shove, no one is responsible.

Best-Practice Method: Information Ownership

The principle of information ownership resolves the conflict described above. The owners of information are now responsible for it. Decision-makers are selected by organizational and content-related aspects. Areas of responsibility are assigned and responsibility for data, processes, systems, and users is distributed. For example, each department creates authorizations, assigns them to users, and controls everything transparently. The IT department provides supporting tasks.

The traditional *black box* of IT is no longer used. All administrative processes are designed more efficiently, erroneous estimates that arise from a lack of knowledge are avoided, and overall risk and operating costs are lowered. Responsibility is distributed to the persons responsible for the processes, data, or departments, because they are best able to evaluate the information to be processed and the relevant risks. Management now enjoys the advantage of increased transparency of information being processed, because it would otherwise be unable to confirm the correctness of the information with a signature. The concept of information ownership also corresponds to the requirement to establish an appropriate internal control system. IT security is increased because those responsible in each user department assign access rights themselves. They can assess the process and risks that arise from overly broad user rights better than a global administrator. As a result, they will grant users only the access rights that they truly require.

Best-Practice Method: Monitoring and Reporting

The use of standardized monitoring and analysis tools like the SAP Audit Information System (AIS), SAP Management of Internal Controls (MIC), Security Audit Logs (SAL), SAP Compliance Calibrator by Virsa Systems (CCV), and other measures round out the required complete solutions. Note that the effectiveness of the control measures must be continually monitored and real events identified.

Without IT-based solutions, you cannot meet the SOX requirements sufficiently. Various manufacturers have made a place for themselves in the market, including SecurInfo. These suppliers' offerings, combined in various ways with SAP solutions, form good comprehensive packages. Here it's a matter of looking closely at the functionalities of the individual solutions and matching them with the requirements and the needs of an individual company. Recognition and monitoring of risks is not the key to long-term success. Rather, the key involves consistent redesign of incorrect processes, risk-related access rights, and creating a comprehensive catalog of measures to meet the requirements of SOX and to guarantee the security of a company's activities.

Best-Practice Method: Integrated, Holistic Solutions

SOX demands the setup of new processes, control methods, and technologies. The more integrated and coherent the strategy and the sought-after solution are, the more successful the implementation of the measures in the company.

The significance of SOX for IT security is also highlighted in a current study of the *Computer Security Institute* (CSI) and the *Federal Bureau of Investigation* (FBI). According to the study, 8 of the 14 companies surveyed think that SOX has increased the importance of IT security (see Figure 4.1).

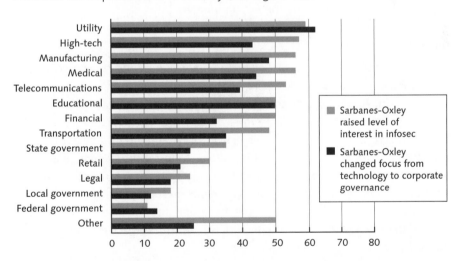

Figure 4.1 Influence of SOX on IT Security (Source: SOX)

The SOX demand for adequate control structures for operative risk management within publicly traded companies will force improvement of international legal standards and rules, and thus improve IT security in general. The benefits of a company's investments depend upon the procedures, the solutions in place, and the stability of those solutions.

4.1.2 Basel II

Operative risk and control management is also the central topic of Basel II. The granting of loans by financial and banking institutions (like the Schneider and Deutsche Bank case in the 1990s) can involve many irregularities. The evaluation of risks in the financial sector is one of the most important economic activities of financial institutions. Worldwide liberalization of financial markets has also increased the risk involved in every type of financial transaction. That's why special supervisory rules for banks and financial institutions were created to promote and control the granting of loans and careful handling of all types of financial transactions. The Basel Committee on Bank Supervision works to ensure that financial markets remain as stable as possible.

The Committee has existed since the mid-1970s and is supported by the regulatory financial agencies and central banks of the most important industrial countries. The decisions of the Basel Committee have no legal force in and of themselves, however, legal guidelines of individual states and the European Union can make them law. In Germany, for example, the legal basis for Basel II is the *Banking Act* (KWG in its German abbreviation). By the end of 2006, companies must implement the rules issued by the Act on June 26, 2004.

Content of Basel II

Basel II consists of three pillars: *minimum capital requirements*, *supervisory review*, and *market discipline*. Basel II requires that a creditor has its own capital reserves for each loan. According to this requirement, risks are to be valued higher than they were before, and individual errors or incorrect estimates by participating companies are to be avoided. The objectives of Basel II are to reduce the risk of bank insolvencies with appropriate regulations, to foster the stability of and ability to schedule investments, and thus to provide more secure incentives for economic development. The security of investments must be guaranteed for borrowers and creditors. If a borrower goes bankrupt, the financial institution that granted the loan loses all or part of the money. If such cases accumulate, the creditor will soon develop its own liquidity problem.

To limit this risk, the credit-granting banks even today must reserve a specific amount of their own capital as security against the credit risk. Basel I set the rule in 1992. Basel I defined fixed rates of capital for an institution's own capital reserves. Basel II was intended to make the fixed rules set by Basel I more flexible (see Figure 4.2). Basel II includes two important innovations: the capital requirement according to a risk analysis, along with scoring and rating. Capital requirements are not fixed, but based on the ability of the borrower to pay and the risk that the bank customer cannot repay the loan. Scoring and rating is used to evaluate the risk of individual customers. Financially weak clients must pay a higher rate of interest in the future for their loans. A creditor has to reserve less financial means for a borrower with good creditworthiness. Credit is therefore less expensive for these clients.

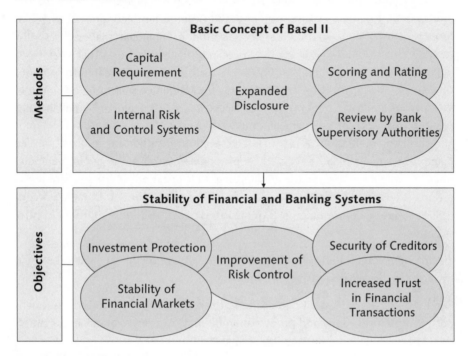

Figure 4.2 Objectives and Methods of Basel II

Supervisory agencies are to see to the continuous improvement of internal risk and control procedures at financial institutions. Now more than ever, internal bank procedures and processes that evaluate internal and economic risks are the standard of evaluation.

Expanded disclosure promotes more transparency in the financial processes of business and supervisory partners. The objective is for banks and financial institutions to increase the amount of information available to partners, the responsibility of upper management, and the effectiveness of risk and control systems.

In Germany, for example, the legal requirements of KWG (§ 25a) and of Basel II are realized with the help of the *Minimum requirements for risk management* (MaRisk in its German abbreviation). MaRisk is an initiative of the German

Bundesbank and the German Financial Supervisory Authority. It contains requirements for the setup of a proper business organization and the introduction of internal control procedures to establish uniform standards along with appropriate and comprehensive risk and control structures in financial institutions.

Effects of Basel II on IT Security

To ensure the security and solidity of national and global financial institutions, the internal (and therefore IT-supported) control systems and management of banks, financial supervision, and transparency are held in higher regard. But capital reserves alone cannot guarantee the security and solidity of a bank. Qualitatively improved risk management and review by bank supervisory authorities are also decisive criteria for meeting the objectives. The implementation of Basel II therefore has a significant influence on the IT security of participating organizations. Adequate risk and control management is achieved with the support of IT systems and the implementation of processes. Protection of important information like data on borrowers is to be secured. Appropriate controls are to avoid manipulations that affect scoring and the credit rating. Authorizations to the relevant applications, along with the correct evaluation of the risk factor and the related controls can thus be appropriate parts of measures to set up a proper internal control structure.

Electronic payment methods must also continue to be secure to ensure the security and functionality of cashless payments.

Basel II demands consistent penetration of risk and control procedures throughout financial institutions and promotes an internal awareness of risk and market-oriented examination and handling of financial transactions.

Best-Practice Method: Integrated, Holistic Solutions

Only the combination of efficient IT systems, internal and external control measures, and managerial awareness can guarantee a reduction in the number of incorrect processes, risk-related access rights, organizational shortcomings, opportunities for manipulation, and incorrect estimates and behavior. Integrated, holistic solutions are therefore of primary importance.

In the SAP environment, solutions like SAP MIC and SAP AIS help establish internal control and monitoring methods. Other solutions can be integrated to enhance and complete these solutions.

4.1.3 GoBS

The *Principles for IT-Supported Accounting Systems* (GoBS in its German abbreviation) is another set of legal rules in Germany and is part of the general fiscal law of the (German) Federal Ministry of Finance. The GoBS provides the regulations for electronic accounting. Regulations include requirements of IT-based accounting systems and rules for their implementation, use, and documentation. The GoBS is a continuation of the *Principles for Accounting* (GoB). Storage media for data and requirements for proper, IT-supported accounting in companies are regulated.The GoBS provides the regulations for electronic accounting. The GoBS is binding and, despite its scope, it is a minimum requirement for companies and organizations with SAP systems.

Content of the GoBS

The GoBS consists of the following content:

▶ **Responsibility**
The person responsible for compliance with the GoBS is the person responsible for accounting.

▶ **Documentation**
The IT systems in use must be able to reproduce all business transactions that are subject to accounting. Such reproduction requires document, journal, and account functions. The document function helps create proof of the business transactions and their financial mapping in the related IT systems. Quantity and time references are just as important as entering the name of the authorized accountant. The journal function serves as a log. Entries must be complete and factually and chronologically correct; legal periods of retention must be taken into account. IT-supported systems must fulfill the document and journal functions with their internal document and archiving processes; verifiability must be guaranteed at all times. The documentation of IT-supported systems must reflect reality and be able to prove that it does.

▶ **Data security**
All data—especially confidential and risk-related data—must be protected with appropriate authorization systems for applications and systems. Authorization for the relevant systems and applications help protect data and transactions. Data and transactions are to be protected from loss, unauthorized disclosure, and change; they must be stored according to legal requirements. Data must be stored according to a schema and controlled at regular intervals. For example, tables and master data are to be secured.

► **Creation and storage of postings**

Access to individual business events and transactions must be possible at all times, and the applications and data for processing must be stored. Plausibility checks and controls are just as important as logging. Follow-up changes to transactions must be documented and traceable.

► **Internal control system (ICS)**

Implementation of an internal control system with established IT-supported and manual controls is mandatory. Best-practice solutions such as *segregation of duties* (SoD) help create a clear separation of functions and responsibilities— even in terms of data and transactions in applications and systems. Control measures must be documented and technically implemented in systems. Specifications for programming, the system landscape, and the use of text systems must exist.

Please see the original text of the GoBS for regulations on the reproduction of documents on storage media, the verifiability of IT-supported accounting, and other instructions.

Effects of the GoBS on IT Security

The GoBS regulates accounting requirements and processes in IT-supported systems in terms of the legality of the accounting transactions, documentation and verifiability, data security, and process control. Accordingly, only an integrated and comprehensive solution can realize the requirements that result from the GoBS for the relevant companies.

SAP applications have numerous solutions to fulfill the requirements of the GoBS, including table logging, archiving, process control, and authorization systems. These solutions must be coupled with related internal flow and control measures to guarantee the integrity and security of accounting processes and data. The separation of functions and their assignment with technical authorizations to transactions and data, the establishment of release processes, and the setup of archiving and external control cycles are all measures covered by standard products from SAP.

Best-Practice Method: Integrated, Holistic Solutions

The GoBS also demands integrative flow and control structures. Risks must be evaluated and requirements must be recorded and implemented in measures. Supplementing standard SAP products with additional security components like archiving systems leads to competent solutions in this area.

4.2 Internal Requirements

Internal requirements for IT security result from influencing factors like the type of company, industry and branch, organizational structure, legal environment, geographical distribution, and the related needs for protection and the risks. The required IT-supported division of labor in a modern company must be accompanied by the appropriate separation of functions, realized as authorizations granted to individual employees.

> **Best-Practice Method: Segregation of Duties (SoD)**
>
> The separation of functions and transactions should allow users of SAP systems to assign authorizations as minimally as possible without withholding from employees the authorizations they need to accomplish their daily work.

In principle, decision-making must focus on risks and legal requirements. Organizational and subjective, historical consideration often plays too great a role, which leads to very complex authorization systems. For example, different authorization components might be developed for user groups with the same functional requirements of SAP software, but without logical or legal reasons for doing so. The administrative costs for such authorization structures can be enormous. Legal requirements and concrete conditions within a company must be adjusted to each other to avoid risk and administrative effort, and thus optimize costs.

A company's experience with SAP systems, the level of training among employees, and the depth of the use of the systems play an important role during the definition of internal requirements for IT security. Evaluation of the required separation of duties should involve those responsible for authorizations in individual user departments, IT security personnel, data protection officers, and internal auditors to define company-specific requirements and use the technology available to translate them into SAP terminology. For example, transactional separations, organizational distribution, and temporary authorizations are important tools in the context of protecting data, establishing process controls, and producing secure reports. However, companies must also ensure that the users of SAP applications have the user rights they need to guarantee the continuity of business flows.

> **Best-Practice Method: Four Eyes Principle**
>
> The Four Eyes Principle is used when critical activities are divided by content and are to be executed by various persons so that the business processes and

related transactions function correctly. The release of purchase orders is a good example.

- ▶ In many countries, the protection of personal data is a legal requirement. In any case, it is the responsibility of all companies to handle personal data carefully and to secure it according to its use in IT-supported SAP systems.

- ▶ Monitoring and reporting are also important internal requirements. Each department has different requirements because of differing functional content and legal conditions. The differences must be identified and documented in the requirements catalog.

- ▶ It's just as important to document business and administrative processes, responsibilities, change-management documents, reporting cycles, and measures for security control and administration reasons as it is for legal and auditing reasons.

- ▶ The authorization system should mirror authorizations based on the identified risks and the related control measures. Persons who leave the employ of a company or external employees may not have access authorization. All SAP systems enable temporal limits for user master data.

4.3 Summary

Legal and internal requirements serve as signposts for the correct choice of IT security measures in an SAP environment. Each company must develop individual procedures and solutions in terms of laws and industry-specific regulations in order to invest appropriately in its future and guarantee its endurance and effectiveness. Internal requirements for security systems and measures should always be defined upon the basis of necessity, especially risks and legal requirements.

Best-Practice Method: Avoidance

To meet all requirements, companies should not only implement methods and solutions to monitor and report on critical activities, but also reduce risk in general with active avoidance measures. Compliance is attained with knowledge and control of requirements and risks. A comprehensive risk management system tuned to the entire company and defined on the basis of legal and internal requirements is the foundation for compliance. Ensuring adherence to these measures and their timeliness is part of the administrative activities of a risk control system that meets the requirements of a company's departments, including the IT department, and also fosters responsibilities.

5   Security Standards

Legal requirements, especially SOX, do not define direct security requirements in the texts of the respective laws. But the requirements should be especially oriented toward security standards so that companies can comply with the requirements. This chapter briefly covers the most important security standards for SOX (ISO 17799, CoBIT, and COSO) and for national standards.

Security standards like *ISO 17799*, *CoBIT*, and *COSO*, the American standard of the National Institute of Standardization (NIST), *Special Publications*, and the German standard, *IT Baseline Protection* of the Federal Office for Information Security (BSI in its German abbreviation) form a risk management and IT security framework to enable companies to meet legal requirements (see Section 4.1). In particular, the requirements of SOX explicitly directed toward the integrity of financial data can be met, if the company establishes an *information security management system* (ISMS) according to ISO 17799. The implementation of standards offers companies an opportunity to make even more future-proof investments for risk management and IT security. This book introduces the most important security standards because they should also be used in an SAP environment. It does so not in terms of special, technical implementation, but in terms of the fundamentals of security defined for management, organization, and processes.

5.1   International Security Standards

The following sections describe the most important international security standards. In addition to ISO 17799, CoBIT, and COSO, which are covered here, *ISO 15408 Common Criteria* also exist. However, they focus on the inspection of detailed, technical security techniques and are therefore inappropriate for establishing an organizational and management-oriented framework. But note that the basic statements of the standards are similar. They often differ only in methodological definition and focus.

5.1.1   International Security Standard ISO 17799

International security standard ISO 17799 was originally developed by the *British Standards Institution* (BSI: the same abbreviation as the German Federal Office for Information Security) and published as a British standard as *BS 7799 Part 1* and *BS 7799 Part 2*[1]. The British standard was published as an international standard in 2000.

---

1 Replaced by the ISO 27001 standard.

Part 1 describes guidelines with 127 standard controls for the management of information security. Part 2 defines specifications for establishing an ISMS within a company.

Part 2 also presents a reference model for setting up an ISMS. Accordingly, companies should consider it as the first step before they simply implement control elements from Part 1 without having previously considered the risks. An ISMS defines the management framework, including the required processes and organization, which is necessary to maintain information security in the company. The following basic principle should be used:

> The organization must create and maintain a documented management system for information security. The task of the system is to deal with the protection of assets, the organization's procedures for risk management, the security objectives and measures, and the required level of guarantee of security. (ISO 17799 Part 2[2])

An ISMS must be set up according to four steps, which continually repeat. The first step is planning, the second step is implementation, the third step is continuous improvement, and the fourth step is inspection. The following tasks are completed in the first step, planning:

1. The information security policy of the company or organization is to be defined and put into effect by management.

2. The area of usage of the ISMS is to be determined. The limits of the organization are to be defined in terms of its characteristics, locations, assets, and technology.

3. An appropriate risk analysis is to be performed. The risk analysis must identify the threats to the assets, the weaknesses, and the effects on the company and determine the level of risk.

4. The risk areas to be managed are to be identified based upon the company's security policy and the required level of guarantee of security.

5. Appropriate security objectives and controls are to be selected for implementation from the 127 standard controls in ISO 17799 Part 1 or supplemented with a company's own objectives and standards. The selection is to be justified.

6. A declaration of usability is to be created. The selected security objectives and controls and the basis for their selection are to be documented in the declaration of usability. The declaration must also contain a record of any exclusion of the controls given in ISO 17799 Part 1.

After the planning step, the selected controls must be anchored in the implementation step. The implemented controls must be documented accordingly. This

---

2 Replaced by the ISO 27001 standard.

book cannot cover all 127 standard controls described in ISO 17799 Part 1, but it does list the most important headings:

▶ **Security policy**
Guidelines for the company's risk management and IT security. Management must define a clear direction in the information security policy and show support and involvement by publishing and adhering to the policy throughout the company.

▶ **Organizational security**
For the administration of risk management and IT security, a framework must be defined to enable the company to reach the security objectives that have been defined. Under the leadership of management, appropriate management forums must be set up to approve the information security policy, distribute roles in security, and coordinate the implementation of security throughout the organization. If needed, an expert help desk for information security should be set up and made available within the organization. Contact with external security experts must be established to keep up with industry trends, monitor standards and methods of evaluation, and create appropriate contact points to handle security issues. An international procedure for information security should be promoted by the cooperation and collaboration of managers, users, system administrators, application designers, auditors, and security personnel, for example. The procedure should also involve experts from areas like insurance and risk management.

▶ **Classification and control of information assets**
Accountability must exist for all information assets. Therefore, persons must be assigned responsibility for them. This ensures that appropriate protection for the company assests is maintained. The same persons who are assigned responsibility for all important company assets should also be responsible for maintaining the approriate security measures. Responsibility for implementing measures can be delegated, however, accountability should remain with the persons responsible for the company assets. This important principle is that of *information ownership*, which plays a critical role in the SAP context, in particular, because very important company assets are processed there.

▶ **Personnel security**
Personal backgrounds must be checked during the hiring process. Applicants should undergo an appropriate background check, especially in terms of confidential tasks (see Section 4.1.2). All users of IT devices—in other words, all employees, including those of external companies—should sign a confidentiality agreement.

► **Physical and environmental security**

Processing devices for important or confidential business data must be located in secure zones protected by a defined security perimeter that must have appropriate security barriers and access controls. They should be physically protected from unauthorized access, damage, and interruption. The protection is to be appropriate to the level of risk that has been determined. It's a good idea to implement a policy for cleaning desks and locking screens to reduce the risk of unauthorized access or damage to paper documents, data storage media, and IT devices.

► **Management of communication and operation**

Responsibilities and procedures for administration and operation of all IT devices should be implemented. That includes the creation of appropriate operating instructions and notification procedures for incidents. A division of duties must be implemented to reduce the risk of inadvertent or intended misuse of the system.

► **Access control**

Access to information and business processes with a business application (like an SAP system) should be controlled on the basis of business and security requirements. Existing guidelines for IT and access control must be considered here. The guidelines must be documented appropriately in an authorization concept. The assignment of access rights must follow the guidelines exactly.

► **System development and maintenance**

These areas include infrastructure, business applications, and in-house developments. The design and implementation of the application that supports this business process determine the level of security that the process can achieve. Security requirements should be identified and agreed upon before developing business applications. All security requirements, including the need for backup plans, must be determined, agreed upon, and documented in the requirements phase of a project.

► **Management of continuing business operations**

A process for the management of continuing business operations must be implemented to reduce downtime to an acceptable minimum in the event of a catastrophe or security failure. The need can arise from natural disasters, accidents, device failure, or intentional damage. The process includes a combination of preventive and restoring controls. The results of catastrophes, security failures, and the loss of business applications must be analyzed. Emergency plans must be developed and implemented to ensure that business processes can be reestablished in the required time. The plans must be secured and practiced so that they become an integral part of all other management processes. The management of continuing business operations also includes measures to identify and reduce risks, to limit the effects of incidents that can produce damage, and to guarantee that basic processes can be quickly resumed.

▶ **Compliance with legal requirements**
Avoiding breaking any criminal or civil laws; legal, regulatory, or contractual obligations; and all security requirements. The development, operation, use, and management of information systems can be subject to legal, regulatory, and contractual security requirements. Such requirements must be met to avoid fines.

After it has been implemented, the ISMS must enjoy ongoing development and continuous improvement. Such development occurs by checking new potential risks and the controls required for them, along with ongoing communication and controls in the company. Ideas and suggestions for improvement from the organization must be recorded and integrated as appropriate into the ISMS.

The last step involves an inspection, or audit, of the ISMS. It involves an external or internal audit of the controls that have been established and a review of the processes and documentation defined in the ISMS. Records must exist that actually document the security management process. For example, auditors must be able to determine how many access authorizations were granted and why and by whom they were approved.

In general, ISO 17799 clearly focuses on establishing a required security management process rather than on the specification of detailed technical security measures. Especially in terms of SOX, these recommendations create an excellent framework to meet legal requirements.

5.1.2   International Security Standard CoBIT

The Information Systems Audit and Control Association developed another important security standard, CoBIT (*Control Objectives for Information and related Technology*), which is completely compatible with the international standard ISO 17799.

The primary objective of CoBIT is to offer an organization or company a general framework that it can use to cover the most important aspects of information security. The following elements are particularly important:

▶ The *CoBIT Security Baseline—39 Steps to Security* defines the most important objectives of security control as a framework that applies to all companies and that can be used as a guideline for establishing security. The following sections describe these steps in more detail.

► Survival guidelines on security (1–6) for private users, professional users, team leaders, middle management, senior management, and upper management in a company.

► Current technical security risks that offer up-to-date information. For example, users can call tests to determine the current vulnerabilities of common Web browsers and which security updates from the manufacturers should be used for the vulnerabilities.

The starting point for the CoBIT Security Baseline is the IT resources in use, such as data, applications, technology, buildings, and consulting personnel. These IT resources are strongly influenced by business objectives for efficiency, availability, confidentiality, integrity, compliance, and reliability. The objectives therefore directly affect the security objectives.

The definition and management of the security objectives is then introduced with the 39 Steps,[3] which are divided into four phases: the planning and organization phase, the customizing and planning phase, the rollout and support phase, and the monitoring and ongoing development phase.

The following steps are relevant to the *planning and organization phase*:

1. **Definition of a strategic IT plan, including the definition of an information architecture**
   Identification of IT systems critical to the company and the derivation of security requirements for the systems.

2. **Definition of the IT organization and its context**
   Identification and communication of responsibilities for security management.

3. **Communication of management objectives and directions**
   Communication of the important strategic security objectives set by management.

4. **Management of personnel in use**
   Recruitment of the correct persons who have the needed abilities and honest background to fulfill the security requirements.

5. **Ensuring adherence to external requirements**
   Ensuring that the IT system functions fulfill legal requirements.

6. **Evaluation of risks**
   Identification, prioritization, and evaluation of risks, including the derivation of the necessary security controls.

---

3 For the sake of clarity, the 39 steps haven been reduced to 20 aspects here.

The following steps are relevant to the *customizing and planning phase*:

1. **Identification of automated process flows**
   The evaluation of these flows in terms of possible and implied security risks.

2. **Customization and operation of the technological infrastructure**
   Security aspects must be considered when customizing the technological infrastructure to business processes. The same is necessary for operations.

3. **Development and maintenance of processes**
   Security aspects must also be considered when developing and maintaining processes.

4. **Installation and acceptance of new systems**
   Acceptance criteria relevant to security must be adhered to during installation and operation of new systems.

5. **Management of changes**
   As is true of the initial installation, changes must also follow a predefined acceptance process.

The following steps are executed during the *rollout and support phase*:

1. **Definition and management of service level agreements**
   Service level agreements (SLA) relevant to security must be considered here.

2. **Management of external services**
   Security aspects must also be realized in services agreements.

3. **Ensuring continuous business operations**
   In this context, all measures must be treated that enable maintenance of critical business applications for the company.

4. **Ensuring technical system security**
   All measures taken must ensure that only authorized persons are granted access to IT systems, according to their roles.

5. **Configuration management**
   Configuration must be designed to guarantee all aspects of security. Sufficiently well-organized patch management is a good example here.

6. **Data management**
   All data must be unchanged, correct, and available as soon as it is accessed during automated system operation.

7. **Building management**
   Building management must ensure that IT devices are not destroyed or stolen.

The following steps are relevant to the *monitoring and ongoing development phase*:

1. **Monitoring and auditing of processes**
   A regular audit must ensure that granting access, for example, follows the defined process.

2. **Obtaining external maintenance of selected measures**
   The hiring of external specialists must ensure that the selected controls meet the security objectives of the company.

Overall, the CoBIT standard offers a generic framework that can help companies attain good basic security. The survival guidelines also offer rules for best-practice behavior that effectively support employees and managers in terms of security.

5.1.3 COSO—Integrated Framework for Company Risk Management

The *Committee of Sponsoring Organizations of the Treadway Commission* (COSO) published an internal and integrated framework for the management of internal controls in the 1990s. It was further developed into an integrated framework for company risk management in 2001. Particularly because of the financial scandals of Enron, WorldCom, and so on, and because of the resulting SOX, the COSO framework enjoys broad usage in numerous companies. The reason is that the COSO framework is especially dedicated to the primary demand of SOX: effective management of all risks to the company related to finance and of the related controls.

Company risk management forms the foundation of the COSO framework, which can define and control the following primary objectives of a company:

▶ **Balance between the company's possible risk acceptance and business strategy**
   The equivalence is reached by balancing possible business strategies and their associated risks.

▶ **Improved decision-making on risks**
   Improved risk reporting can help a company decide more quickly if a risk is to be accepted, avoided, lessened with a control, or shared by taking out insurance.

▶ **Reduction of operating losses and surprises**
   Effective risk management helps minimize operating losses by identifying and evaluating possible risks ahead of time.

- ▶ **Improved use of capital**
  The use of capital can be improved by considering the possible financial risks before investment planning.

- ▶ **Adherence to legal requirements**
  If you include legal requirements in risk management, you can effectively ensure the adherence to these requirements.

Company risk management is defined in the COSO framework as follows:

- ▶ It is an ongoing process anchored in all parts of the company, and it is initiated and controlled by upper management.

- ▶ It must be something shared by all persons, regardless of their level in the company.

- ▶ It must be used in the definition of the company strategy.

- ▶ It must be applied in all parts of the company, and specific risks of each part must be considered.

- ▶ It must inform management about current risks at all times.

COSO defines the framework for company risk management in three dimensions: first with the definition of a company's security objectives, second with the specification of eight components (tasks), and third with the definition of the geographical scope (company entity, division, department, and so on). Together, these three dimensions create the framework for risk management and define the dependencies among the dimensions. A company's security objectives are also divided into four categories:

- ▶ **Strategic**
  The strategic objectives are to be seen at a high level and can be formulated as follows: A company's success depends on an effective supply chain. Financial losses from purchasing must therefore be kept at a minimum.

- ▶ **Operative**
  The strategic objectives must be translated into detailed operative objectives in this step. For example, all purchase orders must be uniquely authorized. Order quantities above a certain amount (determined by the company's acceptance of risk), must be released by those responsible in the financial department.

- ▶ **Reporting**
  The operative business transactions, such as the entire order quantity and the offsetting supply, must be supported by manageable and, above all, correct reporting. For example, reporting must recognize discrepancies immediately and implement appropriate corrections.

▶ **Adherence to legal regulations**

An obvious security objective is adherence to legal regulations. For companies listed on the *New York Stock Exchange*, the legal regulations involve SOX as administered by the *Securities and Exchange Commission* (SEC). From the viewpoint of the COSO framework, these regulations are the primary, but not the sole, means of mandating that companies create an effective internal control system for the business processes that influence financial data. Similar laws exist in Germany, such as the *Law on Control and Transparency in Enterprises* (KontraAG in its German abbreviation) and the GoBS, which was mentioned earlier in this book. Data protection laws (BDSG in Germany) also define legal regulations for personal data. Industry-specific regulations are often also in effect, especially in the pharmaceutical industry or the financial industry. See Chapter 4 for a detailed overview of legal regulations, including the particular requirements of each.

A company must address the following eight tasks to maintain and fulfill the risk acceptance defined in the strategy:

1. **Preparation of the internal organization**

   The company's security objectives and, in particular, the level of possible acceptance of risk, must be communicated to the internal organization. The organization must be prepared for company risk management; it must accept and use these objectives.

2. **Setting objectives**

   The security objectives must be brought into agreement with other company objectives. The level of risk acceptance must be defined so that it does not put anything in the way of new business models and sources of revenue. It should support the models and sources instead.

3. **Early warning system**

   Negative incidents that endanger the security level of the company must be recognized early on. A clear distinction must be drawn between positive (for example, a new source of revenue) and negative events.

4. **Risk analysis**

   Risks must be analyzed according to their effects on the company and in terms of their likelihood of occurrence.

5. **Risk evaluation**

   The risks must be evaluated after the analysis. The evaluation determines if a risk must be avoided, accepted, lessened, or shared. It defines the necessary steps to bring the risk into line with the risk acceptance of the company.

6. **Control steps**

   The steps described in risk evaluation to lessen, distribute, and avoid risk must be checked accordingly. The check is performed with controls monitored by a management system.

7. **Information and communication**

   The information necessary for company risk management must be obtained and communicated to the persons responsible. Only when these persons are informed as best as possible and in a timely manner can the security objectives themselves be maintained, because the required decisions can be made only then.

8. **Monitoring**

   The entire risk management system of the company is continuously monitored with an appropriate reporting structure. Internal and external audits can provide such monitoring.

Many companies often operate globally and in different industries—consider automobile groups that also operate in the financial services industry. Accordingly, security objectives and risk acceptance can be defined differently for individual local entities. The COSO framework allows such differentiation with the implementation of a geographic or business-specific dimension. Such a dimension must determine the company objectives, types of objectives, and how the objectives are included in overall risk management in the company. Particularly in mixed corporate groups, local characteristics can color the objectives significantly. But the company must clearly recognize that various objectives and tasks depend upon each other to a great extent. The effectiveness of company risk management should always be evaluated on the basis of the eight components (tasks). Particularly in the case of different local security objectives, the objectives must be managed at the local level and ultimately consolidated into the overall risk management of the company. If the objectives are implemented correctly, the overall efficiency of the COSO framework is high. It's also important that senior management, above all, considers the establishment of such a system positively and wants to implement it throughout the company.

The COSO framework to establish effective company risk management thus aims at the important regulations in Sections 302 and 404 of SOX that demand an effective, internal management system of risks and the necessary controls. MIC from SAP follows this model. However, the COSO framework is less usable for the technical security discussed in Section 301 of SOX.

5.2 Country-Specific Security Standards

The following sections briefly describe two important national security standards. The American standard from the *National Institute of Standards and Technology* (NIST) focuses more on technical security than it does on business risks, because the risks arise from missing controls or functional separations in the business processes (see Section 5.2.1). The same is true of the standard from the German Federal Office for Information Security (BSI in its German abbreviation), *IT Baseline Protection* (see Section 5.2.2).

5.2.1 American Standard NIST Special Publications 800–12

The American security standard NIST Special Publications 800–12 is structured like a manual for IT security. It describes concrete control objectives for management, operations, and the technology necessary for secure IT systems. It describes a methodology for risk analysis as a foundation that helps select and implement the required and correct security controls. It describes concrete evaluation methodologies for basic information values and lists the most common threats. To respond effectively to these threats, it lists important control measures, as shown in Table 5.1.

Control Measure	Control Objective	Description
Management controls	Computer security guidelines	The computer security guidelines describe the objectives of IT security and, above all, their importance to the organization—at a high level. It also outlines and defines responsibilities.
	Computer security program management	This control must ensure that the objectives defined for IT security are met. This panel is therefore responsible for establishing additional controls. It must use audits to guarantee that the controls have been implemented.
	Computer security risk management	This control provides ongoing analysis of the risks and lowers them with appropriate security measures.
	Security and planning within computer lifecycle management	This aspect of security must be considered with every implementation of a new IT system.
	Security management	Audits must be used to monitor if the intended security measures have been implemented correctly and according to requirements.

Table 5.1 Control Measures of NIST Special Publication 800–12

Control Measure	Control Objective	Description
Operating controls	Personnel controls	During planning and staffing for security, special checks must be carried out to see if the skills necessary to maintain the level of security are present. The background and integrity of employees must also be checked when they are first hired.
	Planning measures for emergencies and system outages	Appropriate redundancies must be planned for systems whose availability is critical to the company. Such planning especially applies to a situation in which the entire data center is affected by a fire or catastrophe.
	Management of security incidents	All security incidents must be captured by an appropriate system. In this context, it's important that appropriate operative countermeasures are available and that they have already been executed in test runs. The responsibilities must be clearly defined: shutting down the system, for example.
	Improved awareness of security with training and continuing education	The organization's employees must undergo training to be sensitized to and educated on the topic of security. The personnel responsible for operations must also receive training on the correct operation of security technologies.
	Security consideration during operation of IT systems	Correct configuration and change management is evident during operation of the IT systems. Also, documentation must be kept at the most current level. It must indicate the operative security settings that must be implemented in detail.
	Physical security	The correct choice of location for the data center and the correct physical security measures (access control and monitoring systems) are fundamental requirements of IT security.
Technical controls	Identification and authentication	Before they are allowed to access the IT system, business partners, customers, and so on must be clearly identified. These persons are assigned an ID or authentication characteristic that uniquely identifies them whenever they use the IT system. The most important authentication characteristics are the user name and password. But stronger options are available, such as digital certificates created according to the X.509 standard.
	Logical access control	After successful authentication, users are allowed to execute only the functions for which they have authorization. In this context, functional separation must be observed: a failure to do so can result in significant business risks.
	Technical logging	Required technical logging can record access to IT systems and changes to data. The log can monitor any unauthorized changes that might have occurred.
	Cryptography	Cryptography is the foundation of technical security controls.

Table 5.1 Control Measures of NIST Special Publication 800–12 (cont.)

Briefly summarized, NIST Special Publications 800–12 is a manual that describes concrete measures for a secure implementation and operation of IT systems. The descriptions of the measures are not detailed; they simply outline the basic underlying concepts.

5.2.2 German Security Standard IT Baseline Protection of the BSI

The German standard, *IT Baseline Protection*, was developed by the BSI. It provides a way to develop a structured security concept for a company's IT systems. The IT Baseline Protection manual of the BSI takes advantage of the actual situation in which users operate a large portion of existing IT systems and applications in similar ways and in comparable environments. For example, servers run UNIX, client PCs run Windows, and systems include database applications or SAP systems. If no special security requirements are present, the dangers here exist independently of the concrete usage scenario. From this situation, two ideas result for a way to approach the creation of a companywide security concept.

▶ A comprehensive risk analysis is not always necessary. The dangers for IT operations and the likelihood of the resulting damage can be limited in certain situations, particularly when the IT systems do not need increased security.

▶ It is not always necessary to develop new security measures for every concrete situation. Bundles of standard security measures can be derived that offer appropriate and sufficient protection from such dangers in the context of normal security requirements.

Based on these assumptions, the IT Baseline Protection manual suggests a procedure for creating and checking IT security concepts. It describes standard proven security measures for typical IT systems that are to be implemented with the current technology to provide an appropriate level of security, or *baseline protection*. The procedure pays special attention to infrastructure, organization, personnel, technology, and emergencies and thus supports a comprehensive approach. It places special value on procuring the required technical knowledge. Accordingly, the IT Baseline Protection manual is also a reference book.

The development of a security concept based on the methodology of IT Baseline Protection occurs in five phases, as briefly described in the following list:

1. IT structure analysis

2. Determining the need for protection

3. Threat analysis

4. Risk analysis

5. Measures concept

The *IT structure analysis* must catalog all components of an IT system and applications and assign them to the five layers set forth in the IT Baseline Protection manual. Figure 5.1 illustrates the five layers.

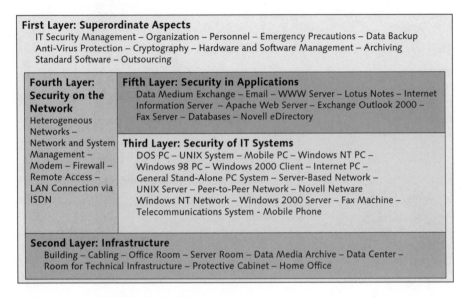

First Layer: Superordinate Aspects
IT Security Management – Organization – Personnel – Emergency Precautions – Data Backup
Anti-Virus Protection – Cryptography – Hardware and Software Management – Archiving
Standard Software – Outsourcing

Fourth Layer: Security on the Network
Heterogeneous Networks – Network and System Management – Modem – Firewall – Remote Access – LAN Connection via ISDN

Fifth Layer: Security in Applications
Data Medium Exchange – Email – WWW Server – Lotus Notes – Internet Information Server – Apache Web Server – Exchange Outlook 2000 – Fax Server – Databases – Novell eDirectory

Third Layer: Security of IT Systems
DOS PC – UNIX System – Mobile PC – Windows NT PC – Windows 98 PC – Windows 2000 Client – Internet PC – General Stand-Alone PC System – Server-Based Network – UNIX Server – Peer-to-Peer Network – Novell Netware Windows NT Network – Windows 2000 Server – Fax Machine – Telecommunications System - Mobile Phone

Second Layer: Infrastructure
Building – Cabling – Office Room – Server Room – Data Media Archive – Data Center – Room for Technical Infrastructure – Protective Cabinet – Home Office

Figure 5.1 Five Layers of the IT Baseline Protection Manual

This phase captures all servers and assigns them to the "security of IT systems—UNIX system" layer. If the security concept also includes buildings, they must be assigned to a second layer. Superordinate aspects, like the operating organization for IT systems, can be modeled with the first layer.

The second phase must determine the protection need for every object in terms of confidentiality, integrity, and availability. This phase primarily involves information or business process owners. Determining the need for protection is an important step, because it is the foundation for the ability to determine the security risk later on. Classification in terms of confidentiality, integrity, and availability occurs in qualitative steps. The BSI provides a possible scale, but the details of the scale must be determined with management in the security policy.

The threat analysis takes the dangers for each object (as defined in the IT structure analysis) from the IT Baseline Protection manual of the BSI and catalogs them appropriately. It is entirely conceivable that multiple UNIX servers exist, in which case the dangers are identical. In this case, bundling is allowed. If the defined need for protection is set to at least "high," additional self-defined dangers can be added.

For example, for an Apache Web server, the dangers listed in Table 5.2 can be taken from the IT Baseline Protection manual:

Low-Level Software of the IT Procedure	Threats for All Objects of the Object Group
Organizational deficiencies	G 2.1 Missing or insufficient rules
	G 2.9 Deficient adjustment to changes with use of IT
	G 2.87 Use of insecure protocols in public networks
Human error	G 3.1 Loss of data confidentiality or integrity because of errors by IT users
	G 3.9 Incorrect administration of the IT system
	G 3.38 Configuration and operation errors
	G 3.62 Incorrect configuration of the operating system for an Apache Web server
	G 3.63 Incorrect configuration of an Apache Web server
Technical failure	G 4.39 Software design error
Deliberate acts	G 5.2 Manipulation of data or software
	G 5.7 Eavesdropping on connections
	G 5.21 Trojan horses
	G 5.28 Denial of services
	G 5.71 Loss of confidentiality of information worth protecting
	G 5.85 Loss of integrity of information worth protecting
	G 5.109 Taking advantage of system-specific vulnerabilities in an Apache Web server

Table 5.2 Sample Dangers for an Apache Web Server

After the creation of a threat scenario, a risk analysis must be performed. According to the IT security manual, the risk analysis is to be performed if data that requires a great deal of protection is being stored and processed. Simple modeling, purely according to IT Baseline Protection, is no longer permitted in this case.

The risk analysis is divided into three steps:

1. The first step assigns all the security measures supported by the IT Baseline Protection manual to the objects defined in the structure analysis. Table 5.3 shows an example for an Apache Web server.

Object Group or Measures Group	Measures
Measures for All Objects of the Object Group	
Organization	M 2.269 Planning the use of an Apache Web server
	M 2.270 Planning the use of SSL with an Apache Web server (additional)
Personnel	M 3.37 Training administrators of an Apache Web server
Hardware and software	M 4.191 Checking the integrity and authenticity of the Apache packages
	M 4.192 Configuration of the operating system for an Apache Web server
	M 4.194 Secure basic configuration of an Apache Web server
	M 4.195 Configuration of access control for an Apache Web server
	M 4.196 Secure operation of an Apache Web server
	M 4.197 Server enhancements for a dynamic website for an Apache Web server
	M 4.198 Installation of an Apache Web server in a Chroot cage (optional)
Communication	M 5.107 Use of SSL with an Apache Web server (optional)
Emergency precautions	M 6.89 Emergency precautions for an Apache Web server

Table 5.3 Sample Structure Analysis

2. The second step now determines which measure found in the first step has already been implemented, and it identifies the danger that prompted this measure to be taken, thereby lowering the risk. If a measure has not been implemented, it must be analyzed in a second risk analysis.

3. First, a probability of occurrence (0–4) of the danger must be implemented and compared to the need for protection defined in phase 2. Probabilities of occurrence can be found in the annual security reports published by the CSI and FBI. A risk is designated as "tolerable," "medium," or "intolerable," which determines if a security measure must be realized. As shown in the risk matrix, the risk scale can be defined (see Figure 5.2). An appropriate measure must be implemented from the IT Baseline Protection manual for every intolerable, high, or even medium risk. In some cases, an additional or optional measure must be implemented. The measure concept defines the necessity.

Amount of Damages = Need for Protection						
4	T	H	I	I	I	I
3	T	H	H	I	I	I
2	T	T	M	M	M	H
1	T	T	T	M	M	M
0	T	T	T	T	M	M
	0-	0	1	2	3	4

likelihood

T – Tolerable risk (no measures required)
M – Medium risk (measures according to IT Baseline Protection Manual recommended)
H – High risk (measures to be implemented as soon as possible)
I – Intolerably high risk (measures are indispensable)

Figure 5.2 Sample Risk Matrix for the BSI IT Baseline Protection Manual

The fifth and last phase must work out the measure concept. This phase defines the security measures that are to minimize the intolerable and high risks identified in the risk analysis. The evaluation should also include a rough estimate of the effort required to establish the measures. If the security measures are implemented, the risk can be reevaluated. A tolerable risk should result in most cases. In this manner, a comprehensive security concept for an application or even for all the IT-based processes of a company can be developed step by step.

As shown, each phase must be worked through iteratively. In this manner, the security concept is always being updated.

The IT Baseline Protection manual of the BSI thus offers a proven methodology for developing a comprehensive security concept based upon standard modules. It deals with the technology and the organization. The measures are described concretely and do not remain at a purely generic level. The IT Baseline Protection manual is less helpful when analyzing and evaluating the risks of fraud relevant to business processes. It focuses on the topic of IT security.

The manual was not particularly helpful in the past when dealing with SAP landscapes because it did not include a module for SAP security. The current edition contains a completely new SAP module. This module can be used to provide basic protection for SAP systems because it describes the required technical measures. Note that for this module as well, the measures treated do not target business-based risks, but deal with technical aspects.

6 Basic Principles of Technical Security

The basic principles of cryptography and, in particular, the method of asymmetric encryption, play an important role for SAP applications. An understanding of these methods and of networks is absolutely necessary to gain a better foundation for appreciating the security mechanisms of SAP NetWeaver that are described in the second part of this book.

The procedures and methodologies used in SAP products are based on important basic procedures of cryptography. Without them, it would be impossible to use SAP NetWeaver securely. In particular, a secure authentication of users would be impossible without asymmetric encryption. Enabling asymmetric encryption for a large number of users, as is the case on the World Wide Web requires the use of a trustworthy *certificate authority* (CA) and a *public key infrastructure* (PKI).

In addition to the basic principles of cryptography and the strong identification and authentication procedures they enable, an understanding of the most important network protocols and of the OSI reference model is also important. The following sections describe these topics in further detail.

6.1 Cryptography

Cryptography describes the methodology for making the transmission of a sender's message to the recipient so incomprehensible that unauthorized third parties cannot view the message and use it for their own purposes. It has it roots in prehistory. In the 19th century B.C., Egyptians used methods to encrypt texts by exchanging blocks of text according to a specific schema. This method was, of course, quite simple and could easily be decrypted with today's utilities. But at the time, it was a widely used and easy-to-use method.

Julius Caesar used a somewhat more complex algorithm in 60 B.C. This *Caesar Code* encrypted a message by juxtaposing it with a secret alphabet. The secret alphabet, however, was simply an exchange of the regular alphabet by x number of places. In general, the value of x could be guessed quite easily.

Table 6.1 shows a simple example of a Caesar Code. In this case, $x = 1$.

Regular Text	S	A	P		N	E	T	W	E	A	V	E	R
Encrypted Text	T	B	Q		O	F	U	X	F	B	W	F	S

Table 6.1 Caesar Code for Message Encyption

Those procedures underwent constant refinement and, basically, remain the foundation of symmetric encryption. Of course, in this age of electronic data processing, encryption occurs at a binary level rather than at the level of letters.

6.1.1 Symmetric Encryption Procedure

In a symmetric encryption procedure, the same key is used to code and to decode a plain-text message.

A simple way of using symmetric encryption is to use the *XOR function* (exclusive "or"). Table 6.2 provides an example of a symmetric encryption for an 8-bit key. The first row of the table displays the data to be encoded as bits. The encryption key given in the second row is then applied to the first row with the XOR function. A bit can only be set for the encoded data record if the record to be encrypted and the encryption key have different bits set. Decryption occurs in the same manner; the last row of the table contains the original data record to be encrypted. That proves the possibility of symmetric encryption with the XOR function.

Data record in plain text	1	0	1	1	0	0	0	1
+ XOR (symmetric key)	0	0	1	0	1	1	0	1
Encrypted data record	1	0	0	1	1	1	0	0
+ XOR (symmetric key)	0	0	1	0	1	1	0	1
Data record in plain text after XOR	1	0	1	1	0	0	0	1

Table 6.2 Using XOR for Symmetric Encryption

The following conditions apply to the use of symmetric encryption:

1. The key cannot simply be determined from the encrypted data record. To prevent such a determination, the key must be long enough and the encryption cannot use a simple function.
2. The key must be kept completely confidential. If encoded data is transferred from a sender to a recipient, both parties must know the key.

Important examples of symmetric encryption today include the *Data Encryption Standard* (DES) and *Triple DES* (3DES). The *Advanced Encryption Standard* (AES) is the successor to the DES. The *International Data Encryption Algorithm* (IDEA) also plays an important role.

Like the DES, AES is a block algorithm with a bit length of up to 256 bits. A contest held by the *National Institute for Standards and Technology* (NIST) in the United States found AES to be the most secure procedure. It was invented by two Belgian mathematicians, Joan Daemen and Vincent Rijmen, and is commonly known as the Rijndael algorithm.

6.1.2 Asymmetric Encryption Procedure

As the name indicates, asymmetric encryption differs from symmetric encryption because it uses two different keys: one for encryption and one for decryption. The procedure is similar to the normal lock on a door; the key is the counterpart to the lock.

Everyday use of asymmetric encryption means that the following requirements must be met:

1. A secret private key, *s*, is implemented for an identity. Messages encoded with this key can be decrypted only with the related public key, *p*. Decryption with the private key, *s*, is impossible.

2. Messages encrypted with an identity's public key, *p*, can be decrypted only with the identity's secret private key, *s*. Decryption with the public key, *p*, is impossible.

3. The correlation between the private key, *s*, and the public key, *p*, is unambiguous. No other pair of keys results in the same encryption.

4. It is impossible to derive the private key, *s*, from the public key, *p*.

5. The pair of keys (*s* and *p*) can be determined by a relatively simple and efficient algorithm.

An asymmetric encryption procedure that meets these requirements was introduced by three American mathematicians—Rivest, Shamir, and Adleman. The algorithm is generally known as RSA. The keys of the procedure are determined as follows:

▶ Public key *p*: A pair of integers (n, *p*)

▶ Confidential private key *s*: A pair of integers (n, *s*)

The number n can consist of 1,024 binary digits, or even 2,048 in a higher quality procedure. The numbers s and p can also consist of up to 1,024 binary digits, but that is not absolutely necessary.

▶ RSA encryption with public key p:

  ▶ Split the plain-text message t into a series of blocks (m_1 ... m_k) with a minimal k so that every block m_i (in binary form) corresponds to a number smaller than n.

  ▶ Calculate $c_i = P(m_i) = m_i p \bmod n$.

  mod is the modulo function that returns the integral remainder of a division of integers.

▶ RSA decryption with the confidential private key, s:

  ▶ Split the coded text c into a series of blocks (c_1 ... c_k) with a minimal k so that every block c_i (in binary form) corresponds to a number smaller than n.

  ▶ Calculate $m_i = S(c_i) = c_i s \bmod n$.

  The entire plain-text message, t, can then be determined from the sum of all m_i.

Multiplication and determination of the coset (modulo function) of 1,024-bit-long numbers requires a great deal of computing. That's why the procedure should not be used for very large quantities of data. The greatest advantage of the asymmetric procedure is that it does not require the exchange of a private key.

6.1.3 Hybrid Encryption Procedure

Hybrid encryption procedures combine the advantages of both methods: the lack of a need to exchange keys with the asymmetric procedure and the obvious performance advantages of the symmetric procedure. The first message between a sender and recipient exchanges the private, symmetric key by using asymmetric encryption between the two parties. For each communication, the symmetric key can be selected at will. After the symmetric key has been exchanged, the actual encrypted transfer of the plain-text information occurs with the fast symmetric procedure.

Figures 6.1 and 6.2 summarize both levels of hybrid encryption. The hybrid procedure is the de facto standard in encrypted communications and is used by the *Secure Sockets Layer* (SSL) protocol.

The following steps are required at the first level (the exchange of keys with the asymmetric procedure, see Figure 6.1):

▶ **Step 1**: The sender selects a random session key for the symmetric encryption that follows (marked as *secret*)

▶ **Step 2**: The sender encrypts the session key with the public key (marked as *public*) of the recipient
→ that produces the encrypted session key

▶ **Step 3**: The sender then transfers the encrypted session key

▶ **Step 4**: The recipient decrypts the encrypted session key with the private key (marked as *private*)
→ that produces the session key for the recipient

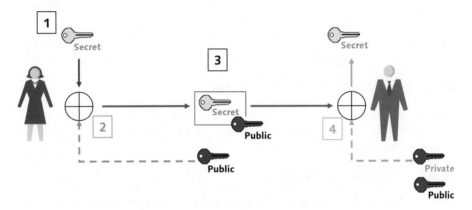

Figure 6.1 Hybrid Encryption (First Level: Exchange of Keys)

The following steps are required at the second level (symmetric encryption of information, see Figure 6.2):

▶ **Step 1**: The sender encrypts the plain text with the symmetric session key (marked as *secret*)
→ that produces the encrypted text

▶ **Step 2**: The sender transmits the encrypted text to the recipient

▶ **Step 3**: The recipient decrypts the encrypted text with the symmetric session key
→ that produces the plain text

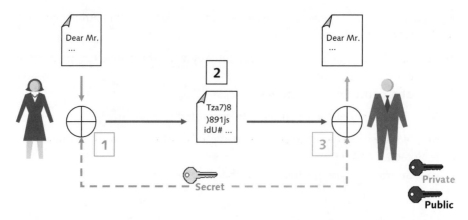

Figure 6.2 Hybrid Encryption (Second Level: Secure Message Exchange with Symmetric Encryption)

6.1.4 Hash Procedures

Hash procedures are used to generate an unambiguous numerical value from a message text or any quantity of data. The unambigiuos numerical value is referred to as the *hash value*.

The following three conditions apply to the hash function:

1. No conclusions about the original message or data record can be drawn from the hash value created by the hash function.

2. The generated hash values do not collide; an unambiguous and unique hash value is generated from each data record. Every hash value must therefore be unique and unambiguous.

3. The hash value must be able to be calculated efficiently.

Figure 6.3 provides an overview of the hash procedure. It shows that when using the hash procedure on large data records, the records must first be split into n blocks (*a*)—of 32 bits, for example. The hash function is then applied to the individual blocks, and the total hash value is calculated by addition. As a variant, a start value for the hash total can also be selected.

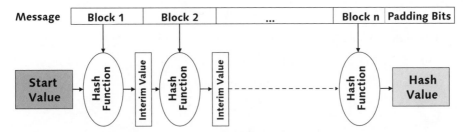

Figure 6.3 Processing Principle of a Hash Procedure with Larger Data Records by Separation into Blocks

Well-known hash functions include the *Secure Hash Algorithm* (SHA) and the *Message Digest Algorithm 5* (MD5). SHA was standardized by the NIST in the United States and is the foundation for the *Digital Signature Standard* (DSS). The mathematician R. Rivest, of the Massachusetts Institute of Technology (MIT), developed MD5. See RFC 1321 for its exact specifications.

6.1.5   Digital Signature

A digital signature can be generated with the interaction of asymmetric encryption and the unambiguous calculation of a hash value. The signature is generated as follows: A hash function (SHA, for example) generates an unambiguous and therefore collision-free hash value from a text—for instance, from an accounting document. The hash value is then encrypted with the secret private key of the signatory and stored together with the document. This procedure is known as *signing*.

Let's say that the recipient of the document wants to check to see if anything in the document was changed during transmission, which means that the document is no longer authentic and by the signatory. The recipient would use the public key to decrypt the attached hash value and compare it with the hash value of the document, which is calculated with the same SHA function. If both hash values are the same, the document comes from the person who signed it, and it has not been changed. If the hash values differ, the document has been changed or the public key does not fit the signatory. When the values differ, the document does not come from the person who signed it. The digital signature is therefore counterfeit.

Figures 6.4 and 6.5 illustrate the steps necessary to generate and validate a digital signature.

Generating the signature involves the following steps:

1. Generating a collision-free hash value for the message
2. Encrypting the hash value with the private key (signing: *private*)
3. Combining the message with the signed hash value

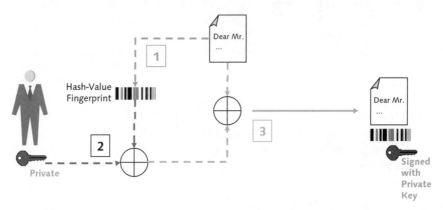

Figure 6.4 Generating a Digital Signature

Verification involves the following steps:

1. Extracting the digital signature from the message
2. Generating a collision-free hash value for the message
3. Decrypting the digital signature with the sender's public key
4. The signature is valid if the generated hash value matches the decrypted hash value of the digital signature. If the values differ, the document was not digitally signed by the sender or it was changed afterwards.

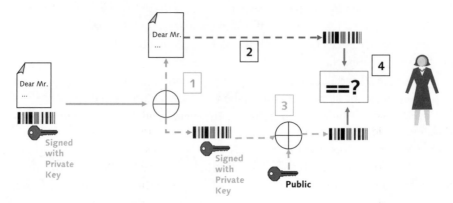

Figure 6.5 Verifying the Digital Signature

The quality level of the digital signature depends on the quality rating of the asymmetric pair of keys being used. Asymmetric key pairs are handled by a public key infrastructure (PKI, see Section 6.2) using digital certificates according to the X.509v3 standard. Some signatures generated with certificates are simply updated, which means they have a rather low level of security. That means that no high-quality registration process occurred to capture the identity. The certificate, particularly the secret private key, is stored at the level of the operating system rather than on dedicated media like a smart card.

Qualified personal certificates must be used to generate signatures like those that meet the requirements of German law. Only an accredited certificate authority (CA) can issue such certificates, which must be stored on smart cards.

Other legal issues may determine which signature can be used. For example, when citizens deal with governmental agencies in Germany and the transactions have legal force, the citizen may use only signatures that meet the requirements of the German signature law.

6.2   Public Key Infrastructure

As noted for the creation and verification of digital signatures, asymmetric encryption methods function only if the public keys of the identities are managed securely and efficiently. For example, the recipient of a message can check the validity of the sender's signature only if it is completely certain that the sender's public key truly belongs to that sender.

This can occur when senders transmit their public key to the recipients ahead of time over a secure and trustworthy channel. In an Internet scenario with numerous participants and an enormous number of identities, it becomes obvious that this way of managing public keys soon reaches its limits and simply becomes impossible.

To avoid this difficulty, the *public key infrastructure* (PKI) was implemented. It helps manage the public keys of individual identities. A PKI consists of two institutions: the *certificate authority* and the *registration authority*.

Think of the certificate authority like a passport office that issues passports so that travelers can identify themselves when they cross into another country. The officials at the border trust the passport office that confirms the identity of the travelers with its seal and signature. The registration authority confirms the true identity of the traveler before the passport is issued. The certification authority issues a passport only when unique characteristics exist to indicate that the traveler truly is who the traveler claims to be.

Now transfer this process to the digital world, and you'll see how the principle is the same. Instead of a passport, a digital certificate is issued for the institution making the request. A certificate is a digital attestation of an institution's public key by a trustworthy certificate authority. Certificates are generated according to the international standard X.509v3, which essentially contains the following attributes:

▶ **Version number**
Specification of the X.509 version being used.

▶ **Serial number**
The unique serial number of the certificate. It may exist only once.

▶ **Signature**
The signature of the certificate and the algorithms and parameters needed to validate the public key of the certificate authority.

▶ **Certificate issuer**
Name of the issuing certificate authority.

▶ **Validity period**
The validity period for this certificate.

▶ **User name**
The name or pseudonym of the certificate owner. This is the *distinguished name* (DN) of the identity. It can also be a server.

▶ **Key information**
The public key of the owner and the algorithms to be used.

▶ **Unique identification characteristic**
An additional identification characteristic is required if the name is used multiple times.

▶ **Enhancements**
Additional specifications on the use of the key, such as several validity periods, and on the conditions of the issue.

The CA must sign the certificate with its secret private key so that the validity of the certificate can be verified at any time. The application must store all the validating certificates of all trustworthy CAs. CAs can also be cascaded in a hierarchy. That means that only a few root-CAs exist that confirm the trustworthiness of another CA by issuing a certificate. The trust relationships between the individual participants (or institutions) are created like a cascade.

In addition to issuing certificates, a CA is also responsible for managing certificates. If, for any reason, a certificate becomes invalid before its validity period expires, the participating institutions must be informed. CAs use a *certificate revo-*

cation list (CRL) to handle this task. With this list, an application can determine if the certificate presented by a user is still valid.

In technical terms, a PKI consists of an LDAP server that stores the certificate according to a defined structure. A PKI must also have an interface for applications, such as those that check the validity of certificates. Redundancy and the absolutely secure setup of the required server systems are extremely important. In many cases, the servers manage not only the public key of the certificate, but also the private key.

The certificates can be issued in various quality classes. The *certificate practice statement* defines the quality classes that a PKI may issue. This statement determines the purpose of the certificate as well as the type of registration process for issuing the certificate.

6.3   Authentication Procedures

Authentication procedures help recognize a previously registered identity before granting permission to execute a specific action, such as starting an application or executing application functionality.

6.3.1   User Name and Password

The simplest and traditionally most common procedure is based on a user ID and password. Upon registration, users are assigned a unique user ID and the required password. The application, such as a database, then stores the values. Users are identified and allowed to access an application only when they enter the correct combination of user ID and password during authentication.

This method is called a *one-factor procedure*, because users are authenticated based only upon "what they know." Authentication does not require a second factor, such as possession of a smart card.

6.3.2   Challenge Response

The challenge-response procedure is primarily used as a schema for authentication in Windows NT networks. It stands for *Windows NT LAN Manager* (NTLM). The target system (a server application) issues a randomly generated *challenge*. The user, which can be a Windows client, for example, who wants to be authenticated on the target system, answers with an appropriate *response*. The response to the challenge is calculated by software or a *token card*.

This procedure is much better than using traditional passwords, because only one correct response to a challenge exists and allows access. Even eavesdropping on the communications between the two partners does not help an attacker gain access. Each challenge is used only once, and no passwords are transmitted over the network.

6.3.3 Kerberos

Kerberos takes its name from a figure in Greek mythology. Kerberos (sometimes written in its Latinate form, Cerberus) is a hound of hell, standing guard at the gates of the underworld. He has three heads and keeps the dead from reentering the world of the living.

In the world of computers, Kerberos is a network authentication procedure developed at MIT at end of the 1980s. See RFC 1510 for its exact specifications. The procedure was first developed for UNIX networks. Microsoft adopted the procedure and has used it as the standard network authentication protocol since Windows 2000. It has since replaced NTLM as the standard in the Windows environment.

Just as the original hound of hell had three heads, Kerberos has three components: the client; the application server to which the client wants to connect; and the trustworthy authentication server, also referred to as a *key distribution center* (KDC).

The Kerberos procedure is relatively complex; it is beyond the scope of this book to describe it in detail. The procedure is essentially based on a symmetric encryption process that does not transmit an encrypted password but uses it as a secret shared between two parties. For example, assume that "Alice" transmits her name and the current time in encrypted form with her password (called an *authenticator*) to a trustworthy institution, "Bob." Bob can then use Alice's password (stored at Bob's location as a shared secret) to decrypt the message and compare the current time in the message with his own current time. If the time systems are sufficiently synchronized, Bob can then authenticate Alice as long as the time specifications lie within the allowed period (five minutes, for example). So that Alice can know that she is linked to Bob, Bob uses the same password to encrypt the time stamp that Alice transmitted and returns it to her as a message. Alice can now use her key to decrypt the message and compare it with the time stamp that she originally sent. If the two are the same, she can securely assume that she is connected with Bob.

Bob can now send Alice a *ticket granting ticket* (TGT) for the day. Alice can use the ticket to access the actual application servers. Bob also manages the application keys of the application servers. Alice receives the keys with the TGT (in encrypted form) when she wants to access the application servers. Alice can then authenticate herself on the application server, using the same principle she did when authenticating herself to Bob. The institution, Bob, is a *key distribution service* and is necessary for effective administration of the symmetric keys, which have a limited period of validity, and to function as a trustworthy instance (much like a CA).

6.3.4 Secure Token

Secure token procedures are typical *two-factor authentication procedures*. In this case, users have a secret password or PIN and a secure token card. Users need the card for authentication on a network or with an application.

The *SecurID* method from RSA Security is one of the most common secure token procedures. With this method, a one-time password, the *passphrase*, is produced, which is valid for about one minute. The SecurID card uses a specific algorithm and a PIN (entered by the user) to generate the passphrase. The passphrase is then transmitted to the required authentication server, which works with the same algorithm to identify the passphrase. If the passphrase is correct, the user is authenticated. The authentication server can then act as a trustworthy instance and transfer the successful authentication to an application server. The transfer can occur with *Security Assertion Markup Language* (SAML).

Because the passphrase is valid for only about one minute during authentication and is used only once, an unauthorized attacker cannot take advantage of the procedure. Two-factor authentication achieves a very high level of security.

6.3.5 Digital Certificate

In certificate-based methods, authentication occurs with a certificate issued by a trustworthy certificate authority. Authentication on an application server must check the validity of the certificate with the asymmetric encryption procedure and the certificate revocation list. The user's unique distinguished name and the unique serial number of the certificate must already be stored in the application, or a directory service must exist that enables access to the certificate.

6.3.6 Biometrics

Biometric authentication procedures are not currently in common use, because they require complex, dedicated devices like iris scanners or fingerprint readers. Most of these devices are prone to error and unreliable.

Authentication is based on unique biometric characteristics of a user. For example, a fingerprint can be used as a unique characteristic because a given fingerprint exists only once in the world. The eye's iris is also absolutely unique. But problems exist when trying to determine the exact differences between the characteristics. In most cases, only a high-resolution scanner can recognize the differences. A biometric procedure requires registration of users ahead of time so they can later be authenticated with the stored biometric characteristics.

As noted, biometric authentication procedures have limitations and are therefore primarily used with access systems for computer centers. Supplemental devices can also use this method to secure access to mobile laptops or *personal digital assistants* (PDAs). Biometric procedures are not currently being used in the SAP NetWeaver environment.

6.4 Basic Principles of Networks

To make the security mechanisms related to networks outlined in the sections above clearer, this section offers a short excursus into network technology, especially because network considerations continue to play an important role when using SAP NetWeaver in the Internet environment.

6.4.1 OSI Reference Model

The *Open Systems Interconnection (OSI) Reference Model* is an open layer model for the organization of communications technology. It was developed in 1979 and is currently the standard for network communications. The OSI model serves as the foundation for a variety of proprietary network protocols that are used almost exclusively in public communications technology in transport networks. It subdivides the various application areas of network communication into seven layers (see Figure 6.6). Each of the layers is designed to be able to perform the tasks assigned to it independently of the other layers.

In a computer network, other participants in the network provide various hosts with the most varied types of services. The communication required to do so is not as trivial as it might seem at first glance. The communication must handle several tasks and fulfill requirements related to reliability, security, efficiency, and so on. The problems that must be solved in the process cover questions about electronic transmission of the signals, a regulated sequence in communications, and abstract tasks that arise between the communicating applications.

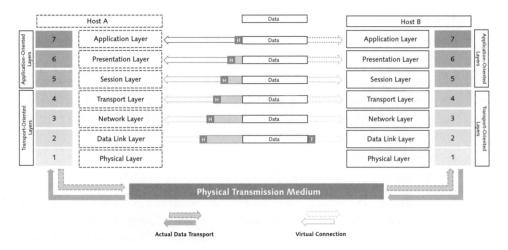

Figure 6.6 OSI Network Reference Model

The number of these problems and tasks makes it reasonable to assign a network's services to specific categories rather than viewing the network as a single service provider. A subdivision of the network into seven layers has proven particularly helpful. In the OSI model, the degree of abstraction of the functions increases significantly from layer 1 to layer 7. Data is redirected from one layer to the next. In other words, communication occurs in a vertical direction. On the sender's side, the communication flows from the top to the bottom; on the recipient's side, the communication flows from the bottom to the top. Seen logically, communication between the sender and the recipient occurs horizontally in every layer.

▶ **Layer 7: Application Layer**

Also referred to as the processing layer or user level

The application layer is the highest of the seven hierarchical layers. It provides applications with a variety of functionalities: data transfer, email, virtual terminal, remote login, HTML, and so on.

▶ **Layer 6: Presentation Layer**

Also referred to as the data presentation layer or data provision level

The presentation layer converts the system-dependent presentation of data (ASCII, EBCDIC, and so on) into an independent form and thus enables a syntactically correct exchange of data between various systems. Layer 6 also includes tasks like data compression and encryption.

► **Layer 5: Session Layer**

Also referred to as the communications control layer, control of logical connections, and the session level

To correct interrupted sessions and similar problems, the session layer provides services for organized and synchronized data exchange. It sets up *check points* that can be used to synchronize a session after a transport connection fails without having to restart the transmission from the beginning.

► **Layer 4: Transport Layer**

Also referred to as end-to-end control or transport control

The tasks of the transport layer include the segmentation of data packages and *congestion control*. The transport layer is the lowest layer that provides complete end-to-end communication between a sender and a recipient. It provides the application-oriented layers 5–7 with uniform access, so that they do not need to consider the characteristics of the communications network. Five different service classes of various qualities are defined in layer 4 for use by the higher layers. They range from the simplest to the most user-friendly services with multiplex mechanisms, error-protection procedures, and error-correction procedures.

► **Layer 3: Network Layer**

Also referred to as the package level

The network layer switches connections for connection-oriented services and redirects data packages for package-oriented services. Data transmission in both directions flows over the entire communications network and includes *routing* between the network nodes. Because direct communications between the sender and the destination are not always possible, the nodes on the path must redirect the packages. The redirected packages do not go to the higher layers, but are given a new, intermediate destination, and are sent to the next node.

The tasks of the network layer include the setting up and updating of routing tables, flow control, and network addresses. Because a communications network can consist of several subnetworks with various technologies, the conversion functions needed for redirection between the subnetworks can also reside in this layer.

► **Layer 2: Data Link Layer**

Also referred to as the connection level or procedure level

The task of the data link layer is to ensure almost error-free transmission and to regulate access to the transmission medium. This includes splitting the bit stream of data into blocks and inserting sequence numbers and checksums.

Recipients can use receipt and repeat mechanisms to newly request blocks corrupted by errors or lost blocks. The blocks are also called *frames*. *Flow control* gives a recipient dynamic control of the speed at which the other side may transmit blocks. The Institute of Electrical and Electronics Engineers (IEEE) in the United States also saw the need to regulate competitive access on a transmission medium, which the OSI model does not support.

▶ **Layer 1: Physical Layer**

Also referred to as the bit transmission layer

The physical layer is the lowest layer. This layer describes the physical characteristics of telecommunications. The characteristics can include electrical signals, optical signals (optical fibers or lasers), electromagnetic waves (wireless networks), or sound. The type of procedure used is referred to as the transmission procedure.

Devices and network components assigned to the physical layer include the network card, transceiver, antenna, amplifier, plugs and sockets for the network cable, the cable itself, the repeater, the hub, the tee, and the terminator.

Digital transmission of bits with or without wires occurs on the physical layer. The topology of the network also plays a role in a wired procedure. Static or dynamic multiplexing can handle common use of a transmission medium at this layer. It requires the specification of specific transmission media (for example, copper wires, fiber optic cables, electrical grid, or air) the definition of plug-and-socket connections, and additional elements. The way that a single bit is to be transmitted must also be determined at this layer.[1]

6.4.2 Important Network Protocols

Table 6.3 provides an overview of the most important network protocols.

Layer	Protocol					
Application	File Transfer	Email	Terminal Emulation	Usenet News	WWW HTML	Domain Name Service

Table 6.3 Overview of the Most Important Network Protocols

---

1 The following is an explanation of the solution. Networks today usually transfer information in as series of bits. Of course, the transmission medium itself (a copper cable for electric transmission or the air for wireless transmission) has no idea of 0 and 1. Every medium thus requires a coding of these values: an electrical impulse of a specific voltage or a radio wave with a specific frequency. These aspects must be defined precisely for a specific network, which occurs with a specification in the network layer of a network.

Layer	Protocol					
Presentation	File Transfer Protocol (FTP)	Simple Mail Transfer Protocol (SMTP)	Telnet Protocol (Telnet)	Network News Transfer Protocol (NNTP)	Hypertext Transfer Protocol (HTTP)	Domain Name System (DNS)
Session						
Transport	Transmission Control Protocol (TCP)					User Datagram Protocol (UDP)
Network	Address Resolution Protocol (ARP)		Internet Protocol (IP)			Internet Control Message Protocol (ICMP)
Data Link	Ethernet, Token Ring, DQDB, FDDI, and ISDN					
Physical Layer	Transmission medium: two-ply cable, coaxial cable, fiber optic cable, or wireless transmission					

Table 6.3 Overview of the Most Important Network Protocols (cont.)

6.4.3 Overview of Firewall Technologies

Traditional firewalls work only at the network and transport layers. Accordingly, the traditional firewall is a package filter at the network layer. Such simple package filters can also be designed to be *stateful* by involving the transport layer. Firewalls that work only at the application level are generally referred to as *application level gateways*. The following sections briefly introduce all three types of firewalls.

▶ **Package Filters**

Package filers represent the simplest form of firewall. They work exclusively at the IP level. Basically, they are network routers with a filtering option. A package filter analyzes the IP header information.

A package filter can define which of the superior protocols (FTP, HTTP, and so on) may pass between two network segments. Communication can also be limited to specific ports, like port 80 for HTTP. Users can also define which IP address of a network segment is allowed to set up communication with another network segment. Communication can be controlled and limited in this manner.

The advantages of such a solution include cost-efficient and high-performance technology. Some disadvantages are also involved. Complex infrastructures can require a great deal of effort to define rules and susceptibility to IP spoofing, in which an unauthorized client uses another IP address to gain access to another network segment.

▶ **Stateful Package Filters**

Stateful package filters work much like stateless package filters and generally provide the same types of rules. But a TCP session can be used to determine which clients have a communications connection with each other. The advantage of this method is that these kinds of firewalls can use this ability to defend against network scanning based on half-open syn queries. In addition, this type of firewall can use both the IP header and the message body to analyze the superior protocol a message is using. Dynamic filter rules can be created in this manner. In other words, the firewall can learn.

▶ **Application Level Gateway**

Because package-filter firewalls cannot defend against attacks at the application level, application level gateways, or *application level firewalls*, are gaining popularity. But only a combination of package filters and application level gateways can provide the required level of security.

Application level gateways offer additional protection against Internet attacks, such as:

▶ Cross-site scripting

▶ SQL script injection

▶ Parameter tampering

▶ Buffer overflow

▶ Stealth commanding

▶ Hidden field manipulation

▶ Directory traversal

▶ URL blocking

The application level gateway can offer such protection because the data flow is actually analyzed at the level of the application. Predefined rules can determine if a query has been formulated correctly. Many users work with a white list, that is, a positive security model. In other words, rules must be defined for acceptable queries. Queries outside the rules are then blocked automatically. But the definition of such rules can create problems. It is especially difficult with very dynamic Internet applications. That's why many manufacturers try to use a learning algorithm that can learn the defining rules.

Use of an application level gateway can often be problematic in terms of performance, which means that another, dedicated computer must be set up for it.

6.4.4 Secure Sockets Layer Encryption

The *Secure Sockets Layer (SSL) protocol* works in two layers. It works best with a reliable transport protocol like TCP. The idea behind SSL is the same as for hybrid encryption—the principle is identical. In a normal case, like with most Internet banking applications, SSL operates so that only the server must identify itself with a certificate. But it can also be configured so that the client has to use a certificate to identify itself to the server. This is referred to as *mutual authentication*.

Encryption of the data occurs as it does with the hybrid procedure, with a symmetric key selected at random for the session. The key is exchanged ahead of time with an asymmetric procedure. Authentication of the server and the exchange of the symmetric key with the server is called the *handshaking phase*.

The phase functions as follows:

1. A client wants to set up a secure communication connection to a specific server with SSL. The client requests the server's certificate with the server's public key.
2. If properly configured, the client can contact the issuing CA and check the validity of the certificate against the certificate revocation list. If the certificate is valid, the client can continue.
3. In this case, the client selects a random number that it uses to encrypt the public key of the server. It then sends the number to the server.
4. The server receives the encrypted random number and decrypts it with its own private key. The decrypted random number is sent back to the client.
5. The client compares the random number sent by the server with the original. If the two numbers are identical, the client can be sure that it's connected to the correct and desired server.
6. If mutual authentication is called for, the same procedure must occur between the server and client in the opposite direction. This step does not usually occur.
7. Next, a randomly generated symmetric key (usually 182 bits, sometimes 256 bits) is exchanged between client and server.
8. Communication can continue with the symmetric key and the appropriate encryption. The key can also be renegotiated after a short time. Such is often the case in *virtual private networks* (VPNs).

Part 2
Security in SAP NetWeaver and Application Security

7 SAP Applications and Technology

This chapter covers the Global Security Positioning System (GSPS), which provides an overview of important SAP applications and related SAP NetWeaver technology. The GSPS map, inserted in this book as a poster, helps you navigate to individual security topics.

7.1 Global Security Positioning System

The *Global Security Positioning System* (GSPS) is a comprehensive overview of SAP applications, SAP NetWeaver components, security aspects, possible solutions, and suppliers. The arrangement of individual components is not static. Instead, the GSPS should simplify your own positioning within the complex landscape of SAP NetWeaver and serve as a checklist for the required security aspects in terms of system, application, and communication security along with risk and control management.

The GSPS is a scenario of many conceivable SAP NetWeaver landscapes. In this example, it does not cover all constellations, service providers, and suppliers of security and compliance solutions. The increasing complexity of the SAP NetWeaver landscape makes it indispensable to have a uniform security strategy that must consider all SAP components in terms of technology, processes, organization, and other issues to achieve comprehensive security with an internal risk and control system.

An overview of the GSPS inserted as a poster in this book (also see Figure 7.1 at the end of this chapter) helps orientation and navigation. Selected chapters describe individual security solutions extensively. Some chapters concentrate on explaining concepts to maintain the character of this book as an overview.

7.2 SAP Applications

The following list provides an overview of the most important SAP applications based on SAP NetWeaver, as found in the GSPS.

▶ **SAP ERP Central Component** (SAP ECC)
SAP ECC consists of all the traditional application components of SAP R/3 and new applications. The functional areas in SAP ECC include analytics (reporting), financials (financial accounting and corporate governance), procurement and logistics execution, product development and manufacturing, sales and services, and corporate services. Chapter 9 describes the risks and controls for SAP ECC.

- **mySAP ERP Human Capital Management** (mySAP ERP HCM)

  mySAP ERP HCM consists of the traditional human resources (HR) application component and enhancements. Functional areas include talent management, workforce process management, and workforce deployment. Chapter 10 describes the risks and controls for SAP ERP HCM.

- **SAP Industry Solutions (SAP IS)**

  SAP Industry Solutions are special applications tailored to the needs of individual industries and industrial branches. Among others, the following SAP industry offerings exist: SAP for Aerospace & Defense, SAP for Automotive, SAP for Banking, SAP for Consumer Products, SAP for Contract Accounts Receivables and Payables (creditors/debtors), SAP for Defense & Security, SAP for Engineering, Construction & Operations, SAP for Financial Service Providers, SAP for Healthcare, SAP for Higher Education & Research, SAP for High Tech, SAP for Insurance, SAP for Media, SAP for Mill Products, SAP for Mining, SAP for Oil & Gas, SAP for Professional Services, SAP for Public Sector, SAP for Retail, SAP for Telecommunications, and SAP for Utilities.

  Based on an important example for SAP for Defense & Security, Chapter 11 describes supplemental control solutions for the SAP industry offerings, not all of which can be treated in this book.

- **SAP NetWeaver Business Intelligence** (SAP BI)

  SAP NetWeaver Business Intelligence is the central application for analysis, evaluation, and overall reporting for mySAP Business Suite and its applications. Chapter 12 describes the essential risk management and control measures for SAP NetWeaver BI.

- **SAP NetWeaver Master Data Management** (SAP MDM)

  SAP NetWeaver Master Data Management is an upper-level system for the central consolidation, creation, and distribution of master data for all SAP applications in a company's heterogeneous SAP NetWeaver landscape. Chapter 13 describes the special considerations for risk and control management with SAP MDM.

- **mySAP Customer Relationship Management** (mySAP CRM)

  mySAP CRM is the central customer and sales management system from SAP. Its functional areas include marketing, sales, service (customer-oriented services), and analysis (market and customer analysis). Chapter 14 describes the important risks and controls associated with mySAP CRM.

- **mySAP Supplier Relationship Management** (mySAP SRM)

  mySAP SRM is the central SAP solution for procurements and the management of suppliers and business partners. Its functional areas include sourcing, procurement, and supplier enablement. Chapter 15 describes the risk and control options for mySAP SRM.

- **mySAP Supply Chain Management** (mySAP SCM)
  mySAP SCM is the central planning and control system. It covers the following functional areas: demand and supply planning (capacity planning), service parts planning (component logistics), procurement, manufacturing (production planning), warehousing, order fulfillment, transportation (transport management), and supply chain design and analytics. Chapter 16 describes the risk and control options.

- **SAP Strategic Enterprise Management** (SAP SEM)
  SAP SEM is the central analysis and control system for business planning and simulation, performance measurement, risk management, and stakeholder relationship management. Chapter 17 describes the risk and control options for SAP SEM.

7.3 SAP NetWeaver

All the SAP solutions listed above use SAP NetWeaver, the new technology and integration platform from SAP. The GSPS covers its main components:

- **SAP Web Application Server** (SAP Web AS)
  SAP Web Application Server is the central unit of SAP NetWeaver. All mySAP and SAP applications run on this platform. In addition to the traditional ABAP stack (ABAP programs and applications), SAP Web AS also offers new Java middleware for Java applications. These components are often referred to as SAP Web AS ABAP and SAP Web AS J2EE. Chapter 8 describes the risks and controls for SAP Web AS.

- **SAP Solution Manager** (SAP SolMan)
  SAP Solution Manager is the central operations management component for complex SAP NetWeaver system landscapes. SAP Solution Manager can be used to manage SAP NetWeaver systems. In addition to implementation and monitoring assistance, SAP Solution Manager provides solutions for technical and functional measures for effective operations management and it supports ITIL core processes. Chapter 18 describes the risks and controls for SAP Solution Manager.

- **SAP Enterprise Portal** (SAP EP)
  SAP Enterprise Portal is the entry point for all users of companywide SAP NetWeaver systems and applications and for all non-SAP systems and applications. SAP EP simplifies navigation for users. Technically, SAP EP is based on SAP Web AS J2EE. Chapter 19 describes the risks and controls for SAP EP.

- **SAP Exchange Infrastructure (SAP XI)**
  SAP Exchange Infrastructure is the integration solution for data and applications. SAP XI provides a central and open interface solution and thus contrib-

utes to simplifying complex landscapes made up of SAP NetWeaver and non-SAP components. The technical solution also supports process modeling. Chapter 20 describes the risks and controls for SAP NetWeaver XI.

▶ **SAP Partner Connectivity Kit** (SAP PCK)
The SAP Partner Connectivity Kit enables the connection of partner solutions with SAP XI. Chapter 21 describes the risks and controls for the SAP Partner Connectivity Kit.

▶ **SAP Mobile Infrastructure (SAP MI)**
SAP Mobile Infrastructure is a component of SAP NetWeaver and offers solutions for the operation and management of mobile applications. Chapter 22 describes the risks and controls for SAP MI.

▶ **Database server**
The database server is the persistent storage area for all data of SAP systems. Chapter 23 describes the risks and controls for the database server.

▶ **SAP Web Dispatcher**
The SAP Web Dispatcher is the load balancer for all SAP system clusters. In addition to load distribution, the Web Dispatcher offers limited security functions like reverse proxy and encryption. Chapter 24 describes the risks and controls for the SAP Web Dispatcher.

▶ **SAProuter**
SAProuter filters access to SAP Web AS systems. Chapter 25 describes the risks and controls for SAProuter.

▶ **SAP Internet Transaction Server** (SAP ITS)
The SAP ITS functionality of SAP NetWeaver is the link between SAP Web AS and the SAP GUI for HTML (web browser). The SAP ITS is needed to format ABAP-based applications in HTML so that a web browser can control them. Chapter 26 describes the risks and controls for the SAP ITS.

▶ **SAP GUI**
The SAP GUI is the graphical user interface for SAP applications. SAP GUI is the client component for non-web-based applications. Chapter 27 describes the risks and controls for SAP GUI.

▶ **Web browser**
The web browser (SAP GUI for HTML) is the graphical user interface for web-based SAP applications. Chapter 28 describes the risks and controls for the web browser.

▶ **Mobile devices**
Mobile devices are used for mobile SAP applications. They include notebooks, PDAs, mobile telephones, and scanners. Chapter 29 describes the risks and controls for desktop security of the mobile devices.

7.4   Security Technologies

The following security solutions and suppliers make a substantial contribution to the improvement of security, control, and compliance measures for SAP NetWeaver products and applications. The list contains only a selection of partner solutions and service providers covered in the GSPS. This does not mean that products from other suppliers do not meet the same level of quality.

7.4.1   Authorizations, Risk and Change Management, and Auditing

The following solutions serve security when dealing with authorizations, the identification of risks, control management, and change management to guarantee compliance with legal requirements and auditing requirements.

▶ **SecurInfo for SAP**
With *SecurInfo for SAP*, SecurInfo offers an integrated solution for risk control, authorization control, user management, and control management that adheres to auditing requirements for a change management process. The focus is on consistent use of the principle of information ownership. It is a preventive solution for reduction of potential risks and minimizing company risks. A predefined risk library within the overall solution can help identify potential risks.

▶ **Approva BizRights**
With *BizRights*, Approva offers a solution for risk analysis and monitoring vulnerabilities in the SAP NetWeaver authorization system. The solution is designed around detective control and enhanced with preventive risk analysis.

▶ **SAP Compliance Calibrator by Virsa Systems**
With *SAP Compliance Calibrator by Virsa Systems*, SAP and Virsa Systems offer a partner solution for risk analyses for SAP applications. The analyses can use predefined risks based on rules to recognize functional separations, critical authorizations, and user master data with a high potential for danger. Predefined controls help minimze the risks. Additional products from Virsa Systems can complete the detective methods of SAP Compliance Calibrator by Virsa Systems to implement control measures in a company.

▶ **SAP Management of Internal Controls** (SAP MIC)
SAP Management of Internal Controls is an SAP product that helps document and manage internal controls. It focuses on compliance with legal requirements like SOX and Basel II. SAP MIC can model processes, assign risks and controls, and measure and evaluate the effectiveness of the controls in use. SAP MIC is a component of mySAP ERP Enterprise Edition.

- **SAP Audit Information System** (SAP AIS)

  SAP Audit Information System is a functionality within SAP ECC to support internal and external system audits. Because audits reveal vulnerabilities in financial and settlement processes as well as in technical applications, SAP AIS is an important component of a comprehensive control and compliance solution for companies. SAP AIS consists of transactions and reports.

- **SAP Profile Generator** (transaction PFCG)

  The *SAP Profile Generator* is the tool for creating ABAP roles and authorization components. It is the standard component for authorization management in SAP Web AS ABAP. The SAP Profile Generator can assign roles to users; it does not consider risks and controls when doing so.

- **SAP User Management Engine** (SAP UME)

  SAP User Management Engine is the tool for creating UME roles and authorization components. It is the standard component for authorization management in SAP Web AS J2EE. SAP UME can assign roles to users. It does not consider risks and controls when doing so.

Particularly in terms of compliance with legal requirements, SAP User Management Engine supports technical solutions from auditing companies like Deloitte, Ernst & Young, KPMG, and PricewaterhouseCoopers.

7.4.2 Identity Management

The management of identities (users of SAP NetWeaver systems and applications and business partner users) is a central task in an internal risk and control system. The opening of applications and systems to the Internet and external partners makes it particularly necessary that information stored on system users is always up to date, audit-proof, and correct. The following sections list some solutions for the SAP NetWeaver environment.

- **Microsoft Active Directory Service** (Microsoft ADS)

  Microsoft Active Directory Service is an LDAP directory service that helps companies manage SAP and non-SAP user master data according to the X.500 standard. Its wide market penetration means that Microsoft ADS is often used in the SAP environment.

- **Siemens DirX**

  Siemens DirX is a metadirectory service for central maintenance of user master data and its assignment to authorizations in various SAP NetWeaver and non-SAP systems.

- **Computer Associates eTrust Admin Server** (CA eTrust)
  With its *eTrust Admin Server* solution, CA offers a metadirectory service for central maintenance of user and authorization assignment data for SAP NetWeaver and non-SAP systems. Employee self-service is also supported on the process side.

- **SUN ONE**
  SUN offers an LDAP directory service with its *SUN ONE* solution. The solution can manage SAP and non-SAP user master data according to the X.500 standard. It is used primarily in web-based applications.

- **Entrust PKI**
  Entrust PKI is a certificate-based, complete solution for the secure and controlled administration of identities. Entrust PKI can be combined with other metadirectory services and offers increased security with digital certificates and their audit-proof management.

- **mySAP Human Capital Management** (mySAP HCM)
  mySAP HCM can manage employees and users of SAP Web AS applications. It uses the organizational structure in mySAP ERP HCM to accomplish this task. Authorizations can also be assigned to users via the organizational structure — for jobs, for example. Linking administrative processes and mySAP HCM to central user management or LDAP directory services leads to a comprehensive identity management solution.

- **BMC Control/SA**
  BMC Control/SA is a comprehensive solution to manage identities in SAP NetWeaver systems and non-SAP systems. BMC Control/SA is used primarily in heterogenous landscapes.

- **IBM Tivoli Directory Server** (IBM Tivoli)
  IBM Tivoli Directory Server helps administer user identities in heterogeneous system landscapes.

- **Novell eDirectory**
  Novell eDirectory is an LDAP directory service used to maintain and manage SAP and non-SAP identities. The X.500 standard is also used.

7.4.3 Secure Authentication and Single Sign-On (SSO)

Secure authentication is one of the most important methods of granting controlled access to internal SAP NetWeaver systems and keeping unauthorized persons at bay. SAP has developed procedures that can be enhanced or replaced by partner solutions.

- **User ID and Password**
  In the standard version, SAP uses one-factor authentication. Each user is granted a unique user ID and a password. This authentication method is used

as the basic procedure throughout the entire SAP NetWeaver environment. Password rules can be defined.

▶ **SAP Logon Tickets**
SAP offers *logon tickets* as an authentication method for single sign-on. The logon ticket is a cookie created and signed on a primary SAP Web AS or SAP EP upon successful initial authentication. All connected SAP systems use the logon ticket for further authentication.

▶ **Computer Associates eTrust Single Sign-On and eTrust SiteMinder** (CA SSO)
With *eTrust Single Sign-On* and *eTrust SiteMinder*, CA offers additional SSO solutions for SAP and non-SAP systems.

▶ **SecurIntegration WebLogonPad Server** (SecurIntegration WLP)
SecurIntegration LogonPad is an SSO authentication solution for various SAP Web AS systems. The leading system is the *WebLogonPad Server* (WLP), which also produces SAP logon tickets and transmits them to the LogonPad. The procedure can be used for the SAP GUI for HMTL and the SAP GUI for Windows.

▶ **iT Sec Swiss Secude signon&secure** (iT Sec Swiss)
iT Sec Swiss Secude signon&secure is an SSO solution for authentication based on digital certificates. It uses the SAP–SNC interface. Various security levels can be configured.

▶ **Kobil eSecure**
Kobil eSecure also handles SSO authentication on the basis of digital certificates with a chip card. It offers a secure storage medium for the SSF function.

7.4.4 Technical Security

Technical security is a basic precondition for linking all components of an SAP system landscape together. To guarantee secure identity and authorization management, secure and encrypted communication, and other technical components, in addition to offering its own solutions, SAP collaborates with numerous partners to support the open system architecture of SAP NetWeaver.

▶ **RSA Security**
RSA offers *RSA ClearTrust*, a pluggable solution for the authentication of identities with the use of the SAP ITS WGate functionality. It also offers *RSA Federated Identity Manager (FIM)*, an SSO solution for authentication on SAP NetWeaver systems with SAML.

▶ **Entrust**
With its numerous products, Entrust offers a comprehensive portfolio for network and communications security, encryption, and secure store and forward.

▶ **BeSeQure**

BeSeQure Business Security Framework (BSF) uses a comprehensive and modular design to offer solutions for the authentication of users, security of Web services, and authorization of users for Web services.

▶ **F5**

F5 TrafficShield Application Firewall (F5) secures Web applications at the application layer. It offers security solutions for attack scenarios for web applications.

▶ **Computer Associates**

CA eTrust Access Control is a control solution for proactive server protection. It guarantees security like protection from unauthorized access at the level of the operating system. *CA eBusiness Server Security* is a server management tool that recognizes vulnerabilities at the level of the operating system. *CA eTrust Community Command Center* is a detective control solution that uses incident analysis.

▶ **iT Sec Swiss**

With its *Secude Secure Notebook* solution, iT Sec Swiss offers a technical encryption solution for the security of mobile devices, especially notebooks.

▶ **SAP**

SAP itself offers several security solutions like *SAP WebDispatcher*, *SAProuter*, encryption for communications links based on the *SAP Cryptographic Library* (SAP CRYPTOLIB).

7.4.5   Influencing Factors

A number of influencing factors determine the value and need of the magnitude and depth of security solutions. Considerations of risk, legal requirements, adherence to security guidelines, security standards, and physical security must be embedded in comprehensive risk and control management. The GSPS shows SAP NetWeaver components worth protecting, influencing factors, and security solutions in their totality. Every company must define its own security requirements in consideration of the influencing factors and the evaluation of risk.

All components of the GSPS are part of a necessary and comprehensive security strategy. The following chapters focus on determining potential risks to help you define the correct security strategy and any related controls. The presentation of standard SAP methods, notes, and best-practice solutions helps readers understand the controls.

Global Security Positioning System (GSPS)

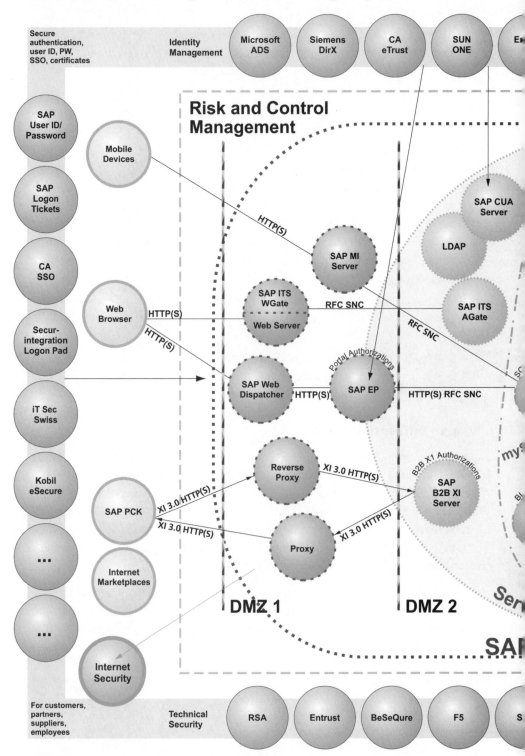

Figure 7.1 Global Security Positioning System

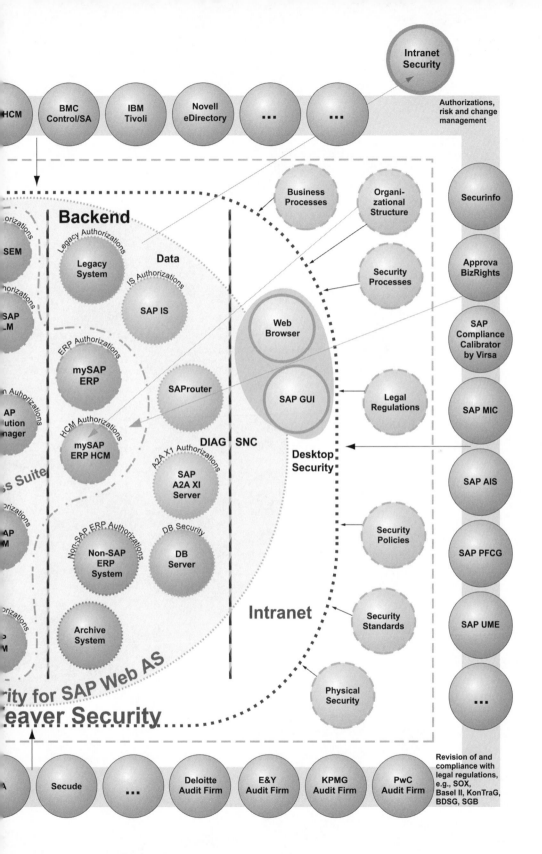

Intranet
Security

Authorizations,
risk and change
management

HCM BMC Control/SA IBM Tivoli Novell eDirectory ... ...

Business Processes Organizational Structure Securinfo

Backend

Legacy Authorizations

SEM

Legacy System Data Security Processes Approva BizRights

IS Authorizations

SAP IS Web Browser SAP Compliance Calibrator by Virsa

SAP _M

ERP Authorizations

mySAP ERP SAProuter SAP GUI Legal Regulations SAP MIC

HCM Authorizations

mySAP ERP HCM DIAG SNC Desktop Security

A2A XI Authorizations

SAP A2A XI Server SAP AIS

Non-SAP ERP Authorizations

DB Security

Non-SAP ERP System DB Server Security Policies SAP PFCG

Intranet

Archive System Security Standards SAP UME

ity for SAP Web AS

eaver Security

Physical Security ...

Secude ... Deloitte Audit Firm E&Y Audit Firm KPMG Audit Firm PwC Audit Firm

Revision of and
compliance with
legal regulations,
e.g., SOX,
Basel II, KonTraG,
BDSG, SGB

8   SAP Web Application Server

This chapter explains IT security concepts—including both ABAP and Java solutions—for the server security (SAP Web AS) area of the Global Security Positioning System (GSPS).

8.1   Introduction and Functions

8.1.1   Overview

The *SAP Web Application Server* (SAP Web AS) is the main technical component of SAP NetWeaver and serves as the application platform for all ABAP-based and Java-based applications. The SAP Enterprise Portal, the SAP Exchange Infrastructure, and the SAP Mobile Infrastructure are likewise all based on the SAP Web AS.

In the past, the role of the SAP Application Server was to function as the technical basis of SAP R/3, and all SAP programs used ABAP only. Then, with SAP NetWeaver, the purely ABAP-based runtime environment was expanded to include Java, on the basis of a J2EE engine. This move marked the beginning of a trend towards incorporating more and more Internet-based technologies. In keeping with this trend, the name was changed to SAP Web Application Server.[1] The SAP Web AS is thus not just a "classic" server for R/3 client-server applications; rather, it is more accurately described as a *middleware technology platform* for Web-based applications.

Besides ABAP applications, the SAP Web AS also supports *Business Server Pages* (BSP), *Java Server Pages* (JSP), and *Web Dynpro* for ABAP and Java. Web Dynpro-based applications are the SAP technology of the future and will gradually replace the classic ABAP dynpros.

Besides the usual application server tasks for various program environments, the SAP Web AS also provides integration services on the basis of Web services using *Simple Object Access Protocol* (SOAP) or *Remote Function Calls* (RFC) for *Business Application Programming Interfaces* (BAPIs).

Thus, SAP Web AS middleware technology makes it possible to gradually switch over what could be described as somewhat monolithic business programs—such

---

1 As of the next release of SAP NetWeaver, the name "SAP Web Application Server" will probably change to "SAP NetWeaver Application Server." In this book, however, we'll continue to use the old name.

as Financial Accounting, Controlling, and Materials Management—to a service-oriented application architecture: the *Enterprise Services Architecture* (ESA).

8.1.2 Technical Architecture

The central component of the SAP Web AS is the *ABAP stack* (hereafter referred to as the *SAP Web AS ABAP*), which contains the runtime environment for ABAP-based applications. These are applications or Business Server Pages that are developed directly in ABAP or ABAP Objects. The ABAP Workbench can be used to develop these applications and to analyze them in order to detect any errors. The applications use the *database abstraction*, a neutral access layer for a range of database manufacturers, to access the database. The SAP Web AS also has its own logical database, which is separate from the SAP Web AS J2EE engine. All ABAP-based applications use the same authorization principles, which are described in Chapter 9.

As we mentioned at the beginning of this chapter, a Java part, namely the *Java stack* (hereafter referred to as *SAP Web AS J2EE*), was added to the ABAP architecture in the SAP Web AS. This was necessary due to the need to open up SAP's existing proprietary architecture and to be able to integrate it into other existing Internet technologies more successfully, such as Java application servers (IBM WebSphere, BEA WebLogic) and .NET (from Microsoft).

The SAP Web AS J2EE is a J2EE server (*Java 2, Enterprise Edition*) that provides the runtime environment for Java-based programs such as *Java Server Pages* and *Enterprise JavaBeans*. The SAP Web AS J2EE also accesses its own database by means of the database abstraction. Communication between the SAP Web AS J2EE and the SAP Web AS ABAP is enabled by the *Java Connection Architecture*. This architecture allows the SAP Web AS J2EE to call ABAP function groups by means of Remote Function Calls. Java also has its own development environment: the *Java Integrated Development Environment* (Java IDE).

Figure 8.1 illustrates the architecture of the SAP Web AS.

Web dynpro applications can be developed using either ABAP or Java. The *Internet Communication Manager* (ICM), using HTTP(S), is used to handle all Web-based programs—that is, programs for both the Internet and intranets. This is the case not only for installations that consist of the SAP Web AS J2EE only, but also for ABAP dynpro applications, as the ITS is integrated into the ICM.

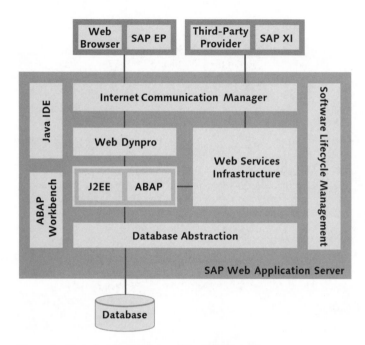

Figure 8.1 Technical Architecture of the SAP Web AS

The ICM also controls *Web services*. It is thus the communication and integration interface both to the user and to other services that use it to call specific functions. The SAP Exchange Infrastructure also uses this interface. All the usual standard protocols, including HTTP(S), SMTP, and SOAP (XML), are available.

Software Lifecycle Management is standardized for the SAP Web AS ABAP and the J2EE. Java applications, too, can have a classic three-system landscape consisting of development, quality assurance, and production systems, although the application development landscape and the development environment are different from ABAP Transport Management and the ABAP Workbench.

8.2   Risks and Controls

In this section, we shall use a simplified version of the proposed risk analysis methodology described in Chapter 2 to identify the main security risks and the necessary controls. Subsequent sections describe these controls in greater detail and illustrate them by means of examples. References to these sections are provided in Table 8.1 below, in the rows entitled **Section**.

No.	Classification	Description
1.	Risk potential	Missing or incomplete authorization concept for technical administration of the SAP Web AS.
		Administrators or even regular users are assigned write access to critical administrative transactions and functions. The "four eyes principle" (a predecessor of pair programming) is being disregarded or incorrectly implemented.
	Impact	Administrators or regular users can view highly-confidential and integral business information and make unauthorized modifications to this information. This makes it possible for secret business information to leak to the outside world and poses a serious threat to the integrity of the system. The negative economic effects for the enterprise could be enormous.
	Risk without control(s)	Extremely high
	Control(s)	Define and implement an administration authorization concept that makes full use of the four eyes principle. This applies both to SAP Web AS ABAP and to SAP Web AS J2EE.
	Risk with control(s)	Normal
	Section	8.3.1
2.	Risk potential	No authorization concept for Java applications.
		There is no authorization concept for Java, which could allow users to access business data that they are not authorized to access.
	Impact	The lack of an authorization concept for Java could lead to unauthorized technical system changes being made. However, because current SAP Java applications are not used in critical business areas such as Financial Accounting or Controlling, this situation cannot cause extreme financial losses for the enterprise. Nonetheless, your system may still be compromized.
	Risk without control(s)	High
	Control(s)	Introduce an authorization concept for Java-based applications on the basis of JAAS or UME roles (Java Authentication and Authorization Service, User Management Engine).
	Risk with control(s)	Normal
	Section	8.3.2

Table 8.1 Risks and Controls for the SAP Web AS

No.	Classification	Description
3.	Risk potential	No authorization restrictions for RFC calls.
		With RFCs from the SAP Web AS to another client or to another instance that uses an RFC user, the RFC authorizations both in the calling and the called systems have unrestricted authorizations.
	Impact	Even if the RFC user is only of the type "Communication" or "System," the full authorization status can still be taken advantage of to create a new dialog user with full authorizations in the target system.new dislation can still be taken advantage of to create a new dislhe called systems have full authorizat This could leave the system vulnerable to unauthorized financial transactions with extremely negative consequences for your enterprise.
	Risk without control(s)	Extremely high
	Control(s)	Restrict the scope of authorizations for RFC communication connections, using the authorization objects designed for this purpose.
	Risk with control(s)	Normal
	Section	8.3.3
4.	Risk potential	Passwords that are too numerous and too simple.
		In order to authenticate themselves to all the different applications or clients running on one or more SAP Web AS installations, users have to log themselves on using a different password in each case. To make it easier to remember their passwords, users either write them down or make them as simple as possible.
	Impact	Application passwords that have been written down or that are very simple represent a weak link in the user authentication chain. This situation can enable unauthorized users to abuse applications and to carry out unauthorized transactions. The financial damage from such abuses can be enormous.
	Risk without control(s)	Extremely high
	Control(s)	Introduce a Single Sign-On (SSO) procedure. This is a stronger, less vulnerable user authentication method.
	Risk with control(s)	Normal
	Section	8.4.1

Table 8.1 Risks and Controls for the SAP Web AS (cont.)

No.	Classification	Description
5.	Risk potential	No central user persistence store.
		Master data is stored in several different user persistence storage locations. In addition to this, there is no unified enterprise-wide employee identifier. The master data storage concept thus contains redundancy and the data is inconsistent.
	Impact	Inconsistent user master data causes a large amount of redundancy in user management, not to mention a lack of transparency. Thus, when changes need to be made (for example, if an employee leaves the enterprise), user accounts are not managed in an appropriate manner. The result may be the existence of user accounts with excessive authorizations, which could be exploited by other unauthorized users. There are also the additional administrative costs of maintaining redundant user accounts.
	Risk without control(s)	Extremely high
	Control(s)	Connect the SAP Web AS to a central LDAP directory that contains the master data of all users in one central location.
	Risk with control(s)	Normal
	Section	8.4.2
6.	Risk potential	Default user passwords that have not been changed.
		The initial default passwords have not been changed for the default users "SAP," "DDIC," and so on.
	Impact	Usually, the default passwords for default users are generally known. Therefore, these passwords should be changed as quickly as possible, to prevent unauthorized users from using the full authorizations of these default user accounts to make illicit financial transactions.
	Risk without control(s)	Extremely high
	Control(s)	Change the default passwords for default users.
	Risk with control(s)	Normal
	Section	8.4.3

Table 8.1 Risks and Controls for the SAP Web AS (cont.)

No.	Classification	Description
7.	Risk potential	The SAP Gateway is not configured.
		The SAP Gateway controls RFC communication between one SAP Web AS and another, or between an SAP Web AS and a CPI-C application. In many cases, this gateway has not been secured.
	Impact	The lack of security in the SAP Gateway could allow unauthorized commands to be executed on the target system; for example, a new administrator account could be created. The user of this new, unauthorized administrator account would then have total control over the target system.
	Risk without control(s)	Extremely high
	Control(s)	Make RFC communication on the SAP Gateway secure using the *secinfo* file.
	Risk with control(s)	Normal
	Section	8.4.4
8.	Risk potential	No restriction on operating system access.
		Even regular users can access the operating system from within the SAP Web AS.
	Impact	Operating system commands that are executed using SAP transactions (such as SM49) could compromise the entire operating system. The integrity of the system is thus not adequately protected, which poses a serious risk to the system.
	Risk without control(s)	Extremely high
	Control(s)	Take measures to prevent operating system commands from being executed from within the SAP Web AS.
	Risk with control(s)	Normal
	Section	8.4.5
9.	Risk potential	Security parameters are not configured.
		Important security parameters—such as those setting down password rules—are not defined.
	Impact	Parameters that have not been configured, or parameters that have been incorrectly configured, cause new weak points in the system. These weak points can allow unauthorized users to carry out illicit financial transactions or to manipulate data for unauthorized purposes.
	Risk without control(s)	Extremely high
	Control(s)	Correct configuration of system security parameters.

Table 8.1 Risks and Controls for the SAP Web AS (cont.)

No.	Classification	Description
	Risk with control(s)	Normal
	Section	8.4.6
10.	Risk potential	Unencrypted communication channels.
		The communication channels either between the SAP GUI or Web browser and the SAP Web AS, or between different SAP Web AS instances, are unencrypted.
	Impact	Unencrypted communication channels can allow unauthorized users to view or manipulate secret business information. This is likely to cause financial losses for the enterprise.
	Risk without control(s)	Extremely high
	Control(s)	Introduce SSL encoding on all HTTP communication channels, or SNC encoding for DIAG or RFC connections.
	Risk with control(s)	Normal
	Section	8.4.7
11.	Risk potential	Unnecessary and unsecured Internet services are active.
		The ICM enables access to and communication with services on the Internet Connection Framework (ICF) of the SAP Web AS. These services should not be accessible via the Internet.
	Impact	Services that should not be generally accessible are used by unauthorized users to exploit potential holes in these services—such as a lack of proper authentication—and possibly to initiate further unauthorized accesses. In the worst-case scenario, the whole system may be compromised.
	Risk without control(s)	High
	Control(s)	Deactivate services that are not required and that do not need to be accessible from the Internet.
	Risk with control(s)	Normal
	Section	8.4.8
12.	Risk potential	No network strategy.
		The SAP Web AS is not sufficiently secured on the network level. If the network is divided up into trustworthy and non-trustworthy areas, firewalls have to be used to separate the various areas.

Table 8.1 Risks and Controls for the SAP Web AS (cont.)

No.	Classification	Description
	Impact	If a firewall configuration is not used, the security of the SAP Web AS on the network level is inadequate in the Internet context, and any weak points that there may be in the system can be exploited on the operating system level. This can allow system attackers to obtain administrator authorizations, which in turn may compromise the SAP Web AS. The end result may be unauthorized manipulation of data or unauthorized execution of transactions.
	Risk without control(s)	Extremely high
	Control(s)	Protect and secure the SAP Web AS network by dividing up the network segments into trustworthy and less trustworthy areas. Do this by appropriately configuring and setting up network-based firewalls.
	Risk with control(s)	Normal
	Section	8.4.9
13.	Risk potential	External attacks on Internet applications. Web-based applications (such as Web Dynpro, BSP, and JSP) do not perform adequate checks on the input transferred by the client on the application level, such as URL parameters, form field input, and so on. This allows hackers to carry out the following application-level attacks (these are the main methods of attack): ▶ Stealth commanding: changing transfer parameters in order to obtain a different application status or to modify price information ▶ Cookie poisoning and token analysis: enable the hacker to carry out session hijacking ▶ Buffer overflow: enables a denial-of-service attack ▶ Cross-site scripting: enables the hacker to divert the user to a compromised site
	Impact	Inadequate checking of input parameters means that the application is compromized, and therefore unauthorized users can obtain advanced permissions on the application level. This also means that back-end applications can be accessed, and unauthorized users can thus modify and abuse back-end application data.
	Risk without control(s)	Extremely high
	Control(s)	Transfer parameters and input fields have to be checked for plausibility and correctness on the server side. It is also recommended that you introduce an application-level gateway. This kind of gateway is especially important for in-house applications that will be provided with the SAP Web AS for Internet use.

Table 8.1 Risks and Controls for the SAP Web AS (cont.)

No.	Classification	Description
	Risk with control(s)	Normal
	Section	8.4.10
14.	Risk potential	Lack of hardening measures on the operating system level. The SAP Web AS operating system has not been hardened, resulting in the existence of superfluous operating system services that have not been deactivated.
	Impact	An attacker has gained access to the SAP Web AS, which means that the SAP Web AS can now be used in other attacks on the enterprise's back-end applications.
	Risk without control(s)	High
	Control(s)	The SAP Web AS has to be hardened on the operating system level. For example, some services that are not required by the overlying applications have to be deactivated. Also, an intrusion detection system can be established on the host level. This system can be used to detect possible attacks and to initiate the required countermeasures.
	Risk with control(s)	Normal
	Section	8.4.11
15.	Risk potential	No software transport and release system. There is no quality assurance process for newly developed or modified software (such as ABAP or Java applications).
	Impact	The lack of a quality assurance process for developing software and transporting it to the production system can cause faulty software to be imported to production servers, where it can seriously damage the integrity of the system. It is thus very likely that the system will be compromised.
	Risk without control(s)	Extremely high
	Control(s)	Introduce a quality assurance process for developing and releasing software, and for transporting it to the production SAP Web AS.
	Risk with control(s)	Normal
	Section	8.4.12

Table 8.1 Risks and Controls for the SAP Web AS (cont.)

8.3 Application Security

8.3.1 Technical Authorization Concept for Administrators

The authorization concept for administrators for the ABAP stack is based on the ABAP standard authorization concept, as described in section 9.3.2.

The authorization concept for authorizations in the ABAP environment should reflect the relevance, risks, and complexity of the SAP systems. This concept defines the procedures, rules, and roles that apply to administrators, and specifies the administrative functions of the SAP Web AS. As is the case with business-department-specific authorizations, you should also perform a risk analysis of the critical functions in the technology-specific area of the SAP Web AS, so that you can make the appropriate functional separations when setting the authorizations (see Figure 8.2).

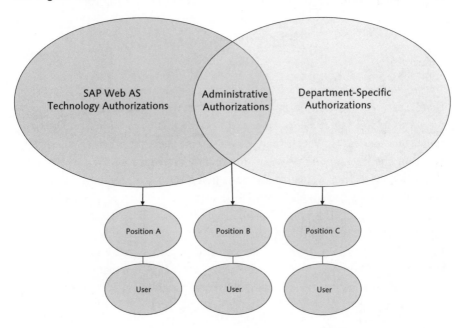

Figure 8.2 Technology Authorizations Are an Integral Part of a Holistic Authorization Concept

Unfortunately, it is still often the case that very generous authorizations are assigned to the administrators of SAP Web AS systems. It is the responsibility of every enterprise to assess the potential risks of its own situation. However, a technology authorization concept is a central component of the overlying authorization and IT security concept, and it should always form part of the enterprise's approach to ensuring that the SAP ECC processes and the processes of all other SAP Web AS systems run smoothly.

The basis of a solid authorization concept for SAP Web AS technology is formed by task-based roles, which, for organizational reasons, are grouped into position roles. Because the size and quality of SAP Web AS technology and development teams can vary, we assume here that a work center consists of multiple administrative task roles. A task role in this context is defined in terms of the quantity of transactions that have a logical relationship with each other and no functional risks. Task roles contain the authorizations that are required to execute all transactions of the role. Because an individual task role usually covers only some of the activities of the basic user, multiple task roles, in most cases, are assigned in aggregated form to a basic user as a basic single role. This ensures that tasks and the monitoring of these tasks are kept logically separate.

If at all possible, an administrative user should be assigned to only one work center—that is, to only one position. If multiple positions are involved, transactions are grouped into either a single role or a composite role and then assigned to the employee.

Example

An employee may be working as a developer and a customizer at the same time. These roles are often implemented as generic roles in the technology area. This means that they do not contain any restrictions in terms of organizational boundaries. However, there can also be roles that are specially developed for the development system, the quality assurance system, or the production system. Thus, the authorizations that a developer has in the development system may be more extensive than those that he or she has in the production system. This creates a situation where the developer has different positions in the development system, the quality assurance or test system, and the production system. However, like with other authorizations, the scope of technology authorizations can be restricted; in this case, the main elements are user group, role name, development class, and program or table authorization group.

The risk analysis process for technology authorizations has the advantage that roles can also be analyzed in terms of their incompatibility with each other. Two technology roles are considered to be incompatible if, for system security and risk-related reasons, they cannot both be assigned to the same user.

Application areas usually describe the functions and objectives of specific task areas, and are used to delimit the functions that are assigned to employees. The following are some of the application areas in the technology area:

▶ ALE

▶ Authorization management and user management

▶ Authorization management

▶ Customizing and development

▶ Operations

▶ System administration

▶ Workflow management

Once the risk analysis has been used to divide up the tasks, the organizational factors can be incorporated into the design of the authorization concept. The process of assigning work areas to specific positions in the technology area is also useful in developing and assigning roles and authorizations on the position level. For example, the project coordinator, developer, customizer, and quality specialist positions may be assigned to the "Customizing and Development" work area. The positions assigned to the "Operations" work area could be as follows: archiver, batch user in the business department, batch job administrator, help desk worker, and operator. The following are examples of positions in the technology area:

▶ **ALE developer**
   This position requires authorizations for the following tasks, among others: developing ALE applications, maintaining ALE Customizing settings, using IDoc test tools, displaying IDoc types, IDoc record types, and segments, configuring ALE partner agreements, ports, and change pointers, adapting ALE controls

(process code, status), and implementing ALE monitoring. There are also other ALE positions, such as ALE customizer, ALE administrator, and ALE monitor.

▶ **Auditor/reviser**
This position requires authorizations for the following tasks, among others: using reports in the audit information system, the security audit log, and the authorization information system, and displaying tables that are relevant to users and authorizations.

▶ **Batch users in business departments**
This position requires authorizations for the following tasks, among others: scheduling, modifying, and monitoring batch jobs that are relevant to the business department, and analyzing their results.

▶ **Batch job operator**
This position requires all authorizations for the job management—for example, for scheduling, modifying, monitoring, and analyzing internal and external background jobs.

▶ **Authorization administrator (central control)**
This position requires authorizations for the following tasks, among others: maintaining all authorization components, displaying users and tables with authorization data, creating transport requests, and all transactions that restrict or manage authorizations, authorization groups, and authorization views, among others. Authorization administration is not purely a technology task; it is a general position that also includes business department authorizations. Because of the higher relevance of this position, it is important that you put in place control and monitoring measures.

▶ **Customizer**
This position requires authorizations for the following tasks, among others: making client-specific and cross-client Customizing settings, using maintenance functions in the development system and display functions in the quality assurance and production system, and maintaining transaction variants, global field values, tables, hypertexts, SAPscript texts, fonts, number range buffers and intervals, transport requests, and so on.

▶ **Developer**
This position requires authorizations for the following tasks, among others: performing development activities in the development system, performing display activities in the quality assurance and production system, carrying out Web developments, developing CATT processes, creating and administrating queries, maintaining hypertexts, SAPscript texts, and fonts, and how they are displayed, displaying Customizing projects and settings, maintaining transaction variants and global field values, maintaining table content, using the

authorization information system, performing internal basic system administration functions for all trace functions, and generating transport requests. Remember to watch out for users with different authorizations in different systems.

▶ **Help desk**
This position requires authorizations for the following tasks, among others: administrating printers, displaying spool requests and user data, locking and unlocking users, modifying user passwords, and other help functions within SAP ECC that are adapted to each real-world situation.

▶ **Operator**
This position requires authorizations for the following tasks, among others: displaying the CCMS system configuration, CCMS DB administration functions, system and client changeability, work processes and user sessions, carrying out performance analyses, and displaying transport requests.

▶ **Project coordinator**
This position requires authorizations for the following tasks, among others: displaying Repository development work, authorization objects and fields, CATT processes, Customizing settings, and Customizing objects, using the Cross System Viewer, and displaying table content. In quality assurance and production systems, it is very important that these authorizations be restricted to table authorization groups, in order to prevent access to sensitive data relating to transactions for table maintenance (SM30, SM31) and table display (SE16, SE17).

▶ **Quality specialist**
This position requires authorizations for the following tasks, among others: departmental acceptance of transports containing development and Customizing work, displaying and releasing transport requests, and releasing tasks.

▶ **Security officer**
Among other things, this position requires authorizations for the following: all transactions to do with authorizations, user management, and IT security, including maintenance and display transactions, monitoring functions, trace activities, master data maintenance, creating new authorization objects and fields, the Profile Generator, the check indicator, administrating profile parameters, creating transport requests, administrating the audit information system, locking and unlocking transactions, and so on. The position of security officer has very wide-ranging authorizations and therefore has to be subject to appropriate monitoring controls.

- ▶ **System administrator for SAP data center**

  This position requires authorizations for creating, deleting, and copying clients, modifying the CCMS system configuration, carrying out CCMS DB administration tasks, defining and executing logical commands in a controlled manner, displaying the changeability of systems and clients, administrating work processes and user sessions, maintaining RFC and CPI-C connections, configuring National Language Support, authorizations for various display functions, including for number range buffers and intervals, carrying out performance analyses, configuring and analyzing the security audit log, sending system messages, locking and unlocking transactions, activating and analyzing system traces, creating, modifying, and deleting background jobs for spool management, displaying user and authorization data, configuring the Central Transport System (CTS) by setting up transport routes and administrating transport requests. These tasks can be divided up into smaller units, depending on the organizational structure of the task assignments.

- ▶ **Workflow developer**

  This position requires authorizations for development work in workflow management (WFM), making Customizing settings in WFM, administrating workflows, maintaining organizational structures for WFM, using runtime tools, and using Utilities and the WFM information system. Workflow development includes workflow administration and workflow monitoring. These positions can be defined either together or separately and can be mapped in roles.

- ▶ **Central user administrator**

  This position requires authorizations for creating and administrating user data, either with transaction SU01 or with the central user management functions. These tasks include locking and unlocking users, making password changes for users, assigning roles and authorizations to users (this task can also be handed over to the business departments as an independent task, at which point the departments take over information ownership), displaying roles, authorizations, authorization objects, authorization object fields, and displaying the Workbench and the tables of the Profile Generator (USOBT_C, USOBX_C). Usage of security audit logs can also be included as a task of this position.

The transactions of the individual positions can be grouped together in a single role or a composite role and assigned to the technology user.

There are currently no selective administrator authorizations for administrating the SAP Web AS J2EE using the Visual Administrator or the Config tool. Therefore, the Config tool can be started on the operating system level without any authorizations. Thus, you must ensure that access to the operating system is subject to very tight restrictions. You can do this using access control lists for Windows or the correct configuration of UIDs for UNIX, for example. You can define an initial administrator account during the installation process for the Visual Administrator, which is connected to the J2EE Engine by the P4 protocol. However, in this case, as before, you should place extra restrictions on operating system access.

You should also implement measures on the network side to ensure that access to the Visual Administrator is restricted:

▶ Access to the P4 interface (by default, port 50004 for instance 00) must be protected from unauthorized access via a firewall. However, because the P4 protocol can be tunneled via HTTP (by default, port 50001 for instance 00), this port also needs to be protected.

▶ The Telnet administration service of the SAP Web AS J2EE (by default, port 50008 for instance 00), which enables target-oriented administration, should be deactivated if it is not in use.

Table 8.2 contains a list of actions for administrating Java roles on the basis of the SAP User Management Engine (UME), the principle of which is explained in more detail in the next section. These actions can be grouped together as appropriate to form UME roles. UME administration is called using the URL *http://<SAP_Web AS_Server>:<J2EE_Engine_port>/useradmin*.

UME action	Description
UME.Manage_All	This action assigns full maintenance authorization—including for ABAP users, if the persistence store has been configured accordingly—for the J2EE Engine, including permissions to perform the following tasks: ▶ Administrate users in all departments and subsidiaries, including creating, modifying, deleting, locking, and unlocking users, and confirming new user creation requests ▶ Create, modify, and delete user groups ▶ Assign UME roles to users ▶ Import and export user data ▶ Manually replicate user data with external persistence storage
UME.Manage_Users	This action authorizes the recipient to manage users in their own departments or users in subsidiaries. These users can include the administrator to whom this action is assigned. Chapter 19 explains how to configure assignments to a department or a subsidiary in more detail. This action authorizes the recipient to perform the following tasks: search, create, modify, delete, lock, unlock, reset passwords, and confirm new user creation requests.

Table 8.2 Java Actions for J2EE Administration

UME action	Description
UME.Manage_Groups	This action authorizes the recipient to view, add, modify, and delete user groups. It also authorizes him or her to assign users to groups. Administrators to whom this action is assigned can perform these tasks only for users in their own department or subsidiary.
UME.Manage_All_Companies	This action authorizes administrators to maintain users in all department and subsidiaries. Thus, this action can be assigned in conjunction with the UME.Manage_Groups action, for example.
UME.Sync_Admin	This action authorizes the recipient to synchronize user data with external persistent storage.
UME.Batch_Admin	This action authorizes the recipient to import and export users and user groups. However, it is restricted to users and user groups in the authorization holder's own department or subsidiary.
UME.Manage_My_Profile	This action authorizes the recipient to display and modify his or her own user profile. It does not grant any authorizations for assigning new roles. (If the UME property ume.admin.allow_selfmanagement is set to True, this action is not checked, with the result that this authorization stays in place indefinitely.)

Table 8.2 Java Actions for J2EE Administration (cont.)

8.3.2 Authorization Concept for Java Applications

The SAP Web AS supports two authorization concepts for Java applications (that is, Java Server Pages and Web Dynpro for Java):

▶ Java Authentication and Authorization Standard (JAAS) for J2EE

▶ SAP User Management Engine (UME)

These two concepts are described briefly below, but not in too much detail, as an understanding of the Java security architecture requires in-depth knowledge of how to program Java applications using Enterprise JavaBeans. However, because SAP regards the Web Dynpro programming environment as a strategic area and only the UME roles concept, which adds an improved role concept to JAAS, is available for this environment, we shall now briefly explain the principles of JAAS as an aid to understanding the UME concept.

JAAS Concept

The most effective way of creating JSP applications is to use *Enterprise JavaBeans* (EJBs). EJBs are independent standard components that first and foremost provide the developer with business logic operations. They are managed inside the SAP Web AS J2EE with the help of an EJB container and can be run only within this container.

The EJB container handles the following standard tasks for the programmer: lifecycle management, security management in accordance with JAAS, transaction management, persistence services, and naming convention management. There are three different types of EJBs: *session beans*, which are responsible for communication with the client; *entity beans*, which take care of data retention and its persistence in the database; and *message-driven beans*, which are required for communication with other beans or objects, including those on back-end systems.

Next, we shall describe the security mechanisms of the JAAS. However, in order to help you understand this as fully as possible, we shall first describe the *Deployment Descriptor*. Because EJBs run inside the EJB container, the container has to be aware of their existence, their available methods (in object-oriented programming, methods define program-based access to an object), and their use. This is done using the Deployment Descriptor (an XML file called *web.xml*). The Deployment Descriptor enables declarative programming, which means that the properties, security attributes, or authorization concepts of the EJB can be described. We shall now explain the latter in more detail.

The JAAS authorization concept uses the concepts of *principals* and *roles*. A principal is a user of the application who has already been authenticated by the application and is thus known to the application. A role in the JAAS context represents a group of principals which, through the role, is assigned certain application permissions. Thus, application permissions are assigned to a role, which in turn assigns these permissions to a group of principals (and therefore, ultimately, to the user). An application permission defines the right, or the absence of the right, to run a specific bean and the methods it contains.

The definitions of application permissions are either *declarative* or *program-based*. In the case of a declarative authorization concept, the roles are defined in the Deployment Descriptor of the EJB. The granularity of the security concept is based on the EJB level and the methods it contains. Thus, a role describes which EJB and which of its methods the role may run and execute. It is possible to authorize a role to run all methods or some of the methods in an EJB; this is the maximum level of granularity. If necessary, the programming concept has to cover these requirements. Two methods are available to the developer for this purpose: `getCallerPrincipal` and `isCallerInRole`.

`getCallerPrincipal` returns the identity of the user and `isCallerInRole` checks whether a principal has been assigned to a role. The developer can use these methods to program more authorization checks, such as a rule-based query. However, we do not recommend that you use program-based authorization concepts too much, as "hard-coded" security checks are always time-consuming and troublesome to manage afterwards, and are therefore very inflexible. The ABAP authorization concept, with its individuality and flexibility, cannot be used with the JAAS, or at best, can only be used with the JAAS if an enormous amount of time and effort is invested.

The following is an example of a declarative authorization concept, described using the Deployment Descriptor. The Deployment Descriptor is located in the JAR file, which contains all the EJBs that have been developed. All the possible roles are defined in the *assembly section* of the Deployment Descriptor (see Listing 8.1).

```
...
<assembly-descriptor>
   <security-role>
      <description>
         Description: general user
      </description>
   <role-name>all</role-name>
   </security-role>
   <security-role>
      <description>
         Description: administrator
      </description>
      <role-name>admin-user</role-name>
   </security-role>
...
</assembly-descriptor>
```

Listing 8.1 Assembly Section of the Deployment Descriptor

The example given in Listing 8.1 defines the names of the roles **all** and **admin-user**. This is always done inside the `<security-role>` tag. You can also use the optional `<description>` tag to provide a description.

Now these roles have to be assigned to the EJBs and the available methods inside the JAR file (or Java component, as the case may be). This is done using the `<method-permission>` tag inside the assembly section (see Listing 8.2).

```
...
<method-permission>
   <role-name>admin-user</role-name>
   <method>
      <ejb-name>SystemLogin</ejb-name>
      <method-name>*</method-name>
   </method>
```

```
</method-permission>
<method-permission>
   <role-name>all</role-name>
   <method>
      <ejb-name>LoginMaintenance</ejb-name>
      <method-name>modifyPersInfo</method-name>
   </method>
</method-permission>
...
```

Listing 8.2 Assigning Allowed Roles to Java Methods Inside the Assembly Section of the Deployment Descriptor

In Listing 8.2, execute access to all methods of the **SystemLogin** EJB is granted to the administrator role **admin-user.** The general **all** user, on the other hand, is granted execute permissions only to the modifyPersInfo method of the **Login-Maintenance** EJB. This is the approach that should be used to granting execute access to the various EJBs and component methods for the various roles. It uses positive declaration; that is, only roles that are explicitly named are assigned permissions, and all other roles get no permissions.

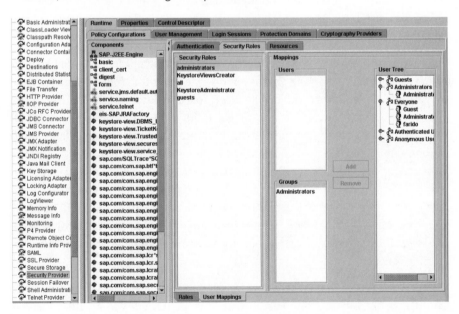

Figure 8.3 Assigning J2EE Roles to User Groups with the Java Visual Administrator

In the next step, we shall assign J2EE roles to users, or more accurately, to user groups. This is done in the SAP Web AS using the Java Visual Administrator, as shown in Figure 8.3. The available J2EE roles are displayed under the **Security**

Provider service for a specific Java component and can then be assigned to the defined SAP Web AS J2EE users.

As you can tell from the above remarks, the J2EE authorization concept very much depends on how the developer configures it, and is thus more flexible than, for example, the ABAP authorization concept. For this reason, SAP extended the basic JAAS concept and further developed it within the User Management Engine. This is explained in the following section.

UME Authorization Concept for Java Applications

The User Management Engine (UME) is the core of user and role management for Java-based applications in the SAP Web AS J2EE. It also fulfils an indispensable function as the basis of the SAP Enterprise Portal, as the SAP Enterprise Portal uses the SAP Web AS J2EE as a runtime environment. Portal roles are based completely on the UME. The technical architecture and functions are therefore described in more detail in Chapter 19, SAP Enterprise Portal.

The UME can be configured in such a way that either its own J2EE database, an LDAP directory, or the SAP Web AS ABAP can be used as the user persistence storage medium (master data and logon data). This is also the case for the SAP Enterprise Portal and is therefore not described until Chapter 19, which also describes the exact configuration.

This section focuses on the details of the UME role concept for Java applications, which is different from the portal role concept. Portal roles define content (iViews, worksets, and so on), while UME roles are used to specify the actual authorizations for Java applications. Unlike in the JAAS, the UME role concept for Java is a program-based approach to authorization. The developer defines application permissions in the application, which he or she then bundles together to form actions using the declarative file *actions.xml*. Because the individual application permissions can become very complex, bundling the actions has the advantage of imposing a logical structure on the permissions. The action `UME.Manage_Roles` contains all application permissions required to manage UME roles, without the authorization administrator having to know all the methods necessary for creating roles.

Ultimately, actions can themselves be bundled to form UME roles, using the UME Console (a Web-based front end that can be called via a URL, such as *http://myserver.mycompany.com:50000/useradmin*), and then assigned to users. Figure 8.4 illustrates the UME role concept for Java applications. Actions can also be bundled into roles and administrated in the UME Console.

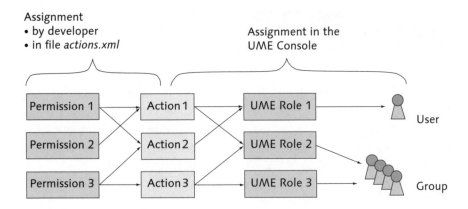

Figure 8.4 UME Role Concept for Java Applications

If the SAP Web AS ABAP is used as the persistence storage for the users, a problem arises: there is no group definition for users in ABAP. This problem is solved by the fact that the users who are assigned to a specific ABAP role in the SAP Web AS ABAP are shown as a group definition in the UME Console; in other words, the ABAP role name appears as a group name in the UME. All users who are assigned to this ABAP role are also assigned to this UME group.

8.3.3 Restricting Authorizations for RFC Calls

In an SAP Web AS group, or in a situation where different clients are used for production on one SAP Web AS, one program part (such as one within a specific transaction) often has to call data on another client or another SAP Web AS instance. This is usually done using a *Remote Function Call* (RFC). In an RFC, an SAP Web AS can be either server or client.

The process of calling ABAP function groups, which then read the required data, takes place in the server system by means of an RFC destination. An RFC destination describes a data record that is stored in the RFC client and contains two types of information: data that describes the network connection, and authentication data for the RFC user. Authentication data is required only if the server system is an SAP Web AS. The RFC user is used for logons in the server system. This user is active in the server system and has specific authorizations, which we shall now look at in detail.

RFC calls can be one of two basic types: *untrusted* and *trusted*. The difference between these two types is that if an untrusted RFC call is made, the client has to authenticate itself to the server using the proper RFC user credentials. If a trusted RFC call is made, no authentication is necessary, as the server system trusts the client.

Figure 8.5 shows the basic procedure of an untrusted RFC call and the authorization objects that are checked in this procedure. With this type of call, a user in SAP Web AS system A starts a particular transaction in which an RFC call is made to SAP Web AS system B.

In system A, the authorization object S_ICF is checked, which contains the **ICF_FIELD** and **ICF_VALUE** authorization fields. The **ICF_FIELD** field can have either of the values "Service" or "Dest". "Service" has to be defined if an Internet Connection Framework service is called. "Dest" can be selected if the call is an RFC call, defined in transaction SM59. The **ICF_VALUE** field can contain the ICF services or RFC destinations for the user, or better still, for the role. Table RFCDES contains a list of the possible RFC destinations.

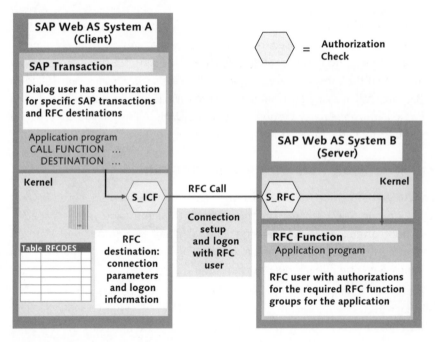

Figure 8.5 Untrusted RFC Call

To make the RFC call to SAP Web AS system B, the client has to log on using the RFC user that has been defined in SAP Web AS system B for this call. Then, in SAP Web AS system B, the RFC call is granted the authorizations that have been defined for the RFC user in authorization object S_RFC. Authorization object S_RFC has the following authorization fields:

▶ **RFC_TYPE**
Type of the RFC object that is to be protected. Currently, this field can take only the value "FUGR" (function group).

▶ **RFC_NAME**

Name of the RFC object that is to be protected. This field contains the name of the function groups that can be called by the RFC user. It is important that full authorization—that is, "*"—is not entered here, or else the user would be able to call critical function groups for creating users. Unfortunately, this rule is often not adhered to. For this reason, we shall now show you how to use a security audit log to find the function groups that are necessary for the application in question and to restrict these function groups.

▶ **ACTVT**

Activity. Currently, this field can take only the value "16" (execute).

If an RFC call is made between trusted systems, the call proceeds as follows (as shown in Figure 8.6). There is no need for the client to log on using an RFC user. Instead, the user ID of the dialog user that is active in SAP Web AS system A is transferred. In this case, this dialog user becomes an RFC service user. For this reason, it is important that there is an additional authorization check in SAP Web AS system B, using authorization object S_RFCACL. This check establishes whether the user who is logged on in the client system is allowed to log himself or herself on to the server system under the user ID in question.

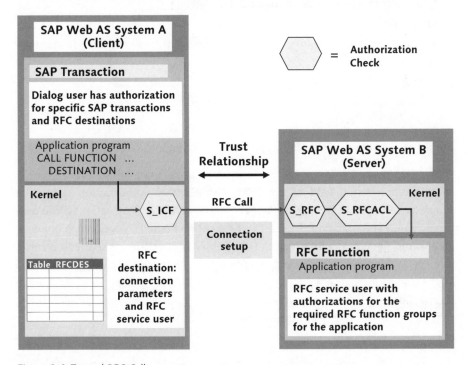

Figure 8.6 Trusted RFC Call

The authorization object S_RFCACL has the following authorization fields:

▶ **RFC_SYSID**
System ID of the calling SAP Web AS system A (that is, the client system)

▶ **RFC_CLIENT**
Client of the calling SAP Web AS system A

▶ **RFC_USER**
User ID of the calling user in SAP Web AS system A. It is important that full authorization ("*") is not entered here, or else every user in SAP Web AS system B would be able to call the function groups in the S_RFC object. This could be a critical problem if, for example, full authorization has been defined, as is often the case. It is precisely because of this problem that in many cases trusted RFC calls are not used. We likewise recommend that you use this type of call only in exceptional cases.

▶ **RFC_EQUSER**
Indicator that shows whether the RFC service user can be called only by a user with the same ID ("Y"=Yes, "N"=No).

▶ **RFC_TCODE**
A calling transaction code of minor importance.

▶ **RFC_INFO**
Additional information from the calling SAP Web AS system that is currently inactive.

▶ **ACTVT**
Activity. Currently, this field can take only the value "16" (execute).

As mentioned already, from the security point of view, trusted RFC calls are more problematic, and so you should avoid using them widely.

It is very important that the correct form of authorizations be used for the **RFC_NAME** authorization field of the S_RFC object. Full authorization should be avoided at all costs in this case. However, implementation instructions often only allow for full authorization. The concept described below is a way of circumventing this problem, as it allows you to specify the function groups that you want to call. This is done using the Security Audit Log, which is activated using transaction SM19 and can be analyzed using transaction SM20. Unlike the system trace (transaction ST01), the Security Audit Log is not particularly resource-intensive, so it can remain active over quite a long period of time.

The Security Audit Log has to be activated for all clients, users and events in the "RFC calls" audit class. This is done in transaction SM19. After approximately two months—we can assume that in this time period, the function groups that are necessary for the application will have been called at least once—the audit log can be analyzed, using transaction SM20 (SM20N). The log can then be downloaded to an Excel table and the called function groups filtered out. These can then be entered into the **RFC_NAME** authorization field. The scope of the authorization is thus set to exactly these function groups.

You should follow this procedure for all documented RFC call destinations, so that full authorization can be gradually eliminated.

8.4 Technical Security

8.4.1 Introducing a Single Sign-On Authentication Mechanism

There are a number of different procedures for introducing a Single Sign-On (SSO) authentication mechanism, which allows users to log themselves on to various SAP Web AS systems at once. Which procedure you choose depends on the particular scenario in each case.

Scenario 1: SAP Enterprise Portal used

If an SAP Enterprise Portal is in use, in order to provide the user with a consistent user interface, you should choose one of the SSO mechanisms outlined in Chapter 19. In this case, the leading logon system is always SAP EP. The most secure procedure in this context is an SSO mechanism that is based on digital certificates (in accordance with the X.509 standard), as this mechanism is based on a dual-factor approach.

Scenario 2: SAP Enterprise Portal not used

If an SAP Enterprise Portal is not in use but you still want to implement an SSO mechanism for multiple SAP Web AS systems, there are, again, a number of ways of doing this, which likewise depend on the type of SAP Web AS front-end connection that you are using.

▶ If only the SAP GUI for Windows is in use, choose one of the options described in Chapter 27. In this case, as before, because of security concerns, you should seriously consider a certificate-based solution.

▶ If only the SAP GUI for HTML (Web browser) is in use, choose one of the options described in Chapter 28. Again, we recommend that you choose a certificate-based approach.

▶ On the other hand, if you want to use the SAP GUI for Windows and the SAP GUI for HTML together, and if you also want to include Business Server Pages, Web Dynpro for ABAP and Java, and Java Server Pages, you should configure an SAP Web AS system to be the main system and the one that issues SAP logon tickets. SAP logon tickets are Web browser cookies that confirm that a user has successfully authenticated himself or herself to a main SAP Web AS, using that user's digital signature. When this user sends his or her next request, the browser sends the cookie along with it, enabling other SAP Web ASes that trust the main SAP Web AS to use the cookie. The cookie, or the logon ticket, as it is more accurately called, can also be transferred to an SAP GUI for Windows, although only with the special shortcut version of the SAP GUI.

However, there can be only one main system, or else the trust relationships would cross over each other, incurring a high level of administrative work and reducing the level of security. All trust relationships have to be defined in accordance with the SAP EP scenario. There is one system—that is, either the SAP EP or an SAP Web AS—that issues SAP logon tickets, and all other systems must accept this system as trustworthy. How this is technically achieved depends on whether the user first logs himself or herself on to the main system using the Web Dynpro for Java applications or, as is the usual case, whether he or she logs on to the SAP Web AS ABAP. In the former case, the SAP Web AS J2EE has to be configured as the system that issues SAP logon tickets; in the latter case, it is the SAP Web AS ABAP that has to be configured. If the SAP Web AS J2EE is the main system, the integrated Windows-Kerberos authentication method can be used instead of the simple user ID and password method. The Windows-Kerberos method is described in greater detail in Chapter 19.

In all cases, a trust relationship has to be set up between the SAP Web AS ABAP and J2EE and the issuing system on each system that is to accept SAP logon tickets. This applies in particular to the SAP Web AS J2EE if Java applications—such as Web Dynpro for Java—are to be incorporated into the SSO mechanism.

We shall now briefly look at the configuration steps that you need to take if you want an SAP Web AS system in an SAP Web AS ABAP to create SAP logon tickets and these tickets to be accepted by an ABAP application on another SAP Web AS (this is a very common scenario).

▶ **Step 1**

Configure the SAP Web AS ABAP to issue SAP logon certificates:

▷ A PKI (public trust center, such as SAP CA) has to issue and sign a digital certificate for the server on the basis of the X.509 standard. Alternatively, self-signed certificates can also be used. However, this is advisable only in test scenarios.

- Transaction STRUST is used to import the certificate into the *Personal Security Environment* (PSE) of the SAP Web AS. In the case of SSO, this is system PSE.

- Configure the following three system parameters to create SAP logon tickets:

  - `login/accept_sso2_ticket`
    Set this to "1" to specify that the SAP Web AS can itself accept SAP logon tickets.

  - `login/create_sso2_ticket`
    Set this to "1" to specify that the SAP Web AS can itself create SAP logon tickets and embed its own digital certificate in these. You can also set "2" here, but you should do this only for self-signed server certificates.

  - `login/ticket_expiration_time`
    This value specifies the validity time period of the SAP logon ticket. It should not be greater than "8" (eight hours). This approximates the duration of a normal working day.

▶ **Step 2**

Configure the SAP Web AS ABAP to accept SAP logon certificates:

- Set the `login/accept_sso2_ticket` parameter to "1" to activate acceptance of SAP logon tickets.

- Run the SSO Wizard (transaction SSO2). In this transaction, you have to enter either an RFC destination for the server that issues SAP logon tickets, or alternatively, the server name and the system ID. The "Activate" button activates the trust relationship. If errors occur, transaction STRUSTSSO2 can be used to track down these errors.

Once you have completed the configuration, the user can then log on to the main SAP Web AS using an SAP GUI for HTML and, for example, start the BSP application that is stored as a link in his or her menu. There can be no simultaneous logons to this SAP Web AS.

8.4.2   Connecting the SAP Web AS to a Central LDAP Directory

It is strongly recommended that you use a central LDAP directory to store the user master data of the employees in your enterprise, especially if multiple production SAP Web AS systems are in use in conjunction with an SAP EP. This scenario is discussed in detail in Chapter 19, which also explains the possible hierarchy definitions for a *flat or deep* LSAP directory.

In an SAP EP scenario, the LDAP directory should be used as the main user persistence storage location for all connected SAP Web ASes. However, unlike an SAP EP, an SAP Web AS ABAP cannot access the LDAP directory "online"—that is, during the process of authenticating a user; instead, it has to synchronize the user master data with its own user storage (ABAP user storage). As mentioned at the start of this section, changes should be permitted to be made only in the LDAP directory, so that no inconsistencies arise. The SAP Web AS J2EE, on the other hand, can connect to the LDAP directory online using the User Management Engine. This is done in the same way as for the SAP EP, which also accesses the LDAP directory using the UME. However, the SAP Web AS J2EE can also be configured in such a way that the main user persistence storage is the ABAP user storage. This is the recommended variant, because in this case no inconsistencies can arise between SAP Web AS ABAP and J2EE, and it also allows the assignment of users to groups to be managed using ABAP roles.

The following user master data is usually stored in the LDAP directory and can be synchronized in the SAP Web AS ABAP using the LDAP Connector:

▶ HR data (name, department, organization)

▶ User data and security information (user account, authorizations, public key certificates)

▶ Information about system resources and system services (system ID, application configuration, printer configuration)

As mentioned already, the LDAP protocol and the LDAP Connector are used for the purposes of synchronization with the LDAP directory. The LDAP Connector is called via ABAP functions and communicates with the LDAP directory server. Various logon methods can be used to establish a connection with the LDAP directory server, such as simple connection (user ID and password) or anonymous connection (guest account without password). It is also possible to use a stronger authentication method on the basis of digital certificates using the LDAP protocol, LDAPS. Currently, synchronization can be performed using Microsoft Active Directory, Novell eDirectory, and the Sun ONE LDAP Server. The technical configuration depends on each individual manufacturer, and so we shall not discuss it in detail here.

However, after the LDAP Connector has been configured (this handles synchronization), the directory schema also has to be adapted. This involves defining which directory attribute is to be mapped to which SAP attribute. SAP provides the relevant mapping rules for the manufacturers mentioned above. These rules can then be adapted to the requirements of the individual enterprise.

8.4.3 Changing the Default Passwords for Default Users

The default passwords for the following default users are widely known, and therefore have to be changed immediately once the SAP Web AS is installed:

▶ **SAP***

The SAP* user in clients 000 and 066 is a super user with comprehensive permissions to set up a new SAP Web AS system. This user has the initial password "06071992". The SAP* user is also used to set up a new client and in this case has the initial password "pass".

▶ **DDIC**

The DDIC user in client 000 is used for transports and corrections, mainly in the Data Dictionary. It has the initial password "19920706".

▶ **Early Watch**

The Early Watch user in client 066 is used by SAP specialists for monitoring and performance management in the system. It shoud never be deleted, and it has the initial password "support".

The user information system (transaction SUIM) or the technical reports provided by the Audit Information System can be used to check whether the default passwords have been changed for these critical default users.

The user ID and password for the SAP Web AS J2EE administrator can be set to anything you like during the installation process. In this case, you should of course choose a password that is as unpredictable as possible, and that adheres to the following complexity rules:

▶ Password length to be a minimum of eight characters

▶ At least one special character

▶ At least one letter

▶ At least one number

8.4.4 Configuring Security on the SAP Gateway

The SAP Gateway is a work process that is activated on the operating system level in order to manage communication between various systems, such as SAP Web AS systems, using the CPI-C protocol. RFC calls are also based on the CPI-C protocol. Besides an SAP Web AS, RFC communication partners can also be older R/3 or R/2 systems. Other external applications can also communicate via the SAP Gateway and run programs on remote systems. This involves some security risks, but these can be minimized with the correct security configuration.

The SAP Gateway is activated on every SAP Web AS instance. Transaction SMGW is used to monitor its status. The *sideinfo* file contains data about all the possible RFC destinations, and thus has to be protected from unauthorized access. This is done using an access control list on the operating system level. This file is on every SAP Web AS instance on which an SAP Gateway is active.

Because all RFC destinations can be maintained using transaction SM59 and are stored in table RFCDES, authorization for transaction SM59 should be assigned only with great care, including to administrators. For this reason, you should regularly check the entries in table RFCDES for any changes that may have been made.

It is important to correctly configure the authorization to execute a specific external CPI-C program or an RFC call. It is also necessary to monitor the registration of an external CPI-C program on the SAP Gateway. A registration means that this program is being made known to the Gateway and can be called from that moment on. This is done using the *secinfo file*, which by default is stored in the data directory of the instance. Alternatively, its location can be specified using the gw/sec_info parameter.

An external program that is allowed to register itself on the SAP Gateway must be specified in this file. The syntax is as follows:

USER=*, HOST=<host>,TP=<tp>;

If, for example, the values USER=*, HOST=hw1414, and TP=TREX are set, this means that the TREX program on host hw1414 may register itself on the SAP Gateway.

The *secinfo* file can also be used to restricted access to a registered program for specific users. The users are the same as the registered users in the SAP Web AS.

In this case, the syntax is as follows:

USER=<user>, [PWD=<pwd>,] [USER-HOST=<user-host>,] HOST=<host>, TP=<tp>;

In the case of USER=HUGO, HOST=twdf0595, and TP=remote_serv, for example, the user HUGO is permitted to start the program remote_serv on the host twdf0595. The parameter USER-HOST specifies the host on which the program may be started. The PWD (password) parameter has to be specified if an external CPI-C program that requires a password is started. Figure 8.7 gives an overview of the functions of the *secinfo* file.

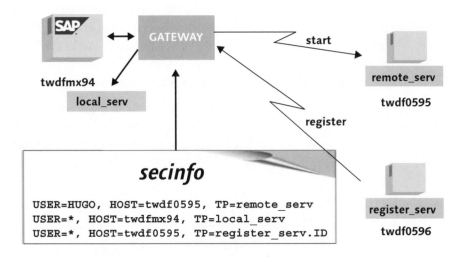

Figure 8.7 Configuring the SAP Gateway with the secinfo Configuration File

8.4.5 Restricting Operating System Access

Transaction SM69 (administrate external system calls) and transaction SM49 (execute external system calls) are used for external operating system access and to start operating system commands. Authorizations that are assigned for these two transactions must therefore be correspondingly restricted.

If these transactions are specified in the authorization, the execution of external operating system commands has to be restricted accordingly, using authorization objects S_RZL_ADM and S_LOG_COM. Authorization object S_RZL_ADM assigns authorization to maintain external system calls using transaction SM69. It has only one authorization field, **Activity**, in which only "01: Create" and "03: Modify" are of major significance.

The authorization object S_LOG_COM has the authorization fields **Command**, **Operating System**, and **Host**, which allow you to specify which operating system command can be executed on which operating system, and on which host.

Because external operating system command calls again use the SAP Gateway—in this particular case, using the *sapxpg* program—access to *sapxpg* using the *secinfo* file should be restricted to specific authorized users. Ideally, authorization should be restricted to users who have access to transactions SM49 and SM69.

The example below restricts permission to execute external operating system commands on the host `twdf0595` to the user HUGO:

```
USER=HUGO, HOST=twdf0595, TP=sapxpg
```

Thus, the *secinfo* file should contain this kind of entry. If the *secinfo* file is missing altogether, this authorizes every user to execute external commands using the *sapxpg* program. Obviously, this is a situation you should avoid at all costs.

8.4.6 Configuring Important Security System Parameters

To operate the SAP Web AS in a secure manner, it is necessary to correctly define some important security-related system parameters using transaction RZ10. Table 8.3 contains some important system parameters and a recommended "best practice" setting for each one.

System parameter	Short description	Recommended setting
login/min_password_lng	Minimum length of logon password (3 to 8 characters)	At least 5 characters
login/password_expiration_time	Validity period of the password in months (0 to 999)	3 to 6 months
login/fails_to_user_lock	Maximum number of failed logon attempts before user is locked (1 to 99)	3 failed attempts
login/failed_user_auto_unlock	Automatic unlocking of user by batch job at night (0: no, 1: yes)	0
login/fails_to_session_end	Maximum number of failed logon attempts before logon attempt is terminated (1 to 99)	3 failed attempts
login/disable_multiple_gui_login	Suppression of multiple user sessions (0: multiple logons possible, 1: multiple logons not possible)	1: multiple logons not possible
login/multi_login_users	List of users who are permitted to use multiple logons	List of users, if parameter login/disable_multiple_gui_login = 0
login/min_password_diff	Minimum number of characters that have to be different from the old password in the new password (1 to 8)	At least 5 characters
login/password_max_new_valid	Validity period of passwords of new users (0 to 24,000 days)	4 days

Table 8.3 System Configurations That Are Relevant to Security

System parameter	Short description	Recommended setting
`login/password_max_reset_valid`	Validity period of reset passwords (0 to 24,000 days)	4 days
Table USR40	Specifies trivial passwords that are not allowed	There should be at least 100 entries, such as name, month, and so on
`rfc/reject_expired_passwd`	Allows RFC connections to log themselves onto the system with an expired password (0: allowed, 1: not allowed)	1: not allowed (SAP Note 622464 must be applied first)
`gw/sec_info`	Location of *secinfo* file to secure the SAP Gateway	A file should be specified, otherwise there is no security.
`gw/monitor`	Allows the SAP Gateway to be monitored from a remote system (0: allowed, 1: not allowed)	1: not allowed
`gw/accept_remote_trace_level`	Allows trace information about the SAP Gateway to be transferred to an external system (0: not possible, 1: possible)	0: not possible
`rdisp/j2ee_start`	Start SAP Web AS J2EE (0: is not started, 1: is started)	SAP Web AS J2EE should be started only if genuinely required
`icm/HTTP/j2ee_<XX>`	Defines whether internal communication between the ICM and the J2EE Engine is encrypted	Parameter should be greater than 0 for every J2EE Engine (serially numbered using `<XX>`)
Root group for the Telnet administration service of the J2EE Engine removed?	Root group includes all users of the SAP Web AS J2EE, including guest users	Manually remove root group (see SAP Note 602371)
Guest user	J2EE Engine has a guest user by default	Lock guest user
Password rules	Password rules can also be set for the J2EE Engine using the Visual Administrator	Define password rules in accordance with the guidelines above

Table 8.3 System Configurations That Are Relevant to Security (cont.)

8.4.7 Configuring Encrypted Communication Connections (SSL and SNC)

Communication connections should be encrypted in order to maintain their integrity and confidentiality. For this purpose, the SAP Web AS provides the standard encryption methods *Secure Sockets Layer* (SSL) and *Secure Network Communication* (SNC), which are available for important communication connections on both the SAP Web AS ABAP and J2EE.

Important Communication Connections for the SAP Web AS ABAP

Figure 8.8 shows all the important communication connections for the SAP Web AS ABAP, while Table 8.4 lists its protocols and encryption mechanisms. As you can see in Table 8.4, all the important communication connections can be encrypted. In the case of the database connection, however, the question of encryption depends on the database manufacturer. In most cases, for performance reasons, no encryption is used for the database connection.

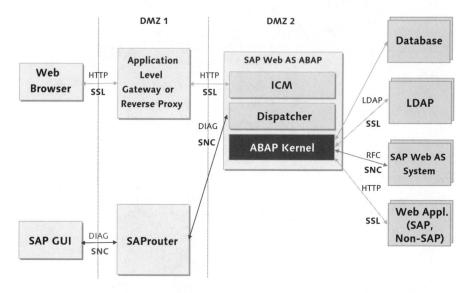

Figure 8.8 Communication Connections That Can Be Encrypted for the SAP Web AS ABAP

Protocol	Encryption method	Communication connections
DIAG	SNC	SAP GUI to SAProuter, SAProuter to SAP Web AS dispatcher
RFC	SNC	SAP Web AS ABAP kernel to other SAP Web AS ABAP kernel or other external CPI-C program

Table 8.4 Overview of Communication Connections of SAP Web AS ABAP

Protocol	Encryption method	Communication connections
HTTP	SSL	Web browser to application-level firewall (SAP Web dispatcher, reverse proxy, etc.), application-level firewall to ICM, ABAP kernel to SAP or non-SAP Web applications
ldap	SSL	ABAP kernel (LDAP Connector) to LDAP directory server

Table 8.4 Overview of Communication Connections of SAP Web AS ABAP (cont.)

Important Communication Connections for the SAP Web AS J2EE

Figure 8.9 shows all the important communication connections for the SAP Web AS J2EE, and Table 8.5 lists its protocols and encryption mechanisms.

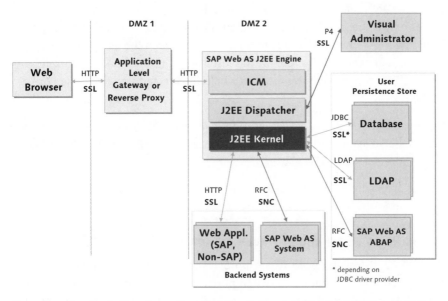

Figure 8.9 Communication Connections That Can Be Encrypted for the SAP Web AS J2EE

Protocol	Encryption method	Communication connections
DIAG	SNC	Not required in the SAP Web AS J2EE environment
RFC	SNC	J2EE kernel (using Java Connector) to SAP Web AS ABAP, J2EE kernel (using Java Connection Architecture) to SAP Web AS system
HTTP	SSL	Web browser to application-level firewall (SAP Web dispatcher, reverse proxy, etc.), application-level firewall to ICM (or directly to J2EE dispatcher, if it is a pure SAP Web AS J2EE installation without ABAP), J2EE kernel to SAP or non-SAP Web application

Table 8.5 Overview of Communication Connections of SAP Web AS J2EE

Protocol	Encryption method	Communication connections
ldap	SSL	J2EE kernel (using Java Connection Architecture) to LDAP directory server
JDBC	SSL	J2EE kernel to database server (SSL encryption is possible only if the JDBC or ODBC driver permits it)
P4	SSL	Visual Administrator to J2EE dispatcher, J2EE dispatcher to J2EE kernel
Telnet	VPN only	Telnet administrator to J2EE dispatcher (not recommended)

Table 8.5 Overview of Communication Connections of SAP Web AS J2EE (cont.)

It should also be noted at this point that the configuration shown in Figure 8.9 applies only if the installation in question is a complete SAP Web AS installation (including ABAP and Java) and communication between the available Web applications is managed via the ICM. If the installation in question were a pure SAP Web AS J2EE one, this communication would be directed straight to the J2EE dispatcher.

Also note that the use of an application-level gateway is optional. For security reasons, however, at least one SAP Web dispatcher should be used. See Chapter 24 for more details on this matter.

Next, as an example, we shall explain the installation steps necessary to configure SNC on an SAP Web AS ABAP and SSL on an SAP Web AS J2EE.

Configuring SNC for the SAP Web AS ABAP

SAPCRYPTOLIB can be used to set up SNC communication between two SAP Web AS systems; it is not necessary to purchase any partner software. However, you will need to purchase new software if you want to set up SNC between the SAP GUI and an SAP Web AS system (see Chapter 27).

The following are the steps you need to take to configure SNC on an SAP Web AS ABAP:

1. Install SAPCRYPTOLIB on all SAP Web AS systems that you want to be able to contact by SNC communication.

2. Set up the *SNC Personal Security Environments* (PSEs) for each SAP Web AS system. Alternatively, you can also use an SNC PSE for each system that is involved, but although this option reduces the amount of administration work involved, we still do not advise you to use it. The better option from a security standpoint is to use individual SNC PSEs, each with a special certificate for each system, as this enables stronger authentication between systems. Transaction

STRUST is used to create the SNC PSE. In this transaction, you have to select the SNC PSE and enter a *distinguished name* with the host name, the organizational unit, the name of the organization, and the country. Alternatively, you can specify these details in parameter `snc/identity/as`. You also have to set a password in order to make access to the SNC PSE secure.

3. In this step, the digital certificates of the SAP Web AS systems that are stored in the SNC PSE have to be exchanged between the systems so that a trust relationship can be established. As before, this is done in transaction STRUST. In this transaction, the digital certificate has to be exported to every participating SAP Web AS system. To do this, you again have to select the SNC PSE and use the **Export Certificate** function under the certificate list to export the relevant system-specific certificate and save it to a local hard disk. The **Import Certificate** function is also available at this location. This can be used to import the certificates of the relevant SAP Web AS systems.

4. In this last step, you have to set the relevant SNC system parameters. The most important of these are as follows:

   ▶ `snc/enable` (activate SNC)
     = 1

   ▶ `snc/gssapi_lib` (path for SAPCRYPTOLIB)
     = */usr/sap/<SID>/SYS/exe/run/libsapcrypto.so* (UNIX)
     = *D:\usr\sap\<SID>\SYS\ exe\run\sapcrypto.dll* (Windows)

   ▶ `snc/identity/as` (SNC name of the SAP Web AS application server)
     = `Syntax:  p:<Distinguished_Name>`, which has to be the same as the SNC PSE

   ▶ `snc/data_protection/max` (maximum security level)
     = '1: authentication only', '2: integrity protection', or '3: confidentiality protection'

   ▶ `snc/data_protection/min` (maximum security level)
     = '1: authentication only', '2: integrity protection', or '3: confidentiality protection'

5. Restart the SAP Web AS systems and test the SNC communication connections.

Configuring SSL for the SAP Web AS J2EE

To configure SSL for an SAP Web AS J2EE, you can use the Visual Administrator, which connects to the relevant J2EE server via the P4 protocol.

The installation steps are as follows:

1. Install the SAP Cryptographic Toolkit for Java (this package consists of the following: *iaik_jsse.jar, iaik_jce.jar, iaik_ssl.jar, iaik_smime.jar,* and *w3c_http.jar*) on the SAP Web AS J2EE system.

2. Configure the start mode for the certificate storage location (*keystore*) and set the SSL service to "Always" (this is done with the Config tool). Here, select the appropriate server node and set the start options for both services to "Always."

3. You now have to create a certificate (key pair, consisting of a public key in accordance with the X.509 standard and a private key). This is done in the **Keystore** service of the Visual Administrator. You can also create a *Certificate Signing Request* (CSR) there, if the certificate has to be signed by a CA. This will be necessary to connect Web applications for the Internet via the SAP Web AS system. In the case of test installations, self-signed certificates can also be used.

4. In this last step, asign the certificate to a specific HTTP port that has to be configured for SSL. This is done in the Visual Administrator using the **SSL service** for the corresponding SAP Web AS J2EE system.

8.4.8 Restricting Superfluous Internet Services

If the SAP Web AS is used in an Internet scenario and provides Web-based applications via the Internet Communication Manager, as shown in Figure 8.1, any applications—also known as *services*—that do not need to be accessible have to be deactivated.

This is done using transaction SICF (Administrating the Internet Communication Framework) in Web Dynpro for ABAP-, BSP-, or ITS-based services on the SAP Web AS ABAP. Figure 8.10 shows an example of this. By right-clicking on the relevant service (such as **IT13: Test Service for IACs**), you can deactivate the service. However, you should not use the option to deactivate the whole ICF tree hierarchy under an ICF object at once. Instead, always deactivate services one at a time, or else you may overlook dependencies, which in turn could cause problems with functionality.

The SAP Web AS J2EE also provides external services, even though not all of these are required in every scenario. The problem in this case is that there may be dependencies between services, with the result that if one service is required, other services may also have to be activated at the same time. We also have to differentiate between system services and non-system services.

We recommend that you use the following procedure to identify and deactivate superfluous services:

▶ Identify the system service that is required to execute the application (such as the service `servlet_jsp` for servlet-based applications).

▶ Next, filter out mutual dependencies between the services. You can view these dependencies on the **Dependencies** tab page. Usually, only the services with a high degree of dependency are required.

▶ You should deactivate those services that do not have any dependencies. When doing so, be aware that some services are will still be required to operate the SAP Web AS J2EE, regardless of their degree of dependency.

▶ Also, you should use the Deployment Tool to remove any applications that are not required.

▶ HTTP aliases that are not required should likewise be removed.

▶ After the services are deactivated, you should check whether the application can still run.

▶ If the application or the SAP Web AS J2EE can no longer run, you will have to check the logs. Usually, the logs will contain error messages that relate to services that are required but that have been deactivated. Otherwise, you will have to use trial and error to pinpoint the required combination.

▶ For system services, you have to change the start setting "always" so that the SAP Web AS J2EE can run again. You do this using the XML configuration file *runtime.xml* in the services directory or the Config tool (value: "never" or "manual").

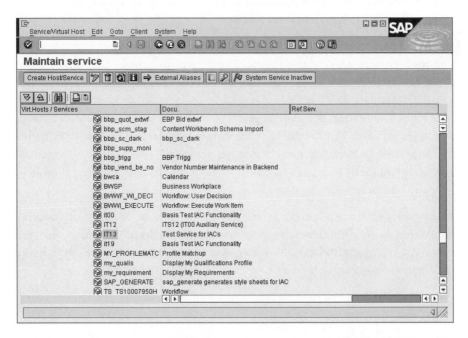

Figure 8.10 Transaction SICF, Used for Administrating the Internet Communication Framework

Because of the level of complexity involved, it is advisable to identify the service combinations that can be deactivated, and to carry out the actual deactivations only after you have established that the risks are sufficiently high to warrant this. A system that provides very sensitive Internet applications, for example, counts as a high-risk system, and so the hardening procedure outlined above should be carried out in this case.

8.4.9 Secure Network Architecture for Using the SAP Web AS with the Internet

Which network architecture you choose for using the SAP Web AS for the Internet will depend on the individual scenario. If you will be providing only Internet applications on the basis of the SAP ITS, the network topology proposed in Chapter 26 can be used.

On the other hand, if you are mainly interested in BSP, JSP, and Web Dynpro applications for ABAP and Java, you should choose the kind of network topologies shown in Figures 8.8 and 8.9. For more information, see Chapter 24, in which the SAP Web dispatcher can be used as a simple reverse proxy in the configurations shown.

8.4.10 Introducing an Application-Level Gateway to Make Internet Applications Secure

An application-level gateway will be of most use if you are mainly using BSP, JSP, and Web Dynpro applications for ABAP and Java that are all accessible via the ICM. The security functionality of the SAP Web dispatcher (see Chapter 24) is somewhat limited, and therefore it should be replaced by a reverse proxy, which is of higher value from the security point of view, or, even better, by an application-level gateway. The functions of the latter are described in detail in Chapter 19, as an SAP EP is usually used in Internet scenarios. That chapter also explains the typical methods of attacks on the Internet, against which an application-level gateway may provide protection.

Nonetheless, we must not fail to mention that in these cases, the transferred parameters, such as those in form fields, are always checked. This usually happens on the Web application's side. This is especially important in the case of in-house development work.

8.4.11 Introducing Hardening Measures on the Operating System Level

SAP Web AS systems that are used for Internet purposes, in particular, have to be hardened on the operating system level. This applies to all areas of application of the SAP Web AS—for example, a SAP Web AS that is used as a runtime environment for the SAP Enterprise Portal, the SAP Exchange Infrastructure, or the SAP Mobile Infrastructure.

The manufacturers of the individual operating systems now provide good, detailed instructions on how to carry out hardening measures. A detailed description of these measures is beyond the scope of this book; however, you should note the following basic principles in relation to hardening:

▶ Any applications (such as Office applications) on a server that is intended for SAP EP should be removed. This also applies to additional administrative tools. Such tools sometimes make administrative tasks easier, but they often contain security weak spots that a potential attacker could exploit. Note in relation to this that you should activate services and applications one at a time, so as not to jeopardize the availability of the SAP system.

▶ Guest accounts have to be deleted or at least deactivated.

▶ Standard operating system passwords have to be changed.

▶ Appropriate access permissions have to be assigned to critical operating system directories (such as /etc in UNIX). This applies in particular to the technical service users under which the SAP Web AS system instances run.

In addition to these measures, you can also set up an *Intrusion Detection System* (IDS) on the server level. In particular, this kind of system monitors any changes made to critical operating system files and triggers an alarm if any change is made to this kind of file without the prior authorization of the administrator. On the other hand, this kind of IDS also often triggers false alarms. Therefore, during installation, you should take this into account in your configurations. The *Tripwire* system is widely used for UNIX systems, and Microsoft provides an IDS solution for Windows.

8.4.12 Introducing a Quality Assurance Process for Software Development

Quality assurance systems or change management systems, or both, are now taken for granted when new SAP systems are rolled out. Because process design always has to be adapted to the individual circumstances of the organization and the details can be very complex, an explanation of this topic would be beyond the scope of this book. We shall therefore present only a brief overview of some tips and tools here.

Quality Assurance and Change Management Process for the SAP Web AS ABAP

Normally, the quality assurance and change management process in a pure ABAP development environment is a three-stage one. The system landscape consists of a development (DEV) system, a quality assurance (QA) system, and a production (PROD) system. New development work, or changes to existing ABAP programs, can be carried out only in the development system. Likewise, customizing work on client-specific and cross-client tables and entries can only be done in the development system. The quality assurance system is used to check the correctness of any newly developed programs. Development work is transported on to the production system only once all tests have been carried out in accordance with a pre-defined test plan and have achieved positive results.

SAP provides tools for the process that we have just roughly outlined. Transaction SE06 is used to make the settings for the areas that can be changed. Transaction SE03 allows you to view and check all the system modifications that have been logged. Transaction SCC4 is used to specify permitted and forbidden settings for maintaining client-specific and cross-client tables and transports. These settings are stored in table T000, which means that this table also has to be protected from being accessed via transactions SM30 and SM31. To ensure that a client—especially the production client—cannot be overwritten, you have to make the corresponding setting in transaction SCC4 on level 1 ("No overwriting").

The following are critical authorizations that you should not assign, at least in the production system:

▶ Table maintenance S_TABU_DIS: activity "02 (change)" should be assigned for non-critical tables only where necessary. In particular, the table group that contains table T000 should not be assigned at all.

▶ Thus, cross-client Customizing via S_TABU_CLI should not be set to "X", or else it would be possible to assign table T000.

▶ For ABAP software development, authorization object S_DEVELOP should be restricted, activity "02 (change)" should be OBJTYPE PROG, and DEBUG should be avoided, as this allows the authorization holder to modify existing programs and to carry out debugging and replace existing code.

The Transport Management System (transaction STMS) is used to transport software packages. It contains a release process that releases packages for transport only once they have been approved by the responsible development team leader or a quality assurance specialist. You can thus use this tool to set up a standardized change management process with a step-by-step release procedure. You can also choose the number of required release steps.

Quality Assurance and Change Management Process for the SAP Web AS J2EE

A quality assurance and change management process can also be set up for the SAP Web AS J2EE. As before, this process can have a three-stage structure consisting of development, quality assurance and production environments. However, the tools that are required are different from the ABAP tools.

Java applications are developed using the SAP NetWeaver Developer Studio, and software components are stored in the *Design Time Repository* (DTR). The DTR is also responsible for distribution to the various environments; developer and release roles can again be specified for this purpose. The following are the fixed roles in this area: **developer**, **quality manager**, and **software change manager**. These roles can be adapted to suit the individual requirements in each case, so that it is possible to set up a Java development process that is compatible with the ABAP quality assurance process.

9 SAP ERP Central Component

This chapter deals with IT security concepts for the SAP ERP Central Component area of the Global Security Positioning System (GSPS). It describes general authorization concepts and solutions for best-practice control methods in SAP ECC applications.

9.1 Introduction and Functions

The term *SAP ERP Central Component* (SAP ECC) applies to all modules (as they were previously called) of the classic central R/3 system, as well as new function modules such as mySAP ERP HCM. SAP ECC is the "typical" backend system and is based on SAP NetWeaver.

Because SAP ECC manages and stores such a wide range of business information and transactions having to do with backend systems, all SAP ECC components must be secure. Therefore, the system has to be designed and configured with all the technical, legal, and organizational requirements in mind. Functional applications such as Financial Accounting (FI), Controlling (CO), Materials Management (MM), Sales & Distribution (SD), Project Management (PM), and Human Resources (HR) are still the core components of SAP ECC, albeit in modified and consolidated form. The volume of interactive points of contact between application and user means that the central backend systems, in particular, need to be protected from user errors, manipulation attempts, data theft, and similar unauthorized access. Applications such as Logistics and Human Capital Management and industry solutions such as IS Banking are potential targets of these kind of attacks. Identity management and authorization management play an important role in distributing functions in the applications and in taking the risks and requirements into account.

9.2 Risks and Controls

The security methods and solutions that you choose for SAP ECC depend on an objective assessment of the requirements and the risk potential of each individual situation. However, different corporate cultures can produce different evaluations of these factors, with the result that in the authorization area, there are as many solutions as there are SAP implementations. Risk evaluation is the central starting point for evaluating security solutions in the SAP environment. The risks that should be evaluated include the situation where the enterprise does not comply with the regulations and guidelines of any relevant industry associations, or statutory regulations and guidelines. Table 9.1 contains the main risks in SAP ECC.

No.	Classification	Description
1.	Risk potential	No authentication.
		Users of the various SAP ECC applications receive their user ID and initial password in an unencrypted email, or the initial password is always the same. This allows unauthorized users to access SAP ECC applications and potentially commit criminal offences.
	Impact	Unauthorized users use loopholes in authentication mechanisms to access data in backend systems. Identity theft and unauthorized use of third-party authorizations to access SAP ECC data and transactions are potential effects of this risk.
	Risk without control(s)	Extremely high
	Control(s)	The authentication mechanism and the associated administrative processes must be strong enough to protect the integrity of authorized users and to allow access only to these users.
	Risk with control(s)	Normal
	Section	9.3.1
2.	Risk potential	Inadequate authorization concept.
		Users of the various SAP ECC applications have authorizations that are too extensive for their actual requirements in terms of information and functions. Reason: The authorization concept is used only as a means of assigning functional authorizations and not as an effective instrument for controlling access and minimizing risks.
	Impact	Users have greater authorizations than are necessary for their position and the scope of their work. They thus have read and modify access to high-risk information and data. This is a violation of both internal company requirements and statutory requirements. It creates a situation where process, administrative, and system risks are not controlled. The risk potential is therefore increased rather than minimized.
	Risk without control(s)	Extremely high
	Control(s)	The authorization concept has to take into account both organizational and functional requirements, and make administration simpler and more effective. The relevant risks have to be taken into account in the authorization design process, and methods of continuous management have to be integrated into the change management process.
	Risk with control(s)	Normal
	Section	9.3.2

Table 9.1 Risks and Controls in SAP ECC

No.	Classification	Description
3.	Risk potential	Inadequate responsibility structure.
		The IT department cannot cope in an orderly and organized fashion with the workload of managing users and authorizations. The complexity of the task is increasing, as is the functional workload on the SAP ECC applications. There is also a need for coordination with the user departments, but these leave the task of authorization management up to the IT department. Also, the authorization components are not sufficiently transparent. This results in authorizations that do not accurately reflect the actual requirements of the enterprise.
	Impact	Authorizations are centrally assigned by administrators, even for users in other geographical regions. The actual persons who are responsible for information design—such as process, data, or application owners—are not properly involved in the design of authorization concepts and their daily administration. Thus, not enough attention, or no attention at all, is paid to the basic requirements. The segregation of functions therefore becomes blurred over time. Users are assigned more and more authorizations, and because of time pressures, analyses of the current situation and current requirements never take place. This results in errors and ineffective methods in authorization design, and extra work in terms of technical implementation, distribution, monitoring, and auditing. The security of the SAP ECC applications is thus not guaranteed, and statutory requirements are violated.
	Risk without control(s)	Extremely high
	Control(s)	Introduce and ensure the consistent implementation of the information ownership principle in order to effectively control authorizations and users in SAP ECC.
	Risk with control(s)	Normal
	Section	9.3.4
4.	Risk potential	Authorization concept is not fully defined.
		The authorization concepts for SAP ECC and SAP Enterprise Portal (SAP EP) are implemented individually rather than as a whole. Because there is no synchronization mechanism, SAP ECC and SAP EP users have different authorizations. Therefore, either too many or too few authorizations are assigned, which compromises the continuity of the process and the effectiveness of authorization management.
	Impact	Authorization errors and inconsistencies compromise operational processes. For example, certain transactions cannot be used, which in turn causes financial losses. Systems and employees are not used effectively.

Table 9.1 Risks and Controls in SAP ECC (cont.)

No.	Classification	Description
	Risk without control(s)	High
	Control(s)	The authorization concepts of the individual applications and systems should usually be part of an overlying comprehensive authorization concept. SAP ECC authorizations should be synchronized with SAP EP authorizations, and the shared concept should be the basis for this. Both conceptually and technically, this synchronization process has to ensure that the authorizations exist in all the various systems, and that the authorizations that have been agreed on are assigned to the users.
	Risk with control(s)	Normal
	Section	9.3.2
5.	Risk potential	Identity management and change management.
		There is no central user master data system. Because of the different types of users of SAP systems, there are a number of different solutions, however, the reasons for why they have arisen are not known. The master data storage system therefore contains redundancies and inconsistencies. The administrative processes do not permit you to make quick organizational changes to employee data or to modify or lock the corresponding authorizations. Because the HCM organizational structure is not incorporated into the process of assigning authorizations to positions, errors can occur with assigning the correct authorizations to certain user groups. This has an effect on the number of active users in SAP ECC, and it increases the threat from unauthorized employees with corresponding permissions.
	Impact	The consistency of user master data is not guaranteed, and modifications are either not implemented or are implemented only after a delay. Employees who have left the enterprise can therefore continue to use their authorizations and access table data and transactional process data in SAP ECC applications while remaining undetected. When an employee changes to a different department or user group, any new authorizations are simply added to their existing ones, which means that their authorizations mount up, along with those that arise as a result of combinations of authorizations. Unwanted authorizations, faulty transactions, unauthorized running of reports, and serious system errors can all result from excessive authorizations. These risks, in turn, can lead to ineffective administration, a lack of transparency, low levels of control, violations of data protection laws, low levels of security, and potential criminal activity. They can also lead to violations of statutory regulations, such as SOX.
	Risk without control(s)	Extremely high

Table 9.1 Risks and Controls in SAP ECC (cont.)

No.	Classification	Description
	Control(s)	Introduce proper user master data administration by including a central administration system (such as LDAP or CUA), and set up a comprehensive, unified identity management system that takes into account all administrative situations that arise in user management.
	Risk with control(s)	Normal
	Section	9.3.2
6.	Risk potential	Password rules.
		Access to SAP ECC is usually controlled by passwords. However, the minimum standards in the system are often not enough to ensure the secure operation of the system. Passwords that are too short can easily be guessed, and old passwords that are not changed regularly lose security as time passes.
	Impact	Potential attackers can get ahold of passwords that are easily accessible or too simple, and thus gain access to data and transactions. Depending on the authorizations that the user holds, the results of an identity attack can be very serious, and can have financial and internal operational consequences for the enterprise. There may also be violations of statutory regulations.
	Risk without control(s)	Extremely high
	Control(s)	Passwords must be subject to rules that are defined in accordance with the security requirements of the enterprise.
	Risk with control(s)	Normal
	Section	9.3.1
7.	Risk potential	Technical problems with authorizations.
		Authorization components, such as roles, are implemented in the system in such a way that the number of roles increases excessively over time, or the build-up of content causes complexity to increase on an ongoing basis. This affects the degree to which authorizations can be administrated, how roles are assigned to users, the degree to which simple monitoring is possible, and the feasibility of technical checks and audits. This all gives rise to potential risks, both in terms of administration and in the whole area of authorization for SAP ECC authorized users.

Table 9.1 Risks and Controls in SAP ECC (cont.)

No.	Classification	Description
	Impact	Ineffective authorization management, errors in assigning authorization components to users, and a lack of transparency and clarity leads to higher costs in authorization management and to an increase in the risk potential caused by excessive authorizations that have arisen due to the purely technical structure of SAP ECC authorization components. Some functional segregations can no longer be implemented. There may also be violations of internal corporate regulations and statutory regulations.
	Risk without control(s)	Extremely high
	Control(s)	An agreed authorization strategy must go hand in hand with a clear concept of the technical implementation of authorizations in SAP ECC. To this end, an appropriate authorization and role concept has to be set up. This concept should incorporate all components of the theoretical and practical aspects of an authorization system. It should also include best-practice solutions.
	Risk with control(s)	Normal
	Section	9.3.2

Table 9.1 Risks and Controls in SAP ECC (cont.)

These general risks have to be considered carefully by means of detailed risk analyses. Table 9.2 shows some of the risks involved with certain transactions and combinations of transactions.

Risk	Transaction code
User can open accounting periods that have already been closed and post documents after the month-end report has been run.	S_ALR_87003642, FBCJ
User can create fake General Ledger accounts and make unauthorized modifications, and start a posting outside the normal reporting period.	FS00, F-02
User can create a fake stock transport and cause an automatic payment to be made.	ME27, F110
User can make unauthorized changes to a purchasing request and create a purchase order.	MASS, ME52
User can make unauthorized changes to vendor master data and thus cause an unauthorized payment to be made.	FK02, F110
User can create a fake goods receipt, make unauthorized changes, and cause automatic payments to be made.	MB01, F110
User can create purchasing orders and associated credit orders.	ME21, F-41

Table 9.2 Examples of Risks in Certain Transactions

Risk	Transaction code
User can create fake profit accounts and related entries.	KE51, 3KE5
User can make unauthorized changes to vendor master records and create associated invoices.	FK02, F-43
User can make unauthorized changes to material master records and create a related fake purchasing order.	MM02, ME21
User can make unauthorized changes to a vendor master record and cause payments to be made.	FK02, F-44
User can post a credit item and cause an unauthorized payment to be made.	F-02, F-18
User can post a credit item and post and remove fake payments.	F-04, F-18
User can enter a fake goods receipt and post a payment to go with it.	MB01, F-18
User can create a fake vendor master record and make unauthorized changes to a purchasing request.	FK01, MASS
User can make unauthorized changes to agreements or contract data and post a corresponding goods rceipt.	ME31, MB01
User can make unauthorized changes to main accounts and assign documents.	FS02, FB02
User can make unauthorized changes to asset data and create purchasing orders.	AS02, MASS
User can create fake internal orders and post receipts to go with them.	KO01, F-02

Table 9.2 Examples of Risks in Certain Transactions (cont.)

9.3   Application Security

9.3.1   Authentication

Every user requires a correct user ID and password to log on to a system. This authentication mechanism can be improved, supplemented, or substituted by additional procedures, such as *Single Sign-On* (SSO), digital certificates, magnetic cards, tokens, biometric identification, and others. SAP ECC supports authentication by user ID and password, SSO, and other methods, including certificate-based solutions. If a Web browser is used as the frontend client, SAP ECC supports the use of logon tickets for SSO. The users are issued with a logon ticket after they have authenticated themselves to the original SAP system. This ticket then functions as an authentication token for other SAP systems. Thus, to authenticate himself or herself, the user has to enter neither user ID nor password;

instead, he or she can directly access the SAP ECC system once this system has checked his or her logon ticket. As an alternative to user authentication with user IDs and passwords, users who use a Web browser as their frontend can also use an X.509 client certificate for authentication purposes. The *Secure Sockets Layer* (SSL) protocol is used to authenticate the user on the Web server. This protocol does not transfer any passwords.

With authentication methods that use a user ID and password, on the other hand, password rules are particularly important. These rules can be defined in the instance profiles, using Transaction RZ10. They specify, for example, the minimum length of passwords, the validity period of passwords, whether certain passwords are allowed, rules for automatic locks in the case of incorrect entries, and so on.

9.3.2 Authorizations

Most enterprises that use SAP systems still use the classic variants of the R/3 system. Application security, in terms of roles and authorizations, is exactly the same in these systems as in SAP ECC. An enterprise's requirements in terms of application security and the required authorization design are defined as part of an authorization concept for SAP ECC.

Role Concept

The role concept is the central starting point when designing and developing the required authorizations. In SAP ECC, authorizations are required for different application functions. Transactions, reports, tables, programs, and activities are protected by means of authorization checks. Transactions are the basic form of access to SAP ECC. As well as protecting transactions and their data, transactional authorizations also restrict organizational and functional elements. Table 9.3 shows an example.

Transaction	Transaction code	Restricted to
Create material	MM01	Company code

Table 9.3 Transaction MM01 with Company Code Check

The necessary authorizations are developed in roles and assigned to the individual users. It is also possible to assign roles on the organizational level of a specific organizational unit, such as by position. The users then receive the relevant authorizations via the organizational unit in the form of roles.

A transaction usually consists of multiple screens in which data can be either created, modified, or displayed. For example, Transaction MM01 is used to create a material master record, Transaction MM02 is used to modify a material master record, and Transaction MM03 is used to display a material master record. The company code is displayed in the company code field, while the material number is displayed in the material number field. Some of these fields contain information that needs to be protected or controlled, and these control points have to be checked accordingly during the running of the transaction.

Usually, there is an ABAP program behind every transaction. The connection to this program is created using Transaction SE93. Authorization checks are built into the program code and have to achieve a positive result when the programs are in use. To this end, the corresponding authorizations are linked to the user master records. In the SAP standard, authorization checks in ABAP programs use what are known as *authorization objects* in order to assign authorization or restrict access to transaction codes, activities, and data.

Programmers use various methods to build authorization checks into their programs. The most common method is an authorization check using the AUTHO-RITY-CHECK statement, which is used to check a specific authorization object at a specific point in the program. If the check has a positive result, the user of the transaction will have the necessary authorizations in their user master record. If the user does not have sufficient authorization, the program encounters an error, outputs a corresponding error message, and terminates at this point. This intentional termination occurs at the point of control, which is either accepted or rejected.

In the case of error messages, a user or administrator can use Transaction SU53 to display more detailed information about the authorization fields.

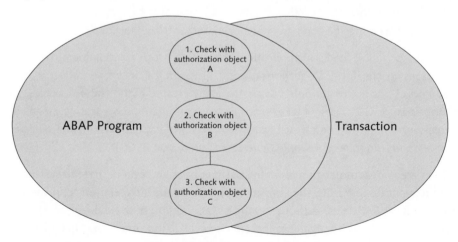

Figure 9.1 Authorization Check in Program Code

In the SAP standard, every transaction is subject to a check using at least the S_TCODE authorization object. S_TCODE is checked when the transaction is started. This is the first restriction of users on the transactional level. All other authorizations check access to specific organizational units and activities inside the transactions. Table 9.4 shows an example of authorization objects for Transaction MM01.

Authorization object	Authorization fields	Meaning	Value
S_TCODE	TCD	Transaction code	MM01
M_MATE_BUK	ACTVT BUKRS	Activity Company code	01 $BUKRS
M_MATE_LGN	ACTVT LGNUM	Activity Warehouse number	01 $LGNUM
M_MATE_VKO	ACTVT VKORG VTWEG	Activity Sales organization Sales channel	01 $VKORG $VTWEG

Table 9.4 Example of Authorization Objects in Transaction MM01

The authorization objects shown in the example are subject to two checks. Firstly, they are checked with a fixed authorization value, which is "01" in the case of Transaction MM01. Secondly, there are authorization fields, which do not contain any fixed check value. The system dynamically awaits the user's entry in each field to be checked, and then checks the input value against the authorizations.

Authorization objects thus check access to transactions, information groups, and data (such as MM01, master data, material), and also to certain organizational units such as a specific company code or material storage location.

The authorization checks in applications make it necessary to implement user permissions in the form of authorizations. The technical implementation of the authorizations no longer depends on manually created authorization profiles, as in the past; instead, it now takes place in semi-automated processes by means of roles.onm oups, and data (such as MM01, master data, matyerhorizati Roles are developed using the *SAP Profile Generator* (Transaction PFCG)).

Roles are known as *design roles* in the design phase. As soon as these design roles are mapped to SAP ECC, they become roles. Roles are also referred to in various situations as SAP roles, authorization roles, application roles, and user roles. The predecessor of roles, activity groups, are also used in individual cases in tables and entries in SAP ECC. However, it is roles that are meant in every case, even if the technical names seem to signify activity groups.

A user needs specific permissions and access options within systems so that he or she can properly use his or her work center. These access permissions are defined by means of organizationally structured roles. Authorization is therefore the key. An authorization is a set of permitted value assignments that are assigned to users by means of authorization objects. When transactions are called in SAP ECC, authorization objects and authorization values are checked and queried in the user master record. The checked access permissions in the program code of the transaction are assigned in the user master record by means of the relevant authorizations. An authorization is thus a form of permission to access certain transactions under certain conditions. A role contains all the relevant authorization components and can be assigned to users both individually and in combination with other roles.

Authorization Components

The main technical components of the SAP authorization system are as follows:

▶ Authorization object with

  ▷ Authorization fields

  ▷ Authorization field values

▶ Authorization

▶ Authorization profile

▶ Role

  ▷ Single roles

  ▷ Composite roles

▶ Users

The role is the unit that contains all of the above authorization components (see Figure 9.2).

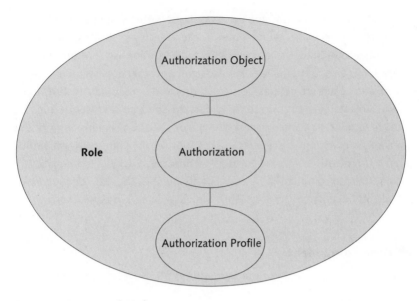

Figure 9.2 Structure of a Role

From the point of view of authorization checking, authorization objects are templates that can be used in program code in order to implement authorization checks in the various SAP ECC applications. SAP provides over 700 authorization objects as standard. These can be used in standard transactions and programs in ABAP. An authorization object can contain up to ten authorization fields (see Figure 9.3). Authorization objects are divided up in accordance with the individual module, are subject to special naming conventions, and, in conjunction with other authorization objects, can ensure that a program or transaction is protected. Authorization objects are assigned to authorization object classes, which are structured into modules and sub-modules. This makes it much easier for programmers, administrators, and system auditors to use them and navigate in them.

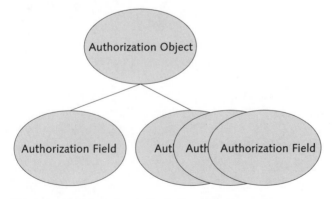

Figure 9.3 Structure of an Authorization Object

As mentioned above, authorization objects are templates for (technical) authorizations. An authorization is a specific instance of an authorization object in the SAP system that ensures special functional or organizational accesses within the SAP system. Field content is assigned to an authorization field in the form of authorization field values and is saved as an authorization. Authorizations are assigned to authorization profiles; Table 9.5 shows an example.

Transaction code	Check	Check with BO	Authorization field	Authorization field value
MM01	Company code	M_MATE_BUK	Activity Company code	01 for Create XXXX

Table 9.5 Example of Authorization Object and Authorization Object Field Value in Transaction MM01

If an authorization object contains multiple fields, the check always uses an AND operation. The overall check of the authorization object is considered successful only if the authorization check for each individual authorization field is successful.

An authorization itself is a technical component of the overall authorization system. "Authorizations" in this context refers not to user permissions, but to the technical component that is part of the role.

As many authorizations as you like can be created on the basis of an authorization object. Because this is now done by using roles, rather than manually, it has no effect on authorization design or authorization management. An authorization contains one authorization object with authorization fields (see Figure 9.4).

Authorizations are assigned in an authorization profile, and a profile can contain one or more authorizations (see Figure 9.5).

Authorization profiles, in turn, are a component of the role. Roles themselves are the most important authorization component. The authorizations and authorization profiles with the corresponding content are assigned to users via the role. After roles and the relevant authorization profiles have been assigned to a user, the user then has the permissions to create, display, or change data in SAP ECC. This ensures a controlled form of access to functions, activities, and data. When a user attempts to log on, the R/3 system obtains the relevant authorizations from the user master record in the user storage location. The system then checks the data in this storage location to see whether the required permissions are sufficient. Normally, if the permissions are not sufficient, a corresponding error message is output and the selected function terminates.

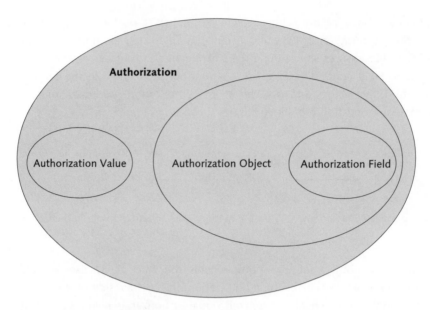

Figure 9.4 Structure of an Authorization

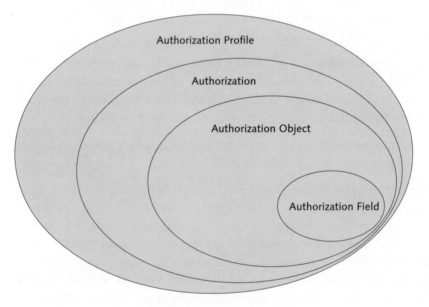

Figure 9.5 Structure of an Authorization Profile

Figure 9.6 provides a schematic summary of the role concept.

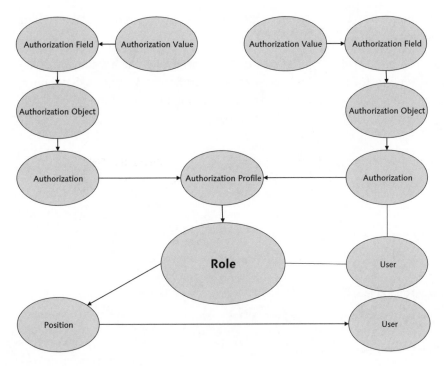

Figure 9.6 Role Concept

Role Categories

There are two technical role categories: single roles and composite roles. Single roles are schematically structured in accordance with the role concept described earlier. Composite roles, on the other hand, combine two or more roles to form a combined function role. Role categories can be used to create simple or complex authorization structures. Which role categories are selected as part of the authorization design process should depend on the individual implementation objectives, such as ease of administration, transparency, and security.

Role types

In terms of content, roles can be grouped into role types (see Figure 9.7). Depending on requirements and various criteria, roles can be subdivided, for example, into roles for users, positions, tasks, individual transactions, or for authorization objects only. For example, employees who work in the Accounting department most likely will require access to Financials transactions for their work. They can then be authorized to access these transactions in a role that suits their function. This kind of role is a *function role*. However, these employees may also require access to transactions in other areas, such as Controlling. *Task roles* are used to add on these types of smaller, additional authorizations. The whole set of authorizations is then assigned to the employees by means of a combination of both role types in a composite role.

Value roles are a special type of role that do not involve the assignment of any transactions. Instead, they contain only specific authorization objects that serve as a set of authorizations for a position or a user group in terms of the specific form they take and in conjunction with other roles.

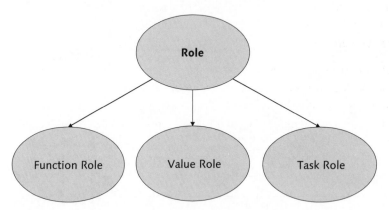

Figure 9.7 Role Types

What role type(s) are selected depends on whether SAP standard solutions or other solutions are used to implement the authorizations. You should critically analyze the requirements in advance and carry out a cost/benefit analysis.

SAP Profile Generator

SAP ECC contains the Profile Generator, a tool for the technical implementation of authorization components that is used to create, modify, and delete roles and to assign roles to users (transaction PFCG). The SAP Profile Generator can also be used to group transactions into logical units and to assign authorizations to them. Transactions, reports, and other authorizable elements are selected using the menu or by directly entering the transaction code.

The assignments of authorization objects to transactions is set down in tables such as USOBT_C and USOBX_C. The Profile Generator collects together the relevant authorization objects, including authorization fields and pre-set authorization field values, and then, in the next step, creates the authorizations within the role. In doing so, the Profile Generator shows both preset values and the fields that need to be maintained. A traffic light icon indicates the status of the authorizations to be maintained. Authorization objects can also be set to "inactive" if they no longer need to be maintained.

Check Indicators

Setting up and maintaining roles has become simpler and clearer thanks to the introduction of the check indicator concept. While in the past, authorization objects had to be laboriously identified in the program code, there are now tables that come with this information. Tables USOBT and USOBX in the SAP standard contain the transactions and the associated authorization objects. Customer tables USOBT_C and USOBX_C are generated first so that every SAP client can individually maintain their transaction values and authorization values without changing the standard. Transaction SU24 is used to maintain these tables.

Check indicators ensure that authorization objects are flagged in accordance with their relevance to the authorization check. Various different check indicators are used to define whether or not an authorization check is used for a specific transaction. This takes place independently of the ABAP program code of the transaction. The check indicators can deactivate these checks both on the transactional and on the global level. "Transactional" in this context means that check indicators can set an authorization object to "inactive" for a specific transaction. In other words, no check will then be carried out. "Global" in this context means that an authorization object is deactivated for all transactions in which it was previously checked. These locked authorization objects are then no longer displayed when roles are created.

Another use of check indicators is in relation to the SAP Profile Generator. Check indicators can be set to allow the authorization check to take place, and to display in the Profile Generator the authorization object in question so that the corresponding authorizations can be created there.

Obligatory authorization checks specify that an authorization object must always be checked while the program is running. The authorization object likewise becomes an obligatory authorization object in this case. The check indicator is set to "PP" for a specific transaction, which has the result that when a role is created, the authorization object is proposed for processing in the Profile Generator (example: authorization objects for company code checks).

Optional authorization checks specify that you can choose whether an authorization object is checked or not. The authorization object in this case becomes a dynamic authorization object. The check indicator is set to "PP" for a specific transaction, which has the result that when a role is created, the authorization object is proposed for processing in the Profile Generator (example: authorization objects for authorization groups).

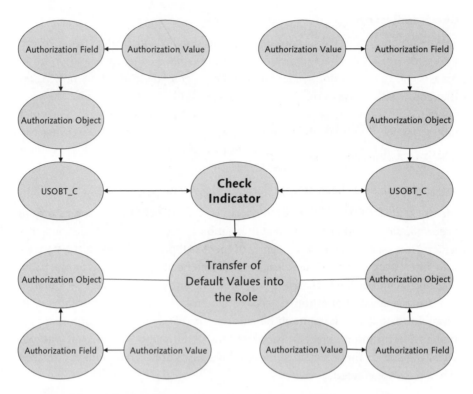

Figure 9.8 Effect of Check Indicators on Transfer to Transaction PFCG

Obligatory and optional authorization checks can also be globally defined using the check indicators. Table 9.6 shows the four types of check indicators and their effects on authorization checks.

Check indicator	Meaning	Explanation	Authorization objects displayed in Profile Generator?
PP	Check and maintain	The authorization object in question is always chekked.	Yes
P	Check	The authorization object in question is checked in certain cases.	No
N	Do not check	The authorization object in question is never checked.	No

Table 9.6 Check Indicators

Check indicator	Meaning	Explanation	Authorization objects displayed in Profile Generator?
U	Unmain-tained	The authorization object in question is not entered in USOBT (USOBT_C) and USOBX (USOBX_C). This indicator has no effect on the relevance of the check.	No

Table 9.6 Check Indicators (cont.)

After the profile has been created and the authorizations maintained, the authorization profiles can be generated and the role activated.

Menus

Role menus can also be created in the Profile Generator. Folder and menu structures can also be defined. This is done based on the order of the transactions, reports, and other functions that are to be authorized along with the role. Menus make navigating in and controlling transactions easier for the user. They can also be imported from other menus, such as the SAP menu or area menu, and from other roles or external files, and then further processed. The **Menus** tab page in the SAP Profile Generator is intended for this purpose.

SAP ECC also allows you to create area menus using transaction SE43. Area menus are used to simplify and standardize navigation aids for organizational and functional units, such as business departments. User groups that need authorization largely to the same functions can control their transactions using an area menu (example: area menu for sales staff).

Organizational and Functional Authorizations

Transactional segregation is not sufficient to guarantee security. In the case of geographical differentiators that require different authorizations, organizational levels with organizational standard fields such as company code or plant can be centrally maintained for the whole role. The authorization values for these fields then no longer have to be individually maintained for every authorization object; instead, they are filled automatically.

The inheritance principle is used for identical roles that are intended to authorize different organizational units. For this purpose, the SAP Profile Generator allows derivation roles, which consist of a fixed part (transaction and authorization objects outside of the organizational levels) and a variable part (organization levels). Various authorization values can then be assigned to the fields on the organizational levels. All other fields in the function role, which functions as the source of the derivations, are stable. Changes to the function role are passed on via the derived roles. Individual changes to single roles need to be made individually using the SAP Profile Generator. The menu for the derived roles is likewise inherited (see Figure 9.9).

Another way of creating roles with organizational divisions is to use value roles. The value role concept assumes that a risk analysis has confirmed the necessity of organizational and functional divisions. The affected authorization objects are not maintained in the roles; instead, they are set to "inactive." However, the authorization checks for these authorization objects still take place. Special authorization object roles, also known as value roles, are created for these authorization checks. These value roles can then be flexibly assigned to different function roles, depending on their own organizational assignment (see Figure 9.10).

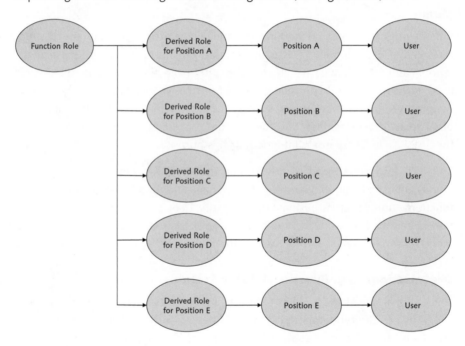

Figure 9.9 Derived Roles

The benefit of this solution is the flexibility and transparency that its structure provides. The organizational data and other authorization data is no longer "hidden" in all the roles; instead, it is always freely accessible in roles specifically intended for this purpose. Not all function and task roles have to be derived—you can also restrict them with a small number of value roles to specific organizational units or other authorization fields.

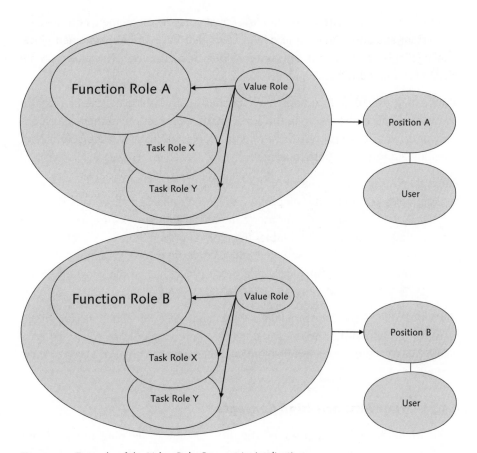

Figure 9.10 Example of the Value Role Concept in Applications

Creating and Maintaining User Data

Before you can assign authorizations to users, you have to create user data in SAP ECC. You do this using transaction SU01 for user master data, or centrally in the *Central User Administration* (CUA) function using transaction SCUG. The CUA allows you to administrate user data, both for SAP ECC and for other SAP systems. Both options can be used with centralized and decentralized user maintenance functions. Transaction SU10 is used for mass changes, that is, if you want to change data such as role assignments, parameters, fixed values, or logon data for a group of users. Users can also be created as reference users and can then function as a template for the creation of other users. Users can also have an alias name. While the standard user ID is 12 characters long, alias names can use up to 40 characters.

The CUA is required for maintaining user master data and for assigning roles. The following preparations are required: connect the SAP clients to the logical systems; enter the ALE distribution model with any partner agreements on the central system and subsystems; and define fields that have to be maintained either locally (client-specific), centrally (systemwide), or by the user. These settings are made in transactions SCUA and SCUM.

Maintaining user data in a consistent manner across multiple systems leads to consistency and transparency in the administrative process. Nonetheless, responsible persons in the business departments should still have a leadership role in assigning authorization data to users.

Either the SAP Profile Generator or the user master data transaction SU01 is used to assign roles and authorization profiles; the SAP Profile Generator has a tab page specifically for this purpose. The user comparison function is an important one here, as it allows all user master tables to be synchronized. You can start this comparison process either from the SAP Profile Generator, using transaction PFUD, or you can set it to run automatically in a batch process using the program *PFCG_TIME_DEPENDENCY* (call program *RHAUTHUPDATE_NEW*).

The SAP Profile Generator provides a wide range of other functions for implementing and administrating roles in a logical manner. It enables you to copy or delete roles, to choose any profile name you like, and to carry out single or mass changes.

9.3.3 Other Authorization Concepts

There are many other ways, besides the role concept, of defining authorizations for specific functions and using them in combination with roles.

Authorization Group Concept

Authorization groups are used to indirectly assign SAP values to authorized users (see Figure 9.11). Value assignments are made by means of a group and are then checked as an authorization value. The element to be protected cannot be accessed directly through a special authorization field; instead, it is accessed only through the authorization group for the element. There are authorization groups for different fields; for example, to restrict table authorization groups, document types for Financials via transaction OVA7, or apply in material master authorization groups.

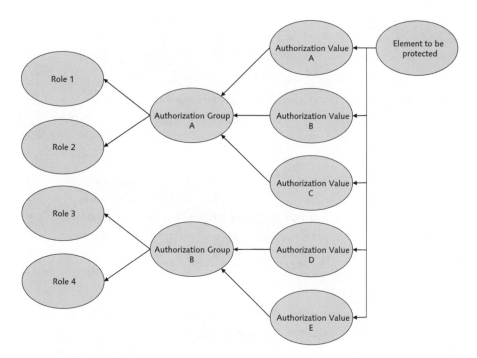

Figure 9.11 Authorization Group Concept

Authorizations for Tables

Like all other data, authorization data is stored in tables in SAP ECC. It is particularly important to protect the content of tables. It is a generally valid rule that in most cases, users do not need direct access to table information. Tables are usually displayed and maintained using transactions and views. For this purpose, parameter transactions are created and assigned to the users via roles. In exceptional cases, direct table maintenance can be used to perform special activities in tables. If you want to control tables directly, this can be done using a number of different transactions, including transactions SE16 and SM31. The kind of protection that the table has depends on table authorization groups, which are checked by means of the authorization object S_TABU_DIS.

Tables are protected in accordance with the authorization group concept. Several tables already have a table authorization group when the system is shipped by SAP. Make sure that every table is assigned to an authorization group; this applies especially to customer-specific tables. This should be set down in any programmers' guidelines. Table authorization groups are maintained using transaction SM31 and the table maintenance view TDDAT in table TBRG.

Table 9.7 gives an overview of some important tables in the authorization system.

Technical name of table	Meaning of table
AGR_1016	Name of role profile
AGR_1250	Authorization data for role
AGR_1251	Authorization data for role
AGR_1252	Organizational levels of authorizations
AGR_PROF	Profile name for role
AGR_SELECT	Transaction code for role
AGR_TCDTXT	Transaction code for role with text
AGR_TCODES	Transaction code for user
CRMC_BLUEPRINT	Customizing CRM
TACT	Standard values for activity codes
TACTT	Standard values for activity codes with text
TBRG	Authorization groups
TDDAT	Table authorization groups
TOBJ	Authorization objects
TOBJC	Authorization objects and object classes
TOBJT	Texts for authorization objects
TSTC	Transaction codes
TSTCA	Authorization values for transaction codes
TSTCP	Parameters for transactions
TSTCT	Transaction texts
AUTHA	Application authorization fields
AUTHB	Basic application authorization fields
USER012	Authorization information for user maintenance
USH04	History of authorization changes
USH10	History of authorization profile changes
USH12	History of authorization value changes
USKRI	Critical authorization combinations (transaction code)
USOBT	Transaction code for the authorization object
USOBT_C	Transaction code—authorization object for customers

Table 9.7 Authorizations and User Data

Technical name of table	Meaning of table
USOBT_CD	History of authorization field changes
USOBX	Check table for table USOBT
USOBX_C	Check table for table USOBT_C
USORG	Organizational level for SAP Profile Generator
USOTT	Transaction code for authorization object
USPRO	Authorization profile
USR07	Authorization object and authorization field values of last authorization check that encountered an error
USR08	User menus
USR09	Work areas of user menus
USR13	Authorization short texts

Table 9.7 Authorizations and User Data (cont.)

Authorization object S_TABU_CLI is used to control the maintenance of cross-client tables. Authorization object S_TABU_LIN allows row-based table authorizations.

Field Group Concept

Some transactions contain specific information that requires protection because of certain risks. The fields in which this information is contained are also protected separately. To do this, the fields in question in the transaction are assigned to a field group. Users obtain their access permission to the information in these fields by being assigned to the field group (see Figure 9.12). The transaction with all other authorizations is assigned to positions or users by means of a role in accordance with the role concept, as before. If users are not assigned to the field group, these users do not have access to the content of the fields that are protected separately. Various applications contain transactions for maintaining field groups, such as AO92, BC65, BUBN, BUCN, and CACS_CSB0103.

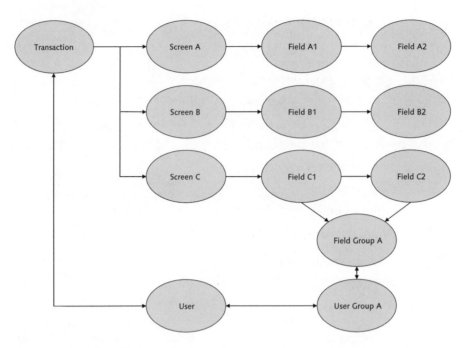

Figure 9.12 Field Group Authorization Concept

Authorizations for Reports

Reports and programs are among the most critical elements of information, and thus require a high degree of protection. Reports can be controlled by means of transactions and authorization objects, and are therefore to be authorized in accordance with the role concept. Calls of reports and programs by means of standard transactions such as SA38 or SE38 should be banned, as the risk of errors or serious system complications is very high. In general, programs are not assigned to any authorization group. If the above-mentioned transactions were assigned, this would also mean that authorization to start all programs was assigned as well. You should not allow this kind of authorization in any circumstances.

Reports can be added to a transaction using either transaction SE93 or the SAP Profile Generator. In the SAP Profile Generator, you can select reports and assign to them a transaction code that is generated by the SAP system. Because these generated transaction codes do not follow any general naming convention, you should decide in advance whether you want all report transactions to have their own naming convention. If you do want this, the convention will have to be included in the authorization management processes and their documentation.

Authorizations for Batch Processing

Batch jobs are programs that run in the background of an application. Authorizations for background processing are defined in a batch job authorization concept (see Figure 9.13). The assignment of authorizations in this case is controlled by the background user, the name of the background job, and the activities. In general, all background jobs have the following criteria:

▶ Job type (technical, functional, risk)

▶ Periodic use (daily, weekly, monthly)

▶ Sporadic use (yes or no)

▶ Short description of job

▶ Assignment to role, user, or position

A batch job administrator is responsible for administrating batch jobs. No other user besides the administrator should have administrator permissions. Administrator permissions are controlled by the authorization object S_BTCH_ADM.

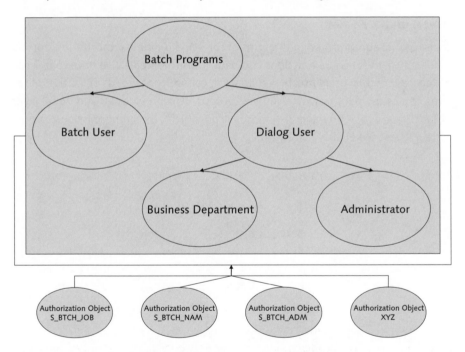

Figure 9.13 Batch Job Authorizations and Related Authorization Objects

Batch jobs run under the authorization of either a dialog user or a system user (batch user). It is a common practice to use just one system user that has the SAP_ALL standard profile as the batch user for all background jobs. However, this is not a good practice, as it contains many risks. There should be several system users for different job categories—for example, one user for all Logistics background jobs. The batch users then get exactly the authorizations and permissions that they need to run the relevant batch programs. The authorization object S_BTCH_JOB is used to define these permissions.

Spool requests that are created by background jobs of the logged-on user are handled in the same way as dialog spool requests. Spool requests that are created by background jobs of other users can be viewed only if the user who wants to view them is explicitly named in an authorization with the authorization object S_BTCH_NAM. However, note that in this case, this user can then view all spool requests of the other user. If spool requests are created by a batch user and another user wants to view these requests, the user name of the batch user also has to be explicitly specified.

The various batch programs are subject to further authorization checks, so these authorization objects also have to be defined and assigned for the batch roles.

User Group Concept

Transactional authorization in the form of roles and defined authorization objects is not sufficient for some functions and data. These elements also have to be separately assigned to users in tables that are specifically intended for each application. This assignment process uses user groups. This provides an additional layer of functional protection and also makes it possible to assign permissions to only certain users (see Figure 9.14).

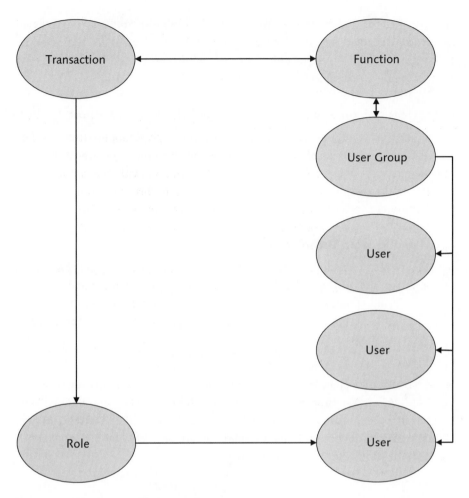

Figure 9.14 User Group Authorization Concept

Authorizations for Queries

"Queries" in this context refers to individual user queries to the SAP database. Access to queries and their maintenance functions is controlled by query transactions such as SQ01, SQ02, SQ03, and SQVI. Query authorizations are assigned by means of a combination of views, users, and user groups, and also by using the Quick Views function. Queries and InfoSets should generally be created in the development system and tested in the test or quality assurance system, as they do involve some risks in terms of security, data protection, and performance. Specific user groups and positions for these queries can then be authorized in the production system. Every authorized user has to be assigned to a query user group; this guarantees that the users can access only queries in their work area. There are special authorization objects for queries, such as S_QUERY, that make access to and activities for queries secure. The details of which InfoSets may be accessed have to be specified for each user group. InfoSets themselves are protected by authorization groups. Authorization for queries is then carried out by assigning queries to query user groups.

Authorizations for the Report Writer and the Report Painter

These functions should be made available only to a small number of users, as they can also perform user-specific analyses using specific data and collect this information in reports. The procedure is similar to that of query authorizations. Authorization restrictions are set for reports, the report group, the libraries, and layouts, by means of authorization groups.

Spool and Printer Authorizations

Security for sensitive spool entries, such as spool entries in the Financials area, is set up using the **Authorization** field in the properties of the relevant spool request. For all sensitive Financials reports that are started in the dialog or in background mode, the corresponding value, such as "YFI" for the **Authorizations** field, for example, is maintained. This protects the spool requests from third-party access.

Spool authorizations (activities and value assignments) are assigned by means of the S_ADMI_FCD and S_SPO_ACT authorization objects. The **SPOACTION** authorization field is used to set the authorized actions, while the **SPOAUTH** field allows specific spool entries to be assigned that are protected by the corresponding **Authorization** field (see Figure 9.15).

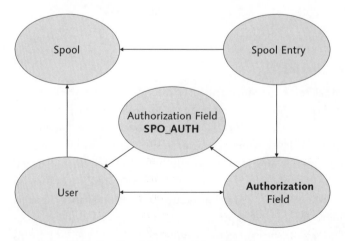

Figure 9.15 Protecting Spool Requests Using Authorizations

User-specific spool entries are called using transaction SP02. The administration transaction SP01 requires special protection. To display and maintain employee-specific spool requests for the YFI authorization group—for example, for the Accounting department staff—the authorization values shown in Table 9.8 have to be added to the authorization for authorization object S_SPO_ACT.

Spool authorization object	Spool authorization field	Authorization value
S_SPO_ACT	SPOACTION	ATTR
S_SPO_ACT	SPOACTION	BASE
S_SPO_ACT	SPOACTION	DELE
S_SPO_ACT	SPOACTION	DISP
S_SPO_ACT	SPOACTION	PRNT
S_SPO_ACT	SPOACTION	REDI
S_SPO_ACT	SPOACTION	REPR
S_SPO_ACT	SPOAUTH	YFI

Table 9.8 Example of Authorizations for User-Specific Spool Entries

For Accounting department staff to be able to see the spool requests of all other employees in their department, and the contents of these requests, all spool requests created in this department need to be protected by the "YFI" authorization value in the Authorizations field. Transaction SP01 has to be assigned for this activity. Then, authorization object S_SPO_ACT has to be defined and authorization object S_ADMI_FCD has to be maintained (see Table 9.9).

Spool authorization object	Spool authorization field	Authorization value
S_ADMI_FCD	S_ADMI_FCD	SP01

Table 9.9 Defining Authorization Object S_ADMI_FCD for Use with Transaction SP01

These settings allow users to view all spool requests that are protected with the "YFI" authorization value and to view their own spool requests that were created without an authorization value. Spool requests that are created by background jobs of the logged-on user are handled in the same way as dialog spool requests. Spool requests that are created by background jobs of other users can be viewed only if the authorization is explicitly specified in the S_SPO_ACT authorization object.

Printer authorizations and other output authorizations are protected by the authorization object S_SPO_DEV. A printer concept with its own consistent naming convention will make the administration work a lot easier.

The list of other authorization concepts is a long one: view authorization concept, authorizations for HR, transaction variant concept, transaction group concept, batch input concept, group authorization concept, and many others. These concepts help to safeguard and optimize the security requirements of the enterprise.

Monitoring and Control

Authorization management has to be controlled and monitored because of the risks involved, and because of the major significance of this area in terms of assigning and dividing up authorizations, and in restricting functions in SAP ECC and other SAP systems. The aim of controlling and monitoring this area is to reduce the risks associated with authorization management tasks. SAP provides a wide range of methods and solutions for these purposes. Reports in the Audit Information System (AIS) can be used to analyze financial data for auditors, and also for system audits and monitoring. Security information logs, the authorization information system, table logs, and other tools can all be used for controlling purposes for the control functions of the SAP systems. The AIS consists of several evaluation reports that provide information on the authorization system and system settings, as well as reports for business and balance sheet audits. Lastly, the reports contain analyses of the following:

▶ System configuration with clients, parameter settings, tables, database and system logs, security audit log analyses, and status displays

▶ Authorization information, change documents, and access statistics for the Repository Information System

▶ User authentication information with logon procedures and password rules, settings for SAP standard users such as "SAP*" and "DDIC"

▶ Authorization management for users with settings for the SAP Profile Generator, check indicators, system parameters, user overview, information on critical authorizations, and their distribution among users

▶ Change and transport system

▶ Batch job processing

▶ Data protection information

▶ Information on development and Customizing

These analyses are used for internal monitoring and control within the enterprise, but are also actively used for system checks by external auditors. Access to the AIS is assigned by means of SAP standard roles. The **SAP_AUDITOR** role is defined as a composite role and is made up of all the individual roles of the AIS and the menu structure required to call reports. There are two different kinds of standard roles in the AIS: transaction roles, which contain the role menu structure, and pure authorization roles, which contain the authorization objects and definitions. The authorization roles contain the authorization objects necessary for executing the reports defined in the transaction role, plus definitions. In terms of results, the reports can be either displayed or loaded into the SAP system for further processing. However, this and other AIS functions can be executed only with other authorizations.

9.3.4 Best-Practice Solutions

The authorization design concept for SAP ECC must be completely incorporated into an overlying SAP security concept. The objective is to customize the functionality of the application to the requirements of the enterprise. This affects the authorizations, which grant access to functionalities, restrict user permissions, and prevent unauthorized activities.

The authorization system is one of the most important preventive controls in the SAP system. Its functions are intended to prevent potential risks from becoming reality, to minimize risks, and to ensure that the applications can be controlled. These functions reveal the clear necessity for a strategically sound definition of the authorization design concept, its effective technical implementation in the SAP ECC system, and an optimized administration procedure for authorizations and users.

It is therefore hugely important that the authorization system be incorporated into the internal control and monitoring system in the enterprise. Authorizations should be granted not only on the basis of functional and work-related requirements, but also should be regarded as a wide-reaching control option. The amount of time and attention that the issue of designing and implementing authorization structures receives depends on the type of enterprise, people's individual assessment of the security requirements and statutory regulations, and individual experience, and is in direct proportion to the amount of resources that are assigned to it. It is important in all cases that a requirements analysis is carried out in plenty of time, so that the appropriate controlling and monitoring objectives can be set and incorporated accordingly into the authorization design process.

User and authorization management should be as integrated, controlled, transparent, and effective as possible. When SAP standard tools such as the SAP Profile Generator and CUA are used, authorization management and user administration should be kept separate, for technical, organizational, and control reasons. If other integrated solutions are in use, such as *SecurInfo for SAP*, then this separation is not necessary, as different, more complex controls are implemented using the information ownership principle.

The amount of work involved in administration and the associated control functions can be very high. This leads to the necessity of having requirements of authorization design and the administrative processes that keep this administration work at a predictable and manageable level—via clear authorization structures, standardized procedures, a clear definition of tasks and the distribution of responsibilities, a limited number of roles if possible, and balanced training measures.

Authorization management comprises the creation of roles and all authorization components in use in the system, with the objective of ensuring that the processes in question run smoothly. This means that the responsible persons must be notified of configuration changes immediately, as these changes could affect the assignment of authorizations. Also, an application guide should be created that describes the administrative processes and the application areas of the relevant tools and methods, such as the SAP Profile Generator and authorization concepts. This guide should also describe technical best practices for using the tools.

User administration includes activities such as creating, modifying, and deleting users, changing passwords, locking, unlocking, and assigning roles and authorization profiles, and many more. The process that applies in the case of problems or changes should also be documented in a guide, and this guide should be made available to all of the responsible persons.

The overall process of authorization and user administration is divided into four main categories:

▶ Application
▶ Release
▶ Implementation
▶ Information

The information is both a concurrent and a subsequent process to cases in the other three categories. In general, this process can be used to process the cases listed in Table 9.10.

Category	Case
Application	New user requires SAP authorizations
	User switches organizational unit
	User leaves company
	User needs more authorizations
	User cannot log on
	Transaction missing in assigned role
	Transactions have to be removed
	Authorization values are missing
	New authorizations have to be distributed across multiple roles
	Roles are missing
	Authorizations outside of the role concept are missing
Release	New user requires SAP authorizations
	User switches organizational unit
	User leaves company
	User needs more extensive authorizations
	User cannot log on
	Transaction missing in assigned role
	Transactions have to be removed
	Authorization values are missing
	New authorizations have to be distributed across multiple roles
	Roles are missing
	Authorizations outside of the role concept are missing
Implementation	New user requires SAP authorizations
	User switches organizational unit
	User leaves company
	User needs more extensive authorizations
	User cannot log on
	Transaction missing in assigned role
	Transactions have to be removed

Table 9.10 Cases in Authorization and User Administration

Category	Case
	Authorization values are missing
	New authorizations have to be distributed across multiple roles
	Roles are missing
	Authorizations outside of the role concept are missing

Table 9.10 Cases in Authorization and User Administration (cont.)

The better the business departments are integrated into the design and authorization management processes, the more successful the implementation of the authorizations and the security of the application processes will be.

The following factors are of central importance for a successful authorization system that is defined in the authorization strategy:

▶ **Functionality**
The users have to be guaranteed that they will receive the authorizations necessary to complete their work. The minimal principle should be used here.

▶ **Risk**
As well as being taken into account in the authorization design process, risk and control analyses should rank along with functional aspects as a central basis for defining and implementing authorizations. This approach ensures that potential risks are identified, and authorizations can then be used to neutralize, restrict, and control these risks. This also creates the possibility of creating a highly effective authorization system, as minor authorization checks do not have to be included and can thus be deactivated. One of the most important control options in this context is functional segregation of duties (SoD), which can be mapped and enforced by the authorization system.

▶ **Strategy**
Make sure that a unified concept is developed. Components and requirements such as risk management, change management, ease of implementation, ease of administration, transparency, ease of control, completeness, ease of auditing, costs, and vision are all part of the strategy. You also have to specify the members of the authorization team, and define how the team is incorporated into the overall strategy and an overlying SAP risk management and IT security team. It is particularly important in this context that you integrate IT staff and staff in the individual business departments in a way that ensures the most efficient form of cooperation possible during the design and implementation phases, and that the business departments take responsibility for authorization management, the applications, and the continuity of the solution. The infor-

mation ownership principle is a central factor in the long-term success of the investments in this context.

▶ **Solution**
The solution(s) should be authoritative and integrated, and have a high degree of automation, so that the implementation team is free to concentrate on quality control and detailed aspects of creating the authorization concept. Because risk potential in general is growing and statutory requirements are increasing all the time, conventional authorization systems are no longer sufficient. This is why solutions that combine integrated controls with risk management, authorization management, user administration, and compliance management are becoming more widespread.

Example

The *SecurInfo for SAP* solution provides a combination of risk and control management, authorization and role management, user administration, change and task management, and integrated workflows (see Figure 9.16). By integrating all the essential components of a comprehensive authorization and user administration solution, and by allowing for the inclusion of the business areas in a logical way, this solution enables a new standard of quality to be reached, both in the area of technical administration and in the analysis and control of process and application risks.

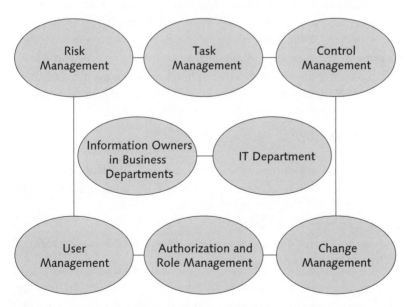

Figure 9.16 Comprehensive Authorization Concept with Securinfo for SAP

- ▶ **Technical implementation**

  Before the technical implementation, you should evaluate the options in the SAP standard tools for identifying risks, creating roles and authorizations, and carrying out the necessary administration and control tasks, and combine them with solutions from other providers, if required.

- ▶ **Concepts**

  In the case of role concepts, make sure that the roles follow a clear logical system. Selecting the correct types of roles is just as important for the success of the concept as the role types themselves and their content-related aspects. In most cases, it makes sense to select a combination of role types. Make sure to define in advance the purpose for which a specific role type is intended. It is advisable to use more authorization concepts, if this is required.

- ▶ **Transparency**

  It is essential that the authorization concept and the associated processes are simple, easy to understand, and easy to follow for both users and administrators, business departments, and auditors. The responsible persons in the business departments, process owners, data owners, and role owners must clearly understand their own role in the internal control process chain and where they fit into the overall process in order to be able to make effective and correct decisions. Therefore, transparency of the processes and activities is essential for the success of the established internal control systems.

- ▶ **User administration**

  User administration is a confidential and highly responsible activity, and should therefore be handled with extreme care. Because it deals with protecting confidential information, authorizations should also be included in the protection area. The processes of creating and modifying user master records and distributing authorizations should be automated as much as possible and should have the highest possible level of control. Solutions such as CUA should be evaluated and used, if required.

- ▶ **Naming conventions**

  Assigning a naming convention for every authorization component is part of the design process. Using naming conventions just for user IDs and roles is not enough. Every authorization component, such as table authorization groups, user groups, and material master data authorization groups, should be set in advance in accordance with a naming convention. Make sure when doing this that the names are unique and that they start with a customer-specific element such as "Y" whenever possible.

Table 9.11 shows some transaction codes that are relevant to authorization and user administration. There are more than 1,000 transactions that can be relevant to good authorization management. The following table contains a selection of these.

Transaction code	Transaction
AL08	Display logged-on users (all instances)
AUTH_DISPLAY_OBJECTS	Switch global authorization object check on and off
AUTH_SWITCH_OBJECTS	Display global authorization object check
BALE	Administration area menu
BALM	ALE master data
OOAC	HCM main authorization switch
PFCG	SAP Profile Generator
ROLE_CMP	Role comparison for menus
RTTREE_MIGRATION	Report tree migration
RZ10	Maintain system profile parameters
RZ11	Maintain system profile parameters
SALE	ALE Customizing
SCC4	Maintain system change option
SCUA	CUA administration (ALE landscapes)
SCUG	CUA administration (user maintenance)
SCUL	CUA administration (distribution logs)
SCUM	CUA administration (fields)
SE01	Maintain special transport requests
SE03	Utility programs for transport and correction system
SE06	Set up Workbench Organizer
SE09	Maintain transport requests
SE10	Maintain transport requests
SE11	Maintain ABAP/4 Dictionary
SE16	Table display
SE43	Maintain area menus
SE93	Transaction administration
SECR	Audit Information System

Table 9.11 Selected Transactions for Authorization Management

Transaction code	Transaction
SICF	Protection for service level accesses
SLG1	Application protocol for authorization objects
SM01	Lock and unlock transactions
SM04	Display logged-on users (per instance)
SM12	Delete locks
SM19	Configure security audit
SM20	Analyze Security Audit Log
SM21	Online analysis of system log
SM31	Table maintenance
SM59	Display and maintain RFC destinations
SM69	Define and maintain logical commands
SMT1	Trusted systems
SMT2	Trusted systems
SO70	Display Customizing
SP01	Spool administration
SPAD	Set up printer
SPOR	Spool administration
SQ01	Query: administration of query user groups and functional areas
SQ02	Query: administration of InfoSets
SQ03	Query: start queries
SSO2	SSO administration
SSO2_ADMIN	SSO administration
ST01	System and authorization trace functions
STAT	Static anaylsis of user actions
STMS	Administration of transport system
STRUST	Trust manager
STRUSTSSO2	Trust manager for SSO
SU01	Maintain users
SU02	Maintain authorization profiles

Table 9.11 Selected Transactions for Authorization Management (cont.)

Transaction code	Transaction
SU03	Maintain authorizations
SU3	User parameters
SU10	Mass changes to user master data
SU20	Maintain authorization fields
SU21	Maintain authorization objects
SU24	Maintain check indicators
SU25	Upgrade and migration: authorizations
SU53	User information for authorization checks
SU56	Display authorization checks (if an error occurs)
SUIM	Authorization information system
SUPO	Maintain organizational levels
TU02	Profile parameters
VUSREXTID	User link (SAP—external)

Table 9.11 Selected Transactions for Authorization Management (cont.)

9.4 Technical Security

Solutions for the technical IT security of SAP ECC components have already been described in Chapter 8. Because all applications run in the SAP Web AS, the IT security controls of this runtime environment apply.

10 mySAP ERP Human Capital Management

This chapter describes IT security concepts for the Global Security Positioning System (GSPS) component, mySAP ERP Human Capital Management (mySAP ERP HCM). It covers general authorization concepts and solutions for best-practice control methods in the HCM applications of SAP ERP Central Component (ECC).

10.1 Introduction and Functions

Application security in the HR department is particularly important as the protection of person-related data is required by law (e.g., data protection law). This means that companies are not only morally, but also legally obligated to secure data that is related to persons and employees and stored in SAP systems, and to protect this data from unwanted external access. In the evaluation of security solutions, *mySAP ERP Human Capital Management* (mySAP ERP HCM) must also be analyzed for potential risks.

10.2 Risks and Controls

Appropriate control solutions must ensure, for instance, that only authorized users can delete an employee in the system. In particular, the individual transactions and activities available to perform such tasks must be protected—in the event of deleting an employee, Transaction PU00. In other scenarios, the control measures involve a multitude of transactions. For example, only authorized users should have the permission to change the wage and salary details for an employee (Transactions PU03 and PA30, Infotype 0003). A detailed risk analysis should therefore provide information on general and detailed risks.

The following main risks exist for HR data and HR systems:

▶ Unauthorized access to personal data

▶ Unauthorized execution of master data reports

▶ Unauthorized downloading of personal data that should be particularly protected

▶ Unauthorized use of standard SAP tools like Transaction SM31 or SA38 to access HCM data

▶ Unauthorized direct access to personal data with database tables

▶ Unauthorized use of ad-hoc queries to obtain information on employees and other HCM-related information

Due to the legal requirements regarding data protection and the required control of personal information, the protection needs in the HR and personnel management areas are especially high. For this reason, mySAP ERP HCM contains some advanced authorization solutions in addition to the role concept and all the authorization concepts described in Chapter 9. As a rule, authorizations are also defined on the basis of transactions, roles, authorization objects, authorizations, and the other authorization components described earlier in this book. Choosing the right security solution in this context depends on the risk level, the organization, and the internal requirements of a company. In many cases, the role concepts are sufficient to ensure proper protection of personal data.

Table 10.1 provides an overview of the risks related to mySAP ERP HCM.

No.	Classification	Description
1.	Risk potential	Inadequate authorization concept.
		Users of the various SAP ECC applications have authorizations that are too extensive for their actual requirements in terms of information and functions. This also affects employee details, which are to be particularly protected due to their confidential nature (for example, date of birth, income, or qualifications). Since HCM doesn't consist of separate systems, the authorization concept is the most important means available to separate HCM authorizations from other functional authorizations.
	Impact	Users have greater authorizations than are necessary for their position and the scope of their work. This includes read and write access to confidential information and data. This situation violates legal requirements such as data protection laws, internal requirements, and the personal rights of employees. Violations of the law on the protection of personal data are evident. The risk of a penalization by the legal authorities exists. Other risks that result from the knowledge of confidential personal data depend on the type and circumstances of the breach of trust.
	Risk without control(s)	Extremely high
	Control(s)	The authorization concept must acknowledge the specific role of HCM-relevant data. The design and implementation of the authorization concept must account for the acknowledgement and application of legal requirements (which data should be protected?), and it must be ensured that the authorizations and administration processes grant access to sensitive personal data only to those employees who have the necessary permission.

Table 10.1 Risks and Controls for mySAP ERP HCM

No.	Classification	Description
	Risk with control(s)	Normal
	Section	10.3
2.	Risk potential	Inadequate responsibility structure.
		The IT department cannot handle the workload of managing users and authorizations in an orderly and organized fashion. The complexity increases along with the functional workload on the SAP ECC applications; this also affects the applications in the HCM area. This means that the individual departments must be coordinated; the authorization management is handled by the IT department. Also, the authorization components are not sufficiently transparent. This results in authorizations that do not accurately reflect the actual requirements of the enterprise. This is particularly critical for personal data as the IT administrators are usually not familiar with the legal requirements.
	Impact	Personal data is not protected or is insufficiently protected. This is a violation of legal requirements, internal company requirements, and the personal rights of the employees.
	Risk without control(s)	Extremely high
	Control(s)	Introduction and consistent penetration of the principle of information ownership for an efficient control of authorizations and users in mySAP ERP HCM, thereby integrating the HCM personnel and the data protection officer.
	Risk with control(s)	Normal
	Section	10.3
3.	Risk potential	Authorization concept is not fully defined.
		The authorization concepts for mySAP ERP HCM have not been set up together, but as individual solutions. Users have different authorizations for HCM data in different systems. This has the result that either too many or too few authorizations are assigned, which compromises the continuity of the process and the effectiveness of authorization management. Moreover, actual data from the production system can be transferred to the QA or other systems. Information to be protected that has been transferred to a printer outside of the "protection zone" can be accessed by any person. There is no integration with other authorization concepts like the spool and printer concept.
	Impact	Authorization errors and inconsistencies compromise operational processes. Data with a high need for protection can sometimes be accessed by everyone. The effects extend from the creation of a bad company atmosphere to identity theft, which is a serious violation of legal requirements and a reflection of the company's failure to meet its responsibilities.

Table 10.1 Risks and Controls for mySAP ERP HCM (cont.)

No.	Classification	Description
	Risk without control(s)	High
	Control(s)	The authorization concepts of the individual applications and systems should usually be part of a overlying, comprehensive authorization concept. Authorizations in SAP ECC should be defined along with the authorizations of mySAP ERP HCM. The common concept serves as the basis for the design, implementation, and administrative follow-up processes.
	Risk with control(s)	Normal
	Section	10.3
4.	Risk potential	Identity management and change management. There is no central user master data system. The master data storage system therefore contains redundancies and inconsistencies. The administrative processes do not permit you to make quick organizational changes to employee data or to modify or lock the corresponding authorizations. There is no integration of the HCM organizational structure into the process of assigning authorizations. The users in mySAP ERP HCM and all other SAP systems are affected by this.
	Impact	The transparency of user master data is not guaranteed, and modifications are either not implemented or are implemented only after a delay. Employees who have left the company can thus continue to use their authorizations and access table data and transactional process data in the applications while remaining undetected. When an employee moves to a different department or user group, any new authorizations, including those that arise as a result of combinations of authorizations, are simply added to the user's existing ones, which means that his or her authorizations build up. Unwanted authorizations, faulty transactions, unauthorized running of reports, and serious system errors can all result from excessive authorizations. These risks, in turn, can lead to ineffective administration, a lack of transparency, low levels of control, violations of data protection laws, low levels of security, and potential criminal activity.
	Risk without control(s)	Extremely high
	Control(s)	Introduce proper user master data administration by including a central administration system (such as LDAP or CUA), and set up a comprehensive, unified identity management system that takes into account all administrative situations that arise in user management.
	Risk with control(s)	Normal
	Section	10.3

Table 10.1 Risks and Controls for mySAP ERP HCM (cont.)

The general risks listed in Table 10.1 must be supplemented by detailed analyses for mySAP ERP HCM to enable a more profound view for specific cases (see Table 10.2).

Control Objective	Transaction Code	Infotypes
The organization plan must be securely maintained and controlled to avoid violations of the functionality of the organizational structure.	PPOME/PPOM_OLD/PPOC_OLD/PPME/PO13/PO10/PO03	
An applicant can only be hired if all necessary application documentation and information is available and meets the requirements.	PB30/PB40	4000
Segregations of duties (SoD) must be defined between employees who are responsible for recording applicant information, those who hire the applicant, and those who initiate the payment of wages.	PB30/PB40/PC00_M99_CALC	4000/0001/0002/0008
Only authorized users are allowed to delete an employee's master recod.	PA41	
Only authorized users are allowed to delete employee data.	PU00	
Only authorized users can change the infotype for status information on wage and salary lists.	PU03/PA30	0003
Authorized HR staff and the relevant employees themselves are the only persons who can change the bank data of an employee.	PA30	0009
Authorized HR staff are the only persons who can change the bonus payments for employees.	PA20/PA30/P16B_ADMIN	0002/0006/0008/0009/0011/0014/0015/0149/0150/0151/2010

Table 10.2 Sample Risks for mySAP ERP HCM

Control Objective	Transaction Code	Infotypes
The work plans of employees are kept up to date to ensure they are correct when an employee terminates work.	PA61/PA63	0007
Only those absences of employees that have been agreed on and approved can be applied and authorized correspondingly according to the employee regulations.	PA30	2001
The authorization of changes to absence data must be controlled correspondingly.	PA30	2013
The employees should be authorized to perform only a selected range of changes to their additional benefits.	P16B_ADMIN/ PC00_M99_CALC_SIMU	0008/0014/0015/2010
Employees can only view their own wage and salary data.	PC00_M16_CEDT	
Uncontrolled deletion of salary data results for an employee can lead to a change of salary data clusters and a loss of the entire set of salary data.	PU01	
Only authorized personnel are allowed to view and maintain salary data.	PA30	0008/0014/0015/2010
Salary and wage types must be verified by a second set of eyes prior to being actively used.	PA30	0008/0009/0014/0015/2010
Salary increases have been correctly authorized and controlled in accordance with the internal requirements.	PA30/C138	
Segregations of duties (SoD) exist between users who maintain master data and those who trigger and start payment runs.	PC00_M99_PA03_RELEA/ PC00_M99_PA03_END/ PC00_M99_PA03_CORR/ PC00_M99_PA03_CHECK/ PA03	
Only authorized employees are allowed to trigger external payments.	PC00_M99_CIPE	

Table 10.2 Sample Risks for mySAP ERP HCM (cont.)

Control Objective	Transaction Code	Infotypes
Employees must not be allowed to approve their own travel requests.	TRIP/TP04/TP03/TP02/TP01	
Travel expenses can only be approved by authorized persons.	PR05	
Necessary control measures must be put in place to ensure that only authorized employees can access and create bonus data.	PW01	
The organization plan must be securely maintained and controlled to avoid violations of the functionality of the organizational structure.	PPOME/PPOM_OLD/ PPOC_OLD/PPME/PO13/ PO10/PO03	

Table 10.2 Sample Risks for mySAP ERP HCM (cont.)

10.3   Application Security

The ABAP part of mySAP ERP HCM consists of a relatively small number of transactions that are protected by a small number of authorization objects. However, the transactions and authorization objects contain many functions and can therefore be used for many different aspects of authorization checks and the assignment of authorizations. In addition to assigning HCM transactions via the general authorization components in HCM (roles, authorization objects like P_TCODE for transaction code checks, or P_PCLX for cluster IDs), specific authorization concepts are also needed to meet the data security requirements, particularly for the use of personal data. Additional authorization checks are centrally enabled or disabled by means of a main authorization switch.

Along with the authorizatons, infotypes determine the level of security in mySAP ERP HCM. Infotypes are logical groups of data fields.

The main authorization switch can be used to configure the use of individual authorization objects, the use of HCM inspection procedures, the tolerance period of authorization checks, and the use of structural authorizations. The main authorization switch can be activated in Customizing by using Transaction OOAC. Thus the transaction itself is also a component of the authorization management and must be protected accordingly.

The following inspections can be enabled or disabled using the main authorization switch:

► Tolerance period of the authorization check

► Inspection procedure

► Customized authorization checks

► Master data inspections

► Extended master data inspections

► Structural authorization checks

► Personnel number checks

The main authorization switch (Table T77SO) enables specific inspections in mySAP ERP HCM, and it automatically corrects and updates the entries in the USOBT, USOBT_C, USOBX, and USOBX_C authorization tables (see Figure 10.1).

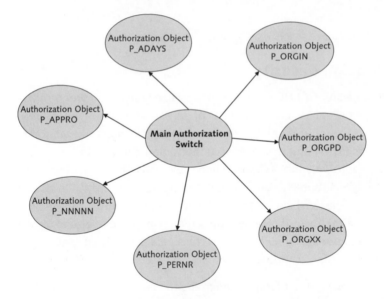

Figure 10.1 Authorization Control Using the Main Authorization Switch

mySAP ERP HCM supports both types of standard authorization checks: extended and customized (see Figure 10.2).

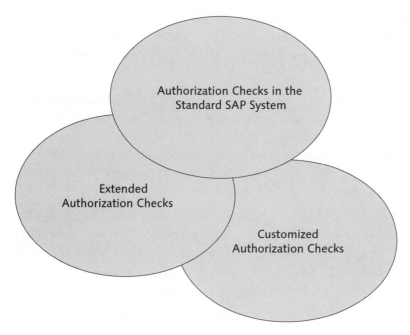

Figure 10.2 Possible Authorization Checks in HCM

10.3.1 HCM Master Data Authorizations

Because the information in mySAP ERP HCM usually consists of master data, the protection of master data using specific authorization objects is particularly critical.

The P_ORGIN authorization object restricts the authorized access to HCM master data. The authorization object permits authorization checks on transaction data according to criteria like information type and subtype, personnel area, and organizational key. The **Authorization Level** authorization field is used for assigning activities like read and write access. Accesses in the context of asymmetric and symmetric four eyes principles can also be stored in this field.

In an asymmetric authorization procedure, different users are assigned different activity rights for manipulating an infotype. This ensures the separation of the creation and release activities in the system by different authorization levels according to the four eyes principle. In a symmetric authorization procedure, the users have the same rights; locked data records can only be released by a second user.

The P_ORGIN authorization object can be used together with the P_ORGXX authorization object, as a complement of the latter, or P_ORGXX can be used separately and replace P_ORGIN. However, additional or substitutional effects are only possible if the main authorization switch is either enabled or disabled.

The P_ORGXX authorization object is used to define responsibilities for personnel administrators. In this context, adminstrator information from Infotype 0001 is used. It is possible to put restrictions on infotypes and to define different authorization levels.

The P_PERNR authorization object controls the access to data of individual users and can be activated, for instance, to ensure that users can't change their own data. The check is only possible if the user ID of the respective user is linked with the personnel number of the corresponding employee. This process is referred to as a *personnel number check*. The relationship between the personnel number and the user ID is mapped through the link in Infotype 0105.

The **AUTHC** authorization field defines the authorization level, and the P_SIGN authorization object defines the authorizations of the personnel number assigned to the user. The authorizations for activities and personnel numbers interact with the **INFTY** authorization field for HR master data, applicant data, and organizational management. Infotypes are authorized or restricted.

The use of *Employee Self-Service* (ESS) is also controlled via the P_PERNR authorization object. For this purpose, the main authorization switch must be activated, and the **PSIGN** authorization field must be set to authorization value "1".

10.3.2   HCM Applicant Authorizations

Information on applicants is controlled via applicant infotypes and checked using the P_APPL authorization object. The time-dependent values of Infotype 0001 enable time-dependent authorizations. The main authorization switch can't be used for deactivation in this case.

The authorization object uses the **VDSK1** authorization field (organizational key). The organizational key enables the definition of more complex roles for the authorization check. In the standard SAP system, the **VDSK1** authorization field is a combination of the "Personnel Area" and "Cost Center" values. In Customizing you can replace these default values with your own rules that allow combinations of fields from Infotype 0001. This results in new and complex authorization structures (see Figure 10.3).

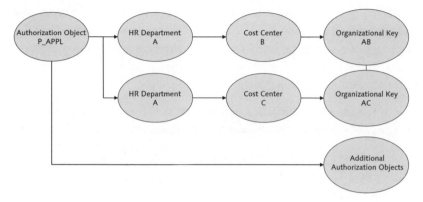

Figure 10.3 Organizational Key for P_APPL Authorization Object

10.3.3 HCM Personnel Planning Authorizations

The personnel planning components can be checked using the PLOG authorization object. The activities are defined using the **Function Code** authorization field.

10.3.4 HCM Reporting Authorizations

The authorization check in HCM reporting is subdivided into a person-related authorization and a data-related authorization.

The P_ABAP authorization object enables you to restrict authorization checks. In contrast to the general regular checks, authorization checks are suspended here although they are available. The degree of simplification for the authorization check is defined in the **COARS** authorization field. If the authorization value is set to "2", no authorization check will be performed on the authorization objects of the HCM master data; if the value is set to "*", no checks will be performed at all. If you want to perform an authorization check independently of infotype and organizational assignment, you must use authorization value "1".

10.3.5 Structural Authorizations

Structural authorizations define the access rights for organizational units that are defined within the HCM organizational structure. The HR data to be protected are defined via Object Type P. Since the individual organizational hierarchies originate from object links (**Organizational Units · Positions · Persons**), different evaluation paths and hence different ways of access are available. Those evaluation paths are defined using structures and can be addressed via structural authorizations. An evaluation or linkage path is defined on the basis of a start object that provides access to personal data. This combination represents the structural profile that enables a user to access organizational units.

For example, the definition of structural profiles determines the object types, the start object, the processing type, the evaluation path, the level of display, and the period. User-specific structural profiles can be created using function modules. Combined with the PLOG authorization object structural authorizations are also used to protect resource planning data in HR.

To be able to use structural authorizations you must set the main authorization switch for the **ORGPD** authorization field to the value of "1".

Structural authorizations can't be assigned via roles that were generated in the SAP Profile Generator. The authorizations are defined using Transaction OOSP. The assignment of structural authorizations to users is done via Table T77UA.

10.3.6 Authorizations for Personnel Development

Checks that are related to the infotypes for qualification and appraisals (Infotype 0024 and Infotype 0025) can be implemented by activating the main authorization switch. For this purpose, new entries are necessary in the table of the main authorization switch, T77SO. Those entries correspond to the authorization values in the P_ORGIN authorization object.

10.3.7 Tolerated Authorizations

A user's authorizations are often dependent on validity periods and responsibilities, which can both affect the access rights for specific datasets. Therefore, it is possible to define authorizations that are dependent on a time logic. In this context a distinction is made between the responsibility period of a user and the time logic.

The responsibility period defines infotype rights; the time logic, on the other hand, draws upon the access type and the validity period of the dataset. This combination affects the assignment of authorizations. If the main authorization switch "ADAYS" is set, you can specify tolerance periods. Those tolerance periods determine the remaining time in which an HR administrator will continue to be responsible for the data of a specific person who has already left the administrator's area of responsibility. The time dependency of infotypes can be set using the "Access Authorization" switch. The authorization is controlled by the P_ADAYS authorization object.

10.3.8 Authorizations for Inspection Procedures

Infotype 0130 controls inspection procedures that can be defined for different purposes by the company. In this context the main authorization switch "APPRO" must be activated to assign authorizations for inspection procedures. The HCM authorization object P_APPRO is used for assigning the authorizations.

10.3.9 Customized Authorization Checks

The P_NNNNN authorization object can be activated using the main authorization switch "NNNNN" in order to use it for customized authorization checks. In this context it is important that you maintain the necessary assignments of the checks in Table USOBT_C.

Authorizations in the HCM environment can have a very complex and multifaceted structure. A solid analysis of the requirements is therefore one of the prerequisites for the creation of an efficient, transparent, and manageable HCM authorization concept.

10.3.10 Indirect Role Assignment Through the Organizational Structure

Roles can be assigned to users either directly via Transactions SU01, SU10, and PFCG, or indirectly through the organizational structure in HCM, which is also referred to as *HR-ORG*. An assignment can, for instance, occur through a job or position. If an employee moves to a different department, the assigned roles are not withdrawn manually from that user, nor are the new roles manually assigned to them—the assignment of the necessary new authorizations instead occurs through the link **Employee · Position**. Thus, the employee is automatically assigned the roles indirectly through the position. The same procedure is applied for new hirings or employees who leave the company. This means that the HR administrators are also responsible for some areas related to authorizations. Orderly and constant maintenance of the organizational structure is therefore one of the prerequisites for this method to function properly.

> **Best-Practice Method: Indirect Role Assignment**
>
> The employees or users are assigned to a job or position that summarizes their activities. They can assign the authorizations in the form of roles to the object types of the organizational structure, which is defined in mySAP ERP HCM, for example, to a position. When the assignment of authorizations and user management are made a part of identity management, they can be better controlled and are therefore a more effective component of the internal control system.

10.3.11 Additional Transactions Relevant to Internal Controls

In addition to the SAP ECC transactions listed earlier in this book (see Table 9.11), the mySAP ERP HCM transactions listed in Table 10.3 are also relevant to internal controls:

Transaction Codes	
P16B_ADMIN	PC00_M99_PA03_RELEA
PA20	PO03
PA03	PO10
PA30	PO13
PA41	PP01
PA61	PPOME
PA63	PPOM_OLD
PB30	PPOC_OLD
PB40	PPME
PC00_M99_CALC	PR05
PC00_M99_PA03_CHECK	PU00
PC00_M99_CIPE	PU03
PC00_M99_PA03_CORR	PV17
PC00_M99_PA03_END	PW01
PC00_M99_CALC_SIMU	SBWP

Table 10.3 Transactions in mySAP ERP HCM Relevant to Controls

10.4 Technical Security

For the evaluation of technical security risks and controls, the following GSPS components must be considered:

▶ Web browser (see Chapter 28)

▶ SAP GUI (see Chapter 27)

▶ SAP ITS (see Chapter 26)

▶ SAP Web AS (see Chapter 8)

The technical controls described for these GSPS components can also be used without limitation for mySAP ERP HCM.

11 SAP Industry Solutions

This chapter describes the SAP Industry Solutions Global Security Positioning System (GSPS) component. Using the SAP for Defense & Security solution as an example, it examines different aspects of IT security.

11.1 Introduction and Functions

SAP has developed specific solutions for many different industries. These solutions are grouped under the product name *SAP Industry Solutions* (SAP IS). SAP Web AS ABAP and J2EE form the basis of the industry solutions. Each of these solutions must take into account specific types of threats (see Figure 11.1).

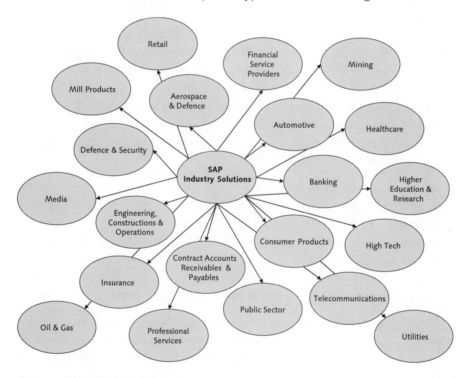

Figure 11.1 SAP Industry Solutions

With its *SAP for Defense & Security* solution, SAP responds to the challenges faced by both the defense and police authorities of Western industrial nations. Growing threats, increased international integration, and global deployment scenarios require an improved synchronization of information and faster decision support.

SAP for Defense & Security provides standardized solutions for deployment planning, maintenance, and materials management as well as for personnel management, accounting, and the logistic support of mobile units. Despite the requirement of a high degree of standardization, the SAP solution is sufficiently flexible to map the transformations that many armed forces experience today.

11.2 Risks and Controls

Like other solutions, the SAP for Defense & Security solution must comply with industry-specific and legal security requirements. However, in contrast to the private economic sector, the correct implementation of those requirements doesn't only involve material assets, but sometimes even human life or issues of national defense. This results in an enormously high need for protection of the defense-relevant processes and the supporting IT systems.

The high need for protection entails problems that can't be solved merely by using solutions that are freely available on the market. Whereas procurement and approval processes in the private sector are primarily price-oriented, these processes in the military sector are additionally defined by other characteristics, such as branch of service, rank, material category, and (organizational) unit. The procurement processes result in the purchase of hand grenades or life jackets. This means that in terms of both data and strategic considerations, the potential risk is very high.

Another area of concern is asynchronous data storage. As military units can be deployed worldwide, additional risks result from the mobile character of those deployments. The SAP systems of the mobile engines on a ship or submarine are not continuously connected to a central system. Therefore, specific functions must be carried out in offline mode, which places additional demands on the technical security of the synchronization, the chronological process, and the authorizations to synchronize purchase order lists that have been created offline, for example.

Authentication represents another risk: How, for instance, can you ascertain the identity of a commander in offline mode? Because a large quantity of military data and processes is subject to a high degree of confidentiality, the data and processes must be particularly protected—in times of peace and during a war.

In a state of defense, mobile devices that contain highly confidential data can fall into the hands of the enemy. For this reason, special requirements exist regarding the storage and transfer of information.

In the following table, we'll primarily consider two specific types of risk (see Table 11.1).

No.	Classification	Description
1.	Risk potential	Support scenarios in the military area.
		Usually an SAP customer operates a dedicated communications line to recreate error messages at SAP, or to browse through the SAP Notes in the SAP Service Marketplace. SAP employees use this line for issue handling. The customer's SAP Solution Manager also uses this line; for example, to send messages or Early-Watch data to SAP.
	Impact	It is possible that military information is transferred and compromised unintentionally. Moreover, the customer systems can be manipulated.
	Risk without control(s)	Extremely high
	Control(s)	From a military point of view, the functions listed above must be separated since the access directions can change, the protocols are not uniform, and logging must be separated according to different activities. Specific qualification criteria must be defined for employees of service organizations.
	Risk with control(s)	Normal
	Section	11.3.1
2.	Risk potential	Deployment scenarios.
		Employees of armed organizations who are deployed in mobile units are assigned to different organizational structures depending on the type of deployment. Authorizations, technical assignments in SAP systems, and other components must be changed according to the deployment scenarios. Because changes in the systems must be taken care of quickly and be carried out within hours in these situations, the standard SAP tools for role changes do not suffice.
	Impact	Employees of unit A move to unit B and must be organizationally assigned there. If the activities, including all those that go along with detailed authorization assignment, can't be carried out immediately, serious consequences during the deployment may result. The system may no longer provide optimal support or any technical support at all. Depending on the type of deployment, national and international interests as well as those of personal security can be at stake.
	Risk without control(s)	High
	Control(s)	The authorization concepts have been extended by an industry-specific solution to meet the requirements. Authorizations are managed via SAP Role Manager. The immediate and efficient processing of entire organizational units is thus ensured.

Table 11.1 Risks and Controls for the SAP for Defense & Security IS

No.	Classification	Description
	Risk with control(s)	Normal
	Section	11.3.2

Table 11.1 Risks and Controls for the SAP for Defense & Security IS (cont.)

11.3 Application Security

In addition to the role concept and all the authorization concepts described in Chapter 9, there are a few more advanced authorization solutions available. We will describe two of them in this chapter: SAP Max Secure and SAP Role Manager.

11.3.1 SAP Max Secure

Functional separations are required, which are supposed to ensure the integrity and protection of data with highly confidential military or defense-related content with regard to the support accesses listed in Table 11.2.

No.	Access	Direction	Dialog
1	OSS	Customer network → SAPNet	No
2	Maintenance (SAP GUI)	SAPNet → Customer network	Yes
3	Maintenance (OS access)	SAPNet → Customer network	Yes

Table 11.2 Types of Access in SAP Support

The critical aspects of these types of access are as follows:

▶ The possibility of an unauthorized, unintentional transfer of data [1]

▶ The possibility of an intended data transfer [2], and in doing so, compromising the data [3]

Control measures for secure authentication [3] and authorization [2] provide protection in this respect. However, in national defense organizations, these controls are not always sufficient. Consequently, the accesses are not approved. And company policies prohibit a remote access by external employees.

For customers with such an increased need for security, SAP offers a support agreement called *SAP Max Secure*, which is also used in other industries. SAP Max Secure is a specific type of support with additional protective measures. Based on a threat analysis and a customer's need for protection, supplemental technical measures can be added to the standard SAP support link to help considerably reduce existing risks.

In addition to the standard controls used in the "Customer–SAP" relationship, the tools, protocols, and system levels of the accesses can be defined.

A terminal server is responsible for the controls. The SAP employee is granted access via ICA client or pnAgent and can only access the applications published by the customer. The redirection through the terminal server allows for an additional, parallel live observation of the activities, which is also referred to as a *shadow session*, and a *session recording* when preserving evidence. The shadow session ensures that legal requirements are adhered to.

The use of encapsulated frontend PCs (SINA, for example) represents another means of control. This method accounts for the physical separation of the SAP network and the customer network. However, this control action is rather complex. Although it positively affects security, it also negatively affects support. In high-security environments, these measures represent an important control option that is mandated by internal policies and legal requirements. When support is needed, an SAP employee takes care of the relevant device, which, if necessary, is located in a specially secured room. The employee opens a terminal session and obtains the tools provided by the customer for a secure logon procedure. Here the encapsulated system allows no data to be printed, buffered, or transferred to other media like USB sticks at the frontend. This means that the customer can exert a high degree of control over the support employees who work remotely.

If the frontend capsule is considered as a component of the customer network, the support employee de facto belongs to the customer and is thus controlled by them.

11.3.2 SAP Role Manager

SAP Role Manager (see Figure 11.2) is an additional industry solution tool and is used to assign roles and authorizations to users who are assigned to an organizational structure consisting of structural elements. SAP Role Manager can be used to reassign users, including their necessary authorizations, from one organizational unit to another, in an individual or mass procedure. The call is carried out via Transaction "Role Manager" (/ISDFPS/ROLE_MANAGER). SAP Role Manager uses reference roles. The following tasks can be carried out using SAP Role Manager:

▶ Defining reference roles
▶ Deriving roles from reference roles and assigning them to the different users
▶ Determining authorization values for the relevant organizational-level fields

- Generating authorization profiles
- Addressing the direct navigation to the SAP user administration applications that are relevant to these actions
- Automating the authorization update process using batch jobs

It is necessary to update existing authorizations if the properties or assignments of an organizational structural element are changed.

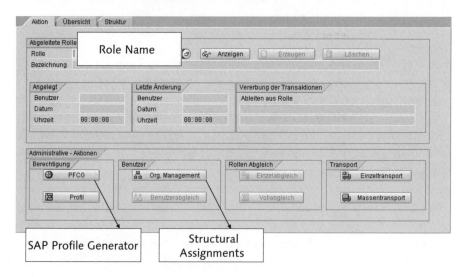

Figure 11.2 SAP Role Manager

As described in Chapter 10, roles can be assigned indirectly via the HCM organizational structure. These indirect role assignments require the existence of a corresponding organizational structure in the relevant SAP system. We distinguish between two different cases:

- A user is assigned the roles that are assigned to the corresponding person or position, to the superordinate organizational structural element, or to other superordinate organizational objects. The "Role–Assignment object" relationship is generated in the SAP Profile Generator.
- A user can be assigned a derived role through the assigned position. SAP Role Manager can be used to assign a role that has been derived from a reference role to a position. Using a business add-in, the derived role is complemented with values for specific organizational-level fields that are determined via the higher-level structural element. The initial authorization assignment is carried out manually via SAP Role Manager. Updates are performed automatically by the system if SAP Role Manager is scheduled as a job in the corresponding system.

A reference role can be created in SAP Role Manager using the **Overview** tab. The required name must be entered for the reference role. Then you must click on the **Create** button to create the reference role. Finally, you must save the role. The **Change** button can be used to perform changes to the reference roles.

The derivation of a role is stored in Table /ISDFPS/AGR_DEF. The organizational level fields are determined for the role and written into Table AGR_1252. The creation and assignment of a derived role is carried out via the **Action** tab in SAP Role Manager. Once you have entered the required name for the derived role, you must click on the **Generate** button. In the subsequent step, the link between the role and the position is defined through the **Create Assignment** action. The SAP system then synchronizes the organizational-level fields. The synchronization of the indirect user assignment must be done manually.

The **Action** and **Overview** tabs in SAP Role Manager are used to perform further administrative steps. It is possible to navigate to the standard applications of the SAP Profile Generator, for example. Table 11.3 lists the functions and the calls they perform.

Function	Call
PFCG	Roles
Profile	Authorizations
Org. Management	User assignments
User synchronization	User synchronization
Individual synchronization	Role synchronization
Full synchronization	Role synchronization
Individual transport	Transport
Mass transport	Transport

Table 11.3 Sample Standard Calls in SAP Role Manager

In an individual synchronization, a derived role is synchronized with its reference role. As a result, it adopts all authorization fields from the reference role. The organizational-level fields are not adopted from the reference role. A full synchronization is necessary when the reference role is changed, provided the change should be transferred onto the derived roles. The necessary synchronization of the organizational level fields is carried out automatically in that case.

To perform necessary role changes in SAP Role Manager, you must select the **Overview** tab. If the role is a reference role, the system displays all roles that have been derived from that role. Changes to a role don't take effect until the respective user logs on to the system again. Changes to an authorization profile are immediately active, but the current transaction must be restarted.

As in the SAP Profile Generator, here traffic lights indicate the status of maintenance actions. Structural assignments of individual derivations to different structural elements (for example, positions) can be controlled via the **Org. Management** function. If the indirect user assignment (to the authorization roles via the organizational structure) step is performed correctly, the traffic light turns green. For this purpose, you must use the synchronization functions. SAP Role Manager assigns the derivation role to an object of the HCM organizational structure to fill the organizational levels of the new derivation that are still empty. The role synchronization then initiates the import of the new auxiliary organizational information for the selected derivation roles. The new structural organizational data originates from different tables that can be addressed using various transactions, such as /ISDFPS/LSP2. The display transactions are /ISDFPS/TOEACC2, for organizational elements used to control the cost centers in Accounting, and /ISDFPS/TOELOG2, which is used to control the supply relationships in Logistics.

SAP Industry Solutions provide a multitude of additional tools that can be used to implement targeted security and control measures, which, in combination with the existing standard solutions, improve the comprehensive internal control structure.

11.4 Technical Security

For the evaluation of technical security risks and controls for SAP Industry Solutions, the following GSPS components must be considered:

▶ Web browser (see Chapter 28)
▶ SAP GUI (see Chapter 27)
▶ SAP ITS (see Chapter 26)
▶ SAP Web AS (see Chapter 8)
▶ SAP XI (see Chapter 20)
▶ SAP MI (see Chapter 22)
▶ SAP EP (see Chapter 19)

The technical controls described for these GSPS components can also be used without limitation for the SAP IS applications.

12   SAP NetWeaver Business Intelligence

This chapter describes the SAP NetWeaver Business Intelligence Global Security Positioning System (GSPS) component, and, in particular, SAP Business Information Warehouse. On the basis of sample scenarios, this chapter focuses on the description of specific security solutions.

12.1   Introduction and Functions

SAP's business intelligence system, *SAP NetWeaver Business Intelligence* (SAP BI), is the central information component within SAP NetWeaver. *SAP Business Information Warehouse* (SAP BW), the integrated information and analysis system (data warehouse), is another Global Security Positioning System (GSPS) component with special security needs. SAP BW stores and processes transactional and analytical data. Figure 12.1 provides an overview of the data warehouse architecture of SAP BW.

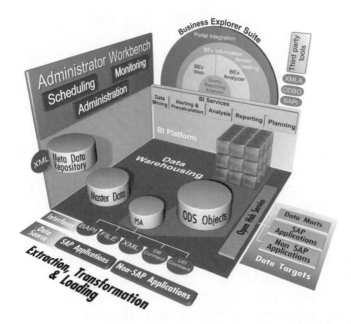

Figure 12.1 Overview of the Integrated Data Warehouse Architecture in SAP BW

In transactional systems such as SAP ERP Central Component (ECC), transactional data is stored in tables and forwarded to other tables for further processing. SAP BW, in contrast, focuses on individual processes from the respective source systems, whereby it extracts and formats information on the individual process. The purpose of this is to provide individual users with the appropriate information. For this reason, historical, non-changeable data must be made accessible to the users as well as operational reporting, aggregated views, and multidimensional analyses that were built on the basis of InfoCubes (see Figure 12.2).

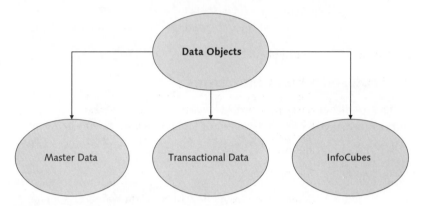

Figure 12.2 Data Objects

Depending on the type of data objects and data, relevance to the company, and the legally defined level of protection, the BW systems and applications must be protected by appropriate control solutions. Here, for instance, analytical data is very important as it provides information on developments and trends, which makes it susceptible to industrial espionage and other risks. SAP BW provides different applications, tools, and dashboards for an analytical evaluation of the transactional data of all SAP NetWeaver processing systems.

Within SAP BI, unstructured and structured data is converted into information that supports both information owners and decision-makers in their areas of responsibility in providing the requested information at the right time and in the right form to the authorized employee. As a central system, SAP BW provides the advantageous option of a consolidated information access and hence a higher degree of security. In contrast to a decentral distribution of data, SAP BW offers a high degree of consistency, a high level of evaluation options, and efficient data access. Program evaluations, ad-hoc reports, and the other tools used for requesting information in operational systems are no longer needed, which eliminates the accompanying additional security risks. The aggregated evaluation of data in a central system results in an aggregated risk evaluation, which prompts you to take the necessary control measures. The central metadata repository facilitates the access to and access control of data and analysis options.

12.2 Risks and Controls

Although the central concept of SAP BI, and in particular of SAP BW, involves aggressive minimization of possible risks, because of its open architecture and integrative design, you must consider the possible risks, protection needs, and implementation of control measures (see Table 12.1).

No.	Classification	Description
1.	Risk potential	Data accesses.
		Data can be presented in different forms. Access to information can be permitted, but under certain circumstances (for example, if the information is available in non-aggregated form), individual transactional data can be compromised, which results in a loss of integrity.
	Impact	For unauthorized persons, evaluations involving real data represent a violation of their scope of authorizations. Even the reading of specific information can lead to potential risks and thus compromise company assets. The effects can be disastrous because the potential risks are often the cause of risks like industrial espionage and the like.
	Risk without control(s)	High
	Control(s)	Data can be classified according to the potential risks involved. An efficient authorization concept can ensure the protection of this data. For example, SAP BW allows for the presentation of data in aggregated form. This enables users to analyze specific groups of data, but they can't drill down to compromising individual data.
	Risk with control(s)	Normal
	Section	12.3.1
2.	Risk potential	Authorization system.
		The authorization system in SAP BW can be designed in a simple or complex manner. Depending on the requirements, authorization objects can be used to implement access and restriction controls for SAP BW objects, such as InfoAreas, InfoCubes, or queries. The higher the number of controls and the more detailed they are, the more complex the monitoring and administrative measures.
	Impact	A higher degree of administrative tasks leads to an increase in costs, a potentially higher error rate, and thus a violation of protective measures.
	Risk without control(s)	High

Table 12.1 Risks and Controls Related to SAP NetWeaver Business Intelligence

No.	Classification	Description
	Control(s)	The identified need for protection must be the basis for control measures, for example in reporting. The SAP BW data must be classified according to its risk relevance and evaluation. The classification of data and evaluation functions in SAP BW result in a targeted authorization concept that reduces the control measures to a necessary minimum and uses them only for an efficient protection of data, processes, and systems. This concept can only be implemented by using appropriate technologies.
	Risk with control(s)	Normal
	Section	12.3.1
3.	Risk potential	Legal requirements:
		As in addition to strategic business information data from the accounting and HR departments are also processed in SAP BW, the areas of data management, data manipulation, and analysis authorization are subject to legal requirements such as Sarbanes-Oxley (SOX) and Basel II. Inappropriate control measures that don't comply with the existing legal regulations thus represent a violation of the legal conditions and requirements.
	Impact	In a best-case scenario, violations of legal regulations can result in a loss of reputation. In the worst case, they can entail penalizations by legal authorities, increased costs, and other business-related and private damages.
	Risk without control(s)	High
	Control(s)	A consistent authorization concept that's in sync with other GSPS areas reduces the risk of violating legal requirements. The authorization concept must be combined with and is an integral part of administrative and process-related control measures.
	Risk with control(s)	Normal
	Section	12.3.1
4.	Risk potential	Design:
		An early integration of risk, authorization, and design tasks is particularly important in the business intelligence area so that the necessary authorization requirements can be included in the design of applications right from the beginning.
	Impact	An erroneous design in the creation of InfoCubes or queries can lead to incorrect reporting results or to an increase in the costs of the subsequent control design.
	Risk without control(s)	High

Table 12.1 Risks and Controls Related to SAP NetWeaver Business Intelligence (cont.)

No.	Classification	Description
	Control(s)	The design of applications and security measures is a basic requirement for a successful and secure use of systems like SAP BW.
	Risk with control(s)	Normal
	Section	12.3.1
5.	Risk potential	Standard: Tables USOBT_C and USOBX_C don't contain the link between the transaction code and the authorization object, which, for instance, is the case in SAP ECC. As a result, the administration effort and error rate increase.
	Impact	Consequently, a higher degree of administrative effort, for instance caused by additional documentation, can be the result. Moreover, an increased number of risks can result when maintaining Transaction SU24 (Check Indicators), which includes the authorization tables. Users could therefore benefit from authorizations that they shouldn't be granted.
	Risk without control(s)	High
	Control(s)	The maintenance of Transaction SU24 is one of the basic rules for best practices in administration. The rule can't be applied in SAP BI. Consequently, external controls, manual authorization maintenance, and sufficient documentation are necessary.
	Risk with control(s)	Normal
	Section	12.3.1

Table 12.1 Risks and Controls Related to SAP NetWeaver Business Intelligence (cont.)

12.3 Application Security

In general, SAP BW complies with the authorization concept and management rules that are based on the SAP role concept. These concepts are described in more detail in Chapters 8 through 10.

12.3.1 Authorizations

The integrity of business data is also ensured by the assignment of roles. Corresponding to the activities contained in roles, authorization profiles are generated that limit the scope of action for individual users or user groups to SAP BW data and evaluation information. Authorizations that are generated on the basis of authorization objects and then automatically added to the profiles of a specific user control access to individual cost center hierarchies. This way you can restrict the drill down process for cost centers.

Authorization checks enable you to protect functions, objects, and data. In an authorization check during the execution of a specific action, the system compares the values for individual authorization fields—of an authorization object assigned to a user via roles—with the values for executing an action that are defined in the relevant program. An authorized user is authorized for a specific activity if the authorization check is successful for each authorization field checked in an authorization object. This way it is also possible to perform complex user authorization checks in SAP BW.

Authorization Elements

Figure 12.3 shows the options available for granting authorizations in SAP BW. Roles are either directly or indirectly assigned to users. They can contain authorization objects for InfoAreas, InfoCubes, queries, and individual InfoObjects. The maintenance effort increases from the tip of the pyramid down to the bottom.

Authorizations must generally be restricted to data, evaluations, transactions, and actions. Depending on their position, users can be authorized for different areas. SAP BW primarily provides authorizations for reporting and *data warehouse management* (DWM). In DWM, for instance, authorizations are required for the creation and modification of queries. These authorizations can be granted using the *Administrator Workbench* in SAP BW, which controls the authorizations for the following activities:

- Data from SAP NetWeaver source systems
    - Structural design
    - Extraction of data
    - Planning and executing the load process
    - Data preparation
- Data Warehouse Management
- Data modeling
- Monitoring and control

The elements relevant for authorization in the data warehouse design are the Administrator Workbench, queries and InfoCube objects, InfoSources, transactional objects, InfoObjects, and source systems.

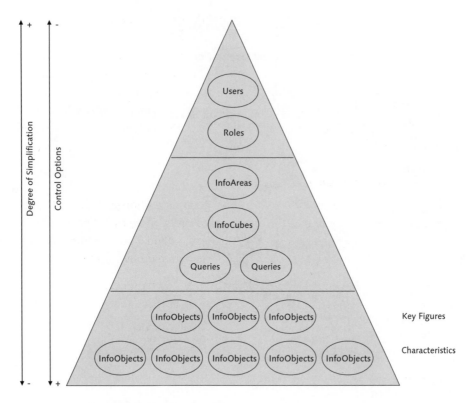

Figure 12.3 Authorization Pyramid in SAP BW

In reporting, for example, authorizations can be restricted to specific reporting objects. You can, for instance, specify authorizations for starting queries. It is also possible to restrict the authorization to specific user and query groups. If a user is assigned to a specific group of evaluations, the authorization can be further restricted to specific characteristics. For instance, it is possible to limit the authorization to data of specific cost centers or of only one cost center. The *Business Explorer* (BEx) in SAP BW controls the authorizations for the following activities:

▶ Query design

▶ Reporting

▶ Data analysis

▶ Display—Web application design

SAP BEx is used as a reporting tool for data analysis and consists of two components: BEx Analyzer and BEx Browser (see Figure 12.4).

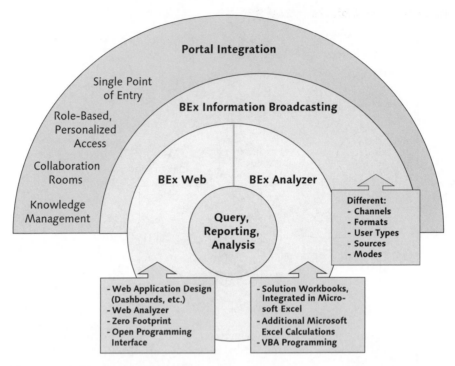

Figure 12.4 Architecture of SAP BW Reporting Components

In *Business Explorer Analyzer* (BEx Analyzer) you can define queries based on a group of InfoObjects or predefined query templates of an InfoCube (*BEx Query Designer*). Queries are embedded in Microsoft Excel-based *workbooks* that can be assigned to roles in SAP BEx. Thus, data can be analyzed and distributed via MS Excel. The SAP Profile Generator assigns the SAP BW roles to the reporting users. Additional query-specific authorizations can be specified in the SAP Profile Generator.

The *Business Explorer Browser* (BEx Web) is used to display the contents of the browser, such as the roles, favorites, and tasks of a user in a specific browser in which you can call reports. You can also address other intranet and Internet pages from the browser. The browser contains drag and drop functionality for folders and objects. This functionality can be modified by a user, provided the user has the corresponding authorization. Moreover, you can maintain user-specific favorites in the BEx Web.

If the BEx Web is used to access data with a mobile device, the communication and the device must be appropriately protected.

Authorization Objects in SAP BW

In SAP BW, authorizations are generally granted via authorization objects for administration and reporting (see Figure 12.5).

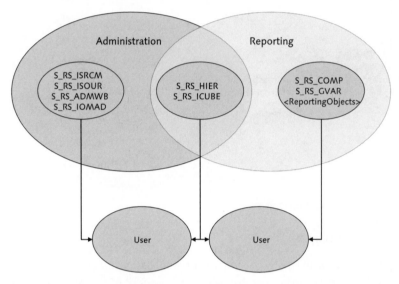

Figure 12.5 Authorization Objects for Administration and Reporting

The reporting authorization objects shown in Figure 12.5 are important for granting and restricting authorizations for InfoCubes and other authorization elements. Sensitive data can be controlled using customized authorization objects that can be created via Transaction RSSM and assigned authorizations through the **Authorizations** menu item. The reporting objects are authorization objects in SAP BW with an additional relationship to InfoCubes. The reporting object authorization fields determine the key figures, authorization-relevant characteristics, and the hierarchy level (see Figure 12.6).

In addition to the authorization objects shown in the figure, there are many other objects available, such as S_RS_IOBJ for InfoObjects, S_RS_ISET for Info-Sets, S_RS _COMP1 for query component authorizations, and S_RS_FOLD for deactivating the overview screen of the *InfoArea* folder so that roles and favorites are only displayed with queries in the BEx dialog. Other authorization objects can restrict MultiProviders, such as S_RS_MPRO.

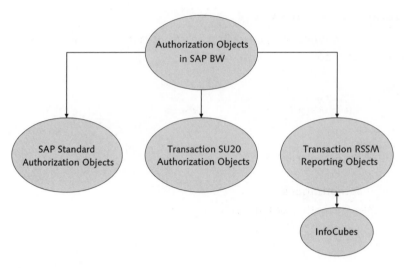

Figure 12.6 Types of Authorization Objects

12.3.2 Other Concepts

Integrating SAP BW with many systems and applications increases security requirements. Integrations may exist, for example, with SAP ECC, SAP MDM, and SAP Industry Solutions. The open concept requires the establishment of specific authorization solutions.

▶ Check indicator concept

As the many different customized reporting objects can't be defined up front in Tables USOBT_C and USOBX_C, and also because specific authorization objects are directly linked to InfoCubes, the normal maintenance of Transaction SU24 isn't possible in this context. On a case-by-case basis, you must determine whether or not certain authorization objects for SAP BW can be maintained using Transaction SU24 and, if so, what the possible effects may be.

▶ Drag and drop authorizations

The drag and drop authorizations are another example of a security concept. Instead of roles, profiles that can be assigned to users and user groups are used.

▶ InfoObject authorizations

The authorizations for InfoObjects can be controlled according to Table 12.2.

Step	Activity	Transaction code
1	Mark InfoObject as relevant for authorization	RSD1
2	Create report authorization object	RSSM

Table 12.2 Authorizations with InfoObjects

Step	Activity	Transaction code
3	Select InfoCubes	RSSM
4	Manually integrate authorization object in role (not via Transaction SU24)	PFCG
5	Maintain authorization values	PFCG
6	Assign role to user	PFCG (or CUA)

Table 12.2 Authorizations with InfoObjects (cont.)

▶ **Hierarchical authorizations**

For hierarchies the authorizations can be controlled as shown in Table 12.3.

Step	Activity	Transaction code
1	Transfer and activate InfoObject 0TCTAUTHH	RSD1
2	Mark InfoObject 0TCTAUTHH as relevant for authorization	RSD1
3	Mark Leaf InfoObject as relevant for authorization	RSD1
4	Create authorization objects with 0TCTAUTHH and Leaf InfoObject	RSSM
5	Definition of hierarchical authorizations including technical descriptions	RSSM
6	Manual integration of authorization object in role (not via Transaction SU24)	PFCG
7	Maintain authorization values	PFCG
8	Assign role to user	PFCG (or CUA)

Table 12.3 Authorizations with Hierarchies

▶ **mySAP ERP HCM data**

For the extraction of data, structural authorizations must also be mapped in SAP BW in order to ensure consistency between the different systems in this area as well. For this purpose, the following tables are relevant in the context of mySAP ERP HCM:

▶ T77PR for structural authorization profiles

▶ T77UA for user assignments

▶ T77UU for users

In Table T77UU you can select users for whom the extraction is to be carried out. You can either select all users or specific ones.

For structural authorizations in SAP BW, the authorizations can be controlled according to Table 12.4.

Step	Activity	System
1	Calling program RHBAUS02 for updating Table T77UU—entering users	mySAP ERP HCM
2	Calling program RHBAUS00 for generating an index for structural authorization profiles	mySAP ERP HCM
3	Activating Data Source 0HR_PA_2	mySAP ERP HCM
4	Replicating Data Source 0HR_PA_2	SAP BW
5	Activating ODS InfoProvider 0HR_PA_2	SAP BW
6	Activating transfer rules for 0HR_PA_2	SAP BW
7	Creating an InfoPackage to perform an extraction for 0HR_PA_2	SAP BW
8	Loading ODS data from mySAP ERP HCM	SAP BW
9	Mark InfoObjects as relevant for authorization: To be able to use the structural authorizations in SAP BW, all characteristic values (for example, position and employee) relevant to reporting must be defined as authorization-relevant InfoObjects.	SAP BW
10	Creating the reporting authorization objects	SAP BW
11	Linking authorization objects to InfoCubes	SAP BW
12	Calling program RSSB_Generate_Authorizations	SAP BW

Table 12.4 Authorizations with Structural Authorizations

SAP BW Transactions Relevant for Internal Controls

Transactions ST01, RSSM, and RSSU53 carry out the different trace functions in SAP BW. Table 12.5 displays the SAP BW transactions for internal controls.

Transaction code	Transaction
RSA1	Administrator Workbench: Transaction RSA1 is the main transaction for administrative functions in SAP BW.
RSD1	InfoObject maintenance: This transaction can be used to mark objects as relevant for authorization.
RSSM	Authorizations: This transaction can be used to create and modify authorization objects in SAP BW. Authorization objects can be assigned to InfoCubes or removed from them. Authorizations can be analyzed using the trace function. The creation and modification of hierarchical authorizations and the corresponding settings occur via this transaction.

Table 12.5 Transactions in SAP BW

Transaction code	Transaction
RSZV	Variable maintenance: This transaction is used to create or modify the variables for the authorization checks.
RRMX	Business Explorer: Business Explorer is the reporting tool in SAP BW and is used for analyzing data.
GLOBAL_TEMPLATES	Global templates: Templates are used for modeling and evaluating data.

Table 12.5 Transactions in SAP BW (cont.)

Users in SAP BW

It is useful to classify the users in SAP BW. In this context it is possible to group users according to administrative, functional, organizational, or other aspects and assign the corresponding authorizations to them.

A subdivision of the user classes into developers, administrators, power users, expert users, and information users is one possible option for the classification. SAP BW uses the concept of user groups. However, with regard to data security and controlled data access, information users who are authorized to use the evaluations and queries must be further classified into subgroups. Information users are only allowed to run queries; they are not authorized to create new queries, or to modify existing ones. This user group is only allowed to display authorizations.

Often *power users* and administrators, in particular, have few restrictions placed on their authorizations. Therefore, their actions must be monitored to determine how best to control their activities on the system (i.e., how often it is necessary that they use the system and for how long a time are they engaged on the system). This relatively small group of users is allowed to create new queries and to modify existing ones. The authorization can, for instance, be restricted to specific InfoCubes. Administrators should be restricted to their work area and should not have access to critical data outside of their own work area.

The use of SAP Business Explorer (SAP BEx) requires the following three types of user groups:

▶ Analysts
▶ Knowledge workers
▶ Information consumers

Figure 12.7 shows the types of BEx user groups and their possible authorization requirements.

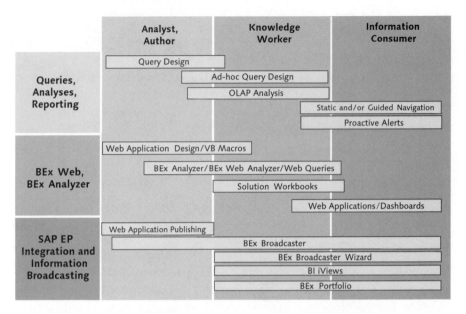

Figure 12.7 Types of BEx User Groups

Transactional systems (OLTP) like SAP ECC focus on current data, transactions, and process-oriented information. Real-time processing and data consistency are important here. SAP BW, on the other hand, is an online analytical system (OLAP). It imports, transforms, and reorganizes historical data based on evaluation criteria, strategic requirements, and statistical aspects, and provides this data for different analytical and informational purposes. The use of reports and collaborative applications such as the user-specific distribution of information (*Information Broadcasting*) via BEx as well as the analysis, alert, and push functions in SAP BW must be complemented by sufficient protective measures. Other potential risks, such as incorrect information caused by an erroneous query design, for example, can produce negative consequences for decision-makers and executives. A protection based on risk classifications in the data area, an evaluation of the protection needs of this data for the entire company, and a comprehensive, immediate collaboration between project teams and security experts are all critical factors when structuring appropriate solutions in the internal control system and ensuring its successful implementation.

12.4   Technical Security

SAP BW is based on SAP NetWeaver. This means that all technically relevant risks and controls of the SAP Web AS GSPS component must be taken into account.

Moreover, depending on individual use, the technical controls of the following GSPS components must also be considered:

▶ Web browser (see Chapter 28)

▶ SAP GUI (see Chapter 27)

▶ SAP ITS (see Chapter 26)

▶ SAP EP (see Chapter 19)

▶ Database servers (see Chapter 23)

The technical controls described there must be applied without limitation to SAP BW.

13 SAP NetWeaver Master Data Management

This chapter describes IT security concepts for the SAP NetWeaver Master Data Management Global Security Positioning System (GSPS) component. In this context, it describes sample solutions for best-practice controls for the Master Data Harmonization and Central Master Data Management applications.

13.1 Introduction and Functions

Master data is subject to specific control requirements. Employees, customers, suppliers, materials—master data is the central type of data that is used and processed in business processes. The information that can be classified as master data must always be correct, available, and up to date. Along with transaction data, master data determines the flow of information and actions within an enterprise. A decentral access to the same master data information is a critical requirement in daily business and administrative processes. This is true for all SAP applications. *SAP NetWeaver Master Data Management* (SAP MDM) is used to centrally create, consolidate, and distribute all master data that's required in a company's heterogeneous SAP NetWeaver landscape.

It is extremely important to protect master data in order to ensure the continuity of business processes that involve the processing of master data, but also because it is critical to the overall success of a company and is therefore of internal and external interest.

The purchasing processes that involve customer, supplier, material, and other types of master data are a good example of the measures taken to protect master data. All the different departments involved must be able to access the same set of data. Another example includes the administration of employee and HR data in SAP MDM. Because customer and supplier data must be protected according to data protection laws, central master data systems are subject to various control measures. SAP MDM can collect and centrally manage data from other systems and also create new data and make it available to other systems (see Figure 13.1).

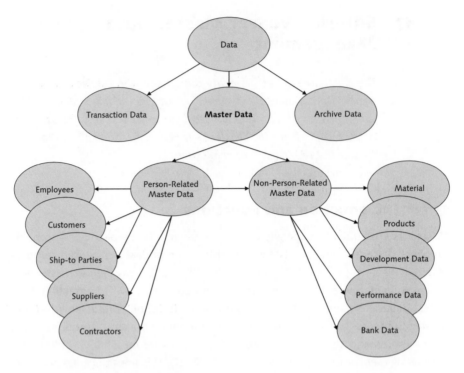

Figure 13.1 Examples of Master Data

13.2 Risks and Controls

The management of HR and partner data also requires adherence to regional data protection laws to ensure a high level of data protection. Data protection regulations apply to person-related data. This includes all data that pertains to an individual person. This kind of data is generally referred to as *master data*. The following data protection objectives are important in this context:

▶ Protection of person-related master data using authentication and authorization controls and security measures like encryption and secure communications.

▶ Person-related data can be managed by only a limited number of specifically trained employees. Access to person-related data must be limited to auditors so they can retrace the data history. This also includes authorizations for administrators.

▶ Persons on which data is stored must be allowed to view this data at any time and be informed about any unauthorized attempts to use this data for purposes other than those for which they are intended.

- Adherence to legal regulations is equally important for the company. Control objectives like ensuring integrity, availability, or traceability must be attained by the implementation of an internal control system. The integration of SAP MDM into this control system is a requirement.

- As soon as person-related data has fulfilled its information storage purpose, and as soon as the end of the determined storage period is reached, the data must be permanently deleted. These requirements are met by archiving solutions.

- "Person-related master data" contains data that must be protected due to their high degree of sensitivity. Among other information, such data includes details on an employee's origin, political opinion, medical data, and their cooperation with a trade union. For the affected people, this data is very important and must therefore be specifically considered when choosing the appropriate protection measures. SAP MDM provides a configuration that meets these data protection requirements.

Person-related master data are subject to the risks described in Chapter 10. Other master data such as material data, product development data, or research results involve different additional risks. Master data in SAP MDM are affected by the following main risks:

- **Person-related data**
  Insufficient protection and therefore violation of legal data protection requirements

- **Creation of customers as consumers using reference customers in the different SAP systems**
  Mapping and data accesses—the use of master data information in distributed systems is not protected to the same extent as in SAP MDM

- **Distributed master data management**
  Data integrity cannot be attained due to user rights with too many authorizations

- **Central data storage**
  If authentications and authorizations are violated, many activities enable access to master data, including manipulating the data

- **Systems**
  Typically, central master data systems store the biggest quantity of master data in a company. Therefore, backup and restore systems are particularly important. Neglecting the security of these systems can result in a loss of data integrity and, worst of all, a loss of information.

- All other risks for SAP MDM are listed in Table 13.1.

No.	Classification	Description
1.	Risk potential	Inadequate authorization concept.
		Master data users have full authorization for maintaining specific types of master data, although they should only have partial authorizations. Due to change authorizations, users can change data for which they have access rights although they aren't authorized to do so. This can result in data inconsistencies and a violation of the master data integrity.
	Impact	The effects comprise disruptions of daily business processes, costly data cleansing measures, and even the complete loss of master data information, including the related process history.
	Risk without control(s)	High
	Control(s)	Authorizations are restricted, and a well-organized management system assigns them only to those users whose positions are assigned the corresponding activities as well.
	Risk with control(s)	Normal
	Section	13.3.1
2.	Risk potential	Inadequate responsibility structure.
		The technical requirements for solid master data management are met by SAP MDM, however, the task- and process-related distribution of master data management functions to concrete departments and employees is missing. The risk of a decentral and uncontrollable master data management exists.
	Impact	The use of available master data is not protected. Neither the integrity and completeness of the data, nor its correctness and up-to-dateness is protected. This affects all processes that involve master data. For example, the integrity of pricing information is no longer ensured, which affects follow-up processes.
	Risk without control(s)	Extremely high
	Control(s)	Implementation and consistent penetration of the information ownership principle to ensure an efficient control of master data using an effective authorization system.
	Risk with control(s)	Normal
	Section	13.3.1

Table 13.1 Risks and Controls for SAP MDM

No.	Classification	Description
3.	Risk potential	Person-related data.
		Master data that is directly or indirectly related to persons (for example, employees, business partners, consultants, and so on) is subject to legal, internal, and ethical requirements. The protection of this data is completely or at least partly jeopardized by insecure authentication, inaccurate user rights, and insufficiently secured interfaces and communication channels.
	Impact	The effects involve the theft of information, the manipulation of person-related master data, and the circulation of data to unauthorized third parties.
	Risk without control(s)	High
	Control(s)	The integrity of technical and process-related controls for the protection of SAP MDM data and master data in the connected systems is an integral part of an internal control system and ensures the protection and compliance of business-relevant master data.
	Risk with control(s)	Normal
	Section	13.3.1
4.	Risk potential	Inconsistent master data.
		The different user management options in an SAP MDM landscape enable the majority of employees to use these systems. This involves the potential risk of inconsistent identity management.
	Impact	Internal and external users are wrongfully authorized to use systems they shouldn't have access to. The datasets in the different SAP systems don't match. Administration, monitoring, and control become increasingly difficult and are constrained, and therefore, it takes more time and a greater expense to carry out these responsibilities.
	Risk without control(s)	High
	Control(s)	Implementation and use of a user management system.
	Risk with control(s)	Normal
	Section	13.3.1
5.	Risk potential	Anonymous user actions.
		In SAP MDM, generic users can be defined for the distribution of master data. SAP MDM users who carry out these actions remain anonymous in the change documents.

Table 13.1 Risks and Controls for SAP MDM (cont.)

No.	Classification	Description
	Impact	Changes to master data can no longer be controlled. This means that the use of a generic user in SAP MDM enables a person to change or create master data, and the change documents don't contain any information on the responsible person.
	Risk without control(s)	High
	Control(s)	The relevant configuration table must contain the ID of the generic user.
	Risk with control(s)	Normal
	Section	13.3.1
6.	Risk potential	Inadequately configured communications connections. A large number of RFC and HTTP communications connections to the SAP NetWeaver systems must be configured specifically for SAP MDM. The internal link between SAP MDM and SAP Content Integrator (CI) is based on HTTP and represents an important and very sensitive connection; SAP CI is implemented on SAP Web AS J2EE.
	Impact	Incorrectly configured RFC connections can easily be compromised by attackers. The internal connection is also used for exchanging highly sensitive master data. If this data is compromised, data inconsistencies in the connected systems can be the result. This endangers the proper operation of the business to a great extent.
	Risk without control(s)	High
	Control(s)	Correct configuration of RFC communication destinations and restriction of RFC system user authorizations. In addition, SNC and HTTPS should be used to encrypt the communications connections.
	Risk with control(s)	Normal
	Section	13.4.1

Table 13.1 Risks and Controls for SAP MDM (cont.)

13.3 Application Security

To ensure the integrity of business transactions and the presentation of information, master data on employees from different departments, subsidiaries of the company, and different geographical regions must always be up to date and complete.

13.3.1 Identity Management and Authorizations

The management of authorizations and users involves the use of different components. SAP MDM uses both the authorization concepts in SAP Web AS ABAP and the J2EE roles in the Java area. Roles and worksets are used in SAP MDM to assign application rights to users.

Identity Management

Solutions that contain LDAP directory services and a central user administration can be used as identity management solutions. In this context, user data is created either in an LDAP directory, in the SAP MDM user administration, or in SAP Enterprise Portal or the integrated User Management Engine (UME).

If an LDAP server is used with SAP EP, the synchronization between SAP Web AS—for example, Central User Administration (CUA)—and the LDAP must be configured, which enables synchronization of data between the backend system and the LDAP. The administration of the SAP EP users must be set to LDAP with Read/Write to make sure users can be created and user attributes and passwords can be changed via the UME of SAP EP. User master data can be managed in SAP EP, SAP Web AS, or in the LDAP directory service. For consistency, user data should only be modified at one location.

Users can also be administrated with CUA and without an LDAP service. The CUA can, for instance, be set up in SAP MDM—a scenario that represents the logical consequence of the master data concept. Users that have been created in the SAP EP UME can also be distributed to the CUA of the connected systems. Therefore, the RFC destinations, technical users with specific standard SAP roles, and CUA subsystems must be defined in the central SAP MDM CUA (Transaction SCUA). This configuration makes it impossible to maintain individual users in the CUA subsystems.

Another option for administrating users in SAP MDM is the integration of *SAP Content Integrator* (SAP CI) to enable a transfer of roles from SAP Web AS to the J2EE Engine. The UME administration option in SAP CI enables you to update the UME of the portal (SAP Web AS ABAP) with the roles.

In SAP EP, users are assigned portal roles that enable them to generate the portal menu. In the SAP Web AS systems (for example, SAP MDM, SAP Solution Manager, Integration Server), all SAP MDM users are assigned the relevant roles of the backend. In the SAP CI user administration, UME roles can be assigned in the UME of the relevant J2EE server.

Roles

In SAP MDM, authorizations are defined via roles and then assigned to the different users. Three different types of roles are used: SAP Web AS ABAP roles, SAP EP roles, and SAP CI roles. If synchronized, these roles provide the required user authorizations.

During the installation of SAP CI, the SAP CI roles are synchronized with the SAP Web AS ABAP roles that are available as groups in the SAP User Management Engine of SAP CI. Because the SAP Web AS roles are also synchronized with the SAP EP roles, all roles required for the SAP MDM systems are synchronized and can be used (see Figure 13.2).

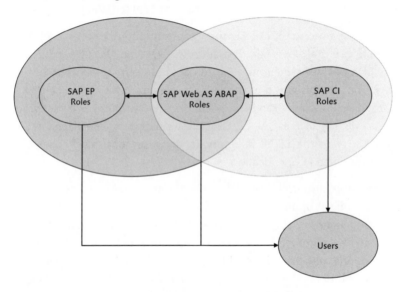

Figure 13.2 Role Types and Role Synchronization for SAP MDM

The following SAP EP roles can be used in the standard SAP version:

▶ **com.sap.pct.mdm.master_data_administrator**
for master data administrators

▶ **com.sap.pct.mdm.master_data_specialist**
for master data specialists

▶ **com.sap.pct.mdm.master_data_manager**
for master data managers

▶ **com.sap.pct.mdm.local_data_manager**
for master data managers (local master data)

▶ **com.sap.pct.mdm.master_data_user**
for master data users

When assigning SAP EP roles to portal users or user groups, the roles from the data source (for example, SAP MDM) are available as user groups in the UME. The assignment of roles to users in SAP MDM is adopted as an assignment of users to user groups. The link between the SAP EP role and the user group is defined in the UME. This means that in SAP MDM, a user is assigned a role and a corresponding SAP EP role.

SAP MDM users must be assigned the default or equivalent roles **eu_role** and **com.sap.pct.mdm.mdm_default_service** if they are to be granted access to personalization functions in SAP EP. These roles also control additional functions in SAP MDM. The following composite roles correspond to the portal roles and can be used as templates for customized SAP MDM roles or as usable roles in the standard SAP version:

▶ **SAP_WP_MDM_MASTER_DATA_ADMIN**
for master data administrators

▶ **SAP_WP_MDM_MASTER_DATA_SPEC**
for master data specialists

▶ **SAP_WP_MDM_MASTER_DATA_MANAGER**
for master data managers

▶ **SAP_WP_MDM_LOCAL_DATA_MANAGER**
for master data managers (local master data)

▶ **SAP_WP_MDM_MASTER_DATA_USER**
for master data users

Additionally, the following SAP CI UME roles can be used in the standard SAP version:

▶ **CI_MasterDataAdministrator**
for master data administrators

▶ **CI_MasterDataSpecialist**
for master data specialists

▶ **CI_MasterDataManager**
for master data managers

The standard SAP version also contains individual roles that are not assigned to any composite roles. Individual and composite roles can be customized according to the requirements of the respective company. In this context, different characteristics and actions can determine and restrict the rights of users. For example, a master data user can be authorized for specific products or business partners.

The Business Server Pages (BSP) applications (mySAP CRM) use the People-Centric UI. For this reason, role-dependent links are defined in SAP MDM Customizing. Accordingly, if roles are changed, those changes must also be made in Customizing to ensure that the links continue to function. These settings can be made using Transaction CRMC_BLUEPRINT (URL generation).

In the MDM environment, users are required for creating ID mappings, starting and executing process chains, and sending and receiving SAP XI messages. These remote users are technical communications users of the user type C that execute RFC or Web service calls. For master data management, default SAP roles are available for remote users.

The following default SAP roles are provided as composite roles for remote users of SAP MDM:

▶ **SAP_WP_MDM_REMOTE_ALE_REMOTE** [external]
for outbound and inbound Master Data Server (MDS) and BW data extraction processes

▶ **SAP_WP_MDM_REMOTE_MDM_REMOTE** [external]
for ID mapping (outbound and inbound processes)

▶ **SAP_WP_MDM_REMOTE_CI_REMOTE** [external]
for accessing SAP CI and filling the ID mapping in the MDS (replication)

▶ **SAP_WP_MDM_REMOTE_XI_MDS** [external]
for receiving and processing SAP XI messages in the MDS

▶ **SAP_WP_MDM_MASTER_DATA_ADMIN** [external]
for master data administrators

Table 13.2 lists some examples of user master records to which the composite roles for remote users listed above can be assigned in SAP MDM.

SAP MDM role	Technical user
SAP_WP_MDM_REMOTE_ ALE_REMOTE	ALEREMOTE As an SAP MDM system user, the ALEREMOTE user is used for communications via ALE.
SAP_WP_MDM_REMOTE_ MDM	MDM_REMOTE The MDM_REMOTE user used to create the ID mapping via a Web service call from the SAP XI to the MDS is defined in MDS Customizing.

Table 13.2 SAP MDM Roles for Remote Users

SAP MDM role	Technical user
SAP_WP_MDM_REMOTE_ CI_REMOTE	CIREMOTE The CIREMOTE user is created during the Content Integrator (CI) installation process.
SAP_WP_MDM_REMOTE_ XI_MDS	<MDSSystemname>_XI_LOGON The user that is required for exchanging messages between SAP XI and MDS is created during the configuration of XI MDS. This user is defined in a communications channel or in an RFC connection in SAP XI.

Table 13.2 SAP MDM Roles for Remote Users (cont.)

Figure 13.3 illustrates the use of SAP MDM composite roles for technical remote users in processes that require the same roles.

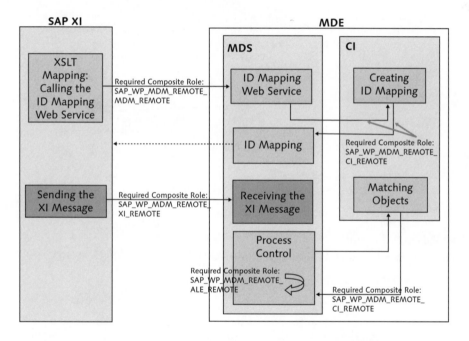

Figure 13.3 Using Roles for Communications Users in an SAP MDM Landscape

The actions for administrative user rights listed in Table 13.3 are relevant for SAP CI roles.

Name of SAP CI Role/Technical Name	Actions in SAP CI
Master data administrator/ **MasterDataAdmin**	This role enables users to perform the following actions in SAP CI: performing initial configurations, displaying version information, creating a system in SAP CI, transporting customizing objects, managing jobs, finding ID mappings, displaying category hierarchies, managing identity check settings, processing change requests, editing UI customizing, managing default categorization settings
Master data manager/ **MasterDataManager**	This role enables users to perform the following actions in SAP CI: managing jobs, editing category hierarchy mappings, displaying category hierarchies, categorizing products, managing default categorization settings, processing change requests, displaying version information, finding ID mappings, managing identity check settings
Master data specialist/ **MasterDataSpecialist**	This role enables users to perform the following actions in SAP CI: displaying category hierarchies, categorizing products, managing jobs, displaying version information, finding ID mappings
Accessibility	This role ensures the accessibility of SAP CI and must be assigned to the SAP CI UME user groups in addition to the other SAP CI roles, because the accessibility role doesn't enable users to perform any separate actions apart from ensuring the accessibility actions that belong to other SAP CI roles.

Table 13.3 SAP CI Roles and Activities

The following SAP CI roles can be assigned during the installation of SAP CI:

▶ **MasterDataAdmin**
is assigned to the UME user group SAP_WP_MDM_MASTER_DATA_ADMIN

▶ **MasterDataManager**
is assigned to the UME user group SAP_WP_MDM_MASTER_DATA_MANAGER

▶ **MasterDataSpecialist**
is assigned to the UME user group SAP_WP_MDM_MASTER_DATA_SPEC

13.3.2 Revision Security

In SAP MDM, generic users are also defined for the distribution of master data. It is possible to define more than one generic user for the inbound distribution process, which facilitates the search for business partners according to change document criteria. Some change documents are not generated with a specific SAP

MDM user ID, but with a generic user of the application. If a business partner change is distributed by the *Master Data Client* (MDC), the change record is generated with a generic user. The ID of the user who performed the change is not displayed. If the object is changed during *staging*, the revision entry is also generated with a generic user ID. If you want to include the entries in the search result, the configuration table must contain the ID of this generic user. The user who is responsible for the distribution is defined as a generic user in Customizing.

The integrative examples from the GSPS emphasize the importance of a holistic view of the SAP NetWeaver components for the definition and implementation of the necessary security and control measures. Separate, individual solutions are therefore a thing of the past. In addition to the technical authorizations and finding identity management measures, it is imperative that the management processes and master data owners are known in order to keep potential risks to a minimum.

13.4 Technical Security

13.4.1 Communications Security

To ensure that the SAP MDM operates efficiently, a large number of RFC connections to those SAP NetWeaver systems, which are to be included into the central master data management process, is required. In this context, the technical default settings for the SAP Gateway must be considered, as well as the authorization restrictions for RFC connections described in Chapter 8. Authorizations for the authorization object S_RFC, whose scope is set too widely, can be used to compromise the system, if the RFC user has the type "system" or "communication".

Moreover, the communications connections should be encrypted using SNC, as described in Chapter 8.

Additionally, an HTTP-based communication link is used between SAP MDM and SAP CI. Because SAP CI is implemented on the basis of SAP Web AS J2EE, the SSL option for the J2EE Engine must be activated; Chapter 8 describes in detail how this can be done. However, the entry for the HTTP provider in the Java Visual Administrator console must be changed. Usually, the entry looks like this:

```
(Port:50000,Type:http)
(Port:50001,Type:ssl).
```

This means that TCP/IP port 50000 can be used to address SAP Web AS J2EE via HTTP, while port 50001 is used for HTTPS connections. The entry must be complemented as follows:

```
(Port:50000,Type:http,BindAddress:127.0.0.1)
(Port:50001,Type:ssl)
```

This means that an internal server communication is used, as the IP address 127.0.0.1 always designates the local server. This way it can be ensured that the communication between SAP MDM (SAP Web AS ABAP) and SAP CI (SAP Web AS J2EE) always occurs internally.

13.4.2 Important Additional GSPS Components

For the evaluation of technical security risks and controls, the following GSPS components must be considered:

▶ Web browser (see Chapter 28)

▶ SAP GUI (see Chapter 27)

▶ SAP ITS (see Chapter 26)

▶ SAP Web AS (see Chapter 8)

▶ SAP EP (see Chapter 19)

▶ SAP XI (see Chapter 20)

14 mySAP Customer Relationship Management

This chapter describes the Global Security Positioning System (GSPS) component, mySAP Customer Relationship Management. Selected examples are used to illustrate the complexity of its mechanisms and possible control solutions.

14.1 Introduction and Functions

With its integrated marketing, sales, and analysis functions, *mySAP Customer Relationship Management* (mySAP CRM) is the central customer and sales component in SAP NetWeaver. Customer relationship management focuses on recording and maintaining a company's relationships with customers. Market and customer analysis functions support the sales department in planning and carrying out targeted actions. Because the technical and business scenarios as well as the control solutions for application and technical security can be very complex, this chapter covers only the most critical solutions, so as not to exceed the scope of this book as a general reference.

14.2 Risks and Controls

mySAP CRM processes important customer and sales data. While customer data is subject to internal and legal data protection regulations, sales data such as product and price information or sales figures often have an enormous strategic importance for the company and therefore must be protected. The control measures depend on the classification of the data and the related need for protection (see Table 14.1).

No.	Classification	Description
1.	Risk potential	Customer and sales data: mySAP CRM processes information on customer data that is either subject to a data protection law or must at least be specifically protected. For example, information on the buying behavior or preferences of customers, or bank and credit information, must be protected, in particular. Sales information such as data on sales within a certain period or region can be anticompetitive if it falls into the possession of unauthorized persons at the wrong time. Furthermore, a transfer of customer data to third parties can only be possible with the explicit permission of the customer. This means that customer and sales data must be protected.

Table 14.1 Risks for mySAP CRM

No.	Classification	Description
	Impact	Information on customer and sales data is of particular interest to competitors. Therefore, the data and its use must be protected.
	Risk without control(s)	High
	Control(s)	The CRM data must be classified according to the required level of protection. Control solutions are defined on the basis of the protection requirements of this data, which are integrated into a comprehensive security strategy. Efficient authorization management helps protect data and activities and ensure that only authorized users have controlled access to it.
	Risk with control(s)	Normal
	Section	14.3
2.	Risk potential	Internal and external users: Depending on the scenario, mySAP CRM can either be made accessible only to internal users or to external users. This entails an increase in the technical security requirements for the mySAP CRM systems.
	Impact	External users may inadvertantly be authorized to access internal mySAP CRM systems. If the technical security measures and the authorization controls are not exactly coordinated, all doors are open for unauthorized access to information.
	Risk without control(s)	High
	Control(s)	As different user groups have access to the CRM data, for external authorizations the protection must be ensured not only by the authorization system, but also by technical control measures.
	Risk with control(s)	Normal
	Section	14.4
3.	Risk potential	Mobile devices: Due to the entry of sales information such as purchase orders, confidential data is stored in databases of mobile devices. This means that the access security for mobile clients, the secure synchronization of CRM data with the CRM server, and the protection of mySAP CRM backend systems must be closely monitored. In a synchronization of data between the mobile client and the CRM server, the data validation is usually performed in the mySAP CRM backend. If the control and protection measures are insufficient, this can result in the loss of individual data records and even of complete database contents, which can subsequently fall into the hands of unauthorized persons.

Table 14.1 Risks for mySAP CRM (cont.)

No.	Classification	Description
	Impact	The consequences are loss or manipulation of data, which can lead to competitive disadvantages, increased costs, or even legal penalties.
	Risk without control(s)	High
	Control(s)	Technical and process-related security measures, such as prompt and secure synchronizations of CRM data with the CRM server and the use of consolidated databases (CDBs), are commonly used standard SAP solutions. In addition, mobile devices must be properly protected by the employees.
	Risk with control(s)	Normal
	Section	14.4.1

Table 14.1 Risks for mySAP CRM (cont.)

14.3 Application Security

mySAP CRM generally adheres to the rules for authorization concepts of SAP Web AS ABAP and SAP Web AS J2EE. These concepts are described in detail in Chapters 8 and 11.

In addition to the role concept, the authorization systems in mySAP CRM are complemented by more advanced concepts that protect access to transactions and Business Server Page (BSP) applications. Internal employees must be assigned roles for the internal CRM system, while external partners require access to CRM data via portal applications. In addition, internal employees want to be able to access mySAP CRM applications from outside the company.

For the different scenarios and the complicated security requirements of CRM applications and systems, different concepts have been established that provide comprehensive protection of data and business activities. SAP Web AS ABAP roles, SAP Enterprise Portal (SAP EP) roles, access control rules, and the business partner principle are some examples of the complex options for controlling authorizations. The central authorization system is implemented using the SAP Web AS role concept. Authorizations for business data and transactions for mySAP CRM are defined and implemented using the SAP Profile Generator or external solutions like SecurInfo for SAP. Additional control options are available for the mobile soutions in mySAP CRM. For channel management, mySAP CRM provides the *Access Control Engine* (ACE), which enables a rules-based distribution of authorizations to users (see Figure 14.1).

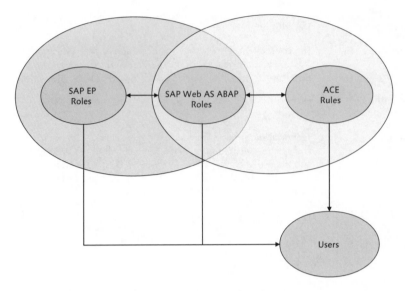

Figure 14.1 Roles in mySAP CRM and Rules-Based Authorizations

mySAP CRM Access Control Engine

The mySAP CRM Access Control Engine (ACE) is an option for controlling user rights in the channel management component of mySAP CRM. The ACE is based on rules instead of roles; the rules-based access control is the security solution for CRM mass data. The effect of the rules, however, is that they complement the authorizations that have been assigned to a user via the roles.

The mySAP CRM ACE function can be maintained in Customizing and can be called using the following path: **Customer Relationship Management · Basic Functions · Access Control Engine**. mySAP CRM then references the users that have been created using Transaction SU01. It also references the assigned roles that have been implemented using Transaction PFCG. The ACE uses user IDs to manage the rules-based authorizations, for instance. This means that changes to users also affect the authorizations that are managed by the ACE.

The ACE can also be used to define additional access rights to business data that are based on rules related to users or user groups. The ACE rules are applied in the interaction with portal and CRM backend roles, for instance, in order to grant different users from different partner companies access to different sets of data. Depending on the configured or activated rules, the ACE filters the general and individual rights of users and then releases the relevant information accordingly. Based on the rules, a user of partner company X can only access information that is related to partner company X. In addition, the rules check the individual rights of the requesting user. The ACE therefore enables you to control dynamic authorizations by using hierarchical business partner structures.

This means that the ACE is a system for defining user-dependent access rights for information objects. The application can check authorizations for different actions like reading, writing, and deleting information objects in mySAP CRM.

For creating the rules, the ACE follows the business partner principle. The involved partner organizations are mapped as business relationships and information objects. The following elements are used:

▶ **Actor**
An actor is an organizational unit that is used as a basis for authorization calculations, such as a business partner, organizational unit, territory/region, or user.

▶ **User context**
The user context describes the organizational units in relation to the users that are used in the ACE.

▶ **ACE group**
The ACE group is a dynamically calculated group of users, which is based on a user's role assignments and the organizational unit the user belongs to.

▶ **Activation tool**
The activation tool is a program that transfers the contents of administrative database tables to runtime information tables. The administrative tables are directly maintained by the administrator, whereas the runtime information tables are used by the ACE for the calcultion of authorizations.

▶ **Actions**
Actions are used to create rules and comprise different individual or composite activities such as writing, deleting, or just reading.

▶ **Rules**
A rule is a group of methods that defines how filters can be used to find actors for a user or for an object, or just to find objects. In addition, rules are used to calculate the relationship between users and information objects.

▶ **Rights**
Rights define the assignment of rules and actions to user groups.

▶ **Roles**
Roles contain authorizations and are assigned to users.

Figure 14.2 shows the hierarchical structure for business partner organizations that are defined as business relationships, as well as the relationships between information objects and those hierarchical structures. It does not refer to the Human Capital Management (HCM) organizational structure.

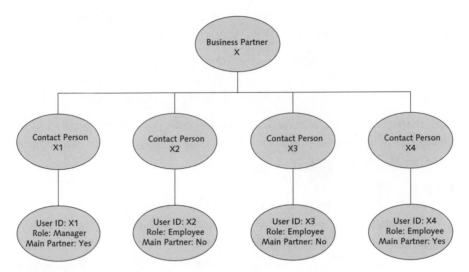

Figure 14.2 Hierarchical Organizational Structure for Business Partners

The ACE uses this information to define the access to individual objects (for example, a list of leads). Once the access to an individual information object has been defined, the result of the authorization check is stored temporarily in the system cache so that it can be used for further accesses. The actor in this case is the partner company (for example, business partner X). The example shown in Figure 14.3 illustrates the relationship between information objects and the hierarchical structure for determining rules-based authorizations.

Example

Due to the rules-based definition of the access to a list of leads, the authorized list can be built and displayed for a specific user.

▶ Rule **A**: Check the contact person the lead entry is associated with

▶ Rule **B**: Check the primary business partner for the contact person

▶ Rule **C**: Obtain contact data of the contact person

▶ Rule **D**: Check the primary business partner for the contact person

▶ Rule **E**: Compare business partners; if identical, the lead data can be displayed to user Z

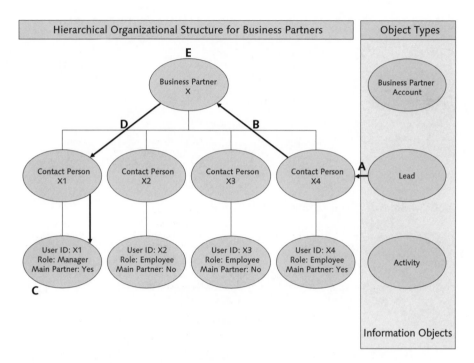

Figure 14.3 Sample ACE Authorization Check

Transaction SM30 can be used to manage the rules for the ACE. The individual object types for information objects such as an activity, lead, or user are equipped with rights and rules in this context. If the rights are activated in the ACE administration in Customizing, the results of the activations can be displayed under **Statistics**. For this purpose, the views listed in Table 14.2 must be maintained.

View	Description
CRM_ACE_ACTTYP	Definition of the actor type
CRM_ACE_AFO_CL	Finding actors of an object
CRM_ACE_AFU_CL	Finding actors of a user
CRM_ACE_ANGRP	Action group for ACE
CRM_ACE_ANGRPS	Action group for ACE
CRM_ACE_CUSTOM	Customizing for CRM portals
CRM_ACE_OBF_CL	Finding objects with filter for ACE
CRM_ACE_OTYPES	Relevant object types for ACE

Table 14.2 mySAP CRM Table Views for Maintaining the ACE

View	Description
CRM_ACE_RIGHTS	Rights for ACE
CRM_ACE_RULES	Rules for ACE
CRM_ACE_ST_ACC	Super types for ACE
CRM_ACE_U_GRP	User group for ACE
CRM_ACE_U_GRPS	User group for ACE

Table 14.2 mySAP CRM Table Views for Maintaining the ACE (cont.)

Table 14.3 displays an example of rule definitions.

Relation ID (Rule ID)	Actor Type	Object Type	GetActorsFrom-User	GetActorFrom-Obejct	GetObjectsBy-Filter
MyLeads	Contact	Lead	UserSContacts	LeadSPartner-Contacts	*
MyCompany Leads	Partner Com-pany	Lead	UserSPartner-Company	LeadSPartner-Company	U.S. Leads

Table 14.3 Rule Definition for the ACE

The **Actor Type** is the type of organizational element used in the relationship between users and information objects. **GetActorsFromUser** determines the actors (for example, the organizational unit) for each user who has been assigned those rights. **GetActorsFromObject** determines the actors in relation to each object that is returned by the rule **GetObjectsByFilter** (see Figure 14.4).

In the administration of rights, permitted actions are defined for the previously defined rules and object types for each user group. User groups are often based on SAP EP roles. Rights describe the relationship between users and objects. Table 14.4 uses the "Lead" CRM object as an example to describe the maintenance of rights by using rules.

Right	User Group	Object Type	Rule	Action
R314	All partner roles	Lead	MyCompaniesLeads	Read
R315	Partner manager	Lead	MyCompaniesLeads	Change
R316	All partner roles	Lead	MyLeads	All

Table 14.4 Rights Definition for the ACE

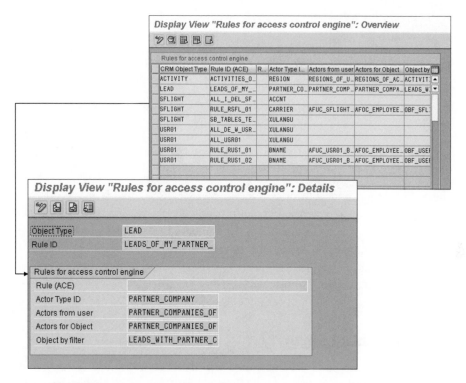

Figure 14.4 Maintaining Rules and Rights for ACE Object Types

The authorizations for SAP EP roles are divided into two categories—rights for administrators and rights for users. In addition to the definition of rights, SAP EP roles are also used to add access controls (ACLs) to the content in SAP Portal Content Management.

The following tables should be logged for monitoring ACE changes:

▶ Definition of the actor type with Table CRM_ACE_ACTTYP

▶ Customizing with Table CRM_ACE_CUSTOM

▶ Object types with Table CRM_ACE_OTYPES

▶ Rights with Table CRM_ACE_RIGHTS

▶ Activated rights with Table CRM_ACE_RIG_RT

▶ Rules with Table CRM_ACE_RULES

▶ Assignment of tables to super types with Table CRM_ACE_ST_ACC

▶ Activated user rights with Table CRM_ACE_UGR_RT

▶ Definition of actors per object with Table CRM_ACE_AFO_CL

▶ Definition of actors for users with Table CRM_ACE_AFO_CL

- Action groups with Table CRM_ACE_ANGRP
- Assignment of actions to action groups with Table CRM_ACE_ANGRPS
- Definition of objects using a filter with Table CRM_ACE_OBF_CL
- User groups with Table CRM_ACE_U_GRP
- Assignment of users, roles, or groups to user groups with Table CRM_ACE_U_GRPS

The logging of these tables can be activated or deactivated in the ABAP Dictionary. The log results can be displayed using Transaction SCU3.

The authorization and control options in mySAP CRM provide many different ways of assigning and restricting authorizations for necessary functions and actions for internal and external users. The standard SAP tools can be used to create functional and organizational authorizations and to define them using roles. Authorization objects can be assigned the corresponding authorization fields. In addition, dynamic access controls are available that are based on the use of flexible authorization rules and individual information objects.

14.4 Technical Security

Depending on operational necessity and security needs, the CRM systems must meet different technical requirements. If mySAP CRM applications should be made accessible only for internal employees, it must be ensured that the CRM systems can't be accessed through the Internet. In that case, the CRM servers should not be outside the *demilitarized zone* (DMZ).

However, due to organizational and sales-related requirements, internal sales employees may need to be granted access to mySAP CRM from outside of the demilitarized zone. This can be the case for employees who work from home or for sales employees who travel in another region. In this case, a *virtual private network* (VPN) can establish an encrypted data communication.

When granting access rights to external users such as business partners, SAP Web Dispatcher can be used to ensure a higher level of security. SAP Web Dispatcher is only used in CRM and BI backend systems, whereby the access to the backend systems is controlled by URL filters. To ensure that all requests from SAP EP to the CRM system pass through SAP Web Dispatcher, the latter should be set up in the DMZ 1 GSPS component. Therefore, each URL that needs access to the backend CRM system must be configured.

14.4.1 Technical Protection of the Mobile Application

For the protection of the mobile CRM application (Mobile Sales), you should consider the technical risks and the corresponding control measures of the SAP MI (see Chapter 22), in particular for mobile devices (see Chapter 29).

14.4.2 Additional Important GSPS Components

The applications contained in mySAP CRM are based on the technical SAP NetWeaver components of the GSPS. The technical risks and controls described for those GSPS components can also be applied to mySAP CRM. Therefore, the technical control measures of the following GSPS components should be considered for mySAP CRM:

▶ Web browser (see Chapter 28)

▶ SAP ITS (see Chapter 26)

▶ SAP Web Dispatcher (see Chapter 24)

▶ SAP Web AS (see Chapter 8)

▶ SAP XI (see Chapter 20)

▶ SAP NetWeaver BI (see Chapter 12)

▶ SAP MI (see Chapter 22)

▶ Mobile devices (see Chapter 29)

15 mySAP Supplier Relationship Management

This chapter describes IT security concepts for the mySAP Supplier Relationship Management component of the Global Security Positioning System (GSPS). It primarily focuses on the authorization concept.

15.1 Introduction and Functions

mySAP Supplier Relationship Management (mySAP SRM) is the SAP solution that includes all business processes for purchasing and supplier management. It is not just one application, but rather it is made up of six different components that can be combined with other SAP solutions and products such as *SAP NetWeaver Business Intelligence* (SAP BI) to map six different business scenarios. The six components are:

▶ **SAP Enterprise Buyer Professional**
SAP Enterprise Buyer Professional (SAP EBP) is the central application for controlling the purchasing process. It enables employees to create puchase orders (POs). The POs must be approved by a manager before the purchasing department can convert them into a delivery request.

▶ **SAP Bidding Engine**
Suppliers can use the SAP Bidding Engine to submit bids for individual purchase orders through the Internet. The SAP Bidding Engine can also be used for negotiating long-term supplier contracts and terms of delivery.

▶ **SAP Supplier Self-Service**
The *SAP Supplier Self-Service* (SAP SUS) web application enables suppliers, who are actually referred to as "business partners," to receive purchase orders and to confirm delivery. In addition, suppliers can provide details on delivery status here. Suppliers can also use the application for issuing invoices. For this purpose, employees on the supplier's side can be assigned specific roles.

▶ **SAP Internet Pricing Configurator**
The *SAP Internet Pricing Configurator* (SAP IPC) is an application that retrieves the purchasing conditions that have been negotiated upfront from the EBP application, when an employee compiles a selection of goods to be purchased. This task is important if, for example, scaled conditions have been negotiated that state that the unit price is reduced when a certain purchase order quantity has been reached.

- ▶ **SAP Catalog Content Manager**

  The *SAP Catalog Content Manager* (SAP CCM) controls the goods catalog that is stored in SAP EBP. Suppliers can send their goods catalogs in different data formats to the company. A catalog manager in the company's purchasing department is responsible for maintaining the catalog.

- ▶ **SAP Live Auction Cockpit Web Presentation Server**

  The *SAP Live Auction Cockpit Web Presentation Server* (SAP LACWPS) can be used for carrying out interactive bidding events through the Internet. Such bidding events are used to determine the quotation price for a specific supplier's bid. The price history can be observed online and the bidding event can be restricted to a certain period of time.

These SAP applications are used to map the following business process scenarios: self-service procurement, plan-driven procurement, strategic sourcing, catalog content management, service procurement, and spend analysis.

15.2   Risks and Controls

Which security methods and solutions you choose for mySAP SRM are determined by an objective assessment of the requirements and the risk potential of each individual situation. As mySAP SRM controls all purchasing processes in a company, its security is very important. Fraudulent activity can happen very easily in purchasing processes due to the lack of a separation of functions. For example, fake suppliers can be created, and services (like cleaning services, for instance) can be procured from these fake companies on a regular basis. The payments for the invoices, which are also fake, then go to a bank account that's part of the fraudulent scenario.

The technical security of mySAP SRM is based on the GSPS components listed in Section 15.4. The main risk for mySAP SRM is described in Table 15.1.

No.	Classification	Description
1.	Risk potential	Inadequate authorization concept.
		Users of mySAP SRM have authorizations that are too extensive for their actual requirements in terms of information and functions. The reason for this can be that the authorization concept is used only as a means of assigning functional authorizations and not as an effective instrument for controlling access and minimizing risks. In the case of mySAP SRM, it means that the entire purchasing process of the company is involved.

Table 15.1 Risks and Controls for mySAP SRM

No.	Classification	Description
	Impact	Users have greater authorizations than are necessary for their position and the scope of their work. This means that specific functional seperations and control steps can't be carried out, enabling employees to perform fraudulent actions.
	Risk without control(s)	Extremely high
	Control(s)	The authorization concept has to take into account both organizational and functional requirements, and make administration simpler and more effective. The relevant risks have to be taken into account in the authorization design process, and methods of continuous management have to be integrated into the change management process.
	Risk with control(s)	Normal
	Section	15.3

Table 15.1 Risks and Controls for mySAP SRM (cont.)

15.3 Application Security

For the main applications of mySAP SRM—SAP Enterprise Buyer Professional, SAP Supplier Self-Service, and SAP Catalog Content Management—the authorization concept for mySAP SRM is based on the ABAP authorization concept that is described in great detail in Chapter 9. For mySAP SRM, the concept is enhanced by specific rules-based queries that can, for instance, be used to determine a manager for approving a list of goods ordered by an employee who's assigned to that manager. When the ordering process is completed, the manager must approve the list of goods before it is forwarded to the purchasing group that actually orders the goods from the supplier. The rules-based queries are controlled by additional attributes that must be assigned to each business partner.

In mySAP SRM, the term "business partner" must be regarded as a stakeholder principle, which means that internal employees are also business partners who are assigned other attributes in addition to their normal user master data. We'll describe this concept in more detail later in this chapter. At this stage we want to first look at the most important authorization objects in mySAP SRM. The best-practice concept described in Chapter 9 can also be applied to mySAP SRM.

15.3.1 Important Authorizations

SAP provides mySAP SRM with standard roles for employees, managers, purchasing assistants, purchasers, purchasing managers, and catalog managers. These roles can also be evaluated for further use in mySAP SRM as many companies typically use a very standardized purchasing process. The standard roles can therefore be customized for specific requirements.

Authorization Control for Document Types

To enable better control of access authorizations for important document types in the purchasing process, such as quotations, POs, invoices, and so on, even at the organizational level, the **Purchasing Organization** (PORG), **Responsible Purchasing Group** (PGR), and **Business Transaction** authorization fields have been included in the authorization objects of the new SAP EBP version that are listed in Table 15.2. This not only enables you to restrict access to action levels, but also to the organizational elements listed above.

> **Example**
>
> A purchaser in purchasing group PGR123 has been assigned the authorization object BBP_PD_PO (place purchase orders) via the role **SAP_EC_BBP_PURCHASER**. The previous SAP EBP version only allowed the restriction to the following actions: create, change, display, print, and delete purchase orders. In addition to that, the new version allows for restrictions to purchase orders of the purchasing group PGR123, the purchasing organization, and the business transaction (for example, the commissioning process).

The authorization objects described in Table 15.2 contain the additional authorization fields.

Authorization object	Authorization field	Description
BBP_PD_AUC	Internet auction	This object can be used for the Live Auction Cockpit application to restrict the purchaser to such an extent that he or she can set up and carry out auctions only for specific purchasing organizations and groups.
BBP_PD_BID	Invitation to bid in an auction	This object can be used for the Live Auction Cockpit and Bidding Engine applications to restrict the purchaser to such an extent that they can invite only specific bidders (i.e., suppliers) that are assigned to a specific purchasing organization and group.
BBP_PD_CNF	Order confirmation	The organization fields listed above are not checked here. You can only restrict the permitted action.

Table 15.2 Authorizion Objects in mySAP SRM

Authorization object	Authorization field	Description
BBP_PD_CTR	Contracts	The access rights of the purchaser for contracts can be restricted using the organizational authorization fields described above.
BBP_PD_INV	Invoice entry	The organization fields listed above are not checked here. You can only restrict the permitted action.
BBP_PD_PO	Purchase order	With regard to raising purchase orders, the purchaser can be restricted to the purchasing organization and group.
BBP_PD_QUO	Quotations	This object can be used to restrict the purchaser in such a way that they can display, accept, and reject only quotations for a specfic purchasing organization and group.
BBP_PD_VL	List of vendors	This authorization object can be used to restrict the purchaser in such a way that they can enter, display, and change only the lists of suppliers of specific purchasing organizations and groups.
BBP_PD_SC	Shopping cart	This authorization object is used to control the creation, change, deletion, or printout of an employee's shopping cart. The organizational fields described above are not checked in this context. On the other hand, the ownership rule does get checked. This means that an employee can only modify his or her own shopping cart. The only exception is an employee's substitute, who can be defined using the **Requestor** attribute.

Table 15.2 Authorizion Objects in mySAP SRM (cont.)

Controlling Authorizations for Displaying Purchasing Budgets

In certain cases, the permissions for purchasers to display purchasing budgets that are assigned to specific accounts must be restricted. The purchasing budgets are defined for specific objects (for example, goods) of an account. The authorization object BBP_BUDGET can be used for ensuring that purchasers display only the information that they are authorized to display. This authorization object contains the following authorization fields, which can be complemented with additional values as required:

▶ Activity

  ▶ 03: Display of the complete overview (via RFC connection to the SAP ERP Central Component (ECC) controlling application component)

  ▶ 28: Display of the detailed chart of accounts via an SAP BW report

- ▶ **Assigned account category**

  Selection of the respective assigned account category

- ▶ **Assigned account object**

  Selection of the respective assigned account object

Controlling Authorizations for Modifying Purchasing Credit Card Master Data

To make the purchasing process as efficient as possible, certain authorized staff can be given purchasing credit cards for specific organizational groups or for a certain department. The M_BBP_PC authorization object can be used to control the access of the purchaser to the master data of the purchasing credit card for maintenance purposes. This authorization object contains the following authorization fields, which can be complemented with additional values as required:

- ▶ **PCINS**

  Purchasing credit card organization

- ▶ **PCNUM**

  Purchasing credit card number

- ▶ **PCBEGRU**

  Purchasing credit card group (Purchasing credit cards can be assigned to specific groups. These groups can be used to restrict the access to certain cards.)

- ▶ **PCMAS_ACT**

  Possible activities:

  - ▶ 01: Change

  - ▶ 02: Change

  - ▶ 03: Display

  - ▶ 04: Display list

  - ▶ 05: Delete

Controlling Authorizations for Maintaining Purchasing Conditions

When considering potential business risks, keep in mind that the maintenance of purchasing conditions is critical. Therefore, the authorizations for maintaining those conditions must be restricted. When restricting authorizations, you can also define which types of contracts can be accessed. In mySAP SRM, this is done using the /SAPCND/CM authorization object that belongs to the cross-application-objects class. This authorization object contains the following authorization fields, which can be complemented with additional values as required:

- **Activity**
  - 01: Create
  - 02: Change
  - 03: Display
- **/SAPCND/AP**

  Because the object is a generic object, the application component for which it is to be applied must be selected here; for mySAP SRM, that's the BBP component.

- **/SAPCND/US**

  Contract conditions method; the maintenance can be restricted to specific contract conditions methods, such as the price determination

- **/SAPCND/CT**

  Contract conditions table; the maintenance can be restricted to specific contract conditions tables, such as the control indicator

- **/SAPCND/TY**

  Contract conditions type; the maintenance can be restricted to specific contract conditions types, such as the contract price

Controlling Authorizations for the Product Master Data Maintenance

mySAP SRM contains several authorization objects for the product master data maintenance. The COM_PRD authorization object controls if a user (typically a purchaser) is generally authorized to maintain product master data or if the user can only display the master data. Therefore, the only authorization field available is the following one:

- **Activity**
  - 01: Create
  - 02: Change
  - 03: Display
  - 06: Delete

The COM_ASET authorization object controls whether a user (typically a purchaser) is authorized to maintain product set types or if the user can only display them. Therefore, the only authorization field available is the following one:

- **Activity**
  - 01: Create
  - 02: Change
  - 03: Display

- 06: Delete
- 21: Transport

To restrict the product master data maintenance the /SAPCND/CM authorization object must be defined as follows:

- Activity: 01: Create and 02: Change
- /SAPCND/AP: BBP
- /SAPCND/US: PR
- /SAPCND/CT: SAP001, SAP118
- /SAPCND/TY: 01PV

Special Authorization Exceptions

Typically, the S_TCODE authorization object controls the authorization for calling a specific transaction, but there are exceptions in SAP EBP for the following transactions, the call of which is controlled by the authorization object BBP_FUNCT:

- **CR_COMPANY**
  Create a new business partner
- **MON_ALERTS**
  Use monitoring functions
- **CR_ASSETS**
  Create asset master data
- **BE_F4_HELP**
  Call an R/3 input help
- **EVAL_VEND**
  Evaluate vendors
- **GLOB_ACCSS**
  Authorization for confirming purchase orders raised by other users

Controlling Authorizations for Maintaining Business Partners

The BBP_FUNCT, PLOG, and B_BUPA_RLT authorization objects are relevant for the maintenance of business partners.

The BBP_FUNCT authorization object described above must have the value "CR_COMPANY", which means that the user is generally authorized to create business partners.

The PLOG personnel planning object from the HR class, which controls checks related to personnel planning and organizational structures, must be assigned the following values:

► **PPFCODE**

This field controls the activities a user can execute regarding information types. The possible values are defined in Table T77FC. The value must be set to "DISP", which stands for "display."

► **PLVAR**

This field specifies which plan version a user is granted access to. The value must be set to "01".

► **OTYPE**

This field defines the object type a user has access to. The object type must be set to "US" and "O".

► **INFOTYP**

This field specifies which infotypes a user is granted access to. The infotypes are HR attributes. They must be set to "1000", "1222", "5500", "5501", "5502", and "5503".

► **SUBTYP**

This field determines the subtypes of the previously defined infotypes a user has access to. A subtype specifically defines the relationships to Infotype 1001. This means that the values "0020", "A490", "0200", and "A002" must be set.

The B_BUPA_RLT authorization object is used to define which roles can be edited for business partners. For instance, **Bidder** can be a possible role. This authorization object contains the following authorization fields, which can be complemented with additional values as required:

► **Activity**

  ► 01: Create

  ► 02: Change

  ► 03: Display

► **BP_ROLE**

Role of the business partner that can be maintained. The following business partners are possible: general business partner, vendor, bidder, component supplier, plant, purchasing organization, service provider, contact person, prospect, employee, organizational unit, Internet user, marketplace supplier, marketplace customer, and financial service provider.

Controlling Authorizations for Bidders in RFQs and Auctions

In SAP EBP, a purchaser can initiate requests for quotation (RFQs) by using the bidding engine. When doing so, the purchaser can invite selected suppliers to submit a bid, which can be submitted via the web application contained in SAP EBP. Another option for this is to use the Live Auction Cockpit for running an online auction over a certain period of time. In this case, many bidders are simultaneously logged on and submit their pricing offers online. This way the purchaser can quickly and efficiently determine the best price offer from all bidders.

The authorizations for bidders can also be complemented with specific values. This is important if a supplier wants to have different bidder roles like, for instance, the trader who is authorized to negotiate prices and also the salesperson who must eventually confirm the bid.

The authorization object responsible for this is the BBP_VEND object, which controls the vendor activities. This authorization object can be used to define the following bidder rights:

▶ Creation of confirmations, such as bid confirmations

▶ Creation of invoices upon delivery of ordered goods or services

▶ Submission of bids for an RFQ or the auction

This authorization object contains the following authorization fields that can be complemented with additional values, as required:

▶ **Activity**

> ▶ 01: Create

> ▶ 02: Change

> ▶ 03: Display

> ▶ 06: Delete

▶ **BBP_OBJTYPE**

Document type that can have the following values:

> ▶ BUS2203: Confirmation

> ▶ BUS2205: Invoice

> ▶ BUS2202: Quotation

Controlling Authorizations for Employees of a Supplier

If SAP SUS is used, which is not necessarily required for mySAP SRM, this web-based application can be used by employees of a supplier (business partner) for processing purchase orders, creating order confirmations, and so on. However, the supplier's employees can also be restricted to specific activities, which is particularly important if the supplier has the large sales organization.

The authorization control is handled by the BBP_SUS_PD authorization object, which contains the following authorization fields that can be assigned the relevant values:

▶ **BBP_OBJTYP**

Object type with the possible values:

▶ BUS2230: Purchase order SUS

▶ BUS2231: Delivery note

▶ BUS2232: Order confirmation SUS

▶ BUS2233: Confirmation SUS (for confirmations, an additional check is performed against the BBP_FUNCT authorization object with the value "GLOB_ACCSS" if a user wants to globally confirm all purchase orders that were sent to the supplier)

▶ BUS2234: Invoice SUS

▶ BUS2235: Message SUS

▶ **Activity**

▶ 02: Create, change

▶ 03: Display

▶ 09: Display price (at time of purchase order)

15.3.2 Rules-Based Security Checks Using Business Partner Attributes

As noted, in mySAP SRM, the underlying ABAP authorization concept is enhanced by specifically programmed, rules-based security queries. The security queries are used on the basis of additional, defined business partner attributes, in particular for release workflows for purchase orders. The business partner attributes are assigned to both internal employees and external suppliers who are both referred to as "business partners" in mySAP SRM. A department is also a business partner that must be assigned attributes as well.

The business partner attributes are assigned to the individual business partners by means of an organizational structure that must be specifically defined. Figure 15.1 shows an example of such an organizational structure. There are actually two types of organizational structures: there is the organizational structure of internal business partners with all areas and departments, including the purchasing organization, and there is the external structure that includes all kinds of suppliers. The attributes can be assigned to the departments. If they are, they apply to all employees of a corresponding department, including any additional person-related information.

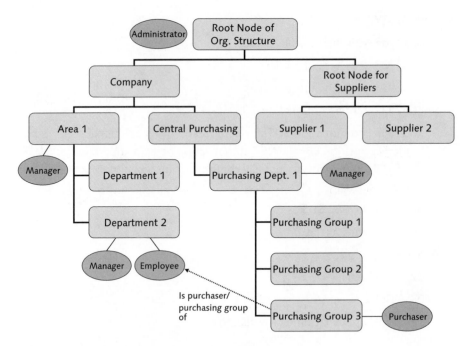

Figure 15.1 Organizational Structure for mySAP SRM

Each department must be assigned a manager. The attributes can also be used to control which purchasing group is responsible for which department. This means, for instance, that purchase orders created in a department must always be processed by the responsible purchasing group.

mySAP SRM can't function without such an organizational structure. The following transactions are used to create the organizational structure:

▶ **PPOCA_BBP**
Initial creation of the organizational plan

▶ **PPOMA_BBP**
Changing and maintaining the organizational structure

If an internal organizational structure is already available, it can be adopted by a mySAP ERP HCM organizational structure. It must, however, be complemented by the supplier structure.

As the business partner attributes are used to run specific security queries, each user must be created as a business partner within mySAP SRM, because a regular SU01 user is not sufficient for the use of SAP EBP. Table 15.3 contains the most important business partner attributes that are used to run rules-based security queries for the release workflow.

Attribute	Name	Description
APPRV_LIM	Approval limit	The total value of a shopping cart ordered by an employee that a user (typically a manager) can approve.
BUK	Company code	Company code in the backend system. Usually the user inherits the company code from his or her area or organizational group. The company code in the backend system determines the company code for which a user can make purchases. The inheritance will only be neutralized if a value is specified.
CAT	Catalog ID	Specifies the goods catalogs from which a user can place purchase orders.
CNT	Cost center	Defines the cost center in the backend system. Default value for the account assignment when creating a shopping cart or a local order. A user can only place orders for his or her own cost center.
LAG	Storage location	An organizational unit that enables the user to distinguish between different material stocks within the same plant.
PM_IPHAS	Phase	Phases divide the lifecycle of an order into several stages (for example, opened and released), and they determine which activities a user is allowed to perform for the order at a certain stage. This attribute is used for selecting orders in the R/3 backend system and is mandatory.
PRCAT	Product category	Defines the product categories for which a user has authorizations. It is advisable to define a default value, for instance, if a user orders only office equipment. In that case, the product category should be restricted to "office equipment."
REQUESTER	Requester	Specifies for which organizational units or users the employee is authorized to create shopping carts. A user can select all users of an organizational unit as deviating requesters if the attribute is maintained, for instance, with the entry "O 50000019". If a specific user is to be selected as a requester, the attribute must be maintained as follows: <US><User ID of deviating requester>, for example, "USMANAGER22". This attribute must also be maintained for the use of the "Purchase as substitute" application. For example, you can specify all employees for whom an assistant is authorized to make purchases.
RESP_PRGRP	Responsible purchasing group	Number of the purchasing group that is responsible for the organizational unit.

Table 15.3 Important Business Partner Attributes for Rules-Based Security Queries

Attribute	Name	Description
ROLE	Role (technical ABAP role)	Specifies the role of the user, such as manager, employee, or purchasing assistant. If no approval workflow is used for new users, a default value must be set for the ROLE attribute, for example, "SAP_EC_BBP_EMPLOYEE". (If no default value is found, the approval workflow is automatically activated.)
SLAPPROVER	Spending limit approver	Specifies the approver used for the approval workflow when the spending limit is exceeded.
SPEND_LIM	Spending limit	Value up to which a user can make expenditures. If the value is exceeded, a workflow starts for approving the spending limit.
TEND_TYPE	Transaction type: RFQ	Specifies the transaction type for automatically created RFQs, for instance, in mySAP PLM (collaborative engineering). The attribute must be defined for the purchasing group that is responsible for the organizational unit of the entry channel. The value of this attribute can be inherited. For example, purchasing groups can inherit it from their purchasing organization.
TOG	Tolerance group	Defines the tolerance group. This attribute can be used for a user group to define tolerance checks if the quantity or tolerance values for deliveries or invoice have been exceeded.

Table 15.3 Important Business Partner Attributes for Rules-Based Security Queries (cont.)

The approval workflow must be activated by a Customizing setting so that the rules-based security queries for the workflow are actually carried out.

15.3.3 User Management

Just as mySAP SRM applications users are treated as business partners with additional attributes, the user management concepts that are based on Transactions SU01 and PFCG can't be used without additional enhancements.

For example, the web-based application should be used for creating internal SAP EBP users, because it directly saves the newly created user as a business partner due to the fact that the user is assigned to a corresponding organizational unit. That would be the ideal way if an administrator created the users. The administrator would also be able to convert existing SU01 users into business partners by using Transaction USERS_GEN. In that case, the attributes are assigned to a corresponding organizational unit using Transaction USERS_GEN, and can then be controlled.

However, the implementation of the information ownership principle is not possible here, which means the best-practice method to be used in this case would be the activation of the Employee Self-Service (ESS). This self-service must also be activated for external business partners such as bidders.

In both cases, the user logs on to the SAP EBP web application and requests a corresponding user ID, including the defined role (for example, employee or bidder). The user can also assign himself or herself to a required organizational unit. This action triggers an approval workflow. For an employee, the responsible manager then receives a request to provide the approval via the workflow. For an external business partner, this request is sent to the responsible purchasing group. The roles can be defined upfront for each user so that it is impossible to assign additional roles at a later stage, and an accumulation of functions can be avoided.

Connecting the SRM server to a central user administration with a corresponding organizational structure according to the mySAP ERP HCM concept is not recommended. The reason for this can be found in the mySAP SRM business partner principle, the additional attributes of which are not mapped in the HCM organizational structure. In this case, a complex conversion of the used HCM infotypes would be necessary.

Alternatively, it is possible to connect the SRM server to a Central User Administration (CUA), but to permit the user maintenance only in the SRM subsystem. The only benefit of this scenario, however, would be that the created mySAP SRM business partners would also be available as SU01 users in the central CUA system. And that's not much of a benefit.

15.4 Technical Security

The mySAP SRM applications are based on the technological SAP NetWeaver components of the GSPS. mySAP SRM contains different predesigned implementation scenarios that can be customized according to specific customer requirements. The technical GSPS components regarding technical risks and controls, which are relevant to those scenarios, also apply to mySAP SRM.

For the self-service procurement, plan-driven procurement, service procurement, and strategic sourcing scenarios, the following GSPS components are relevant:

► Web browser (see Chapter 28)
► SAP ITS (see Chapter 26)
► SAP Web Dispatcher (see Chapter 24)
► SAP Web AS (see Chapter 8)

- ▶ SAP XI (see Chapter 20)
- ▶ SAP BI (see Chapter 12)

For the catalog content management and spend analysis scenarios, the following GSPS components are important:

- ▶ Web browser (see Chapter 28)
- ▶ SAP ITS (see Chapter 26)
- ▶ SAP Web Dispatcher (see Chapter 24)
- ▶ SAP Web AS (see Chapter 8)
- ▶ SAP BI (see Chapter 12)

16 mySAP Supply Chain Management

This chapter describes the mySAP Supply Chain Management Global Security Positioning System (GSPS) component, based on a sample control solution.

16.1 Introduction and Functions

In the SAP world, central planning and control processes are mapped using *mySAP Supply Chain Management* (mySAP SCM). Control measures for the protection of planning, purchasing, production, and stockholding data are processed here. This GSPS component contains essential information on the supply chain of a manufacturing company that must be evaluated and protected. Because the mySAP SCM applications map the foundations for the production processes, which involves a connection between mySAP SCM and other SAP systems, concrete requirements must be considered when evaluating the data and the need for protection.

16.2 Risks and Controls

mySAP SCM processes important information such as planning and production data. The control measures depend on the classification of data and the corresponding need for protection (see Table 16.1).

No.	Classification	Description
1.	Risk potential	Data security: mySAP SCM processes information needed for ensuring a functioning supply chain. This data is of essential importance for maintaining the production processes and must therefore be protected from unauthorized access, modification, delay, and other risks.
	Impact	Unauthorized data access can result in a manipulation of the data, which can severely disturb the production operations and therefore create high extra costs. Securing the undisturbed continuity of those business processes must be a top priority.
	Risk without control(s)	High
	Control(s)	A solid authorization system, including appropriate controls of access rights to mySAP SCM data, functions, and actions is an important measure within the internal risk control system.

Table 16.1 Risks and Controls for mySAP SCM

No.	Classification	Description
	Risk with control(s)	Normal
	Section	16.3

Table 16.1 Risks and Controls for mySAP SCM (cont.)

16.3 Application Security

mySAP SCM generally complies with the authorization concept rules of SAP Web AS ABAP and SAP Web AS J2EE. These concepts are described in more detail in Chapters 8 and 9.

The authorizations for accessing mySAP SCM data and application objects and activities are defined and implemented on the basis of roles. The SAP Profile Generator is one of the main tools used to create roles and authorizations.

SAP provides many predefined roles for mySAP SCM that you can use as templates for your own customized roles. These predefined roles also include the SAP templates for *Advanced Planning and Optimization* (APO). The role concept is supported by some additional authorization solutions. The most important ones are the authorization and filter profiles that are defined in mySAP SCM Customizing, and the *Access Control Lists* (ACLs), which can be used for forecasting and replenishment, for instance.

16.3.1 Authorizations for the iPPE Workbench

For the applications contained in APO and the *Integrated Product and Process Engineering* (iPPE) Workbench, iPPE authorization profiles for master data are created in Customizing. These iPPE authorization profiles are defined in the mySAP SCM Implementation Guide (IMG): **Advanced Planning and Optimization · Master Data · Integrated Product and Process Engineering (iPPE) · Settings for the iPPE Workbench Professional · Define User Profiles for the iPPE Workbench Professional**.

SAP provides standard authorization profiles that can also be used as templates. These profiles include the following:

▶ S_PPEALL
  This authorization profile is used for granting user rights for the iPPE Workbench. This involves authorizations for the entire iPPE Workbench.

▶ S_ASTACT
  This authorization profile is used for granting user rights for process structures within the iPPE Workbench. It involves the *Detail Area* of the iPPE Workbench.

▶ **S_ASTCMP**

This authorization profile is used for granting user rights for product structures within the iPPE Workbench.

▶ **SASTFLO**

This authorization profile is used for granting user rights for line structures within the iPPE Workbench.

The authorizations for the *Navigation Area* in the iPPE Workbench control the model definitions and objects of *Product Lifecycle Management* (PLM). Here the authorizations are maintained via model definitions and the PLM environment.

In contrast to SAP ERP Central Component (ECC), in the iPPE Workbench Professional reports can still be called using the traditional report tree concept. The assignment of reports occurs via iPPE authorization profiles. However, the reports must have been defined for the report trees up front.

16.3.2 Authorizations for Supply Chain Planning

Authorizations for planners—in other words, for the *Supply Chain Planning* application (SCP)—are also defined in Customizing. Responsibilities are defined using the following path: **APO · SCP · Specify the Person (Planner) Responsible**.

16.3.3 Authorizations for Event Management

Information that is used in *SAP Event Management* (SAP EM) is presented in scenarios to which users are assigned. The assignment controls which parameters and conditions are displayed to a user for a specific scenario. This way access to information in SAP EM is controlled.

The assignment occurs in Customizing. For this purpose, authorization profiles with parameters are defined and then assigned to an event handler type, and the users are granted or restricted access to the event handlers. In addition, filter profiles for components of event handlers can be used. The filter profiles are then assigned to the corresponding event handler types, which in turn are assigned to roles. Finally, the role is granted via a user group to the user who is to be authorized (see Figure 16.1).

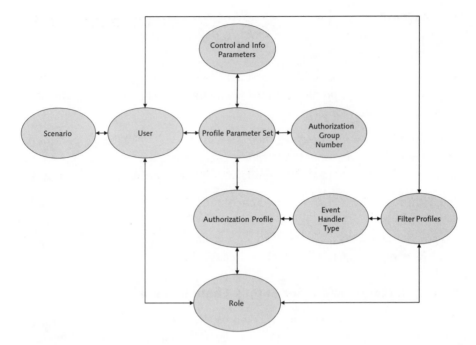

Figure 16.1 Authorizations for mySAP SCM EM

The additional authorization solutions such as ACLs for replenishment applications help install the necessary controls within the complex mySAP SCM solution.

There are, however, some security concerns regarding these solutions, due to the necessity of an RFC connection for a dialog user in the *Available-to-Promise* (ATP) solution, for instance. These solutions must be complemented by technical security measures in order to ensure a comprehensive control system.

16.4 Technical Security

In terms of technical security, the following GSPS components are important for mySAP SCM. In particular, the technical risks and necessary controls of these components should be considered.

▶ SAP Web AS (see Chapter 8)

▶ SAP ITS (see Chapter 26)

▶ SAP GUI (see Chapter 27)

▶ SAP Web Dispatcher (see Chapter 24)

▶ Web browser (see Chapter 28)

▶ SAP BI (see Chapter 12)

17 SAP Strategic Enterprise Management

This chapter describes IT security concepts for the SAP Strategic Enterprise Management Global Security Positioning System (GSPS) component, including its most important transactions and authorization objects.

17.1 Introduction and Functions

SAP Strategic Enterprise Management (SAP SEM) is the strategic solution for analyzing important financial data and other freely selectable business performance indicators. On the basis of the analyses, decisions can be made that keep the company on a secure profitability path. SAP SEM is therefore the functional solution for strategic enterprise management.

SAP SEM enables companies to make faster and more efficient strategic decisions. It is sold in different versions for specific industries, and it can be customized to meet a company's specific requirements. In the following sections, we'll look at the *SAP SEM for Banking* solution, which consists of the following functional areas:

▶ Consolidation and aggregation functions for essential corporate data such as the revenue figures for a specific product by region, or the contribution margin of a particular product.

▶ Financial risk management, which includes an analysis of the investment capital involved compared to the possible revenue that can be achieved. The influence of legal regulations or possible environmental effects can be included in the analysis as well, which, for instance, is a definite requirement for reinsurance transactions.

▶ The Management Cockpit enables excutives to display an overview of important key figures. *Traffic light functions* that provide managers with a clear overview of the company's performance can also be defined here.

▶ A freely definable balanced scorecard can be used to define the most important key figures for measuring company performance. This helps decision-makers tailor their corporate decisions specifically to target weak areas or products of the company.

▶ In addition, a simulation function can be used to project the effects certain decisions will have in future. This simulation can be helpful in the decision-making process.

17.2 Risks and Controls

The security methods and solutions that you choose for SAP SEM are determined by an objective assessment of the requirements and the risk potential of each individual situation. However, different corporate cultures can produce different evaluations of these factors, because SAP SEM processes consolidated enterprise data that is used for making strategic decisions and is therefore exposed to a high risk potential.

Risk evaluation is the central starting point for evaluating security solutions in the SAP environment. The risks that should be evaluated include, for example, the situation whereby the enterprise does not comply with the regulations and guidelines of any relevant industry associations, or statutory regulations and guidelines. Table 17.1 contains a list of the main risks for SAP SEM for Banking.

Note that SAP SEM runs only on SAP Web AS, which is why we don't discuss the technical security risks any further at this stage. In addition, you should note that SAP SEM is based on the ABAP authorization concept, so the controls described in Chapter 9 can be applied to SAP SEM. In particular, the information ownership method described there should be applied as a best-practice method for SAP SEM.

No.	Classification	Description
1.	Risk potential	Inadequate authorization concept.
		Users of SAP SEM are granted authorizations that greatly exceed the actual requirement for information and functionality, because the authorization concept is only used as a means for granting functional authorizations to users, and not as an effective control tool for minimizing risks. With this solution especially, highly sensitive, consolidated enterprise data is processed, the knowledge of which is of extermely high significance, particularly for the competition.
	Impact	Users have greater authorizations than are necessary for their position and the scope of their work. Read and write access to high-risk, consolidated financial data and other enterprise key figures is possible. This is a violation of both internal company requirements and statutory regulations. It creates a situation where process, administrative, and system risks are not controlled. The risk potential is therefore increased rather than minimized. In addition, competitors can take possession of important key figures and use this information to improve their own strategic position.
	Risk without control(s)	Extremely high

Table 17.1 Risks and Controls for SAP SEM

No.	Classification	Description
	Control(s)	The authorization concept has to take into account both organizational and functional requirements, and make administration simpler and more effective. The relevant risks have to be taken into account in the authorization design process, and methods of continuous management have to be integrated into the change management process.
	Risk with control(s)	Normal
	Section	17.3

Table 17.1 Risks and Controls for SAP SEM (cont.)

17.3   Application Security

The authorization concept for SAP SEM is entirely based on the ABAP authorization concept, which is introduced and described in great detail in Chapter 9. Because in SAP SEM a large quantity of data must be imported for analysis from a connected SAP Business Information Warehouse (SAP BW), the authorization concept described in Chapter 12 must also be considered.

17.4   Technical Security

Depending on individual configurations, the following GSPS components may be important in terms of technical security:

▶ SAP Web AS (see Chapter 8)

▶ SAP ITS (see Chapter 26)

▶ SAP GUI (see Chapter 27)

▶ Web browser (see Chapter 28)

▶ SAP BI (see Chapter 12)

18 SAP Solution Manager

This chapter describes IT security concepts for the SAP Solution Manager Global Security Positioning System (GSPS) component. In particular, it focuses on the authorization concept and the cross-system management functions.

18.1 Introduction and Functions

SAP Solution Manager (SAP SolMan) is the central application for implementing, operating, and optimizing a complex SAP NetWeaver system landscape. As shown in Figure 18.1, the term "central" in this context means that the separate SAP system-specific implementation and operation solutions are replaced by SAP SolMan. The big advantage of this is that all customizing settings can be made in only one application. Also, the monitoring of the operation status with regard to available storage space, workload, and so on, which is very important in terms of security, occurs in only one monitoring console. This advantage is obvious, because it enables you to accelerate the implementation of countermeasures, which are needed to stabilize the complex SAP NetWeaver system landscape. In addition, you can stabilize the operating costs since you don't have to create a new implementation and monitoring solution for each SAP NetWeaver system that is added to the landscape. Instead, you can simply integrate those new systems into the existing SAP SolMan.

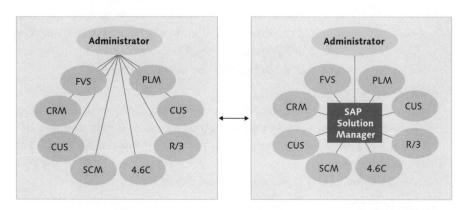

Figure 18.1 Central Concept of SAP Solution Manager

In addition to automated test procedures, SAP SolMan provides a support desk function, since it can also be used as a ticketing solution. A knowledgebase helps support employees find quick and efficient solutions to problems. The knowledgebase can be built step by step during the implementation and execution of the test cycles.

Table 18.1 provides a brief overview of the two different concepts.

Old concept (without SAP Solution Manager)	New concept (with SAP Solution Manager)
Growing number of components	Central point of access
Each new component requires an individual monitoring and management solution	Central monitoring of business processes
Dramatically increasing costs for operation and monitoring	Interrelationships between business applications are taken into account

Table 18.1 System Landscapes with and without SAP Solution Manager

SAP Solution Manager is used in the following scenarios:

▶ **Implementation and Distribution**
This scenario is especially important for the implemenation phase of a new implementation project. SAP SolMan provides complete project management functionality for this scenario, which contains the documentation of a project in addition to project controlling. The automated test run functionality is of great importance in this context as well.

▶ **Support Desk**
Once the implementation phase is finished, SAP SolMan provides a comprehensive support desk functionality. This functionality mainly captures the problems of users and the solution management using a ticketing system. Solutions to problems are found using integrated knowledge management or by forwarding the problems to a support employee at a higher level.

▶ **Monitoring**
The monitoring function can be used at any time to control the current status of the SAP NetWeaver systems that are in use. The status is indicated by traffic lights. In the case of yellow traffic lights, proactive measures can be used to quikly counteract imminent problems to ensure the availability of the SAP NetWeaver systems and hence the business processes.

▶ **Service Delivery**
If problems that arrive at the support desk also require an assignment of on-site personnel (second-level support employees), in order to exchange a hard disk, for example, SAP SolMan can be used to coordinate and control that assignment. All service delivery units connected can therefore be controlled centrally.

▶ **Upgrade**

The import of necessary application and system upgrades for entering a higher release level can be executed centrally using SAP SolMan. This way it is also possible to monitor and trace the release levels of the connected SAP NetWeaver systems centrally.

▶ **Change Request Management**

Change request management or change management is one of the most important *IT Infrastructure Library* (ITIL) processes, as new requirements must first be categorized and evaluated. This must be documented accordingly and be released by the persons responsible for change management. Only when a change request has been released can the necessary test be run, which usually happens fisrt in the development system and then in the QA system before the change is transported into the production system. SAP SolMan supports this entire process.

Figure 18.2 summarizes the entire functional scope of SAP SolMan. You should note that in the future SAP SolMan will continue to play an increasingly important role in complex SAP NetWeaver system landscapes.

Figure 18.2 Functional Areas of SAP Solution Manager

18.2   Risks and Controls

The security methods and solutions that you choose for SAP Solution Manager are determined by an objective assessment of the requirements and the risk potential of each individual situation. Because SAP SolMan can be used to centrally control and monitor a complex SAP NetWeaver system landscape, as well as modify critical technical configurations in all integrated SAP NetWeaver systems, a corresponding comprehensive authorization concept is of enormous importance. However, since SAP SAP Solution Manager provides security functionality such as the proactive system monitoring function, SAP SolMan can also be considered as a control tool for system availability.

The technical security of SAP SolMan is based on the SAP Web AS and SAP GUI GSPS components. Furthermore, SAP SolMan runs within the context of mySAP CRM, which is necessary for the support desk functionality. Table 18.2. lists the main risks for SAP SolMan.

No.	Classification	Description
1.	Risk potential	Inadequate authorization concept.
		Users of SAP SolMan have authorizations that are too extensive for their actual requirements in terms of information and functions. Reason: the authorization concept is used only as a means of assigning functional authorizations and not as an effective instrument for controlling access and minimizing risks. This application, in particular, enables users to set sensitive technical system configurations from a central point.
	Impact	Users have greater authorizations than are necessary for their position and the scope of their work. The access to high-risk, central technical system configuration settings can result in system instabilities, and may even compromise the entire system. Highly sensitive business processes can be affected and this may result in a loss of revenue for the entire company.
	Risk without control(s)	Extremely high
	Control(s)	The authorization concept has to factor both organizational and functional requirements, and make administration simpler and more effective. The relevant risks have to be considered in the authorization design process, and methods of continuous management have to be integrated into the change management process.
	Risk with control(s)	Normal
	Section	18.3

Table 18.2 Risks and Controls for SAP Solution Manager

No.	Classification	Description
2.	Risk potential	No monitoring of the SAP NetWeaver system landscape.
		The technical operation status of a complex SAP NetWeaver system landscape is not monitored centrally. System breakdowns or critical statuses such as system overloads can't be identified.
	Impact	As critical system statuses can't be identified in real time, the availability of the SAP NetWeaver system landscape can't be ensured. Therefore, business processes that must be highly available depending on individual requirements can no longer be ensured. This may lead to an increased loss of revenues. It may also have legal implications, for instance, if a banking application fails and the users affected by this take legal action.
	Risk without control(s)	High
	Control(s)	A complex SAP NetWeaver system landscape must be monitored using SAP SolMan or a similar partner solution. The monitoring function must be configured in such a way that instable system statuses can be identified early so that corresponding countermeasures can be implemented.
	Risk with control(s)	Normal
	Section	18.4
3.	Risk potential	Inadequately configured communication connections.
		Specifically for SAP SolMan, many RFC communication connections to the integrated SAP NetWeaver systems, but also to the SAP OSS system, must be configured. In this context, incorrectly configured RFC connections are a potential risk. If RFC authorizations are too extensive, the risk potential increases even more.
	Impact	Incorrectly configured RFC communication connections can be used to further compromise the system. For example, an RFC system user that has authorizations for all ABAP function groups can be used to create a new dialog user in the target system. That dialog user can be granted a wide range of authorizations and can be used to carry out unauthorized financial transactions.
	Risk without control(s)	Extremely high
	Control(s)	Correct configuration of RFC communication destinations and restriction of RFC system user authorizations.
	Risk with control(s)	Normal
	Section	18.3

Table 18.2 Risks and Controls for SAP Solution Manager (cont.)

18.3   Application Security

The authorization concept for SAP SolMan is entirely based on the ABAP authorization concept that is introduced and described in great detail in Chapter 9. There are no specific additional complements or enhancements available for SAP SolMan such as specific rule-based authorizations, for example. The best-practice method described in Chapter 9 should be adopted for SAP SolMan.

This chapter describes the transactions and authorization objects that are particularly important for SAP SolMan and must be used in order to restrict certain access rights (see Tables 18.3 and 18.4).

Transaction	Description
DMD	Solution Content Repository
DMDDEF	Solution Metadata Repository
DSMOP, DSWP, SOLUTION_MANAGER	SAP Solution Manager
DSWP_WEB, SOLUTION_MANAGER_BSP	SAP Solution Manager (HTML)
SMAP01	Solution Map Object Maintenance
SMSY	Solution Manager System Landscape
SOLAR01	SAP Solution Manager: Business Blueprint
SOLAR01C, SOLAR02	SAP Solution Manager: Configuration
SOLAR_CONF	SAP Solution Manager: Customizing
SOLAR_EVAL	SAP Solution Manager: Evaluation
SOLAR_MIGRATION	Solution Manager Migration
SOLAR_PROJECT_CREATE	Solution Manager Project Creation
SOLAR_TESTPLAN	SAP Solution Manager: Test Plan
SOLMAN_DIRECTORY	Solution Directory
SOLMAN_PROJECT	Solution Manager Project Overview
SOLMAP	Solution Map Maintenance
/SAPTRX/ASC0SD1	Define Solution/Scenario
CRMM_IIA	Interactive Solution Search
ISCB	Define Solution Type
ISCD	Define Solution Categories

Table 18.3 Important Transactions for SAP Solution Manager

Authorization object	Description	Authorization field	Values
AI_SOL_DIR	Controls access to the Solution Manager directory	Activity (ACTVT)	02: Change, modify, delete directory elements
S_SMSYEDIT	Controls the authorization for maintaining the Solution Manager system landscape	Activity (ACTVT)	▶ 01: Create ▶ 02: Change ▶ 03: Display ▶ 06: Delete ▶ 70: Administration (needed to make basic settings; if this authorization is set, the remaining fields are not checked) ▶ D1: Copy
		SMSYETYPE	Type of system attached to SAP SolMan: ▶ SYSTEM: SAP system ▶ COMPUTER: server ▶ DBSYS: database ▶ PRODUCT: product ▶ LOG_CMP: logical components ▶ Other
		SMSYENAME	Name of system attached to SAP SolMan
D_SOLUTION	Controls the access to system data of the system landscape defined in SAP Solution Manager. It can control access to individual customer numbers, installation numbers, and database IDs.	DSWPDCUSNO	Existing customer numbers
		DSWPDINSNO	Existing installation numbers
		DSWPDDBID	Existing database ID
D_SOLM_ACT	Controls the executable actions that are possible within a monitoring configuration (also referred to as a solution)	DSWPSOLACT (Activity)	▶ 00: Display report ▶ 05: Display session ▶ 10: Change session ▶ 12: Delete session ▶ 15: Archive session ▶ 20: Change settings (within a monitoring configuration) ▶ 25: Start service processing

Table 18.4 Important Authorization Objects for SAP Solution Manager

Authorization object	Description	Authorization field	Values
			▶ 30: Create service
			▶ 35: Change global settings
			▶ 40: Create/archive monitoring configuration
			▶ 50: Delete monitoring configuration
D_SOLMANBU	Controls the permitted activities per session type (bundle ID)	DSWPBUNDAC (Action)	▶ 01: Display ▶ 02: Change
		DSWPBUNDLE	Session type ID
D_SOLMAN	Controls the SAP Solution Manager call	Activity (ACTVT)	▶ 16: Start
D_SOL_VIEW	Controls the view that can be displayed in SAP Solution Manager	Solution Manager View	▶ 10: Display Solution Manager settings ▶ 20: Display Solution Manager operations

Table 18.4 Important Authorization Objects for SAP Solution Manager (cont.)

18.4 Technical Security

18.4.1 System Monitoring Function

As noted earlier, SAP SolMan can be used as a central system monitoring and management solution. For this purpose, the systems to be monitored are connected to the SAP SolMan system via the interfaces of the *Computing Center Management System* (CCMS). Figure 18.3 illustrates this relationship.

Within SAP SolMan, traffic light functions are available to the operating personnel. These functions can be used to clearly monitor the operation status on the basis of separately configurable system parameters for the defined monitoring configuration. The central monitoring function enables you to initiate necessary countermeasures for system stabilization in real time, if necessary. The overall availability of the SAP NetWeaver system landscape can therefore be kept at a high level.

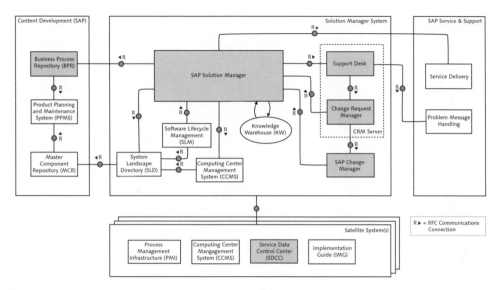

Figure 18.3 Connecting SAP Systems to Be Monitored to SAP Solution Manager

18.4.2 RFC Communication Security

As shown in Figure 18.3, appropriate RFC communication connections must be implemented when setting up a monitoring configuration. In this context, the technical default settings for the SAP Gateway, as well as the authorization restrictions for RFC connections described in Chapter 8, must be considered. Authorizations for the S_RFC authorization object, whose scope is set too widely, can be used to compromise the system if the RFC user has the type "system" or "communication."

18.4.3 Important Additional GSPS Components

The following GSPS components must be considered for the use of SAP Solution Manager:

► SAP Web AS (see Chapter 8)
► SAP ITS (see Chapter 26)
► SAP GUI (see Chapter 27)
► Web browser (see Chapter 28)

19 SAP Enterprise Portal

This chapter explains IT security concepts for SAP Enterprise Portal in the Global Security Positioning System (GSPS) area of server security. The integrative portal concept is discussed in detail.

19.1 Introduction and Functions

Like SAP Web AS, *SAP Enterprise Portal* (SAP EP) plays a critical role in the SAP NetWeaver product strategy. Via a central access point, SAP EP provides important applications and information (for example, documents) to individual employees. In an Internet scenario, business partners can also be directed to various Internet applications of the enterprise via this central access point. To start their applications, employees and business partners only need a web browser to access SAP EP. They no longer need to start every application separately, for example, using SAP GUI. SAP EP controls the entire access to these applications. This is referred to as *people integration*, which is illustrated in Figure 19.1.

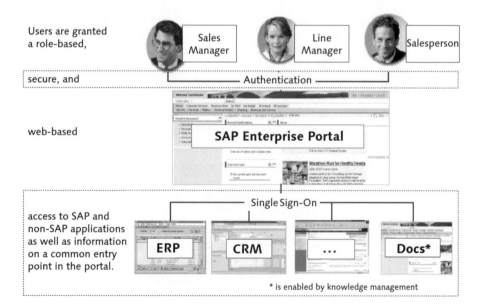

Figure 19.1 People Integration via SAP Enterprise Portal

The authorizations for the applications are controlled using portal roles. Applications are either accessed after an enforced user authentication or anonymously.

Another benefit of SAP EP is the possibility to easily implement a Single Sign-On mechanism for the associated backend applications. Users only need to log on once to SAP EP. SAP EP then takes over any further authentication to the backend applications. In addition to SAP applications, non-SAP applications can also be integrated in SAP EP. Even links to other external resources can be integrated. Additionally, users can customize their content, or they can organize the portal content, like documents, for managing their own know-how. This makes it possible to integrate a knowledge management functionality in the portal.

19.1.1 Technical architecture

SAP EP is based on SAP Web AS J2EE. It is an SAP Application Server that combines with other software components for knowledge management, the Unification Server, and the Connector Framework, to form the SAP Enterprise Portal architecture.

The SAP EP architecture is illustrated in Figure 19.2. Its essential components are:

▶ **Portal server**
The portal server contains the portal's runtime environment, the *portal runtime* (PRT), including the application information that is partially returned by the backend applications (for example, via XML) or other portal content, and which is prepared accordingly for the frontend (web browser) in the Page Builder. The various content is provided to the users in iViews. An iView is the smallest unit for dividing and structuring a portal page.

Portal services comprise the services for managing the iView content. User management (definition of authorizations and roles) via the *User Management Engine* (UME) is significant as well. Another service manages the connections of the individual iViews to the backend applications via the Connector Framework.

Other important services include those that provide the navigation service for the entire portal content, the caching service, the portal content handling service, the URL generation service (for example, via SAP Internet Transaction Server), and the Web service. The latter can be used to access the portal via Web services. In turn, it is also possible to call Web services. The *Portal Content Directory* (PCD) is used to manage the content, that is, all objects (for example, iViews, roles, content, applications, backend applications). PCD sets the portal roles and their accesses to the individual objects and defines the services that can be called.

▶ **Knowledge management**
Knowledge management is an additional component that contains content management, that is, portal content management using administration tools

(for creating iViews, layouts, documents, etc.), and the TREX search and classification engine. TREX is the SAP search engine that creates an index across the
entire portal content and can be used to search the portal content for key-
words or logically related search terms. Users can then store the found documents and information in the portal for their personal knowledge management.

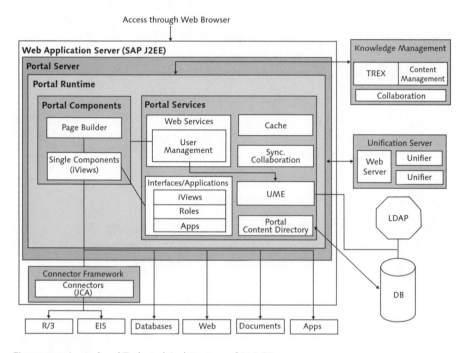

Figure 19.2 Logical and Technical Architecture of SAP EP

▶ **Unification Server**
At the business object level, the Unification Server provides a *Drag&Relate*
functionality. Using this functionality, the user can start a query across several
applications and data sources. For example, the user can simply drag a name to
an author query and will then receive replies for that name from all applications and data sources attached to the portal that are grouped in one view. All
further existing information about a given object can be grouped in this way.

▶ **Connector Framework**
The Connector Framework is based on the standardized *Java Connection Architecture* (JCA). This framework can be used to connect the applications running
in the portal to other backend applications. Connectors for this purpose are
already available (e.g., for R/3 backend applications, JDBC, etc.). Connectors
can also be called via Web services and can be used to connect iViews to the

backend applications. The connectors provide an integration form that is independent of the respective backend application so that the programmer can focus entirely on developing the business logic.

19.1.2 Description of the User Management Engine

In the portal environment, it is crucial to have a basic understanding of the *User Management Engine* (UME), because this architecture service controls all management of users and their authorizations in SAP Enterprise Portal. More sophisticated knowledge of the UME is also important, because many of the technical controls explained are implemented using UME.

Figure 19.3 presents an overview of all architecture services provided by the UME. The central layer provides the *application programming interfaces* based on Java that are required by the SAP EP applications (e.g., Java-based iViews) to perform, for example, the authentication of a user or to maintain the related master data.

These programming interfaces are the following:

▶ **User API**
Using the User API, a portal application can call authentication services for existing users and also validate their authorization.

▶ **User Account API**
The User Account API enables the portal application to create new users, to maintain their master data, and to assign their portal roles, among other things. The User Account API is therefore implemented for management services and, unlike the User API, is not used at runtime.

▶ **Group API**
The Group API can be used to create group definitions. Even at runtime, you can query if a user belongs to a specific group.

▶ **Role API**
The Role API serves for managing the portal roles. It can also be used to assign the portal roles to the users.

The *Persistence Manager* controls the access to user data via the programming interfaces described above. The Persistence Manager performs the task of managing the available storage systems. As persistence storage, the portal database, an external LDAP directory, or SAP Web AS ABAP can be implemented.

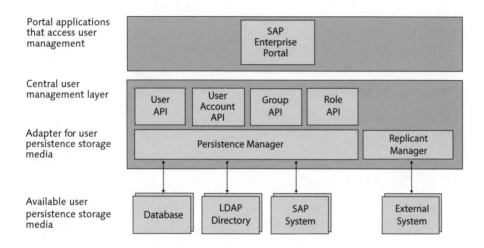

Portal applications that access user management	SAP Enterprise Portal			
Central user management layer	User API	User Account API	Group API	Role API
Adapter for user persistence storage media	Persistence Manager			Replicant Manager
Available user persistence storage media	Database	LDAP Directory	SAP System	External System

Figure 19.3 User Management Engine

The following formats can be used for the database:

▶ Oracle 9.2 or above

▶ Microsoft SQL Server 2000 or above

▶ IBM DB2/UDB

Possible LDAP directories are:

▶ Novell eDirectory

▶ Sun ONE Directory Server

▶ Microsoft Active Directory Server

▶ Siemens DirX

The following SAP system is required:

▶ SAP Web AS 6.20 or above

The Persistence Manager can manage several LDAP directories at a time. You therefore have the option to distribute users among the various storage systems connected to UME, which is particularly important when implementing SAP EP in Internet scenarios. For example, external users can be made persistent in the portal database, and internal users can be made persistent in an LDAP directory. It is also possible to make this division according to user attributes. For example, the assignment of the portal role to the user can be stored in the portal database, and the corresponding master data can be stored in the LDAP directory.

This distribution is controlled via an XML file, the *data source configuration file*, which can be set using the config tool. It is recommended to use one of the UME data source configuration files delivered by SAP. A customized file can be defined only if none of the specified files meets the requirements. The name of the data source configuration file is defined in the following UME property entry:

```
ume.persistence.data_source_configuration=
  dataSourceConfiguration_new.xml
```

The property is `ume.persistence.data_source_configuration`, which in this case is set to the file *dataSourceConfiguration_new.xml*.

Listing 19.1 shows an example of an XML file where regular users are stored in an LDAP directory (CORP_LDAP) and service users are stored in the portal database (PRIVATE_DATASOURCE).

```
<dataSource id="PRIVATE_DATASOURCE"
            className="com.sap.security.core.persistence.
              datasource.imp.DataBasePersistence"
            isReadonly="false"
            isPrimary="true">
    <homeFor>
        <principals>
            <principal type="USER">
<!--
COMMENT: If you set the triple attribute values ($service-
User$,SERVICEUSER_ATTRIBUTE,IS_SERVICEUSER) in a substructure
for the principals (not yet authorized user) of the type "USER"
in your name range, this rule is applied, and the service users
are stored in the PRIVATE_DATASOURCE portal database.
-->
                <nameSpace name="$serviceUser$">
                    <attribute name="SERVICEUSER_ATTRIBUTE">
                        <values>
                            <value>IS_SERVICEUSER</value>
                        </values>
                    </attribute>
                </nameSpace>
            </principal>
        </principals>
    </homeFor>
    <notHomeFor>
```

```
        </notHomeFor>
        ...
</dataSource>

<dataSource id="CORP_LDAP"
            className="com.sap.security.core.persistence.
              datasource.imp.LDAPPersistence"
            isReadonly="false"
            isPrimary="true">
    <homeFor>
        <principals>
            <principal type="USER">
<!--
COMMENT: If no substructure for specific principals of the type
"USER" is defined, except for the "notHomeFor" section, this rule
is applied to all other users. This means that all users except
for those with the service user attribute are stored in the CORP_
LDAP LDAP directory.
-->
            </principal>
        </principals>
    </homeFor>
    <notHomeFor>
        <principals>
            <principal type="USER">
<!--
COMMENT: As explained above, this rule applies if a substructure
exists for principals of the type "USER" and the Serviceuser
attribute.
-->
                <nameSpace name="$serviceUser$">
                    <attribute name="SERVICEUSER_ATTRIBUTE">
                        <values>
                            <value>IS_SERVICEUSER</value>
                        </values>
                    </attribute>
                </nameSpace>
            </principal>
        </principals>
```

```
</notHomeFor>
    . . .
</dataSource>
```

Listing 19.1 Example of the dataSourceConfiguration_new.xml File

The *Replication Manager* is responsible for providing a replication service via XML with additional external applications. Therefore legacy SAP systems like SAP R/3 4.6D up to SAP Web AS 6.10 can be supported, for example.

19.2 Risks and Controls

In this section, we will use a simplified version of the proposed risk analysis methodology described in Chapter 2 to identify the main security risks and the necessary controls (see Table 19.1). The controls are then discussed in more detail in the following sections and illustrated using examples.

No.	Classification	Description
1.	Risk potential	Authorization concept missing or faulty. Due to an inadequate assignment of rights, users gain access to information and applications in SAP Enterprise Portal for which they have no authorization.
	Impact	Due to their authorizations, users are able to view or even change confidential business documents. This enables them to perform fraudulent acts or other activities that jeopardize the business.
	Risk without control(s)	Extremely high
	Control(s)	Portal roles are predefined and assigned the corresponding authorizations. Portal roles enable users to access only specific applications and information.
	Risk with control(s)	Normal
	Section	19.3.1
2.	Risk potential	No information ownership principle. Owners of business processes cannot determine or approve the assignment of portal roles that enable other employees to access their information and applications.

Table 19.1 Risks and Controls for SAP Enterprise Portal

No.	Classification	Description
	Impact	Central administrators assign portal roles and the associated authorizations for business process information without the approval of the business process owner. Because of this, authorization accumulations can occur, or the assigned authorizations can no longer be validated due to a lack of transparency. Users therefore gain access to information for which they are not authorized.
	Risk without control(s)	Extremely high
	Control(s)	A segregation of functions when assigning portal roles is achieved using the delegated administration by involving the information owner (usually the owner of the business process).
	Risk with control(s)	Normal
	Section	19.3.2
3.	Risk potential	No holistic authorization concept between SAP EP and the backend. Users have incongruent roles in the portal and the corresponding backend applications, and therefore have either too little or too much authorization.
	Impact	Due to excessive authorization, users are able to access information or applications for which they are not authorized. Therefore, they have the possibility to manipulate information and to perform fraudulent activities. Additionally, it is likely that they cannot perform their tasks due to insufficient authorization and are therefore not productive.
	Risk without control(s)	High
	Control(s)	Portal roles are synchronized and reconciled with the respective backend applications. For this purpose, portal roles can be downloaded into the bakkend applications, or the roles can be uploaded to the portal. However, this only applies if the bakkend applications are SAP systems.
	Risk with control(s)	Normal
	Section	19.3.3
4.	Risk potential	No approval process for portal content. There is no approval process when uploading and implementing new portal content if SAP EP is used in an Internet scenario.
	Impact	In an Internet scenario, incorrect portal content is published, which damages the organization's external presentation and reputation. Eventually, this may result in a loss of sales.

Table 19.1 Risks and Controls for SAP Enterprise Portal (cont.)

No.	Classification	Description
	Risk without control(s)	High
	Control(s)	An appropriate workflow needs to be established that ensures that portal content is checked before it is published.
	Risk with control(s)	Normal
	Section	19.3.4
5.	Risk potential	No central user persistence storage location. Master data is stored in several different user persistence storage locations. In addition to this, there is no unified enterprise-wide employee identifier. Therefore, the master data storage concept contains redundancy, and the data is inconsistent.
	Impact	Inconsistent user master data causes a large amount of redundancy, not to mention a lack of transparency. Therefore, when changes need to be made (for example, if an employee leaves the enterprise), user accounts are not managed in an appropriate manner. The result may be the existence of user accounts with excessive authorizations, which could be exploited by other unauthorized users. There are also the additional administrative costs of maintaining redundant user accounts.
	Risk without control(s)	Extremely high
	Control(s)	Connect SAP Enterprise Portal to a central LDAP directory that contains the master data of all users in one central location. Alternatively, SAP EP can also be connected to an existing SAP backend system that is then used as the main user persistence storage location.
	Risk with control(s)	Normal
	Section	19.4.1
6.	Risk potential	Passwords that are too numerous and too simple. Every backend application has its own password. Users need to memorize these different passwords, so they often choose simple or even structured passwords, like names of months. In the extreme case, passwords are jotted down somewhere near the desktop.
	Impact	An unauthorized user can easily take on another identity and gain more application rights to effect unauthorized and fraudulent transactions.
	Risk without control(s)	Extremely high

Table 19.1 Risks and Controls for SAP Enterprise Portal (cont.)

No.	Classification	Description
	Control(s)	Using SAP EP, a Single Sign-On mechanism is established based on SAP logon tickets. The user then only has one user name and one password for all applications connected to SAP Enterprise Portal. Additionally, there needs to be a regulation that passwords are not to be written down on notes close to the desktop.
	Risk with control(s)	Normal
	Section	19.4.2
7.	Risk potential	Passwords that are too numerous and too simple.
		Every backend application has its own password. Users need to memorize these different passwords, so they often choose simple or even structured passwords, like names of months. In the extreme case, passwords are jotted down somewhere near the desktop.
	Impact	An unauthorized internal user can easily take on another identity and gain more application rights to effect unauthorized and fraudulent transactions.
	Risk without control(s)	Extremely high
	Control(s)	Using SAP EP, a Single Sign-On mechanism is established based on an external authentication mechanism (Windows authentication) for the Windows system. Users then only need to log on to their Windows accounts on their desktops to access all applications connected to SAP EP.
	Risk with control(s)	Normal
	Section	19.4.3
8.	Risk potential	Passwords that are too numerous and too simple.
		Every backend application has its own password. Users need to memorize these different passwords so they often choose simple or even structured passwords, like names of months. In the extreme case, passwords are jotted down somewhere near the desktop.
	Impact	An unauthorized internal user can easily take on another identity and gain more application rights to effect unauthorized and fraudulent transactions.
	Risk without control(s)	Extremely high
	Control(s)	Using SAP EP, a Single Sign-On mechanism is established based on person-related digital certificates for the individual users. Users are then always authenticated to the portal and its associated applications using their certificates.

Table 19.1 Risks and Controls for SAP Enterprise Portal (cont.)

No.	Classification	Description
	Risk with control(s)	Normal
	Section	19.4.4
9.	Risk potential	Misconfigured anonymous access.
		The portal is misconfigured for anonymous access so that anonymous users can access confidential information.
	Impact	Anonymous users can view or manipulate information for which they are not authorized. Therefore, confidential information is released to the public, which can damage the company's reputation and even result in financial losses.
	Risk without control(s)	Extremely high
	Control(s)	Correct configuration of the portal for anonymous users.
	Risk with control(s)	Normal
	Section	19.4.5
10.	Risk potential	Misconfigured portal.
		SAP EP has been misconfigured for the initial configuration.
	Impact	Due to a misconfiguration of SAP Enterprise Portal, a directory browsing of SAP EP might be enabled, for example. Unauthorized content, like exploits, can then be uploaded to SAP Enterprise Portal. Additionally, it might be possible to gain administrative rights.
	Risk without control(s)	Extremely high
	Control(s)	Adhere to SAP Note 606733, deactivating services that are not required.
	Risk with control(s)	Normal
	Section	19.4.6
11.	Risk potential	Circumventing authentication and authorization mechanisms of SAP EP.
		SAP EP services can be accessed directly, circumventing authentication and authorization, by calling the appropriate service URL.
	Impact	By circumventing the authentication and authorization mechanism of SAP EP, confidential information can be viewed or manipulated.
	Risk without control(s)	Extremely high

Table 19.1 Risks and Controls for SAP Enterprise Portal (cont.)

No.	Classification	Description
	Control(s)	Set up security zones for SAP EP content so that it cannot be called directly by entering the URL.
	Risk with control(s)	Normal
	Section	19.4.7
12.	Risk potential	No network strategy. At the network level, there is no sufficient security for the portal due to the fact that the network is not divided into trustworthy and untrustworthy areas using firewalls.
	Impact	If a firewall configuration is not used, the security of SAP Enterprise Portal at the network level is inadequate, and any weak points that there may be in the system can be exploited at the operating system level. This can allow system attackers to obtain administrator authorizations. The portal can therefore be compromised. The final result may be unauthorized manipulation of data or unauthorized execution of financial transactions.
	Risk without control(s)	Extremely high
	Control(s)	Secure the portal by securing the network. Divide the network segments into less protected areas and trustworthy zones. Do this by appropriately configuring and setting up network-based firewalls.
	Risk with control(s)	Normal
	Section	19.4.8
13.	Risk potential	External attacks on the application. On the application side, the entries transferred from the client at the application level (e.g., URL parameters, form field entries, etc.), are not sufficiently checked. The following attacks can therefore be successful at application level: Stealth commanding: changing transfer parameters in order to obtain a different application status or to modify price information Cookie poisoning and token analysis: enables the hacker to carry out session hijacking Buffer overflow: enables a denial-of-service attack Cross-site scripting: enables the hacker to divert the user to a compromised site
	Impact	Because of inadequate checking of input parameters the application is compromised, and therefore unauthorized users can obtain advanced permissions at the application level. This also means that backend applications might be attacked and that data theft or modifications can take place.

Table 19.1 Risks and Controls for SAP Enterprise Portal (cont.)

No.	Classification	Description
	Risk without control(s)	Extremely high
	Control(s)	Transfer parameters and input fields have to be checked for plausibility and correctness on the server side. It is also recommended that you introduce an application-level firewall. This is particularly relevant for self-developed applications that are to be integrated into the portal.
	Risk with control(s)	Normal
	Section	19.4.9
14.	Risk potential	Unencrypted access. The connection between the frontend (browser) and portal server is unencrypted. Further internal communication channels are unencrypted as well.
	Impact	If a Single Sign-On configuration was implemented in SAP EP by using SAP logon tickets, the session of another user can be copied by "sniffing" and adopting the cookie. Additionally, a *man-in-the-middle attack* is possible, where important business information is accessed by unauthorized persons and can be manipulated by them. Financial losses can be very high for the organization.
	Risk without control(s)	Extremely high
	Control(s)	The communication between frontend and SAP EP and other communication channels is encrypted via SSL.
	Risk with control(s)	Normal
	Section	19.4.10
15.	Risk potential	No virus scan when uploading documents. When uploading documents or other attachments from the Internet to SAP EP, the attachments are not scanned for potential computer viruses or other exploits.
	Impact	An unidentified virus can spread through SAP EP to other systems of the organization and potentially compromise all IT systems of the organization. This can result in substantial damage to the organization due to downtime and recovery of the IT systems. There might also be legal consequences for the organization if the portal turns out to be a "cesspool of viruses."
	Risk without control(s)	Extremely high

Table 19.1 Risks and Controls for SAP Enterprise Portal (cont.)

No.	Classification	Description
	Control(s)	Implement an antivirus scan when uploading attachments to the document via knowledge management. The attachment will then be discarded if it contains potential viruses and will not be posted on the portal server. This scenario is particularly relevant for recruiting portals where attached résumé documents need to be scanned for existing computer viruses or macros.
	Risk with control(s)	Normal
	Section	19.4.11

Table 19.1 Risks and Controls for SAP Enterprise Portal (cont.)

19.3 Application Security

19.3.1 Structure and Design of Portal Roles

Structure of Portal Roles

The structure of SAP portal roles is very different from ABAP-based roles that are traditionally used in most applications (e.g., FI, CO, MM, etc.) in the SAP environment. The main difference is that ABAP-based roles specifically define the access to transactions and also the authorization range of a role via authorization fields. For example, a role specifies that a user may start the "Create material" transaction and create materials for a specific company code. See Section 9.3 for more details on this matter.

Portal roles do not specify the access to individual transactions in an SAP system, but the access to individual objects that are available in a portal. Basically, these are the following objects:

▶ iViews
An iView is an extract from the complete page of a portal. It can either present pure information or access to a specific functionality. An iView can also store the call of a backend application and link it directly to the start of a specific transaction in an SAP system. This is the main purpose of an iView. An iView is the smallest unit in SAP EP.

▶ Worksets
A workset groups various iViews in a logical navigation structure according to the respective business aspect. This means that all iViews concerning "Controlling" are grouped in one workset. Therefore, a workset is a navigation structure below the portal role.

▶ **Pages**
A portal page specifies the visual arrangement of different iViews; it defines the layout. A page can consist of one single iView. It can also be assigned to a workset.

The navigation structure at the highest level is the portal role. It comprises worksets that can, in turn, contain pages and iViews. This structure is shown in Figure 19.4.

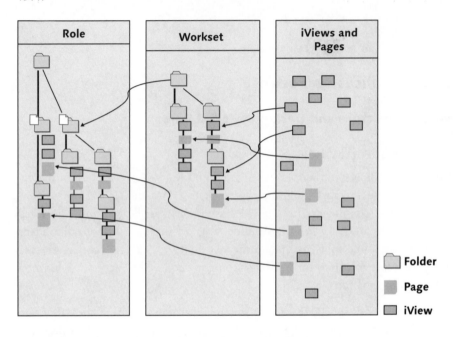

Figure 19.4 Portal Role Defines Navigation Structure in SAP Enterprise Portal

The example in Figure 19.5 shows the **Corporate Home** workset, which exists in the **Administrator** role. The first level of the navigation structure—in this case, the **Corporate Home** workset—always goes to the top portal navigation row of the mandatory and predefined top-level iView. The second level, **About Us** in this example, always defines the second portal navigation row of the predefined top-level iView. The third level goes to the detailed navigation iView. In this example, the pages **About Us** and **Corporate Index** are on the third level and contain more iViews.

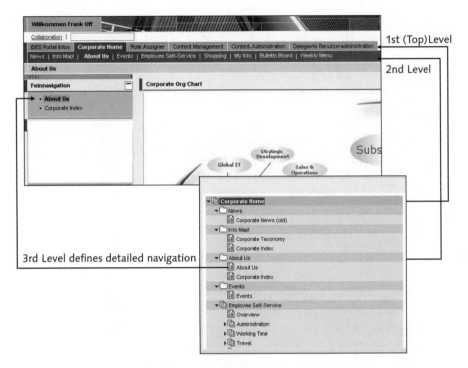

Figure 19.5 The Portal Role During Runtime ("Corporate Home" Workset)

In summary, portal roles can be described as follows:

▶ A portal role defines a collective folder for several worksets, pages, and iViews that are to be accessed by the role.

▶ Portal roles are grouped according to the individual job roles of the positions existing in the enterprise.

▶ A portal role defines the technical navigation structure of a user in SAP Enterprise Portal. The entire navigation structure of a user is defined by the sum of all portal roles assigned to it.

▶ Portal roles can be directly assigned to individual users or user groups.

Technically, the roles are administered in the *Portal Content Directory* (PCD) that is located in the **Content Administration** workset. Using the Role Editor, the roles can be defined in a dedicated directory within a content area. Figure 19.6 shows the **Standard User with Hometab** sample portal role. This portal role contains the **Home** workset, which includes various iViews like the **Outlook Web Access** and **Universal Worklist** application calls. The **Home** workset also contains other worksets, such as **Shopping** and **Employee Self-Service,** which are shown on the second top-level navigation when the role is executed.

Figure 19.6 Sample Portal Role ("Standard User with Hometab")

These objects can be administered using the Role Editor, and the hierarchy of the worksets, pages, and so on can be changed. For example, if more iViews or pages are to be added to the role, you need to navigate to this object in the PCD and right-click to select **Add to Role**. You can then insert the new object as a delta link or as a copy. The delta link has the advantage that changes to the original object, for example, the added iView, are propagated to the portal role; the object properties can be inherited accordingly. If you want to prevent this, you can also dissolve inheritances. The Role Editor can also be used to edit Access Control Lists (ACLs) and other properties. Additionally, you can define worksets of the second level as an entry point so that they are displayed in the first row of the top-level navigation.

Authorizations for Portal Roles

An important difference between ABAP roles and portal roles is that in the portal, no authorizations are defined for the backend application itself. This must still be done within the backend applications (for example, mySAP ERP).

In the portal, however, access to the individual objects (portal roles, worksets, pages, iViews) is defined via ACLs. There are three authorizations for the objects:

▶ **Administrator**
This authorization controls the administration of the portal objects at administration time.

▶ **End User**
This authorization controls the call of an object at runtime if the object is executed in the runtime environment of SAP EP. This does not apply, for example,

if the iView starts a transaction on a backend application, because in this case, only a redirect takes place.

▶ **Role Assigner**

This authorization controls the right to assign a portal role to another user. It therefore only exists for objects of the portal role type and for PCD directories that pass the authorizations on to the objects contained therein.

For the ACL administrator, there are six authorization levels for administering the objects, which are listed in Table 19.2.

	Description		
ACL definition	**Create**	**Delete**	**Edit**
None	The directory of the objects and the objects themselves are not visible in the PCD. This setting only makes sense for pure runtime roles for which the end-user right must be activated.	The directory of the objects and the objects themselves are not visible in the PCD.	The directory of the objects and the objects themselves are not visible in the PCD.
Read	The directory of the objects and the objects themselves are visible in the PCD. New objects can be created as an instance of an existing object, as a delta link.	The directory of the objects and the objects themselves are visible in the PCD. Objects cannot be deleted.	The directory of the objects and the objects themselves are visible in the PCD. Objects cannot be edited.
Write	This ACL selection only applies to directories in the PCD and not to objects. A role that has write authorization for a directory can create new objects in that directory.	This ACL selection only applies to directories in the PCD and not to objects. Objects cannot be deleted, but directories can.	This ACL selection only applies to directories in the PCD and not to objects. Objects cannot be edited.
Read/write	The directory of the objects and the objects themselves are visible in the PCD. New objects can be created as an instance of an existing object, as a delta link.	The directory of the objects and the objects themselves are visible in the PCD. Only the newly created inferior objects of an existing superior object can be deleted.	The directory of the objects and the objects themselves are visible in the PCD. Only object properties and delta links[1] can be edited.

Table 19.2 ACL Definition "Administrator" for the Design Phase of Portal Objects

---

1 New objects that are created on the basis of template objects are only derived from the original. This derivation is referred to as a delta link.

	Description		
ACL definition	Create	Delete	Edit
Full access	The directory of the objects and the objects themselves are visible in the PCD. New objects can be created as an instance of an existing object, as a delta link.	The directory of the objects and the objects themselves are visible in the PCD. All objects can be deleted.	The directory of the objects and the objects themselves are visible in the PCD. Only object properties and delta links can be edited.
Owner	The directory of the objects and the objects themselves are visible in the PCD. New objects can be created at any time.	The directory of the objects and the objects themselves are visible in the PDC. All objects can be deleted.	The directory of the objects and the objects themselves are visible in the PCD. All object properties, including authorizations, can be edited.

Table 19.2 ACL Definition "Administrator" for the Design Phase of Portal Objects (cont.)

At runtime, only the **End User** ACL is checked. It can take on two values: possible or not possible. At runtime, when the user is logged on to the portal, the portal object contained in the portal role can be displayed accordingly. For customizing the layout, the user can only use those objects that have an authorization specified in the **End User** ACL. Direct access to the portal object via the web browser URL is possible only if the **End User** ACL has been set for the security zone as well (see Section 19.4). However, the iView execution restriction using the ACL only works if the called application is executed in the runtime environment of SAP EP and if it is therefore a Java application. For iViews only starting a backend application, this access protection does not work. For this purpose, the authorizations in the backend application must be set properly.

The **Role Assigner** ACL only exists for the portal role object or can only be defined for PCD directories that pass their authorizations on to the portal roles contained therein via inheritance. The **Role Assigner** ACL can also take on only two values: set or not set. A role possessing this ACL is authorized to assign this role to other users. This means that delegated user management is feasible.

Figure 19.7 summarizes the relationship of portal roles, their assignment to users or user groups, and the (still necessary) specification of authorizations in the backend applications (SAP Web AS ABAP authorizations).

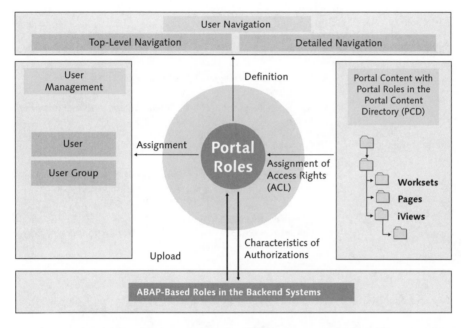

Figure 19.7 Relationship Between Portal Roles and Authorizations in the Backend Applications

In the *Portal Content Directory* (PCD), the portal roles are defined with the existing navigation structures via the workset, page, and iView portal objects. For access control, there are three Access Control Lists for every object for the design phase and for runtime. Within the backend applications, the authorizations are still specified if an iView calls a backend application, for example, from mySAP ERP. You have the option to upload roles from the backend applications and vice versa. The sum of all portal roles assigned to a user defines the user's complete navigation structure.

19.3.2 Delegated User Administration for Portal Roles by Involving the Information Owners

SAP Enterprise Portal is delivered with standard roles that enable delegation, or better distribution, of tasks. Task distribution can be observed in the areas of system, content, and user administration. For this purpose, SAP provides the **Super-administrator**, **Content Administrator**, **System Administrator**, and **User Administrator** standard portal roles. Table 19.3 provides an overview of these portal roles.

Portal role	Description
Superadministrator	This portal role is assigned to the initial "SAP*" user and enables the following: ▶ Full access, including all rights for all objects in the Portal Content Directory ▶ Full access to all tools of the content, system, and user administrators
Content Administrator	This portal role enables access to the following portal tools and content: ▶ Content administration (maintenance of portal content), including the option to define portal roles, worksets, pages, and iViews ▶ Editors for maintaining portal content, such as the Permissions Editor (maintenance of authorizations, ACLs) and Property Editor (maintenance of object properties) ▶ All directories of the PCD if the ACLs have been defined accordingly
System Administrator	This portal role enables access to the following portal tools and content: ▶ System administration, such as system configurator, transports, authorizations, monitoring, support, and portal display ▶ All directories of the PCD if the ACLs have been defined accordingly
User Administrator	This portal role enables access to the following portal tools and content: ▶ All user management tools for creating new users, assigning roles to the users, administering the *user mapping* (mapping of the portal user name to potentially deviating user IDs in back-end applications), user replication with external directories, group administration, and more

Table 19.3 Standard Administration Roles

Standard administration roles can be fine-tuned using authorization control and can therefore be adapted to specific requirements. The significant segregation of functions for defining and assigning portal roles can be achieved in this way.

In terms of the information ownership principle that has been introduced for the management of ABAP roles and ABAP users already, the portal environment provides the option of delegated user administration. It can be set up so that there is still one ultimately responsible user administrator who has the authorization to perform all user management, but who is supported by delegated user administrators.

These delegated user administrators can be specified so that they are only authorized to issue the assignment of users from one subsidiary or department to a portal role. The delegated user administrators need to belong to the same subsidiary or department.

The following technical steps must be carried out to establish delegated user administration for the portal:

1. Define the necessary subsidiaries or departments to which the users can belong. This is done in the config tool for the J2EE Engine underlying the portal. For this purpose, the following entry must be added to the `sapum.properties` property (for example, with the sales, marketing, and development departments):

   `ume.tpd.companies=Sales,Marketing,Development`

   Alternatively, you can import a list of subsidiaries and departments from a partner directory on a backend system into the portal. This option is not discussed here in detail because it depends on the type of directory and on the backend system itself.

2. Set the `Check ACL` parameter for the `com.sap.portal.roleAssignment` iView to **True**.

3. Determine one or several delegated user administrators per company, department, and so on. The user administrator in charge does this by assigning the following portal role to these administrators: **Delegated User Admin**, which can be found in the following PCD directory: *pcd:portal_content/administrator/user_admin/delegated_user_admin_role*.

4. Assign the portal users to a company, department, and so on using the `Org_ID` attribute. This can be done by the user administrator in charge. The following possibilities are available:

   ▶ Use the user administration tool in the portal

   ▶ Use the import function in the portal for inviting users from a directory or a file, and so forth. In this case, the `Org_ID` needs to be defined.

As soon as these steps have been completed, the delegated user administrator can create new users for the respective subsidiary or department and assign portal roles for which the **Role Assigner** authorization has been set.

The delegated user administration can be associated with the self-registration of users with the portal. If a user is to be admitted during the self-registration as a proper portal user by the user administrator responsible for a specific subsidiary, the following parameter must be defined for the portal in the config tool:

```
ume.logon.selfreg=TRUE
ume.admin.selfreg_company=TRUE
```

Additionally, all admissible subsidiaries or departments must be defined. If this is the case, the delegated user administrator receives a notification about the admittance of the user if the user specified his or her company during the registration process. If this is not the case, the self-registered user retains his or her guest status.

Please note that the term "company" can also be interpreted so that this concept is built according to your own organizational structure, and the responsibility of approval can be delegated to the individual departments. Unfortunately, true information ownership is not feasible because the administration of portal roles cannot yet be assigned to the individual subsidiaries or departments.

19.3.3 Synchronization of Portal Roles with the ABAP Roles of SAP Backend Applications

Portal roles and ABAP roles in the SAP backend applications can be synchronized. For this purpose, SAP EP allows you to upload ABAP roles or to import portal roles into the backend applications. However, only the relevant transactions and MiniApps can be uploaded, but not the actual ABAP authorizations that are defined in the authorization objects and profiles. Still, these options are very important, particularly in an SAP application environment, because SAP EP is becoming increasingly important as a central component, but it must be synchronized with the backend applications. For this reason, both possibilities should be considered.

Uploading ABAP Roles in SAP Enterprise Portal

In the first step, let's look at how ABAP roles are uploaded from the SAP backend applications. The following conversion rules are applied:

▶ Simple ABAP roles are migrated as portal roles (or as worksets) to the portal. Simple ABAP roles are stored in the Portal Content Directory as portal roles or worksets using the corresponding menu path.

▶ Composite ABAP roles are created either as portal roles or as worksets in the PCD using the corresponding menu path. The simple ABAP roles contained in the composite role are migrated as well. The menus of the simple ABAP roles are integrated in the main menu of the migrated composite role.

▶ MiniApps are migrated as iViews.

▶ In addition to the migration of ABAP roles, all services containing simple roles and composite roles (e.g., transactions, MiniApps, URLs) are migrated as well. This means that all transactions, MiniApps, URLs, and so on that were contained in the "old" ABAP role are available as portal content objects after migration and can be assigned to more portal roles. The transactions contained in the ABAP roles are automatically migrated to iViews that include the transaction call via the default SAP GUI (either SAP GUI for Windows, SAP GUI for Java, or SAP GUI for HTML). These are stored in the PCD under the *Migrated Content* path.

▶ Even the existing assignment of roles to the users in the backend applications can be migrated. However, this only works if the users exist under the same user ID in both the portal and the backend application.

▶ The authorizations existing in the backend applications due to authorization objects and profiles are not migrated. Eventually, this means that the authorizations for the backend applications cannot be specified via SAP EP. Therefore, this specification of authorizations must remain within the respective backend applications.

▶ Derived ABAP roles are not migrated, because they do not differ from the template ABAP roles with regard to their functions, and authorizations are not migrated.

Figure 19.8 summarizes the migration of an ABAP role to a portal role during the upload process.

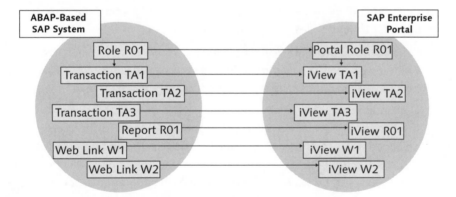

Figure 19.8 Migration of ABAP Roles to SAP EP

However, the following restrictions or notes need to be considered for this functionality:

▶ Simple ABAP roles and composite roles do not have pages that define the layout of the arrangement of the migrated iViews. These pages must be created (e.g., using templates) and assigned to the migrated portal roles. However, this is not mandatory but simply improves the layout.

- The role hierarchy and navigation structure must be adapted. The role menus of the migrated ABAP roles correspond to the menus of an ABAP-based SAP backend application that normally has a deep navigation structure with many hierarchical levels. Therefore, removing superfluous navigation levels is recommended.

- The top navigation level needs to be validated as well because it often contains 10 or more entries. A one-to-one migration would mean that in the portal, the first navigation row in the top-level iView (in the portal header) would be overloaded.

- Often you need to consider whether it is more advantageous to migrate ABAP roles to worksets and not directly to portal roles, which, in turn, can be combined more easily to design self-developed portal roles.

- It is also often recommendable to only migrate single services, like a transaction, for example, instead of a complete (often complex) role. Transactions, and thus iViews, can therefore be grouped in a simpler and more structured way to form new portal roles.

Here is a short description of the uploading procedure:

1. The functionality for uploading the ABAP roles from a backend application can be found in SAP EP under the following menu path: **System Administration · Transport · Upload Roles**

2. In this menu, you need to select a backend application. After selection, a list of available ABAP roles that can be uploaded is displayed. After completing this selection, you can choose the following options in the next screen:

   - **Upload user mapping**
     If this option is set, the assignment of the ABAP roles to the users is also uploaded apart from the ABAP roles themselves. This option only works if the user IDs in the portal and in the backend application are identical. This can be achieved by selecting the ABAP backend application as the user persistence storage location for the portal.

   - **Upload included services**
     If this option is set, not only the role structure is uploaded, but also the transactions, URLs, and so on contained therein. These are created as new objects in the PCD.

   - **Select first folder level as entry point**
     If this option is set, all top navigation levels of an ABAP role structure are specified in the portal role as entry points in the portal main navigation row. However, you need to be careful because the top portal navigation row can quickly be overloaded. This option should therefore not be set.

► **Convert roles to worksets**
  If this option is set, ABAP roles are not directly converted to portal roles, but rather to worksets. These worksets can then be further processed at a later stage and grouped to form a customized portal role.

3. After selecting these options, you can start the procedure via the **Upload** button. After uploading, the migrated portal roles can be further processed in the PCD like any other portal role. The roles are stored in the following PCD directory: **Portal Content · Migrated Content · SAP Component System · Roles · Systems** (system ID plus client of the SAP backend application). The name of the portal role contains the role description of the SAP backend application.

After the upload of the ABAP roles has been completed, the roles can be supplemented with existing predefined SAP business packages. If the uploaded ABAP roles are integrated as delta links into the existing portal roles of the business packages, these are renewed automatically when the ABAP roles are uploaded again at a later stage. This enables consistent portal role maintenance between SAP EP and backend applications.

Possibility of Distributing Portal Roles in the SAP Backend Applications

In addition to uploading existing ABAP roles to SAP EP, you also have the option of distributing portal roles to the associated SAP backend applications. When distributing portal roles to the backend applications, the following must be considered:

► During the distribution, only those iViews that contain transactions, MiniApps, and non-transactional services are taken into account. All other objects, such as documents or links, are not distributed. Non-transactional services include iViews that call backend applications using BAPIs and that can display the results of these backend applications in SAP EP.

► Additionally, the assignments of users to portal roles are optionally distributed to the backend applications as well. In contrast to the uploading functionality, however, only those users that do not exist in the backend applications are newly created. Still, you should take care that the user IDs in SAP EP and in the backend application are the same. If this is not the case, the SAP EP user mapping functionality must be used. Additionally, the user assignment to roles must be adjusted manually using Transaction WP3R.

The role distribution to the backend applications is illustrated once more in Figure 19.9. In this example, Transactions T1, T2, and T6, which are called in the "System 1" backend application via the appropriate iViews, are distributed to the backend application as the ABAP role **A_1**. Using Transaction WP3R, this ABAP role can then be processed, and the authorization objects can be specified accordingly. This ABAP role **A_1** can also be copied to ABAP role **A_2**. This role can then be defined with different authorization values. The assignment of ABAP roles to the users can also be performed using Transaction WP3R. The same applies to Transactions T3, T4, T5, or, respectively, to iViews C, D, and E.

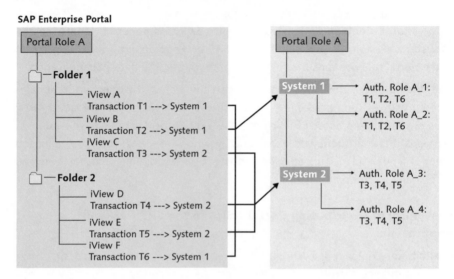

Figure 19.9 Distribution of iViews to the Corresponding SAP Backend Applications

As mentioned above, the ABAP roles can be implemented in the ABAP authorizations using Transaction WP3R after the portal roles have been distributed to the backend applications. Transaction PFCG cannot be used for this purpose.

These maintenance steps should be regarded in more detail:

1. In the first step, the desired portal roles need to be distributed to the corresponding backend applications. For this purpose, you need to navigate to the application **System Administration · Permissions · SAP Authorizations** in SAP EP. There you will find the portal roles that can be distributed. The roles to be distributed are simply selected.

2. In the next step, you need to select the target system to which the roles are to be distributed. As shown in Figure 19.9, only those iViews or transactions, respectively, are distributed from the portal role to the relevant backend application that can be executed there.

3. In the next step, the portal roles with the appropriate name are distributed to the backend application.

4. In the backend system, the authorizations for the ported portal roles can now be maintained using Transaction WP3R. At first, the migrated portal roles themselves need to be maintained. In the initial screen, you need to select the first option, **Maintain authorization roles,** with the corresponding ported portal role.

5. In the next step, the authorizations can be specified as shown in Figure 19.10.

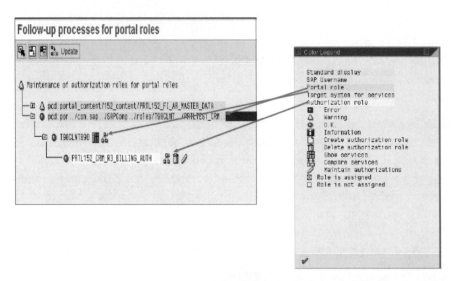

Figure 19.10 Maintenance of Authorizations of Distributed Portal Roles Using Transaction WP3R

6. To be able to assign the distributed ABAP roles to the users, this assignment must once again be distributed in the portal. For this purpose, navigate to **System Administration · Permissions · SAP Authorizations** and go to the **Transfer User Assignment** tab. For portal roles that have already been distributed, you can distribute the respective assignment of users to the backend applications as well.

7. After distributing the users to the backend applications, the second option in Transaction WP3R, **Assign authorization roles to users,** needs to be selected. With this option, the distributed portal roles can be assigned to the selected user.

Selection of the Primary System: SAP EP or Backend Applications

For synchronizing the business roles between SAP EP and the backend applications, you must select a primary system. In this regard, you should consider the following aspects:

- If SAP EP is exclusively used for managing documents or other company-internal content, and if the portal roles for calling the backend applications are rather simple, you should use SAP EP as the primary role design system. However, make sure that the ABAP authorization structure does not need to be specified in a very complex manner with many company codes, plants, and so on, because in that case, the maintenance effort using Transaction WP3R would be very high.

- If the access to backend applications is managed primarily by using SAP EP, you should use the backend applications as primary systems. The roles should be built and managed there and transferred to SAP EP via the uploading functionality.

Assuming that we have a common business scenario, where SAP EP is primarily used as a standard entry platform for the backend applications, we recommend that you continue to use the respective backend applications as primary systems for managing the roles. This solution is much better, because the information ownership principle demanded by the Sarbanes-Oxley Act (SOX) can be implemented best by using currently existing external tools, especially SecurInfo for SAP.

19.3.4 Change Management Process for New Portal Content

For SAP EP, several tools, such as the GUI Machine or the Portal Development Kit, can be used to create new content and store it in the PCD. This content might also be created directly in the PCD using the *iView Wizard*. In any case, however, you need to ensure that an appropriate change management process is implemented, as it is required for changes to traditional SAP systems as well.

For this purpose, SAP EP also provides a transport management system that can be used to transport packages from portal objects. Therefore, a three-system landscape with a development (DEV), quality assurance (QA), and production system (PROD) should exist in SAP EP. The development of the new content must take place on the development system and must then be tested on the quality assurance system by key users of strategic business units. On approval, the new content can then be imported into the production environment.

The following principles and best practices should be considered during portal content change management:

- Changes to objects on the development system should always be made to the originals and not to copies, because existing changes would otherwise be overwritten again during a succeeding transport.

► The development system carries out a transport to a common transport directory, from where the quality assurance and production systems then import its changes.

► Transport packages for the developers must be created at an early stage so that they are able to gradually integrate their modified or newly created objects during the project.

► The developers of new portal content must be responsible for the content they created. They also must confirm when they have placed their content in the provided transport packages.

► The business process owners must be involved in the approval of the new portal content. They must check this content to make sure it functions properly and is textually correct. Additionally, they must give their final approval for import to the production system.

► When finalizing the transport packages, dependencies among objects must be considered. This is important if inheritances are to be transported as well. For this purpose, a multi-package approach should be chosen where the object content, portal structures, and applications are separately exported and imported.

The following transport packages should be created:

 ► **Content transport package**
 This package contains iViews and pages with dependent objects.

 ► **Structure transport package**
 This package contains pages, worksets, and portal roles without dependent objects.

 ► **Application transport package**
 This package contains new application elements (PAR files) that include new portal components and services.

► When importing multi-packages, application packages need to be imported first, then the structure packages, and finally the content transport packages.

The transport manager is available in SAP EP under the following path: **System Administration · Transport**. Here you will find the **Export** and **Import** functions. In export mode, the objects can be selected in the PCD that are to be added to a defined transport package. For this purpose, right-click the appropriate object and select **Add to transport package**.

The transport mechanism is only available to the content administrator to whom the **Content Administrator** portal role was assigned. This role is a standard role delivered by SAP.

19.4 Technical Security

19.4.1 Connecting SAP EP to a Central LDAP Directory or SAP System

Because the application landscapes are increasingly complex in most organizations, connecting SAP Enterprise Portal to a central LDAP directory where all user master data is stored is recommended. In simpler scenarios, the SAP EP user master records can also be stored in an existing SAP system. For this purpose, SAP Web AS version 6.20 or higher is required.

A central LDAP directory has the advantage that the user master records can always be kept consistent across all connected applications. Even when changes occur (for example, due to an employee moving to another department, etc.), this information can immediately be changed in one central place and does not need to be made consistent across several administrative units.

Description of LDAP

Technically, *Lightweight Directory Access Protocol* (LDAP) is based on the X.500 standard of the originally defined *Directory Access Protocol* (DAP), which was relieved of some functionality to increase performance. In the LDAP directory, information can be stored in a *flat* or *deep hierarchy*. The differences between these two hierarchies are illustrated in Figure 19.11.

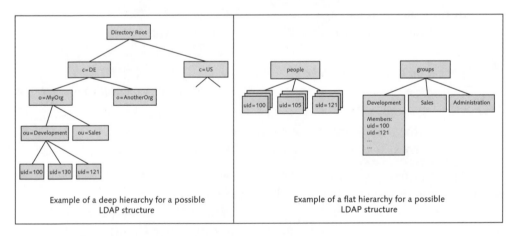

Figure 19.11 Comparison of Deep and Flat LDAP Hierarchies

In a deep hierarchy, the organizational structure is represented by a directory tree. A **distinguished name** (DN) is created using the attributes C (*Country*), O (*Organization*), OU (*Organizational Unit*, like subsidiary, department, etc.), and UID (*User*

ID). In a flat hierarchy, all organizational elements are mapped at the same level and linked to each other using references (links). In the given example, the links are created by entering the members and their user IDs in the appropriate organizational units. The benefit of the flat hierarchy is that employees do not need to be listed several times if they are assigned to an organizational unit more than once. The entire data set that needs to be stored in the LDAP directory can therefore be limited.

Connecting the LDAP Server to SAP EP

An LDAP directory is connected to SAP EP by selecting a data source configuration file (XML file). In SAP EP, this file can be selected using the following function: **System Administration · System Configuration · UM Configuration**. On the **Data Sources** tab, the appropriate data source configuration file (for example, **Read-Only Novell LDAP Server (Flat Hierarchy)...**) can be selected. If no appropriate data source configuration file is available for selection, you can change one accordingly. Otherwise, the standard data source configuration files delivered with SAP EP provide numerous configuration options. If **Read-Only LDAP Server (Flat Hierarchy)...** is selected, for example, on the **LDAP Server** tab you need to specify the server name and the technical user for authentication on the LDAP server, and the directory tree for the users (e.g., OU=Users, OU=Development, O=MyOrg, C=DE). Additionally, you need to enter the group path (e.g., OU=Groups, OU=Development, O=MyOrg, C=DE).

You can also create a secure encrypted connection to the LDAP server by setting the **SSL** option. For this purpose, however, the LDAP server must provide an appropriate option as well. After these options have been set, the configuration must be saved and SAP EP must be booted. Only then will the settings take effect.

Connecting SAP EP to an SAP System

Connecting SAP EP to an existing SAP Web AS ABAP system (SAP Web AS 6.20 or higher) is similar to connecting it to an LDAP server. In this case, however, a different data source configuration file needs to be selected. For this purpose, an XML file can be used to make SAP Web AS ABAP a user persistence storage location. This option should only be applied in rather simple enterprise scenarios, though.

Selecting the Leading User Persistence Storage Location

When connecting SAP EP to an external user persistence storage location, you should consider which system should act as the leading system. If SAP EP is to be used as a self-registration platform, define SAP EP as the leading system. On the other hand, if a mySAP ERP Human Capital Management (HCM) system is already in use and if all employees and their positions in the enterprise are maintained there according to the organizational structure, define the mySAP ERP HCM system as the leading system. MySAP ERP HCM first registers all changes and then effects a transfer to the attached LDAP directory. Therefore in a complex enterprise structure using the mySAP ERP HCM system as the leading user persistence storage location is recommended.

In simpler enterprise structures and when the backend application is the main application in the enterprise, this backend application should be used as the leading user persistence storage location. In this case, complete change management, including the SAP roles, can remain within the SAP backend application.

19.4.2 Implementation of a Single Sign-On Mechanism Based on a One-Factor Authentication

By default, SAP EP provides several kinds of user authentication. The simplest option is the standard authentication based on user ID and password. Nevertheless, appropriate rules should be defined for this method as well (see Section 19.4.6). This one-factor authentication can be either *form-based* or *basic*. In an iView, it is form-based, and if it is an HTTP status request of the Type 401, it is basic. The SAP EP server verifies the entered credentials against the selected user persistence storage.

SAP EP provides a Single Sign-On mechanism based on SAP logon tickets so that the user only has to log on once and doesn't have to re-enter his or her credentials in every single backend application. This mechanism is summarized in Figure 19.12.

The logon process is as follows:

1. The user enters his or her credentials (user ID and password) on the SAP EP server.

2. The SAP EP server validates the data against the values stored in the user persistence storage.

3. If the validation is successful, additional information, such as the *mapping of user information*, is read from the portal database. This mapping is necessary if the user's user name in the backend systems is different from the one used in SAP EP. This assignment is determined in the mapping.

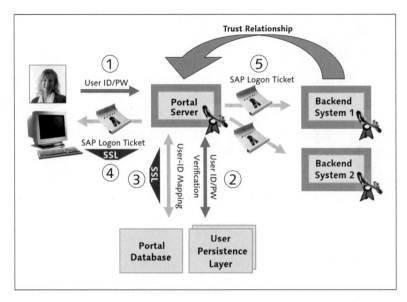

Figure 19.12 Single Sign-On Mechanism in SAP EP Based on User Name and Password

4. The SAP EP server issues an SAP logon ticket (web browser cookie) and signs it with its own certificate. The following information is stored in this SAP logon ticket: the user name used in the backend application (for example, "AliceM"), the logon name in SAP EP (for example, "Alice.Mueller"), the validity period of the SAP logon ticket, and the SAP system ID of the issuing system (for example, "C11" and "Client 000," SAP Web AS J2EE). It does not contain any passwords. Only one different user name can be supported in the backend applications, which again supports the use of an LDAP directory. Additionally, the SAP logon ticket is digitally signed with the private key of the SAP EP certificate and is eventually sent back to the web browser in the form of a cookie.

5. If the user starts a new backend application using an iView within SAP EP, the SAP logon ticket is also sent to the backend application, which then needs to verify it. For the SAP logon ticket to be accepted, the backend application must be configured so that it accepts SAP logon tickets for authentication. The user name specified in the SAP logon ticket must be known to the application as well, and, most importantly, there must be a trust relationship with the SAP EP issuing the ticket. The SAP logon ticket will only be accepted for authentication in the backend application if these requirements are met.

The backend application can also be a non-SAP application. For non-SAP applications, there are several possibilities that are just listed here for the sake of completeness. They will not be discussed in detail. For example, there are web server filters that can be integrated in a web server as ISAPI. There are also Kerberos mapping modules for IIS-based applications (such as Outlook Web Access or SharePoint Portal Server) or Domino filters for Lotus Notes-based web applications.

In the scenario mentioned above, however, it is crucial that you define a leading system to issue SAP logon tickets and that you configure all other backend applications so that these SAP logon tickets are accepted for authentication. Between the backend applications and the issuing SAP EP, there must be a trust relationship based on digital server certificates that are stored on the servers.

The following example assumes that an ABAP backend application is used on an SAP system of a higher release than 6.10. By default, SAP EP is configured so that it creates SAP logon tickets after a user has been successfully authenticated. The J2EE Engine underlying SAP EP is accordingly preconfigured for the portal. For a signature to take place, an appropriate server certificate must be stored in the Keystore service of the J2EE Engine that can be accessed via the Visual Administrator.

In the next step, the SAP ABAP backend system must be configured so that it accepts SAP logon tickets from SAP EP. This requires the following steps:[2]

1. SAP EP must be added to the component list of the SAP backend system: This is achieved using Transaction SM30 for the TWPSSO2ACL table.

2. A new entry must be inserted in this table using "New entry".

3. By default, the **Common Name** (CN) of SAP EP and the ticket-issuing client need to be entered. The CN can be taken from the portal server certificate and is usually identical to the SAP system ID (for example, "C11"). For SAP EP, the default client is "000". However, these can also be defined in a different way.

4. For **Subject Name**, **Issuer Name**, and **Serial Number**, you need to enter the following values:

   For **Subject Name**, the **Distinguished Name** (DN) of the portal server must be entered (e.g., CN=C11,OU=Development,O=SAP,C=DE).

   For **Issuer Name**, the **Distinguished Name** of the issuing Certification Authority that issued and signed the server certificate for the portal server must be entered. For self-signed certificates, this must be the same DN of the portal server that has already been specified under **Subject Name**.

   For **Serial Number**, the serial number of the portal certificate must be entered.

5. After specifying this data, the entry must be saved.

---

2 Prior to performing these steps, some requirements must be met, which are described in detail for the relevant system releases in SAP online help (*http://help.sap.com*).

6. The portal server certificate is then imported to the SAP ABAP backend system using Transaction STRUSTSSO2 or STRUST. For this purpose, the system PSE must be selected.

7. In the **Certificate** section, the **Import certificate** function must be selected. A new window is opened providing the **Import certificate from file** option. This option needs to be selected.

8. In the browser, the portal certificate in DER format must be selected that was previously saved from the Keystore of the portal to a file system location.

9. After selecting the appropriate certificate, the portal server certificate can be imported.

10. The profile parameters `login/accept_sso2_ticket` = 1 and `login/create_sso2_ticket` = 0 must be set.

11. The ABAP backend system is now configured to accept SAP logon tickets issued by SAP EP.

An SSO mechanism can therefore be created based on SAP logon tickets. However, please note that the communication channels among the web browser and the SAP system and the respective backend applications are encrypted via SSL.

19.4.3 Implementation of a Single Sign-On Mechanism Based on an Integrated Authentication

In a pure intranet scenario, it makes sense to combine the authentication to SAP EP with the already performed user authentication to the Windows domain based on NTLM or Kerberos. For the authentication integration, however, Microsoft *Internet Information Server* (IIS) must be used as an upstream web server for SAP EP.

To implement the integration with a Windows Kerberos or NTLM authentication, SAP provides the `HeaderVariableLoginModule` for SAP EP, which is based on the *Java Authentication and Authorization Standard* (JAAS). The following principle applies: A trustworthy instance, in this case the Windows domain server, performs the authentication and returns a header variable (`REMOTE_USER`) with the authenticated user ID in the URL that needs to exist in the user persistence storage of SAP EP as well. If the user ID exists in the selected SAP EP user persistence storage, the user is authenticated to SAP EP.

For this option to be securely applied, the following requirements must be met:

▶ The HTTP and HTTPS services of SAP EP cannot be called directly and must be appropriately secured by a firewall. SAP EP may only be accessed via the upstream IIS web server (configured as reverse proxy).

- ▶ Any HTTP or HTTPS access to SAP EP must be routed via the external IIS web server (configured as reverse proxy) that performs the authentication to SAP EP.
- ▶ Between the external IIS web server and SAP EP, a technically strong authentication based on server certificates must be implemented that results in an appropriate trust relationship between both systems.

For the authentication to the Windows domain controller to be successful, the following configurations need to be carried out:

1. On the IIS web server, the SAP `IisProxy` module needs to be installed. For this purpose, it is recommended to install version 1.7.0.0 or higher.
2. The correct configuration of the `IisProxy` module should be tested.
3. Windows IIS is then configured for an integrated Windows domain authentication.
4. The *Login Module Stack* in SAP EP should be adjusted to contain the `Header-VariableLoginModule` so that it checks for an existing header variable.
5. Finally, the access is tested by entering the following example URL: "http://<Web_server_host>:<Web_server_port>/irj".

Meanwhile, a more elegant and more secure option of integrating the Windows-based Kerberos authentication is provided by SAP Consulting Deutschland as a consulting solution: The new module SAP `SPNegoLoginModule` is available for both SAP EP and SAP Web AS J2EE. It can do without integrating Microsoft IIS and the necessary ISAPI IisProxy. Therefore, it is not necessary to secure SAP EP against direct HTTP access using a network firewall so that the IIS web server is circumvented.

Another secure possibility of integration with a Windows domain is provided by SecurIntegration GmbH with their product *SI EP/Agent*. The SI-EP Agent is connected to SAP EP via JAAS. Instead of using a Windows IisProxy, it requires the placement of an SI-EP Agent server between the user's browser and the SAP EP for the SSO integration with the Windows domain. In this case, the relatively insecure method of header variables authentication, where a session hijacking attack (taking over an authenticated session from another user) can be performed quite easily, can be avoided.

If another SSO authentication to backend applications needs to be carried out, you need to select the SAP logon ticket method again that was presented in the previous section. In this case, the first authentication in SAP EP is effected via the integrated Windows Kerberos authentication. SAP EP then issues an SAP logon ticket that is used by the backend applications for further authenticating the user.

19.4.4 Implementation of a Single Sign-On Mechanism Based on Person-Related Certificates

A more sophisticated and secure authentication mechanism is based on the use of person-related X.509 certificates for the users. In this case, the *Secure Sockets Layer protocol* (SSL) is changed to a mutual authentication. This means not only must the server provide a certificate to prove its authenticity to the user, but also the user has to prove his or her identity using a person-related certificate. However, this should be issued by a trustworthy instance like an accredited Certificate Authority (CA). For SAP EP, the Single Sign-On process is basically the same as the process using a user ID and password. After the first authentication with person-related certificates, an SAP logon ticket is also issued for further authentication to the backend applications. This is illustrated in Figure 19.13.

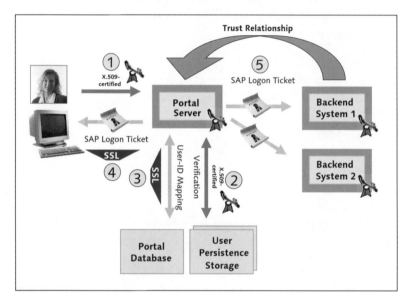

Figure 19.13 Single Sign-On Mechanism in SAP EP Based on Person-Related Certificates

For verifying person-related certificates, the person-related certificates must be stored in the selected user persistence storage. For the portal database, they must be maintained manually or, when using an LDAP directory, they can be automated by mapping the user certificates stored therein.

The following configuration steps must be carried out to enable a certificate-based authentication for SAP EP:

1. For the J2EE Engine underlying SAP EP, the HTTPS service must be enabled.

2. The person-related certificates exist either in DER or Base64-encoded format.

3. Using the **KeyStorage** service (accessible via the Visual Administrator), the Certificate Authority (CA) that issued the person-related certificates must be entered in the list of trustworthy instances. In the standard version, all common external CAs are available there, such as VeriSign, Entrust, and SAP CA.

4. In the **Security Provider** service, the Login Module Stack must in turn be adjusted by adding the optional `ClientCertLoginModule` for all applications that are to accept certificates.

5. Finally, either the person-related certificates must be manually added to the user persistence storage, or the certificate attributes need to be mapped to the LDAP entries.

If the user certificates are stored in an external LDAP directory, the `certificatehash`, `javax.servlet.request.X509Certificate`, and `certificate` attributes need to be set accordingly in the data source configuration file. A data source configuration file can look as shown in Listing 19.2:

```
<dataSource id="CORP_LDAP"
            className="com.sap.security.core.persistence.
              datasource.imp.LDAPPersistence"
            isReadonly="false"
            isPrimary="true">
  ...
  <attributeMapping>
    <principals>
      <principal type="account">
        <nameSpaces>
          <nameSpace name="com.sap.security.core.
            usermanagement">
            <attributes>
              ...
              <attribute name="certificatehash">
                <physicalAttribute name="*null*"/>
              </attribute>
              <attribute name="javax.servlet.request.
                X509Certificate">
                <physicalAttribute name=
                  "usercertificate"/>
              </attribute>
              <attribute name="certificate">
                <physicalAttribute name=
                  "usercertificate"/>
```

```
            </attribute>
          </attributes>
        </nameSpace>
      </nameSpaces>
    </principal>
    ...
  </principals>
 </attributeMapping>
 ...
</dataSource>
```

Listing 19.2 Example of a Data Source Configuration File

The `certificatehash` attribute must be set to *null* because the user certificate cannot be temporarily stored in an LDAP directory. The `javax.servlet.request.X509Certificate` and `certificate` attributes both point to the `usercertificate` LDAP entry. This depends on the LDAP server used, though.

After the configuration has been completed, an SSO mechanism based on person-related certificates can be used. This mechanism can only be effectively implemented, however, if the required certificate management is combined with a PKI (e.g., by Entrust or RSA) and if the certificates are stored in an LDAP directory. This also enables a process for central user management.

19.4.5 Configuration for Anonymous Access

SAP EP can be configured in an Internet scenario so that single pages and iViews can be anonymously started by an Internet user, that is, without previous authentication. If not all of the portal content, but only single iViews, can be viewed anonymously, you need to be particularly careful.

For portal content to be accessed anonymously, named portal users are predefined that are assigned to the group of *anonymous users*. These portal users are either defined as normal users or, more favorably, as service users.

To enable an anonymous call, the following UME properties need to be set:

▶ `ume.login.anonymous_user.mode = 1`

This value should not be changed.

▶ `ume.login.guest_user.uniqueids = <comma-separated list of all anonymous users>`

By default, this is set to `anonymous`. These users are automatically assigned to the **Anonymous users** group.

For these iViews, pages, and worksets to be accessible anonymously, the authentication scheme in the properties can now be set to anonymous. This can be defined in the Portal Content Directory by right-clicking on the appropriate portal object (**iView**, **Page**, **Workset**), starting the Object Editor, and entering "anonymous" as the authentication scheme in the advanced mode of the Property Editor.

After performing this step, the Authorization Editor must be used to add the **Anonymous users** group for the **End User** authorization. The Authorization Editor can be started by right-clicking on the object and selecting **Open Permissions**.

After this configuration, all iViews, pages, and worksets configured in this way can be started via an anonymous Internet access.

19.4.6 Secure Initial Configuration

After the initial installation, you should definitely perform the steps mentioned in the composite SAP Note 606733 if SAP EP is used via the Internet. In particular, this includes the following Notes:

▶ 531495 (How to disable directory browsing in SAP J2EE Engine)

▶ 602371 (All users for telnet authorized for R/3)

▶ 603142 (J2EE users after installation without password)

▶ 604285 (Security vulnerability by unprotected HTTP PUT method)

▶ 622447 (SAP Biller Direct 2.0 installation note (Java component))

▶ 646140 (Security check of Internet Sales)

▶ 705619 (WEB-INF Security vulnerabilities in SAP J2EE Engine 6.20)

This composite note is still valid and should always be adhered to.

Using the config tool, important UME properties should be defined. These properties are all stored under *sapum.properties*. Among other options, the maximum length of user IDs can be specified. If you consider a synchronization with an SAP backend system, you should take into account that it currently only supports a maximum length of eight characters. More password policies like complexity and length can be specified here as well. You should use a minimum length of six characters and at least one numeric character. The UME properties can also be used to define the number of failed authentication attempts. Using a minimum number of three attempts is recommended.

Additionally, the validity period of SAP logon tickets can be defined in these UME properties. For pure intranet scenarios, the maximum validity should be adjusted to the regular business times. In Internet scenarios, however, you should consider setting much shorter validity periods of, for example, 15 minutes.

19.4.7 Definition and Implementation of Security Zones

Security zones offer an additional protection provided by SAP EP to prevent services that are usually called via an iView from being called directly via the service URL. Normally, the user can call a specific iView, page or workset at runtime using his or her portal role and the associated authorizations. If this is not wanted, the user can try to call the service (or a portal component), for example, a file upload functionality that is controlled using the iView, directly by entering the URL.

To prevent this, the components and services can be assigned to security zones. This task must be carried out by the developer for every PAR file (the Portal Archive Repository containing the services and components) using a describing XML file, *portalapp.xml*. The assignments of components and services to the individual security levels can be viewed and modified using the Permissions Editor in SAP EP (see Figure 19.14). The Permissions Editor for security zones is started via **System Administration · Permissions · Portal Permissions · Security Zones**.

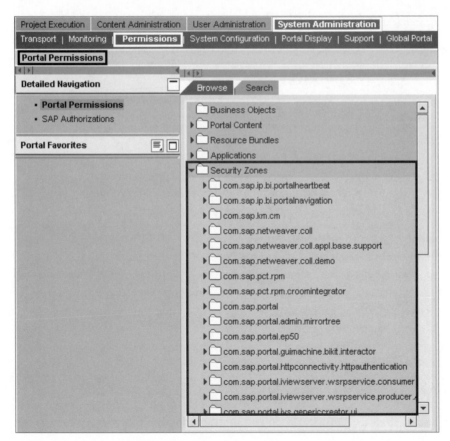

Figure 19.14 Permissions Editor for Security Zones

Like any other objects, security zones can be controlled via the PCD. All security zones can be found under the **Security Zones** directory. The next level is the **Vendor ID** (the provider of the components and services, like SAP), and the level after that is the **Security Area** (like SAP Enterprise Portal or SAP NetWeaver Knowledge Management, etc.). Within the **Security Area**, the **Safety Levels** are defined to which the individual components and services are eventually assigned. These safety levels indicate the protection needs of the individual components and services. Services and components that are particularly sensitive must be assigned to the **High Safety** level.

There are four **Safety Levels**, which are described in Table 19.4.

Safety Level	Description
No Safety	Anonymous users can access components and services assigned to this level.
Low Safety	A user must have authenticated to SAP EP before accessing a service or component assigned to this level.
Medium Safety	A user must be assigned to a portal role that is authorized to access components and services assigned to this level. The authorization of the portal role is defined using iViews.
High Safety	A user must be assigned to a portal role with advanced permissions (e.g., Content Administrator) to be able to access components and services assigned to this level.

Table 19.4 Definition of Security Zones for SAP EP

Listing 19.3 presents an extract from an example *portalapp.xml* file.

```
Security Zones
  <vendor_ID> = sap.com
    <security_area> = NetWeaver.Portal
      <safety_level> = high_safety
        <portal_application_name> = com.sap.portal.prt.cache
              components
          <component_name> = DBTest
              services
          <service_name>
```

Listing 19.3 Example of a portalapp.xml File

In Listing 19.3, the DBTest component is assigned to the **High Safety** level. A service is not defined.

For a user to be able to regularly start or call the service or a component using an iView according to his or her portal role, the user must be assigned to the portal role that has the **End User** authorization for the security level assigned to the service or component. Again, this can be set in the Permissions Editor for the **Security Level**, and again it is possible to use the inheritance of authorizations via the directory. This means that if you set the **End User** authorization for the **High Safety** directory, it also applies to all components and services contained in this directory. However, you can disable inheritance for individual components and services.

In summary, for a user to be able to start the service, you must first activate the **End User** authorization at iView level and then the authorization for the respective component or service in the security zone.

In the standard configuration, however, this check for security zones is disabled, and the `Dcom.sap.nw.sz` parameter must be set to `True` using the config tool.

For a detailed definition of the correct security zones for the initial configuration of SAP EP, you should refer to the document "How To...Secure Permissions for Initial Content in SAP EP 6.0 SP2" (see the SAP Developer Network at *http://www.sdn.sap.com*).

19.4.8   Secure Network Architecture

To prevent SAP EP from being directly accessible at the network level from the Internet, you should establish a network zone structure that is commonly used for Internet scenarios and that consists of *demilitarized zones* (DMZs). Such a network architecture is illustrated in Figure 19.15.

From the Internet, the client (web browser) can only reach the reverse proxy that is placed in the outer DMZ (DMZ 1). It accepts the HTTP(S) requests and forwards them to the SAP EP located in the inner DMZ (DMZ 2). The outer firewall only transfers HTTP requests via port 80 or HTTPS requests via port 441. The internal firewall needs to be configured with filter rules that only permit requests from the reverse proxy to SAP EP. This must be admissible for those ports for which the HTTP or HTTPS services have been defined on the portal. This can be checked easily via the Visual Administrator.

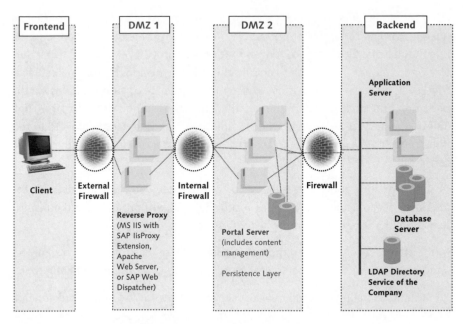

Figure 19.15 DMZ Network Architecture for Implementing SAP EP

In DMZ 2, the portal database can also be installed, which usually acts as the user persistence storage for external Internet users. For internal users, the company-internal LDAP directory can be used that is located in the backend. For this purpose, an appropriate firewall rule must be defined on the backend firewall. In the backend, the critical backend applications, such as SAP systems, the database server, and the search and classification engine (TREX) for SAP EP should be implemented.

Compared to a regular proxy, a reverse proxy functions in exactly the opposite way: In company-wide networks, a proxy fulfills the task of bundling and filtering accesses to the Internet. In this case, not every work center can directly access the Internet, but is routed via the proxy, which then acts as the calling instance toward the website selected by the user. The response is then redirected via the proxy to the user's application (usually a web browser). A reverse proxy performs the exact opposite task. It accepts requests coming from the Internet, checks them for correctness, and forwards them to SAP EP. For SAP EP, the request does not appear to come from the Internet, but from the reverse proxy.

For SAP EP, the freely available Apache web server or the Microsoft IIS web server are mainly used, which can also be configured as reverse proxies. The SAP Web Dispatcher discussed in Chapter 24 can also be regarded as a sort of reverse proxy. However, it only provides limited security filter functionality, but it can still be implemented together with SAP EP.

The Microsoft IIS web server is often used as a reverse proxy because it is more or less freely available in a Windows environment. SAP provides an ISAPI filter, the IisProxy. SAP customers can download it for free from the SAP Service Marketplace (*http://service.sap.com*). Its installation and configuration is very easy if you refer to the available documentation. After configuration, the IIS reverse proxy functions as a forwarding reverse proxy. This means that original requests with a specific URL arriving at the IIS through HTTP port 80, for example, are directed to another SAP EP port (e.g., 4001) with another URL; this is done via a mapping table. The URLs provided by SAP EP can therefore be hidden and protected from direct access.

As mentioned earlier, the Apache web server that is available as open software provides specific security checks at the HTTP application protocol level when it is configured as a reverse proxy. These security checks can be activated when the security module `mod_security` is installed. It is recommended to use at least Apache version 2.x. The security filter functionality of the `mod_security` module must be defined using filter rules. The exact configuration of the filter rules can be viewed under *http://www.modsecurity.org*.

The following security checks can be performed using `mod_security`:

▶ Analyze inbound HTTP requests using predefined filters.

▶ All paths and parameters of the URLs are first untagged to prevent a normal form from being circumvented with escape sequences, thereby rendering it no longer fit to be analyzed.

▶ Even `POST` HTTP commands where the control sequences in the HTTP body are forwarded to SAP EP can be analyzed.

▶ All HTTP requests can be logged so that you can analyze them in detail at a later stage.

▶ The HTTP responses can be checked using output rules to ensure that a complete response is sent to the client and does not arrive in separate stages due to a splitting process that would expose it to potential modifications.

▶ After decryption, HTTPS requests can also be analyzed on the Apache server.

On the whole, a reverse proxy installation of Apache provides numerous possibilities for ensuring effective Internet security. However, the correct configuration with the appropriate filter rules is rather complex, and its performance is a little weaker compared to the commercial application-level gateways (see Section 19.4.9). Still, this alternative should be considered in a cost/benefit analysis.

19.4.9 Introducing an Application-Level Gateway to Make Portal Applications Secure

The network architecture suggested in Figure 19.15 provides sufficient protection against Internet attacks only at the network level. It does not ensure sufficient protection against the most common attacks at the application level, though. To counteract these types of attacks, the application itself should be programmed so that every input made by the Internet user is checked for plausibility and correctness in the portal application before it is processed further. On top of this, the use of application-level gateways or application-level firewalls provides additional protection against attacks at the application level. The most common attacks are outlined in Table 19.5:

Internet Attack	Target	How to Proceed
Cookie poisoning	Taking over another identity, session hijacking	With regard to SAP EP, the authenticity of a user is managed using the SAP logon ticket (a cookie), for example. An attacker can try to take possession of this cookie or to manipulate it and change content so that he or she can take on the identity of a user who has already been authenticated.
Hidden field manipulation	Manipulating data (e.g., price information)	In many eShop applications, price information for offered goods is often transferred to a hidden field in the HTTP body. This hidden field can be changed in order to alter the price of goods. Often, hidden fields also contain information about the session state of an application session that was previously authenticated. By means of manipulation, attackers can try to take over the session of another user.
Parameter tampering	Fraud	Via the URL, a lot of information is transferred to the server using Common Gateway Interface (CGI) encoding. For example, these parameters provide information about the logged on user or about the user's credit limit and so forth. On the server side, the correctness of these parameters is often not verified (for example, when using SAP EP with the external Windows authentication service), so these parameters can easily be modified. Therefore, identities can be obtained by fraud or credit limits can be modified.

Table 19.5 Typical Internet Attacks at the Application Level

Internet Attack	Target	How to Proceed
Buffer overflow	Denial of Service	In normal form fields for entering information and for transferring this data to the server, the amount of data transferred is too large. The application servers, like SAP EP servers, might be brought to a crash.
Cross-site scripting	Identity theft, fraud	Via normal form fields, JavaScript or ActiveX components are transferred to the server and executed when they are transferred back to other users. They then direct those users to fictitious pages that entice them to enter confidential information.
Backdoor and debug options	Taking possession of the server	Often, Internet applications are developed under such a high time pressure that developers forget to remove debug options after going live. These debug options can be abused by external attackers.
Forceful browsing	Taking possession of the Internet application	The attacker tries to quit the normal logical application flow and take possession of the Internet application by calling modified HTTP responses in order to achieve more advanced authorization. In SAP EP, this could be achieved if security zones are not implemented, and services can therefore be called directly via a URL.
HTTP response splitting	Phishing, identity theft	The HTTP responses that are intended for the application server and stored in the cache are split and sent back to the application server in a modified way. Unprotected services can therefore be called on the application server to promote the attacker to a higher authorization level.
Stealth commanding	Introducing malware	Attackers often try to introduce their own malware (like trojans) to application servers using form fields or document upload options. With this malware, further attacks can then be carried out.
Script injection	Fraud, taking over another identity	Using script injection, attackers try to change database entries directly by using the logic of SQL queries. URL header variables are often used to integrate them directly in SQL queries. A modification of these header variables can be used for a script injection.
Known vulnerabilities	Taking over the control of the Internet application	Known vulnerabilities in the operating system, for example, that are reported on a regular basis, can be used by attackers for taking over the Internet application.

Table 19.5 Typical Internet Attacks at the Application Level (cont.)

In order to effectively avert such attacks, server-side checks must be carried out during application development. Along with secure application development, implementation of application-level gateways can provide additional protection.

These application-level gateways must be placed before SAP EP in DMZ 1. They accept all requests from the Internet and check these requests for plausibility and correctness according to rules that were previously defined. Figure 19.16 presents the DMZ network architecture using an application-level gateway.

An application-level gateway considerably improves the options for performing security checks in a normal reverse proxy, as it was described in the previous section. Possible application-level gateways you can use are Kavado InterDo, Net-Continuum NC-1000, F5 TrafficShield, or DenyAll rWeb.

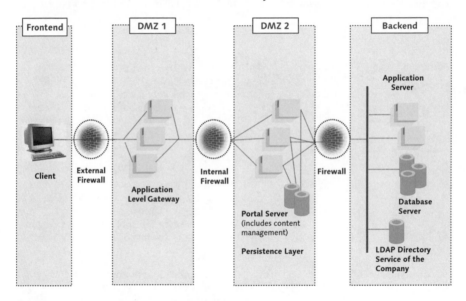

Figure 19.16 DMZ Network Architecture with Application-Level Gateway

All of these commercial products work with a positive security model. This means that Internet requests (i.e., HTTP or HTTPS requests) that are not included on the positive access list are blocked.

For the TrafficShield application firewall by F5, this essentially works as follows: A normal and admissible point of entry is defined for the Internet application, like *http://my.webapplication.com*. Only this URL is permitted as a possible point of entry. If it is called, the HTTP response generated on the application server (in this case, SAP EP) is checked for the new possible links and form fields before it is returned to the client. These potential new branches and input options are stored per user session in the cache of the application-level gateway. This means that the cache is user-specific, which is achieved via an additional cookie. This cache gradually builds the positive list per user throughout the course of the session. If the user issues a new request, it is checked against this positive list. If it is contained therein, the request is forwarded to SAP EP. If it is not, the request is blocked. For example, if the user modifies the URL and given parameters, this request would be blocked, as it is identified as not being part of the positive list.

In addition to this positive list, you can also define black lists (for example, special character strings like <, >, /, etc.) that indicate script input in form fields and are therefore blocked. You can also define form field sizes in order to prevent buffer overflow attacks. Therefore, numerous configurations can be specified that will not be discussed in detail. The challenge is often in finding the right balance between security and functional requirements. It can only be found by performing sufficient tests.

Altogether, the security level that can be achieved compared to a traditional reverse proxy is higher because it's the reverse proxy's level of configuration is more complex. This is the case if the web application is built in a very dynamic way, which is common practice today.

19.4.10 Configuration of Encrypted Communication Channels

To prevent information from being changed or viewed by unauthorized persons during the transport between the individual components, all communication channels can be encrypted using the *Secure Sockets Layer protocol* (SSL) or a *Secure Network Connection* (SNC). Apart from just encryption, the use of SSL provides the benefit of a stronger technical authentication among the architecture components.

Table 19.6 further discusses all connections and explains the encryption methods:

Connection	Encryption	Connection Purpose
Client <> reverse proxy	SSL (HTTPS)	Via this connection, the web browser can send an HTTP request to the reverse proxy and receive the HTML responses.
Reverse proxy <> SAP EP server	SSL (HTTPS)	After the HTTP(S) request has been validated on the reverse proxy, it is forwarded to SAP EP.
SAP EP server <> portal database	SSL (for JDBC)	Under certain conditions, the portal database is also used as the user persistence storage. In this case, it is recommended to use encryption because the users' credentials are then kept in the database.

Table 19.6 Encryptable Communication Channels for SAP EP

Connection	Encryption	Connection Purpose
SAP EP server <> LDAP server	SSL (LDAPS)	If an LDAP server is used as the user persistence storage, it is recommended to use encryption because the users' credentials are stored on the LDAP server and are queried during the authentication process. In this case, the connection is established between the UME and the LDAP server.
SAP EP server <> SAP system	SNC	If the SAP system is used as the user persistence storage, the Remote Function Call (RFC) connection that is used in this case between the portal and the SAP system should be appropriately encrypted. For this purpose, the SNC protocol can be used. The connection is established between the UME and the SAP system. RFC calls can also be used for further function calls on the SAP system that can be secured using SNC.
SAP EP server <> web application	SSL	Other web applications that can be addressed using HTTP (for example, on SAP and on non-SAP systems) can be secured again using SSL.

Table 19.6 Encryptable Communication Channels for SAP EP (cont.)

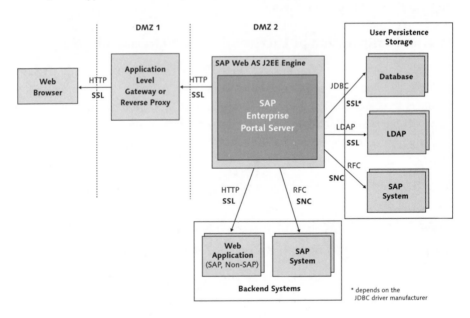

Figure 19.17 Encryptable Communication Channels for SAP EP

The exact steps that are necessary to configure the SSL or SNC connections, respectively, are not further discussed in this chapter because they have already been described in detail in Chapter 8. The required configuration steps are identical. In this context, it should be mentioned that the cryptographic libraries have been installed both for the SAP J2EE Engine underlying SAP EP and for the SAP backend systems to be connected. Additionally, the appropriate certificates for the servers must be implemented because all encryption mechanisms are initially based on asymmetric encryption processes.

19.4.11 Implementation of a Virus Scan for Avoiding a Virus Infection

If SAP EP enables an application to upload a document, there is the risk that this document (attachment) is infected with a virus. In order to prevent this virus from quickly spreading throughout the organization via the existing office communication platform, SAP provides the possibility of using a certified interface to integrate a virus scanner that scans this attachment for potential viruses before it is stored in the database and that prevents further storage in case of an infection.

The certified products for the virus scan interface (VSI) can be found in the SAP Service Marketplace under *http://service.sap.com/securitypartners* (see also SAP Note 786179). The VSI is available both for ABAP programs and for Java programs running on SAP Web AS J2EE.

The essential elements of the virus scan interface are illustrated in Figure 19.18. The virus interface can be called directly on the relevant server (SAP Web AS) or via a Remote Function Call on a dedicated virus scan server. A dedicated virus scan server is recommended if the virus scan software provided by the individual certified vendor cannot be executed on the same SAP Web AS due to its operating system or if a high virus scan load is anticipated. The actual virus scan software product of the respective vendor is then connected via the VSI. For this purpose, an API of the relevant virus software vendor is addressed.

Additionally, it is possible to connect several different virus scan products via the virus scan interface if a product does not provide the desired virus definition. For this purpose, the virus scan products must be assigned to individual virus definition groups. It is then possible that some groups are executed locally on SAP Web AS and others on a dedicated external virus scan server.

The choice of an external virus scan server mainly depends on the expected load of a potential attachment (document) uploading activity. In classic job exchanges where a large number of attachments must be managed, it makes sense to implement a dedicated external virus scan server or even a cluster.

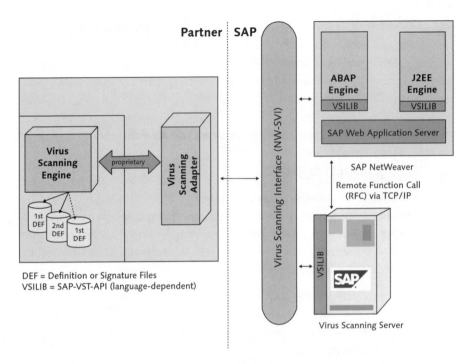

Figure 19.18 Architecture of the Virus Scan Interface

When selecting a virus scanner, you should pay attention to the functionality of the automated update of the virus definition file. It is crucial that this file is always up to date in order to ensure good virus protection. In this respect, a daily update functionality would be ideal.

20 SAP Exchange Infrastructure

This chapter explains the IT security concepts for the Global Security Positioning System (GSPS) component, SAP Exchange Infrastructure. In this regard, we'll focus primarily on message and communication security.

20.1 Introduction and Functions

The *SAP Exchange Infrastructure* (SAP XI) is a central part of SAP NetWeaver. It is the integration infrastructure for distributed business applications and information. The objective is to integrate both SAP and non-SAP applications via a central interface platform. Thus, the number of required direct interfaces between the individual applications can be considerably reduced. SAP XI relies on existing standards like Web services (Simple Object Access Protocol, SOAP), RFC, FTP, and other available protocols. It also uses interfaces (called *connectors* in the SAP XI context) to *Enterprise Application Integration standards* (EAI) like RosettaNet or the chemical integration standard Chemistry Industry Data eXchange (CIDX).

In the future, SAP XI will significantly become more important to *Enterprise Services Architecture* (ESA). In this scenario, SAP XI is the integrating link and therefore the integration service for all Enterprise Services. Even today, SAP XI is the central integration infrastructure for SAP business applications.

Technical Architecture

The logical technical architecture supports three phases during the implementation of SAP XI: the design, the configuration, and the runtime phase (see Figure 20.1). During the *design phase*, the Integration Builder is used to define, design, and store the integration components in the Integration Repository. SAP provides numerous standardized integration components that were especially adjusted to the mySAP solutions.

In the Integration Builder, the integration scenario is then specified. It determines which integration components may communicate with each other or which Web service is called on another backend server when a specific SAP XI service is addressed. This is called the *configuration phase*. The result of the configuration phase is stored in the Integration Directory. Both the Integration Repository and Directory run in the technical runtime environment of the SAP Web AS 6.40 J2EE Engine.

At *runtime*, the integration rules stored in the Integration Directory are applied by the Integration Server when forwarding or routing communication requests. The Integration Server consists of the Business Process Engine, the Integration Engine, and Central Adapter Engine components. Except for the Adapter Engine, these components use the ABAP technical runtime environment of SAP Web AS 6.40. The Adapter Engine, however, requires SAP Web AS J2EE.

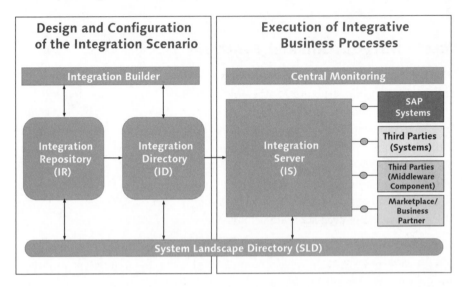

Figure 20.1 Logical Technical Architecture of the SAP Exchange Infrastructure

The Integration Server is the central place where communication requests are received and properly forwarded. For this purpose, it uses the native SAP XI protocol. The interface adapters for IDoc-based and HTTP-based message exchange run directly on the Integration Server as well. Senders and recipients that don't support any XI protocol (exceptions: IDoc and HTTP) must be connected via the Adapter Engine. Which, in turn, provides several protocols like Web services (SOAP), FTP, SMTP, and so forth. The Adapter Engine translates the requests or responses into the XI protocol and forwards them to the Integration Engine. The Adapter Engine can also be installed in a decentralized location on a separate SAP Web AS J2EE. You can also run it on a pure Java Virtual Machine (J2SE environment). If adapters for certain exotic protocols are not available, you can integrate user-developed adapters. Even externally certified adapters provided by partner companies are available.

The *System Landscape Directory* (SLD) now stores all metadata that describes the necessary components, and adapter versions, for example, of the given SAP XI. At runtime, this metadata is read and updated, if necessary, by the other SAP XI components—Integration Repository, Integration Directory, and Integration Server. The technical parameters are defined in the Exchange Profile. In addition, it stores the connection data for the communication among the components using technical service users.

Apart from SLD and the Exchange Profile, the Central Monitoring component is also very noteworthy. It logs all processed messages and communication connections. Using this component, you can later perform error analyses. The Central Monitoring component requires SAP Web AS ABAP as a runtime environment.

Figure 20.2, Figure 20.3, and Figure 20.4 provide a summary of the most important facts for the three phases of design, configuration, and runtime when implementing SAP XI.

From a security validation perspective, the following points are particularly essential:

▶ A direct interaction of a user with SAP XI takes place only during the design and configuration phase. Afterwards, the processes run automatically in the runtime environment and must be monitored via the Central Monitoring component. The configuration data stored in SLD, IR, and ID is accessed by authenticated administration users only during the design and configuration phase.

▶ The security level to be achieved at runtime, particularly the security of exchanged messages by digital signature and encryption, is specified in the *collaboration agreements*. This is achieved by *receiver agreements* specifying that a message is to be encrypted and signed before it can be sent to the final recipient. In the same manner, the sender agreements can define that a signature of an inbound message needs to be validated before the message can be processed further. This holds true whether an application is a sender, or a recipient is always determined by the respective communication partner and not by SAP XI. An application sending a message to SAP XI is therefore a sender.

▶ As mentioned above, SAP XI consists of numerous components like Integration Builder, SLD, Integration Server, and others. Each of these components requires information from the other components, and receives it via one-factor authentications based on technical users.

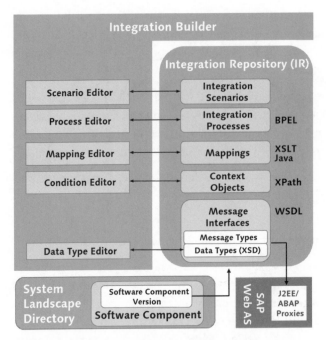

Figure 20.2 Design Phase: Using the Integration Builder for Building Integration Components in the Integration Repository (IR)

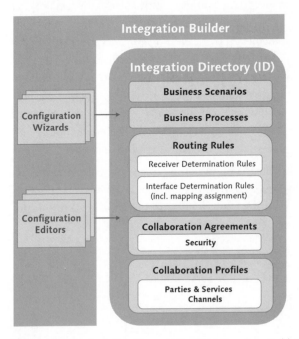

Figure 20.3 Configuration Phase: Using the Integration Builder for Building the Integration Scenario in the Integration Directory (ID)

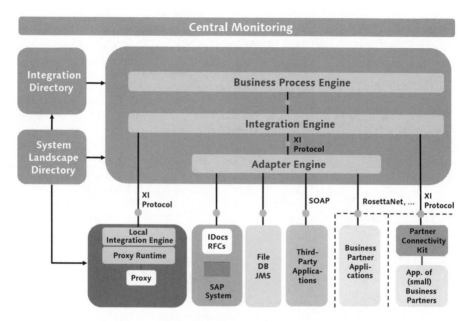

Figure 20.4 Runtime: Processing the Integration Rules on the Integration Server at Runtime

20.2 Risks and Controls

Because the SAP Exchange Infrastructure is implemented on the technical platform of SAP Web AS and also uses it at runtime, the only risks and controls that are significant are those that pertain to the SAP XI functionalities.

We will use a simplified version of the proposed risk analysis methodology described in Chapter 2 to identify the main security risks and the necessary controls (see Table 20.1). The controls are then discussed in more detail in the following sections and are illustrated using appropriate examples.

No.	Classification	Description
1.	Risk potential	No authorization concept for the design and configuration phase:
		Via the Integration Builder, users can access configurations for which they are not authorized. This is enabled by a nonexistent or insufficient authorization concept.

Table 20.1 Risks and Controls for the SAP Exchange Infrastructure

No.	Classification	Description
	Impact	The configuration of the integration scenario causes it to become unstable, leaving message exchange vulnerable to being impaired and manipulated. The availability of the integration platform can no longer be guaranteed. Message recipients can also be changed so that required postings are not affected in the actual target system, but in a system intended for this purpose by a fraudulent user.
	Risk without controls	Extremely high
	Control(s)	Roles are specified for accessing objects and collaboration agreements stored in the Integration Repositories and Integration Directories. This is set in an authorization concept.
	Risk with control(s)	Normal
	Section	20.3.1
2.	Risk potential	Passwords that are too simple. Passwords and authorizations for technical service users, which are necessary for authentication among the SAP XI components, are too simple and can be discovered easily.
	Impact	If insufficient authentications or incorrect authorizations are selected for technical service users, the component can be accessed directly, and the configuration can be changed by unauthorized persons. The stability of the SAP XI configuration and the availability of SAP XI are therefore at stake. Unauthorized users can also read and manipulate component information.
	Risk without controls	High
	Control(s)	The passwords for technical service users must be secure, that is, they must have sufficiently complex characteristics. Standard passwords must be changed in any case. In addition, the authorizations of technical service users must be determined in accordance with the predefined roles.
	Risk with control(s)	Normal
	Section	20.3.2
3.	Risk potential	The selected technical service user is always the same. The same technical service user (XIAPPLUSER) is used for all communication channels from different SAP Web AS systems to the XI server. There is no differentiation of the different SAP Web AS systems.

Table 20.1 Risks and Controls for the SAP Exchange Infrastructure (cont.)

No.	Classification	Description
	Impact	Since there is no differentiation, other communication channels of SAP XI can be used by other SAP Web AS systems as well. Unauthorized transactions can therefore be triggered on other connected SAP Web AS systems.
	Risk without controls	High
	Control(s)	For every SAP Web AS system communication channel via RFC, HTTP, etc., a different technical system user with another password should be selected.
	Risk with control(s)	Normal
	Section	20.4.1
4.	Risk potential	No encryption of communication channels. Communication channels to the XI Server transferring authentication data of technical service users for the communication channel are not encrypted. Furthermore, the communication channels to the connected partner systems to be integrated are also not encrypted.
	Impact	The authentication data of technical service users can be eavesdropped, and therefore, can be used by unauthorized communication partners connected to SAP XI. The unencrypted external communication channels enable third-parties to view the exchanged messages and gain insight into confidence data. Additionally, unauthorized financing transactions might be effected.
	Risk without controls	Extremely high
	Control(s)	The internal communication channels between the SAP XI components must be encrypted. The communication channels between SAP and non-SAP systems connected to SAP XI should be secured via encryption techniques like Secure Sockets Layer (SSL) or Secure Network Communications (SNC).
	Risk with control(s)	Normal
	Section	20.4.2
5.	Risk potential	No signature of XML messages. XML-based messages (per XI or SOAP protocol) are submitted unsigned to SAP XI and forwarded as such to the actual recipient.

Table 20.1 Risks and Controls for the SAP Exchange Infrastructure (cont.)

No.	Classification	Description
	Impact	The problem with unsigned messages is that you can't verify the identity of the exact sender, nor can you check whether parts of the message were changed by a third person during the transfer to SAP XI. Moreover, incorrect postings can be triggered. Also, you can't retrace who initiated the financing transaction as completed transactions can later be denied by the sender.
	Risk without controls	Extremely high
	Control(s)	All inbound XML-based messages must be digitally signed by the sender, especially when using SAP XI in Internet scenarios where business partners are integrated.
	Risk with control(s)	Normal
	Section	20.4.3
6.	Risk potential	No encryption of external communication channels. XML-based messages (per XI or SOAP protocol) are transferred unencrypted to SAP XI.
	Impact	If XML-based messages are transferred unencrypted to SAP XI, the information contained therein can be recorded (sniffed) by unauthorized third persons. If the information is highly confidential, that is, secret business information, the damage potential is accordingly high.
	Risk without controls	High
	Control(s)	The messages should be encrypted, especially when using SAP XI for integration scenarios where business partners have to be integrated via the Internet, and where the business data is highly confidential.
	Risk with control(s)	Normal
	Section	20.4.4
7.	Risk potential	The SAP XI communication channels are not secured. Communication interfaces of SAP XI, particularly in Internet scenarios, are abused by unauthorized third persons. Therefore, unauthorized transactions are triggered on the SAP and non-SAP systems to be integrated via SAP XI.
	Impact	If unauthorized transactions are executed, you can't retrace who initiated them. Rollback—restoring the original state—is also not possible, which can result in considerable damage.
	Risk without controls	Extremely high

Table 20.1 Risks and Controls for the SAP Exchange Infrastructure (cont.)

No.	Classification	Description
	Control(s)	Implement a proxy for outbound messages and a reverse proxy for inbound messages for SAP XI. In an Internet scenario, two consecutive SAP XI systems located in different network segments should be used in addition. One in the frontend DMZ (SAP B2B XI) for communicating with business partners (B2B), and another one for the backend (SAP A2A XI), for the internal application-to-application communication (A2A).
	Risk with control(s)	Normal
	Section	20.4.5
8.	Risk potential	The message exchange is not audited or monitored.
		The executed messages and transactions are not checked for potential processing errors by the central monitor.
	Impact	Processing errors are not discovered at an early stage and therefore result in instabilities in the integration network. In short, transactions that weren't executed properly cannot be determined in time, which, in turn, can lead to financial losses.
	Risk without controls	High
	Control(s)	Constant monitoring of SAP XI using the central monitor provided for this purpose.
	Risk with control(s)	Normal
	Section	20.4.6
9.	Risk potential	No authentication for the file adapter.
		SAP XI enables you to retrieve files from a sending system and to place them on a receiving system using file adapters. There is no authentication for the file adapter—at a technical or user level. This communication channel, therefore, is easily accessible.
	Impact	Files could be introduced to a target system to, for example, overwrite the password file /etc/passwd. Afterwards, the attacked target system could be taken over via a newly created administration account.
	Risk without controls	High
	Control(s)	It is vital that you ensure a correct configuration of authorizations at operating-system level for the SAP XI of the relevant file directories, especially when using the file adapter. In particular, this applies to the SYSADM user, under whose tutelage SAP XI is executed.
	Risk with control(s)	Normal
	Section	20.4.7

Table 20.1 Risks and Controls for the SAP Exchange Infrastructure (cont.)

20.3 Application Security

20.3.1 Authorizations for the Integration Builder

As mentioned above, the SAP Exchange Infrastructure does not involve direct interaction with the users in the departments at runtime. SAP XI is a pure backend infrastructure that transports messages from one SAP or non-SAP system to another target system. Using appropriate mapping rules, messages can be converted and translated so that they're understood by the receiving system. SAP XI therefore fulfills the function of a central integration hub for all applications connected via connectors.

The only interaction between SAP XI and users, except for monitoring, takes place during the design and configuration phase. Using the Integration Builder, these administrative users access the Integration Repository, Integration Directory, and System Landscape Directory. A part of the user authorization is performed in SAP Web AS ABAP and can therefore be defined via the ABAP authorization system. The Integration Builder is a Java application where the access to single objects of the Integration Directory can be authorized.

SAP delivers the following standard roles for administration (design and configuration phase) that can be used in this respect:

▶ SAP_XI_DISPLAY_USER
This role grants the user only read access to the information contained in the Integration Repository and Integration Directory (integration objects, communication interfaces, etc.)

▶ SAP_XI_DEVELOPER
This role can create, delete, and change the integration components in the Integration Repository.

▶ SAP_XI_CONFIGURATOR
This role can create, delete, and change integration scenarios in the Integration Directory.

▶ SAP_XI_CONTENT_ORGANIZER
This role can create, delete, and change the contents in the System Landscape Directory.

▶ SAP_XI_MONITOR
This role can monitor all SAP XI components and all messages that were processed using SAP XI.

▶ SAP_XI_ADMINISTRATOR
This role comprises all roles listed above and is a master role for administering SAP XI.

The access to the individual object types within the Integration Repository and Integration Directory can, as mentioned above, be designed in a more detailed way. For this purpose, the following conditions must be met: The J2EE parameter in the Exchange profile, com.sap.aii.ib.server.lockauth.activation, to be found under *http://server:http-Port/exchangeProfile,* must be set to true. In SAP Web AS ABAP of the SAP XI system, the **SAP_XI_ADMINISTRATOR_J2EE** role must be assigned to the administrator, because it grants access to the Integration Builder role configurator, which is available in the Integration Builder menu via **Tools · Roles**. This ABAP role must therefore be granted in a very restrictive way.

Using this user role administrator, accesses within the Integration Builder to the object types can be limited both in the Integration Repository and in the Integration Directory. In the Integration Repository, the access to individual software component versions, name ranges, and repository object types (software components, integration scenario objects, interface objects, mapping objects, adapter objects, and imported objects) can be limited. The authorizations to create, change, and delete can be granted.

In the Integration Directory, the access to the object types interface determination, recipient determination, receiver agreement, configuration scenario, and special agreement can be restricted. For this purpose, the authorizations to create, change, and delete are also available. In general, read access is granted using the **SAP_XI_DISPLAY_USER** ABAP role.

If new roles are created for the Integration Builder, the corresponding roles are physically stored in the User Management Engine (UME) (see Chapter 8). These UME roles for the Integration Repository then start with XIRep_*, or for the Integration Directory with XIDir_*. In UME, they can either be assigned directly to the existing administrator or to a user group. Please remember: The UME group name is identical to the name of the ABAP role. Therefore, if you assigned a specific role in SAP Web AS ABAP to a specific person group, this ABAP role can be addressed as a group in UME. In the same way, the defined integration builder UME roles can be assigned to the same ABAP users.

20.3.2 Passwords and Authorizations for Technical Service Users

The various SAP XI components listed above, like Integration Repository, Integration Directory, Integration Server, and so forth, must access one another during the design, configuration, and runtime phases to read or write information. During this access, a component; for example, the Integration Directory accessing the Integration Server, reads the relevant technical service user data from the

Exchange profile, in this case XIISUSER, and then uses it to authenticate to the Integration Server.

The service user data is read from XIISUSER via the XILDUSER service user that knows every component.

The following technical service users are used to access the respective component:

▶ **Exchange profile and SLD**
Access via the technical service user XILDUSER using the ABAP role **SAP_BC_AI_LANDSCAPE_DB_RFC**.

▶ **Integration Repository**
Access via the technical service user XIREPUSER using the ABAP role **SAP_XI_IR_SERV_USER**.

▶ **Integration Directory**
Access via the technical service user XIDIRUSER using the ABAP role **SAP_XI_ID_SERV_USER**.

▶ **Adapter Engine**
Access via the technical service user XIAFUSER using the ABAP role **SAP_XI_AF_SERV_USER_MAIN**.

▶ **Integration Server**
Access via the technical service user XIISUSER using the ABAP role **SAP_XI_IS_SERV_USER_MAIN**.

▶ **Runtime Workbench (cache at runtime)**
Access via the technical service user XIRWBUSER using the ABAP role **SAP_XI_RWB_SERV_USER_MAIN**.

These technical service users are set up during the SAP XI installation and are automatically configured. The passwords need to be chosen during the installation as well. It is important that the chosen passwords are sufficiently complex to ensure that they are secure. The following rules should be applied:

▶ Password length to be a minimum of eight characters
▶ At least one special character
▶ At least one letter
▶ At least one number

20.4 Technical Security

20.4.1 Definition of Technical Service Users for Communication Channels at Runtime

At runtime, there are different communication channels that are used to access SAP XI. For these communication channels, an authentication is performed using technical service users.

Scenario 1: Communication Between Sending System and Integration Server Via XI Protocol

In one important scenario, the sender is an SAP Web AS system (Release 6.20 or higher). In this case, an ABAP application can send a message via the ABAP proxy using the XI protocol (XI 3.0 message format). A service user XIAPPLUSER then needs to be set up on the Integration Server that enables the SAP Web AS system to log on to the Integration Server. In the ABAP stack, it has the **SAP_XI_APPL_ SERV_USER** role. For every SAP Web AS system that is logging on, a separate technical service user XIAPPLUSER must be set up. The technical service user XIAPPLUSER is also used when the sending SAP Web AS system connects to the Integration Server via RFC or IDoc. The communication with the recipient (SAP Web AS system) via the XI protocol requires a technical service user as well.

Scenario 2: Communication Between Sending System and Integration Server Via the Adapter Engine and Various Adapters

For the communication between a sending SAP and non-SAP system via an adapter, the authentication scheme that is necessary for the relevant adapter type is used. Normally, technical service users are implemented as well. When using a file, database, or Java Message Service (JMS) adapter, XIAFUSER is used. The Adapter Engine (either central or decentralized) communicates with the Integration Server using the technical service user XIISUSER via the XI protocol. The technical service user XIISUSER must be assigned the ABAP role **SAP_XI_APPL_ SERV_USER** as well. For the communication between the Integration Server and the Adapter Engine, the initial authentication is performed using XIAFUSER, which must be assigned the role **SAP_XI_APPL_SERV_USER** for this purpose. The subsequent communication to the final recipient depends on the respective adapter.

Changing the Passwords for Service Users

The passwords used for the technical service users must be changed regularly, at least once a year. This is critical to prevent potential brute force attacks on passwords. You make this change in the Exchange profile, which can be called via the following path: *http://host:port/exchangeProfile*.

The password must be changed in the corresponding entry `com.sap.aii.<component>.serviceuser.pwd` (for example, `com.sap.aii.integration_directory.serviceuser.pwd` for the Integration Directory). This must also be done in the corresponding entry in SAP Web AS ABAP for the technical service user as well using Transaction SU01.

20.4.2 Setting Up Encryption for Communication Channels

As mentioned above, SAP XI enables you to distinguish between the internal communication based on technical service users and the external communication to the connected partner systems. The internal communication among the components takes place via HTTP. It can be secured using Secure Sockets Layer (SSL) (or HTTPS, respectively).

When securing the external communication channels, the encryption type depends on the adapter. For adapters where the protocol used for communication is also based on HTTP, HTTPS can be implemented as well. For communication interfaces based on RFC, Secure Network Communication (SNC) can be used.

In general, an encrypted SSL or SNC communication can be configured in the same way as the SAP Web AS, because SAP XI is built on this technical runtime environment.

As a general prerequisite for using SSL, the necessary cryptographic program libraries (for example, SAPCRYPTOLIB for ABAP and IAIK security package for J2EE) must be installed both in SAP Web AS ABAP and in SAP Web AS J2EE. In both cases, the appropriate digital certificates (according to X.509 standard) must be requested at a Certificate Authority (CA). Because SSL is also used for technically authenticating the two communication partners, SSL can be configured so that not only the server authenticates itself to the client but that the client also authenticates itself to the server. In the internal XI communication, the components partially function as client and server.

The SSL (HTTPS) communication must therefore be configured in both stacks (SAP Web AS ABAP and J2EE):

▶ For SAP Web AS ABAP, Transaction STRUST must be used to configure SAP Web AS for SSL used for SAP XI; this is where the digital certificate mentioned above must be imported. Additionally, an appropriate HTTPS service with one port must be set up for the Internet Communication Manager (Transaction SMICM, services).

▶ For SAP Web AS ABAP to function as a client as well, the digital certificate must be imported in the client *Personal Security Environment* (PSE) using Transaction STRUST. This can be the same client that was used for the server as well. Otherwise, the HTTPS port of the respective server must be used for all destinations (Transaction SM59) where HTTPS with client authentication is to be used.

▶ Additionally, SAP Web AS J2EE must be properly configured as an HTTPS server. This is done using the Visual Administrator. The certificate requested above must be imported into the key store *service_ssl* under the *key storage* provider. Additionally, the certificate must be assigned to the HTTPS service in the SSL provider, and the port for HTTPS must therefore be configured and activated.

▶ In order for SAP Web AS J2EE to act as a client, in addition to importing the server certificate to the *service_ssl* key store, it must also be imported to the *TrustedCAs* key store if self-signed certificates will be used.

Configuration of the Internal SAP XI Communication

In order to change the entire internal communication to SSL (HTTPS), you must set the following parameters in the Exchange profile:

▶ The `com.sap.aii.connect.secure_connections` parameter must be set to `all`.

▶ The parameters defining the HTTPS communication ports (for example, `com.sap.aii.connect.integrationserver.httpsport`) must be set to the port that has been defined for the HTTPS service—either SAP Web AS ABAP or J2EE, this depends on the technical runtime environment of the component.

More information about configuring a secure internal SAP XI communication can be found in SAP Note 766215.

Configuration of External Communication

For the external communication of messages via the communication channels defined in the Integration Directory, the implementation depends on the relevant carrier protocol. If it is the commonly used HTTP, you can select the corresponding secure equivalent HTTPS in the Integration Directory (provided that the appropriate HTTPS service has been activated on the sender or receiving system, respectively, as described above). Otherwise, it depends on the adapter. For RFC adapters, the secure SNC protocol can be used instead of SSL.

Table 20.2 contains information about the most commonly used adapters and their possibilities regarding protection.

Adapter	Runs on	Outbound	Inbound	Protocol	Protection
XI 3.0	IS	X		HTTP	Possible via HTTPS. This is achieved with the selection via the encrypted communication channel in the Integration Directory.
			X	HTTP	Per HTTPS. This is achieved with the selection via the encrypted communication channel in the Integration Directory.
IDoc	IS	X		tRFC	Possible via SNC. The connection must be defined with a technical service user as a communication channel of the IDoc type. The channel must reference an appropriate RFC connection (type 3) between SAP XI and receiving system (IDoc). The technical service user in the receiving system (IDoc) must have the proper IDoc authorizations.
			X		Possible via SNC. The connection must be defined as a type-3 RFC destination on the sending IDoc system. The used technical service user must have the **SAP_XI_APPL_SERV_USER** role on SAP XI.
Plain HTTP	IS	X		HTTP	Possible via HTTPS. In the Integration Directory, the communication channel of the type HTTPS must be selected. Depending on the configuration of the target system, an anonymous login or the authentication using a technical service user is permitted.

Table 20.2 External Adapters and Encryption Possibilities for the Relevant Communication Protocols

Adapter	Runs on	Outbound	Inbound	Protocol	Protection
			X	HTTP	Possible via HTTPS. To be able to address this adapter, the sender must address SAP XI (Integration Directory) via the *https://<XI_host>:<httpsport>/sap/xi/adapter_plain* service. An authentication scheme must be stored behind the service (to be set via Transaction SICF). The technical service user must have the **SAP_XI_APPL_SERV_USER** role.
RFC	AE	X		RFC	SNC is not possible. In the Integration Directory, only the type RFC can be selected for the communication channel. For this purpose, an appropriate RFC connection (SM59) must be set up between the Integration Server and the receiving system. The RFC service user must have the proper authorizations in the receiving system. (Note: This adapter should only be implemented in an Internet scenario.)
			X	RFC	SNC is not possible. You must define an RFC connection from the Integration Server back to the actual target system that can be used to read the RFC metadata. For this purpose, the adapter should be registered accordingly with the SAP Gateway. There is no authentication via a technical service user. (Note: This adapter should not be implemented in an Internet scenario.)
SOAP	AE	X		HTTP	Possible via HTTPS. In the Integration Directory, the SOAP protocol needs to be defined for the receiving channel. The channel can be authenticated to the receiving application using a technical service user. An anonymous login is permitted as well, though. Additionally, the message can be digitally signed.

Table 20.2 External Adapters and Encryption Possibilities for the Relevant Communication Protocols (cont.)

Adapter	Runs on	Outbound	Inbound	Protocol	Protection
			X	HTTP	Possible via HTTPS. In the sending channel of the Integration Directory, the SOAP protocol must be set. The corresponding technical service user can be authenticated via basic authentication or SSL client certificate. This technical service user requires the **xi_adapter_soap_message** role in the Adapter Engine. This must be set via SAP UME. The signature validation of the message can be enabled as well.
RNIF (Rosetta-Net Inter-Face)	AE	X		HTTP	Possible via HTTPS. In the Integration Directory, the type RNIF needs to be defined for the receiving channel. The channel can be authenticated to the recipient using a technical service user. An anonymous login is permitted as well. Additionally, the message can be digitally signed and encrypted.
			X	HTTP	Possible via HTTPS. In the sending channel of the Integration Directory, the SOAP protocol must be set. The corresponding technical service user can be authenticated via basic authentication or SSL client certificate. The technical service user requires the **SAP_XI_APPL_SERV_USER** role in SAP Web AS ABAP. A signature validation of the message can be enabled as well. Additionally, the message can be decrypted.
CIDX (Chemical Industry Data Exchange)	AE	X		HTTP	Possible via HTTPS. There are the same options as listed for the RNIF adapter.
			X	HTTP	Possible via HTTPS. There are the same options as listed for the RNIF adapter.

Table 20.2 External Adapters and Encryption Possibilities for the Relevant Communication Protocols (cont.)

Adapter	Runs on	Outbound	Inbound	Protocol	Protection
File system	AE	X		NFS	There are security options at operating-system level only. For the SYSADM technical user that runs the SAP XI instance, the access to operating system directories must be restricted. There are no encryption options. We do not recommend using this adapter in implementation scenarios with very high security requirements.
			X	NFS	There are security options at operating-system level only. For the SYSADM technical user that runs the SAP XI instance, the access to operating system directories must be restricted. There are no encryption options. Using this adapter is not recommended in implementation scenarios with very high security requirements.
FTP	AE	X		FTP	Secure FTP is not possible. Otherwise, you can also use technical service users for FTP authentication. We do not recommend using FTP for integration scenarios with high security demands.
			X	FTP	Secure FTP is not possible. Otherwise, you can also use technical service users for FTP authentication. We do not recommend using FTP for integration scenarios with high protection needs.
JDBC (Java Database Connectivity)	AE	X		JDBC	Depending on the manufacturer, the database access might be encrypted. The authentication is again implemented using technical service users at database level. We do not recommend using JDBC for integration scenarios with high protection needs.

Table 20.2 External Adapters and Encryption Possibilities for the Relevant Communication Protocols (cont.)

Adapter	Runs on	Outbound	Inbound	Protocol	Protection
			X	JDBC	Depending on the manufacturer, the database access might be encrypted. The authentication is again implemented using service users at database level. We do not recommend using JDBC for integration scenarios with high protection needs.
Mail	AE	X		IMAP4, POP3, SMTP	Possible via SSL. Except for IMAP4, S/MIME, that is the signature and encryption option of mails, can be implemented as well.
			X	IMAP4, POP3, SMTP	Possible via SSL. Except for IMAP4, S/MIME, that is the signature and encryption option of mails, can be implemented as well.

Table 20.2 External Adapters and Encryption Possibilities for the Relevant Communication Protocols (cont.)

In general, the protection needs for the integration scenario should be determined based on SAP XI when selecting possible adapters. For high protection needs—for example, when connecting systems that are processing highly confidential information and information with high integrity demands—you should implement only those adapters that support digital signatures (high integrity) and encryption (high confidentiality) at message level.

20.4.3 Digital Signature for XML-Based Messages

XML-based messages, like they are used for the XI 3.0 protocol, SOAP, RNIF, and CIDX adapters, can be signed. By digitally signing a message, you can achieve the following security objectives:

▶ The sender of a message can be unambiguously authenticated at message level. It is not necessary to rely on the authentication of the communication channel via technical service users, because it may have been compromised by an attacker. In a purely technical authentication, it is also impossible to retrace the sender in a legally binding way.

▶ Using a digital signature, the integrity of the message can be unambiguously determined. An unauthorized change to the message carried out by an attakker at a later stage can be reliably discovered. In case the message was changed by an attacker, SAP XI can refuse to further process it.

▶ A digital signature attests the originality of the message. A sender cannot discard sending the message at a later stage. This is particularly important if business orders are to be digitally processed. However, you must consider the legal requirements that are to be applied to the business contract. If you want to set up a legally-proof contract, the signature must comply with the policies of the Electronic Signatures in Global and National Commerce Act. Naturally, this can be circumvented if the business partners have not made any other previous agreements.

Using the XI 3.0 protocol, you can digitally sign the SAP manifest and the payloads (that is the actual message), in addition to the SAP main header (similar to the SOAP header in Web services). Using SOAP, however, you can sign only the SOAP body (that is the message only). The RNIF adapter uses S/MIME. CIDX uses the signature standard PKCS#7.

In the following sections, the steps necessary for configuring the implementation of a digital signature will be discussed in detail for the XI 3.0 protocol.

In SAP XI, messages can be signed using the certificates existing in the certificate store of SAP Web AS J2EE (*key storage provider*) in the SAP XI runtime environment of the underlying SAP Web AS. The certificate store of SAP Web AS ABAP is not used in this case. The Integration Server using SAP Web AS ABAP as the technical runtime environment implements an internal Web service for addressing the signature functions of SAP Web AS J2EE.

For digital signatures, you must consider the trust model to be applied. There are two variants that can be implemented in this respect:

▶ There is a direct trust model that does not use a CA: The public keys (certificates) of the sender and the recipient (i.e., the business partners or internal systems) must be exchanged beforehand. In this case, a new key store can be created on the J2EE Engine of SAP XI, where all public certificates of the possible senders are stored. This key store can be freely chosen.

▶ A Public Key Infrastructure (PKI) is used: In this case, there is a trust relationship between the business partners that is confirmed by one or several trustworthy CAs. All implemented certificates of the business partners must be digitally signed by these root CAs. The relevant public certificates of the CAs must be stored in the *TrustedCAs* key store of SAP Web AS J2EE. However, SAP XI does not support multilevel hierarchical trust relationships. Therefore, the used certificates must have been signed directly by the trustworthy CAs. A multilevel certificate hierarchy is not supported.

In order for the access to the key storage provider of SAP Web AS J2EE to function correctly, you must assign the appropriate J2EE roles in SAP Web AS J2EE (see Chapter 8) to the technical service user (RFC user), which is used by the Web service (HTTP carrier protocol) to log on to the Integration Server. This is done using the Security Provider service in the J2EE Visual Administrator and affects the following roles:

▶ On the **Policy Configuration** tab, the `sap.com/tc~sec~wssec~app*wsspro-cess.jar` component needs to be selected. It contains the J2EE role **WSSecurityProcessing** that must be assigned to the RFC service user, so it can be used by the external Web service to log on to the Integration Server (HTTP connection type).

▶ If a new key store has been generated for storing the external business partner system certificates, the aforementioned RFC service user must be assigned to the J2EE role **KeystoreAdministrator**, which is included in the `keystore-view.<Name of the created key store>` component.

To use the J2EE security functions, the IAIK cryptography components first need to be implemented in SAP Web AS J2EE. This is done using the software deployment tool. The collaboration agreements for communication partners that have been stored in the Integration Directory define whether it's necessary to use digital signatures and, if so, specify the validation of a signature.

The receiver agreement (see Figure 20.6) in the Integration Directory defines whether a message is signed before it is forwarded to the recipient in SAP XI. In this receiver agreement, the key store of SAP Web AS J2EE is selected with the corresponding signature certificate (private certificate of the Integration Server). As a prerequisite, either the XI 3.0 protocol or SOAP (or RNIF or CIDX, respectively) must have been chosen for the communication channel with the recipient. In the communication channel, for example, the XI protocol channel is entered for which **Message Security** has been specified, for example "Message_to_XI". In the key store, you specify the **Key store name**, and the key store entry contains the actual certificate. In the communication channel, the **Message Security** radio button must be set (see Figure 20.5) to enable a digital signature in the receiver agreement.

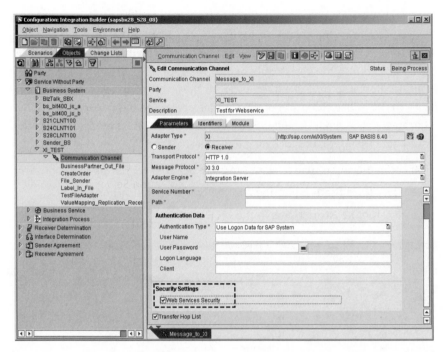

Figure 20.5 "Message Security" Option for the Communication Channel of the XI 3.0 Protocol

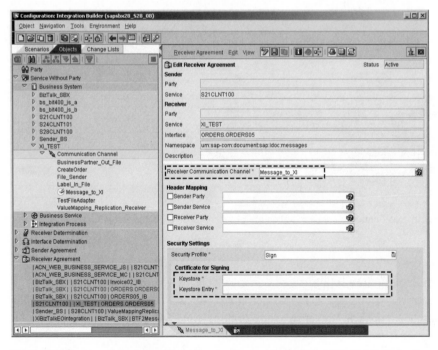

Figure 20.6 Receiver Agreement: Signature of a Message in the Case of an XI 3.0 Protocol

The sender agreement (see Figure 20.7) in the Integration Directory specifies the public certificate of the sender to be used for validating the signed message in SAP XI. For self-signed certificates (see above), the public certificates must have been imported into the key storage of SAP Web AS J2EE. The self-signed public certificate must also have been imported to the *TrustedCAs* key store. The same applies to the public certificate of the CA that signed the business partner system certificates. In the sender communication channel, the **Message Security** option must be set. Therefore, the following must be specified:

▶ The communication channel with **Message Security** set for the XI 3.0 protocol

▶ The issuer (Certificate Authority) and the owner of the certificate

▶ The key store **Keystore Name** in the J2EE stack

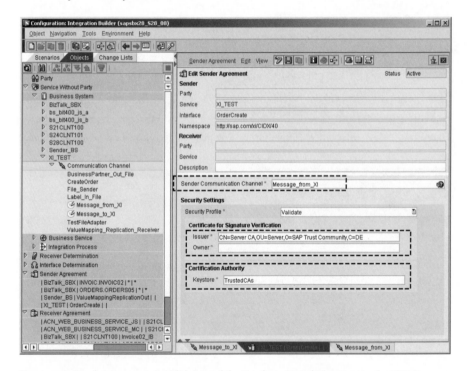

Figure 20.7 Sender Agreement: Validation of the Sender's Digital Signature in the XI 3.0 Protocol

Since SAP XI can sign using only server-based certificates, there might be legal problems if more sophisticated signature policies according to the Electronic Signatures in Global and National Commerce Act are to be observed. For this purpose, SAP provides direct signature options using SAP GUI (see Chapter 27).

There are other possibilities for external Web services offered by the security solution of BeSeQure.[1] The *Business Security Framework* implemented therein is specially designed for Web service security and supports all current Web service security standards like *Webservice-Security* (WS-Security), *Security Assertion Markup Language* (SAML), or *Organization for the Advancement of Structured Information Standards* (OASIS). In this solution, a central server is used to synchronize the access policies with the *Web service adapter* that signs the messages. Person-related certificates can be used for digital signatures as well. The Web service adapters additionally perform authorization checks based on access policies. For example, the Web service adapters are implemented before the communication channel with SAP XI and with the business partner. Therefore, they are always an upstream signature and validation instance.

For SAP XI, these Web service adapters are virtually transparent. This enables both consistent and seamless Web service security without further programming.

20.4.4 Encryption of XML-Based Messages

The encryption of the XML-based message body (SOAP body) itself is currently not supported by the SAP protocols XI 3.0 and SOAP. For this purpose, you need to use the RNIF and CIDX adapters. These protocols enable encryption at message level. They use the public certificate of the business partner system (receiving system) for encryption.

SAP is currently planning to develop the option of encrypting messages for the XI protocol and for SOAP. For now, however, SAP relies on the encryption of the communication channel using SSL for securing messages.

Additionally, message encryption is only possible using the external solution of BeSeQure. As we mentioned in the previous section, this solution encrypts the messages in the upstream *Business Security Framework* (BSF) Web service adapters.

20.4.5 Network-Side Security for Integration Scenarios

Particularly when SAP XI is used in an Internet scenario, for the integration of a business partner (supplier, reseller, customer), for example, the scenario must be secured via the network. As with portal scenarios, a multilevel DMZ concept must be used for network segmentation, as shown in Figure 20.8.

---

1 BeSeQure provides companies with a fast and costeffective solution for the secure connection of all backend systems. For more information, go to *http://www.besequre.com*.

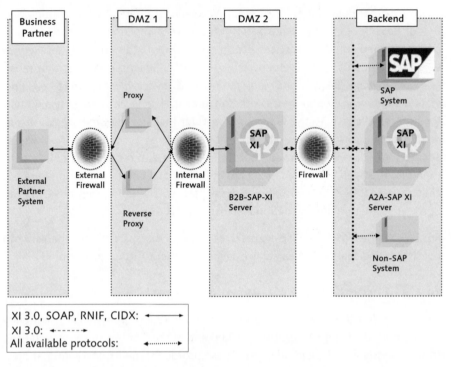

Figure 20.8 DMZ Concept and Implementation of Two SAP XI Instances in an Internet Integration Scenario

In an integration scenario with a business partner where the Internet is used as the network between business partner and your own enterprise, two SAP XI systems should be implemented: one system establishing the integration with the business partners, that is a *business-to-business* (B2B) SAP XI system, and a second system for the internal application integration, an *application-to-application* (A2A) integration hub. This ensures that the A2A integration channels cannot be directly accessed from the Internet. Between the B2B SAP XI system and the A2A SAP XI system, you can establish a dedicated communication channel that can be protected and controlled in a more optimal way. For this purpose, you can use the XI 3.0 protocol, which can implement an additional message signature. Additionally, this communication channel can be encrypted using HTTPS. This also enables a mutual authentication at a technical level between the B2B and A2A integration systems. The firewall between DMZ 2 and Backend may permit the communication between only B2B and A2A SAP XI systems.

If all systems (e.g., SAP Partner Connectivity Kit, see Chapter 21) used by the business partners are known, the outer firewall should also restrict access to these systems. This does not prevent IP spoofing attacks, but it does provide additional protection.

For inbound messages, the communication should be directed via at least one reverse proxy. For outbound messages, from the B2B integration system to the business partner, a proxy should be implemented. We recommend that you use only these protocols—XI 3.0, SOAP, RNIF, and CIDX—for communicating with business partners, because this is the only way to achieve good message security with digital signature and encryption.

As a reverse proxy, you can use the SAP Web Dispatcher in this integration scenario, which provides only very limited security functions. Only the URL services, which must be called externally, can be restricted.

Preferable solutions would be application-level gateways (or application-level firewalls) that are specifically designed for XML-based message communication, that is, Web services. They provide the security functionalities necessary for a secure communication based on Web services. The Web services application-level gateways can check the contents of the SOAP header and body for *malformed* contents like attempted SQL script injections. Additionally, they provide the full range of Web services security standards such as SAML for an additional authentication or Web service security.

The following are manufacturers of an application-level gateway:

▶ Xtradyne XML/SOAP Gateway

▶ Datapower XS40 XML Security Gateway

▶ BeSeQure Business Security Framework (Web services security)

20.4.6 Audit of the Integration Builder and the SAP XI Communication

The investigative security objective—within the security management—can be implemented and achieved by using an audit An audit enables you to detect changes made to the configuration or security violations and to take proper countermeasures. By using an audit, you may also find potential security weak spots that require new security controls. The SAP Exchange Infrastructure provides numerous possibilities for an audit.

Change History in the Integration Builder

In the Integration Builder, a change history can be called for every object in the Integration Repository and Integration Directory that has been changed. Using this change history, you can retrace who made what change to which object at

what time. The change history can be called in the object's detail view by selecting **History** from the main menu of the object.

Monitoring Outbound Messages

The entire message processing can be monitored in the Integration Server and the
Adapter Engine. There you can see if a message transfer failed, or if a recipient is
still not reachable. The monitor for the Integration Server is started via Transaction
SXMB_MONI (see Figure 20.9). The administration of the Integration Server and
of the archive function for processed XML messages is accessible via Transaction
SXMB_ADM. The monitor for the Adapter Engine is accessible in SAP Web AS
ABAP via Transaction SXMB_IFR. This transaction starts the web frontend, which
also starts the Integration Builder. You can start the monitoring function with a
mere click on the **Runtime Workbench** link (see Figure 20.10).

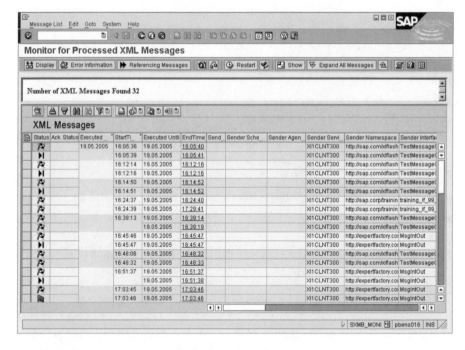

Figure 20.9 SXMB_MONI Monitor in the Integration Server

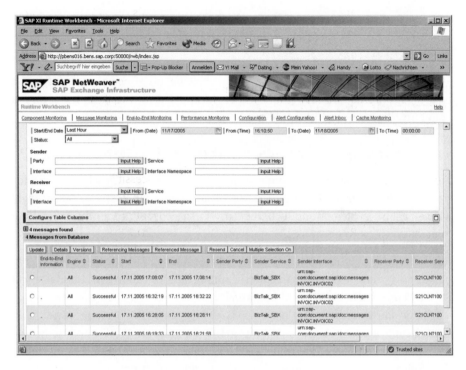

Figure 20.10 Monitor Runtime Workbench for the Adapter Engine

By default, only XML messages processed in an asynchronous way are made persistent in the Integration Server. XML messages that are processed synchronously are made persistent only if errors occur, or if the logging function has explicitly been switched on. Incorrect message transfers are never deleted automatically. They have to be removed manually by the administrator.

Only messages that were successfully processed in an asynchronous way can be archived or deleted. The archiving of the processed messages can be controlled using Transaction SXMB_ADM. Two archiving jobs need to be set up:

1. One archiving job that writes those messages to an archive that were made persistent in the Runtime Workbench.

2. One deletion job that deletes those messages that were made persistent in the Runtime Workbench.

Messages that were processed using the **Message Security** mode (i.e., that were digitally signed) are always archived. This applies both to messages that were asynchronously processed and to those that were synchronously processed.

Apart from mere monitoring, an alert function can be defined as well (Transaction SXMB_MONI) that triggers an alarm if messages were not correctly processed.

This function can also be linked to the SAP Computing Center Management System (CCMS) so that these alarm messages can also be reported centrally to an SAP Web AS system.

The important aspect here is that a process has been defined that specifies the measures to be taken if a high-priority alarm is raised. In this case, the required countermeasures need to be initiated.

20.4.7 Securing the File Adapter at Operating-System Level

The file adapter provides an immense security leak, because it allows unauthorized access to the NFS file directories of an integration system. We strongly advise against implementing it, particularly in the context of an Internet-based integration scenario.

But, if there is no other option, you should take appropriate security measures at operating-system level. This includes granting authorizations to the technical SYSADM user running SAP XI at operating-system level that enable access to only a specific file directory. On Windows-based systems, this can be done using Access Control Lists (ACLs). On UNIX systems, the correct user ID needs to be set. You should specifically define an exchange directory. All other system-critical directories must be protected using special access restrictions.

21 SAP Partner Connectivity Kit

This chapter explains the IT security concepts for the Global Security Positioning System (GSPS) component, SAP Partner Connectivity Kit. As was the case with SAP Exchange Infrastructure, here, too, we'll focus primarily on message and communication security.

21.1 Introduction and Functions

The *SAP Partner Connectivity Kit* (SAP PCK) is a supplement of the SAP Exchange Infrastructure (SAP XI) and only requires SAP Web AS J2EE as a technical runtime environment. As the name implies, SAP PCK is designed for integrating the business partners of an enterprise in the existing SAP XI via the XI 3.0 protocol. The advantage here is that the integration can be simplified and the improved security mechanisms of the XI 3.0 protocol can be used.

The SAP PCK is implemented specifically when integrating smaller supplier companies with a bigger regular supplier or manufacturer. In this case, SAP PCK is included in the license price of SAP XI. As in SAP XI, the administration is done via web frontends whose graphical user interfaces (GUIs) are similar to that of the Integration Builder. This enables a simple installation and configuration of SAP PCK.

The connection of SAP PCK to the SAP XI Integration Server of the integration partner via the XI protocol is shown in Figure 21.1. Therefore, all security mechanisms addressed in Chapter 20, like the digital signature, are already available at message level.

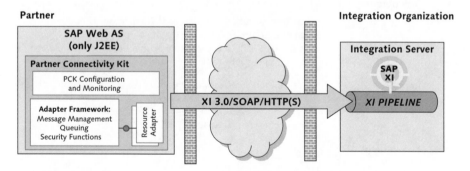

Figure 21.1 Connecting SAP PCK to the SAP XI of the Integration Organization

21.2   Risks and Controls

The risks and controls for SAP PCK are essentially identical to those of SAP XI. In the following, we will discuss only those risks for which the control possibilities differ from those of SAP XI. Again, the simplified risk and control management methodology will be applied (see Table 21.1).

No.	Classification	Description
1.	Risk potential	No authorization concept for the design and configuration phase.
		Via the SAP PCK web frontend, users can access configurations for which they are not authorized. This is enabled by a nonexistent or insufficient authorization concept.
	Impact	The configuration of the integration scenario technically results in an unstable state so that message exchange can be considerably impaired. The availability of the integration scenario can no longer be guaranteed. Message recipient data can also be changed, so that potentially required postings are not effected in the actual target system but rather, in a system intended for this purpose by a fraudulent user.
	Risk without controls	Extremely high
	Control(s)	Appropriate roles are specified for accessing the objects and collaboration agreements stored in SAP PCK. This is set in an administrative authorization concept.
	Risk with control(s)	Normal
	Section	21.3
2.	Risk potential	The selected technical service user is always the same.
		For communication channels in an integration scenario, the technical service user chosen for the partner systems is always the same (PCKRECEIVER). There is no differentiation between the various systems to be integrated.
	Impact	Because there is no separation, other communication interfaces of SAP PCK can be exploited by other partner systems. Therefore, unauthorized transactions can be triggered on other partner systems connected to SAP PCK.
	Risk without controls	High
	Control(s)	For every SAP or non-SAP system connected to PCK, a different technical service user should be set up to enable differentiation. A technical collective service user for all connected partner systems should be avoided.

Table 21.1 Risks and Controls for the SAP Partner Connectivity Kit

No.	Classification	Description
	Risk with control(s)	Normal
	Section	21.4.1
3.	Risk potential	No encryption of external communication channels. XML-based messages (per XI or SOAP protocol) are transferred unencrypted to SAP PCK.
	Impact	If XML-based messages are transferred unencrypted to SAP PCK, the information contained therein can be viewed by unauthorized third persons.
	Risk without controls	High
	Control(s)	Since SAP PCK is exclusively used in Internet scenarios, all external communication channels should be encrypted.
	Risk with control(s)	Normal
	Section	21.4.2
4.	Risk potential	No signature of XML messages. XML-based messages (per XI or SOAP protocol) are transferred unsigned to SAP PCK.
	Impact	With unsigned messages, the exact sender cannot be verified, and therefore it cannot be determined whether parts of the message were changed by an unauthorized third person during the transfer to SAP PCK. This can eventually lead to incorrect postings. Furthermore, you cannot retrace who (i.e., which legal person) initiated a posting. Requested transactions can later be denied by the sender.
	Risk without controls	Extremely high
	Control(s)	SAP PCK is exclusively used in Internet scenarios. Therefore, digital signatures should always be used when exchanging messages.
	Risk with control(s)	Normal
	Section	21.4.3
5.	Risk potential	The SAP PCK communication channel is not secured. Communication interfaces of SAP PCK, especially in Internet scenarios, are exploited by an unauthorized third person, and unauthorized transactions are therefore triggered on the SAP and non-SAP systems connected to SAP PCK.

Table 21.1 Risks and Controls for the SAP Partner Connectivity Kit (cont.)

No.	Classification	Description
	Impact	When unauthorized transactions are executed, it's often impossible to retrace who requested these transactions. A rollback to the original state is also no longer possible. This can cause considerable damage.
	Risk without controls	Extremely high
	Control(s)	Implement a proxy for outbound messages and a reverse proxy for inbound messages for SAP PCK.
	Risk with control(s)	Normal
	Section	21.4.4
6.	Risk potential	The message exchange is not audited or monitored. The executed message transfers are not checked for potential processing errors using the central monitor.
	Impact	Processing errors are not discovered at an early stage and result in instabilities in the integration network. Important transactions might not be carried out, and this can lead to financial loss.
	Risk without controls	High
	Control(s)	Constant monitoring of SAP PCK using the central monitor provided for this purpose.
	Risk with control(s)	Normal
	Section	21.4.5
7.	Risk potential	No authentication for the file adapter. SAP PCK enables you to retrieve files from a sending system and to place them on a receiving system using file adapters. There is no authentication for the file adapter—at a technical level, or at the user level. Therefore, this communication channel is very accessible.
	Impact	Due to the lack of authentication, files can be introduced to a target system to overwrite the password file /etc/passwd, for example. A new user can be created in this way. The attacked target system can be controlled by using the new user.
	Risk without controls	High
	Control(s)	It is vital that you ensure a correct configuration of authorizations at operating-system level for accesses from SAP PCK to the relevant file directories, especially when using the file adapter. This applies to the SYSADM user, in particular, in whose context SAP XI is executed at operating-system level.

Table 21.1 Risks and Controls for the SAP Partner Connectivity Kit (cont.)

No.	Classification	Description
	Risk with control(s)	Normal
	Section	21.4.6

Table 21.1 Risks and Controls for the SAP Partner Connectivity Kit (cont.)

21.3 Application Security

For the design and configuration phase (see Chapter 20), SAP PCK is delivered with predefined roles by default. Because SAP PCK is based on the technical runtime environment of SAP Web AS J2EE, we're dealing with J2EE roles (see also Chapter 8) that can be assigned to the administrative users via the Visual Administrator. The following J2EE roles are available by default (see Table 21.2).

PCK role	J2EE component	Description
Administrate	`sap.com/com.sap.xi.pck*` `aii_ib_sbeans`	This J2EE role enables a user to fully access the configuration interface of SAP PCK. The user can therefore administer the integration scenario according to the Integration Builder of SAP XI.
Display	`sap.com/com.sap.xi.mdt*mdt`	This J2EE role gives the user read access to the processed messages in the message monitor.
Modify	`sap.com/com.sap.xi.mdt*mdt`	This J2EE role enables a user to modify the messages processed in the message monitor.
Payload	`sap.com/com.sap.xi.mdt*mdt`	This J2EE role gives a user read access to the *message payload*. This role should therefore be assigned very restrictively.
xi_af_adapter_ monitor	`sap.com/com.sap.aii.af.app*` `AdapterFramework`	Using this J2EE role, the state of the Integration Adapter for SOAP, HTTP, etc., can be viewed.
Support	`sap.com/com.sap.xi.pck*pck`	This J2EE role enables access to the administration of system parameters of SAP PCK.

Table 21.2 J2EE Administration Roles for SAP PCK

21.4 Technical Security

21.4.1 Separate Technical Service User for Every Connected Partner System

As in SAP XI, a separate technical service user should be chosen for SAP PCK as well. In the standard delivery, this is the technical service user PCKRECEIVER. This user should be copied and renamed for every connected system. In SAP PCK, the role **xi_af_receiver** is designed for this purpose. It is included in the J2EE component sap.com/com.sap.aii.af.ms.app*MessagingSystem. This role must be assigned to the set up technical service users using the Visual Administrator.

21.4.2 Setting Up Encryption for Communication Channels

The encryption of communication channels for the SAP PCK adapter—HTTP(S)— is set up just like it is in SAP XI. Therefore, the exact details have not been repeated here. Instead, simply refer to Section 20.4.2 for more information.

21.4.3 Digital Signature for XML-Based Messages

The mechanisms for establishing message-based security are also identical to those of SAP XI. The XI 3.0 protocol supporting this is used precisely for this purpose (see Section 20.4.3). The configuration editor is called via the URL *http://<PCK_host>:<port>/pck/start* (for example, *http://supplier.pck.de:50000/ pck/start*).

21.4.4 Network-Side Security for Integration Scenarios

Like SAP XI, SAP PCK can be secured on the network side using a proxy for outbound messages and a reverse proxy for inbound messages. This means that you must transfer the DMZ structure shown in Figure 20.8 to the business partner. The application-level gateways for XML-based communication, which is recommended for SAP XI, can be implemented here as well.

21.4.5 Audit of the Message Exchange

As for SAP XI, you should monitor the message exchange in SAP PCK. For this purpose, the monitoring tool can be called from the PCK start (URL: *http://<PCK_ Host>:<port>/pck/start*). Using the monitoring tool, you can archive critical messages, that is, those messages that have been digitally signed.

Besides monitoring messages, you can also monitor the adapter state. Using graphical symbols, you can easily detect whether problems have occurred during the forwarding and processing of messages.

To perform the audit of SAP PCK at an early stage and to take quick countermeasures if errors occur, we recommend that you combine SAP PCK with the SAP CCMS monitor if it is already implemented for monitoring other SAP systems.

21.4.6 Securing the File Adapter at Operating-System Level

The file adapter is secured in the same way here as it is in SAP XI. And, as in SAP XI, here again, you are strongly advised not to implement this adapter in an Internet scenario. If there are no other options, you must ensure that the operating system access of the technical user, who is running SAP PCK on the server, is greatly restricted. You should assign an authorization to this user for only those directories in which the files for further processing—by the actual target application—are to be stored.

22 SAP Mobile Infrastructure

This chapter describes IT security concepts for the Global Security Positioning System (GSPS) component, SAP Mobile Infrastructure. The security of replicating applications and data are the primary considerations.

22.1 Introduction and Functionality

The use of mobile end devices is clearly becoming increasingly more important in many business scenarios. In particular, logistics uses mobile scanners that capture goods receipts and goods issue on site and post them directly to inventory. In addition, sales staff needs a way to close an order directly at a customer's site. The use of mobile devices enables sales staff to improve their relationships with very important customers. For that reason, the use of mobile applications in various business processes will increase significantly. Moreover, the use of *radio frequency identifier technology* (RIFD) provides yet another push in that direction.

Within mySAP Business Suite, SAP offers several mobile applications implemented on the basis of *SAP Mobile Infrastructure* (SAP MI). The applications include mobile asset management within mySAP Product Lifecycle Management (mySAP PLM), mobile field sales within mySAP Customer Relationship Management (mySAP CRM), mobile warehouse management within mySAP Supply Chain Management (mySAP SCM), and many more. The mobile devices involved include traditional notebooks, but also *personal digital assistants* (PDAs), mobile phones, and other devices. The prerequisite is that the mobile device can run the mobile client component, SAP MI.

SAP MI supports two scenarios for mobile use. In the *online scenario*, the mobile device uses a middle layer to connect directly to the backend application. Data is exchanged directly online. In the *offline scenario*, the mobile device works independently of the backend application. Data is exchanged periodically during a synchronization process. The second scenario occurs more often, because an opportunity to establish a direct connection with the backend application is not a frequent occurrence. Therefore, the offline scenario is considered to be the more important scenario, and is the model on which the following security considerations are based. The architecture of SAP MI is identical in both scenarios, as shown in Figure 22.1.

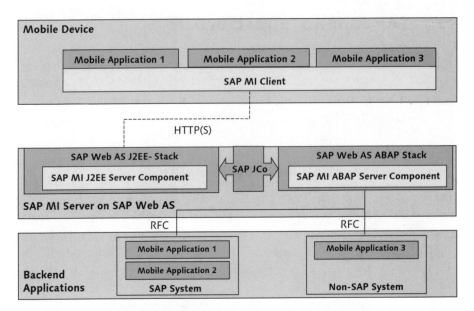

Figure 22.1 Technical Architecture of SAP MI

The mobile SAP MI client is installed on the mobile device as an independent, technical runtime environment. With this component, applications can be developed independently of the operating system on the mobile device. The following operating systems are currently supported: Windows NT/2000/XP, Pocket PC 2002/2003, Linux Embedix by Sharp, and Windows CE .NET 2.4. The SAP MI client assumes responsibility for the following tasks and provides the required application programming interfaces (APIs):

▶ Local data storage

▶ Data synchronization between the mobile device and the SAP MI server

▶ Application management

▶ Tracing and logging on files that can also be transmitted to the SAP MI server

▶ Configuration management for setting application and user parameters

▶ User-interface programming models based on JSP/AWT

▶ User management

The SAP MI server serves as the middleware and controls the mobile device with its options for data synchronization. Once again, it uses SAP Web AS as the technical, runtime environment. SAP WEB AS consists of two components: one based on J2EE and one based on ABAP. The J2EE component is responsible for the following tasks:

- Synchronization of configuration, application, and user data with the SAP MI client
- Distribution of applications on the individual mobile devices that are connected
- Establishing an encrypted connection to the SAP MI client
- Compressed transfer of information
- Control of the relay or communication of application data with the ABAP component

The ABAP component is responsible for the following tasks:

- Control of the processing of asynchronous queuing
- Control of communication with the backend applications that have been called for synchronous or asynchronous communication
- Management of user rights (authorization concept) and control of the distribution of user rights to the mobile devices that are connected
- Management of applications and control of the distribution of applications to the mobile devices that are connected

22.2 Risks and Controls

The risks and controls described in this chapter refer exclusively to SAP MI. Risks that arise because of the mobile transfer protocol being used (such as GPRS, GSM, UMTS, or WLAN) are not addressed in more detail here. See Chapter 29 for risks related to the mobile devices. See Chapter 8 for risks related to SAP Web AS; this chapter does not describe these risks.

We'll now apply the methodology for risk analysis, which we introduced in Chapter 2, in a simpler form to SAP MI to determine the primary, critical security risks and the required controls (see Table 22.1). The sections that follow provide a greater specification of the controls and illustrate them with examples.

No.	Classification	Description
1.	Risk potential	Missing authorization concept for the mobile application.
		A missing or incomplete authorization concept can give unauthorized users access to functionalities in the application for which they do not have rights. Other users might have access to a functional scope that is too wide, because no concept for a separation of functions exists. Legal frameworks can also be disregarded.

Table 22.1 Risks and Controls for SAP MI

No.	Classification	Description
	Impact	Unauthorized transactions or a missing separation of functions means that fraudulent actions can be started. Such actions can include unauthorized financial transactions or violate legal requirements. Section 4.1 reviews important legal requirements.
	Risk without controls	Extremely high
	Control(s)	Design and implementation of an authorization concept that considers the principle of information ownership and separates functions. This control is an important requirement of the Sarbanes-Oxley Act (SOX). The control also applies to mobile applications.
	Risk with control(s)	Normal
	Section	22.3.1
2.	Risk potential	Missing authorization concept for the administration of SAP MI. Unauthorized administrators obtain access to the configuration parameters of SAP MI. Administration also lacks the related separation of functions.
	Impact	Unauthorized administrators obtain access to the configuration settings of SAP MI, particularly the mechanisms of user management and application distribution. Such access endangers the stability of the mobile infrastructure and might allow unauthorized devices to log on to the SAP MI server. Ultimately, unauthorized persons can execute fraudulent actions, like financial transactions.
	Risk without controls	Extremely high
	Control(s)	Design and implementation of an authorization concept for the administration of SAP MI.
	Risk with control(s)	Normal
	Section	22.3.2
3.	Risk potential	Authorizations of RFC users are too broad. A technical RFC user is required to establish an RFC connection to the backend applications. The scope of authorizations assigned to this user is too broad. In some cases, the complete authorization "SAP_ALL" is granted.
	Impact	Although the user types "communication" and "service" are typically set, authorizations whose scope is too broad allow for the unauthorized creation of new dialog users in the backend applications. In this manner, SAP MI can become compromised.

Table 22.1 Risks and Controls for SAP MI (cont.)

No.	Classification	Description
	Risk without controls	High
	Control(s)	Restriction of RFC authorizations for the current RFC users to the ABAP function groups that are actually called.
	Risk with control(s)	Normal
	Section	22.3.3
4.	Risk potential	Unencrypted communications connections.
		The communications connections between the mobile device and the SAP MI server, between SAP Web AS J2EE and SAP Web AS ABAP (via JCo), and between the SAP MI server and backend applications are unencrypted.
	Impact	The information being transmitted can be viewed or manipulated by unauthorized parties. Authentication data between the SAP MI client and the SAP MI server can also be spied on. That means that an unauthorized external device can log on to the SAP MI server and execute application functions or exchange data. Fraudulent activities like unauthorized financial transactions can be triggered.
	Risk without controls	Extremely high
	Control(s)	Encryption of the most important communications connections for SAP MI.
	Risk with control(s)	Normal
	Section	22.4.1
5.	Risk potential	The selected password is too obvious.
		The authentication mechanism between the SAP MI client and the SAP MI server is based on the user ID and password method. The selected password is too obvious (i.e., too easy for hackers to deduce) and authentication on the mobile device itself was deactivated.
	Impact	Unauthorized mobile devices can log on to the SAP MI server simply by guessing the password in a brute-force attack. Consequently, data can be exchanged with the backend applications and unauthorized financial transactions can be executed.
	Risk without controls	Extremely high
	Control(s)	Selection of a complex password for authentication of the SAP MI client to the SAP MI server for data synchronization.
	Risk with control(s)	Normal
	Section	22.4.2

Table 22.1 Risks and Controls for SAP MI (cont.)

No.	Classification	Description
6.	Risk potential	Superfluous services on the SAP MI server.
		Services on the SAP MI server have been activated, although they are not required for the synchronization of application data or for online access.
	Impact	Superfluous services can be used to compromise the SAP MI server.
	Risk without controls	Extremely high
	Control(s)	Deactivation of the superfluous services on the SAP MI server.
	Risk with control(s)	Normal
	Section	22.4.3
7.	Risk potential	Missing network segmentation.
		At the network level, inadequate security of the SAP MI server exists, because of not separating the network into trustworthy and non-trustworthy areas with firewalls.
	Impact	Inadequate security, with appropriate firewall configuration on the network side, leaves any vulnerabilities at the operating-system level open to possible attacks. Hackers might be able to receive administrator rights. Unauthorized access to confidential information can be achieved in this manner; unauthorized financial transactions or manipulations are also possible.
	Risk without controls	High
	Control(s)	Protection of the SAP MI server with network security is achieved by dividing the network segments into unsecured and trustworthy segments. The control can be implemented by configuring network-based firewalls appropriately.
	Risk with control(s)	Normal
	Section	22.4.4
8.	Risk potential	Missing monitoring concept.
		No monitoring concept is present for the SAP MI system landscape.
	Impact	System availability or unavailability cannot be recognized. Users cannot access their applications. The synchronization mechanism is unavailable. Sales revenues can suffer if orders cannot be scheduled in production in a timely manner.
	Risk without controls	High
	Control(s)	Implementation of a system monitoring concept with the required reaction and problem-resolution processes.

Table 22.1 Risks and Controls for SAP MI (cont.)

No.	Classification	Description
	Risk with control(s)	Normal
	Section	22.4.5

Table 22.1 Risks and Controls for SAP MI (cont.)

22.3 Application Security

22.3.1 Authorization Concept for SAP MI Applications

The basic authorization concept for SAP MI applications essentially corresponds to the ABAP authorization concept. The same basic principles (information responsibility by business units, risk management, and so on) implemented in stationary SAP applications are applicable to mobile applications integrated in the portfolio of SAP applications. This observation is an important aspect of compliance with SOX.

However, mobile applications do have special characteristics, which we will examine more closely. Also noteworthy is the fact that SAP MI is used primarily only when it deals with offline applications that synchronize their information with the backends and therefore execute the appropriate transactions. Consequently, authorizations must be controlled on the mobile device and in the backend applications that are called by the mobile application.

Authorization objects are also used to define the scope of authorizations for mobile applications. But the authorization objects used in the mobile application are not created individually and locally in each mobile device. Instead, they're created centrally in the SAP MI ABAP server component using the *Mobile Component Descriptor* (MCD). The MCD defines and describes all parameters of the mobile application: the name of the required mobile software components, version, description, component type (an additional required technical runtime component for the mobile device), and so on. The MCD also defines the authorization objects that should be checked in the mobile application. This setting is made in the dependency definition of the MCD under the **Environment** tab. The dependency is defined with three parameters:

▶ `DEPENDENCY_TYPE`
This parameter must be set to `AUTH_OBJECT`. It determines the type of dependency to be defined. This example involves a dependency definition for an authorization object.

▶ `DEPENDENCY_NAME`
This parameter specifies the name of the dependency definition.

▶ **DEPENDENCY_VALUE**

This parameter defines an existing ABAP authorization object (like M_MATE_ BUK, creation of a material master for a specific company code) that should be checked in the mobile application. The developer must program this authorization object in advance, so that it can be included in the dependency definition. The developer must also provide default values for the dependency definitions.

The dependency definition determines which authorization objects in the SAP MI ABAP server component must be assigned specific characteristics for the mobile application (for example, using Transaction PFCG) and must later be loaded into the mobile application during synchronization. Accordingly, the authorization objects can be managed just like all other ABAP applications.

In addition to the business authorization objects defined in the dependency definition, the authorization objects must be assigned to and given characteristics for a role. Roles are listed on the **Authorizations** tab in the MCD. These authorization objects have a technical orientation and define synchronization authorizations and so on. Table 22.2 lists the most important authorization objects and fields. They must be maintained for all users.

Authorization object	Field	Value	Description
S_ME_SYNC	**ACTVT** (Activity)	38 (Execute)	This authorization must be assigned to each user. It enables synchronization between the SAP MI client and SAP MI server for installation of the mobile application or other components, and for the exchange of business data with backend applications.
S_RFC	**ACTVT** (Activity)	16 (Execute)	This authorization must be assigned to each user. It enables execution access to the function group defined in the following. The function group is required for synchronization between the SAP MI client and server.
	RFC_NAME (Name of the function group)	RFC1 SDIRRUNTIME SYST SG00 SRFC SYSU	This authorization must be assigned to each user. It enables implementation of the Java Connector (Jco).

Table 22.2 Technical Authorization Objects for SAP MI

Authorization object	Field	Value	Description
		ME_USER	This authorization must be assigned to each user. It enables changes of the synchronization password.
		BWAF_MW	This authorization must be assigned to each user. It enables synchronization of business data with backend applications.
	RFC_TYP	FUGR	Only the value "FUGR" (function group) can be defined.

Table 22.2 Technical Authorization Objects for SAP MI (cont.)

In order for a user to work with mobile applications, the ABAP role assigned to that user must include a definition of the mobile application—much like the concept of the S-TCODE for stationary transactions. A MiniApp is created in the SAP MI ABAP server component for the mobile application. The MiniApp has the same name as the mobile application described in the MCD. The MiniApp must then be assigned to a role (for instance with Transaction PFCG, **MiniApps** tab). The role can then be assigned to the user. Figure 22.2 illustrates the relationship between mobile application authorizations and authorizations that apply to the server side. The example shows that the MCD and dependency definition can also set the authorization object (Object 3) to **not checked**.

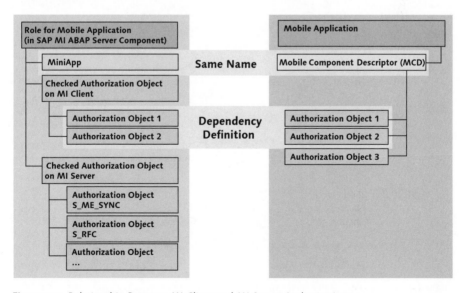

Figure 22.2 Relationship Between MI Client and MI Server Authorizations

Once an ABAP role for each mobile application has been determined for the SAP MI ABAP server component, the next step assigns the role to the user, after which the mobile application can be distributed to the mobile devices by synchronization. That occurs in two steps. The first step uses the report WAF_DEPLOYMENT_ FROM_ROLES to consolidate all roles. It then writes the MiniApps and the corresponding mobile applications (according to the report) to a synchronization directory.

The synchronization directory can be controlled from the *SAP MI Web Console*, which enables you to view and edit the pending distribution of mobile applications for the mobile devices that are available. Theoretically, the SAP MI Web Console can be used to distribute the mobile application to a user without prior definition of a role. Such an action should be used only as an extreme measure, however, and therefore, we will not elaborate further on this rare exception. The Web Console can also be used to distribute the mobile applications to the mobile devices that are available. This feature can be helpful when a mobile application should not be distributed to all mobile devices. Service **SyncBO MIAUTH** can be started from the SAP MI Web Console; it handles the final distribution of authorizations and mobile applications to the mobile devices.

22.3.2 Authorization Concept for Administration

The administration of SAP MI requires the authorizations listed in Table 22.2 and the definition of the authorizations listed in Table 22.3.

Authorization object	Field	Value	Description
S_RFC	**ACTVT** (Activity)	16 (Execute)	This authorization enables execution access to the following defined function group: This function group is required for synchronization between the SAP MI client and the server.
	RFC_NAME (Name of the function group)	MEREP_ INSTTK_ MPC	This authorization is required to use the installation kit.
		BWAF_ MOMO	This authorization is required to start the SAP MI Web Console.
	RFC_TYP	FUGR	Only the value "FUGR" (function group) can be defined.

Table 22.3 Authorization Objects for the Administration of SAP MI

Authorization object	Field	Value	Description
S_TCODE	TCD (Transaction code)	SMOMO	This authorizes the transaction to call the SAP MI Web Console.
		MEREP*	This authorizes the transaction to control intelligent synchronization.
		MI_MCD, MCD	The editor for the mobile component descriptor is started with MI_MCD or MCD.
S_MI_MGMT	ACTVT (Activity)	01 (Create) 02 (Change) 03 (Display) 06 (Delete) 78 (Assign)	This authorization defines the administration rights permitted for defining SAP MI components in the MCD and the SAP MI Web Console.
	MI_GROUP	Administrator group	Groups can help divide the administrators into various levels of authorization. Some groups should include activities 01, 02, 03, and 06, but not 78. Another group should contain rights 03 and 78. A separation of functions can be achieved in this manner. The groups can be maintained using Table MEMGMT_AUTH_GRP and Transaction MGMT_AUTHORITY.
S_MI_CCMS	ACTVT (Activity)	*	This authorization can maintain the alarm notifications sent to the CCMS. Complete authorization can be assigned to all administrators here.
S_MI_ALERT	ACTVT (Activity)	36	This authorization is used to maintain the alarm notifications displayed in the SAP MI Web Console.
S_DATASET	ACTVT (Activity)	34	This authorization can store the alarm notifications on the SAP MI server.

Table 22.3 Authorization Objects for the Administration of SAP MI (cont.)

22.3.3 Restricting the Authorizations of the RFC User to Backend Applications

As shown in Figure 22.1, backend applications are accessed with an RFC access. Access requires the setup of a technical RFC user in the backend applications. The SAP MI ABAP server component logs on with the technical user. The type of RFC user is either "communication" or "service." Even if the user type appears not to be critical because no dialog logon is possible, the RFC user may not be assigned a full authorization like "SAP_ALL." Instead, the user should contain authorization object S_RFC, which can granularly control the call of the function groups in the backend applications that are actually needed for the application with authorization field RFC_NAME. Authorized function groups must be at least the same as those of the mobile application itself and of all wrapper and BAPI wrapper function groups.

See Chapter 8 for the exact method of limiting the function groups to be assigned properties in authorization object S_RFC. Chapter 8 also describes how an authorization check with trusted RFC calls differs.

22.4 Technical Security

22.4.1 Setting Up Encrypted Communications Connections

SAP MI includes the following three major types of communications connections:

1. Communication between the SAP MI client and the SAP MI J2EE server component. This communication is primarily used to distribute the software components, parameter settings, and authorizations, and to synchronize business data and objects. The standard protocol used is HTTP. The underlying carrier protocols are either GSM, UMTS, GPRS, or other mobile protocols. SSL (HTTPS) can be used to encrypt the connection.

2. Internal communication between the SAP MI J2EE server component and the SAP MI ABAP server component over the internal Java Connector (JCo) connection, which corresponds to an RFC connection. The connection can be encrypted with a secure network connection.

3. Communication between the SAP MI ABAP server component and each backend application via RFC. This connection can also be encrypted with SNC.

Encryption of the first type of communication noted above is imperative, because the SAP MI client is authenticated to the SAP MI J2EE server component with a user ID and password. Encryption of the internal JCo and RFC connections with Secure Network Communication (SNC) is recommended, but not required.

Depending on the potential risks of the mobile application, encryption should be used. The use of SNC should result in a stronger technical authentication among the server components—another reason to recommend implementation. See Chapter 8 for information on how to set up an SNC encryption.

Both sides must be configured to set up the HTTPS connection between the SAP MI client and the SAP MI J2EE server components. The first step configures the SAP MI J2EE server component for the HTTPS service. See Chapter 8 for information on the configuration. The next step converts the configuration of the SAP MI client to HTTPS communication. Conversion occurs in the file *MobileEngine.config*, which is located in the *SAP MI Client Component Installation Path/Settings* directory. The following parameters must be set as indicated below in the file:

▶ `MobileEngine.Security.SSLSupport = True`
   SSL support is activated in the SAP MI client.

▶ `MobileEngine.Security.HostnameVerifying = True`
   When calling the mobile application with a URL, the server name given in the URL is checked with the server certificate of the SAP MI server.

▶ `MobileEngine.Sync.ConnectionTimeout = -1`
   This technical parameter optimizes the synchronization performance when SSL is used as the communication protocol.

If no trustworthy Certificate Authority (CA) has issued the server certificate of the SAP MI J2EE server component (see the list of trustworthy CAs in SAP Note 602993), either the issuing CA certificate or the SAP MI server certification must be defined as trustworthy. Definition occurs in the SAP MI client with *keytool* from Sun Microsystems. The complete command then appears as follows:

```
keytool -import -alias <Alias-name> -file
<server-certificate-file> -keystore truststore
```

The alias name is a short form of the digital certificate that is considered as trustworthy. This name must be identical to the name of the server certificate.

Once configuration is complete, the communication between the SAP MI client and the SAP MI J2EE server component occurs with SSL.

22.4.2 Securing the Synchronization Communication

As described in the previous section, the communication that occurs between the SAP MI client and the SAP MI J2EE server component helps to synchronize business transaction data after all components have been installed on the mobile device. Users of the mobile application on the mobile device can have up to three passwords. One password is for authentication to the operating system of the mobile device; the second password is for logging on to the SAP MI client; and the third password is for authentication to the SAP MI J2EE server component for synchronizing the business data. The following minimum criteria apply to all three passwords:

▶ Length of at least eight characters
▶ At least one special character
▶ At least one letter
▶ At least one number

A configuration file on the mobile devices stores the password for logging on to the SAP MI client as a hash value. The user can change it at will. Only the SAP MI server stores the password for synchronization, however. Various options can force a logon during synchronization with the SAP MI J2EE server component. In the file *MobileEngine.config*, the parameter `MobileEngine.Security.Synchro-nizationPasswordHandlingOption` can be set as follows:

▶ `atsync`
The local password for logging on to the SAP MI client does not correspond to the synchronization password. The synchronization password must be entered at every synchronization. This is the default setting and is also recommended.

▶ `local`
The local password for logging on to the SAP MI client corresponds to the synchronization password. The synchronization password need not be entered for each synchronization. This setting is not recommended.

This setting is a good idea only when automatically scheduled synchronizations (controlled with the `Timed Sync` parameter) are to be executed. In this case, it is the only feasible option. However, the risk potential is greater, because synchronization can still occur if the mobile device is stolen, which can lead to erroneous postings.

▶ `once`
The local password for logging on to the SAP MI client does not correspond to the synchronization password. The synchronization password must be entered only once for each logon to the SAP MI Client—at the first synchronization. Follow-up synchronization in the same logon session does not require you to enter the password. This setting is also not recommended.

The logon session must be deactivated after three incorrect logon attempts on the SAP MI server to avoid successful brute force attacks. Deactivation is defined with parameter `login/fails_to_user_lock`. The user account should be locked after three incorrect attempts to log on.

Administrators must be informed if a mobile device is stolen so they can lock the user account immediately.

When a JSP-based application (Java application) is installed on the SAP MI client, a local web server with a configurable log function exists on the SAP MI client. The `Information` or `Debug` parameters must not be set to display mode (verbosity level), because the Jasper log function would also log the synchronization password on the side of the mobile device in this case. The default setting is

"FATAL," and should be used. You can check the setting in the installation directory of the SAP MI client on the side of the mobile device in the file *server.xml* in subdirectory *conf*.

22.4.3 Deactivating Superfluous Services on the SAP MI Server

Superfluous services should be deactivated when using SAP MI. Deactivation is important for HTTP-based services, because they're made available externally with the Internet Communication Manager (ICM) and called by entering the URL. Demo services can be called in this manner, for example. But those services have a drawback—they enable attackers to obtain additional system information or non-secured demo services that can compromise the integrity of the SAP ABAP server. This is why extraneous services must be deactivated in the SAP MI ABAP server component using Transaction SICF.

The services that SAP MI doesn't need for administration and runtime should also be deactivated for the SAP MI J2EE server component. Chapter 8 describes a possible strategy.

22.4.4 Secure Network Architecture

Secure network architecture can also be set up for SAP MI according to the concept of a demilitarized zone (DMZ). The SAP MI server can be placed behind the first firewall in the external DMZ 1. The use of an upstream reverse proxy with SAP MI is difficult to configure because of the synchronization mechanism. Figure 22.3 shows the proposed network architecture; however, the figure does not display the intermediate transmission paths, such as a telecommunications provider with a receiving station, conversion of wireless into wired communications, and so on.

As noted in the previous section, the communication between the individual technical components should be encrypted. If possible, the backend applications can be placed in the internal DMZ 2. Because intelligent synchronization temporarily stores business data on the SAP MI server, special hardening measures must be used for this server at the operating-system level. The hardening measures correspond to those of SAP Web AS. See Chapter 8 for more information.

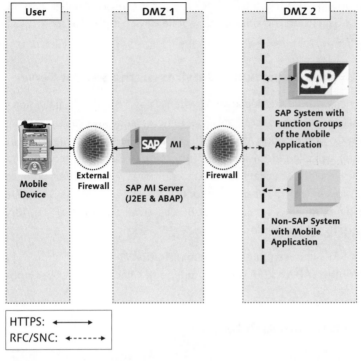

Figure 22.3 DMZ Network Architecture for SAP MI

22.4.5 Monitoring

As holds true for all other SAP systems, SAP MI can also be connected to the Computing Center Management System (CCMS) (Transaction RZ20). A monitoring template for SAP MI already exists; it can be tailored to meet individual needs. The template supports the following monitoring functions:

▶ Configuration of SAP MI, including all mobile devices, SAP MI server, and backend applications

▶ Heartbeats: all functions of the SAP MI server are active

▶ Tracing functions for successful synchronization between the SAP MI client and the SAP MI server

▶ Alarm notifications for memory problems, unavailable services, and so on

▶ Logging of the intelligent synchronization functions

▶ Tracing of the SAP MI client distribution functions and configurations

Activation of CCMS monitoring for SAP MI occurs with the report SAP_CCMS_MONI_BATCH_DP, which collects all the data of the passive data collector MI_*. Transaction RZ21 controls the data collector; it runs every 60 minutes by default.

This value can be controlled via Transaction SM36. The connection of the SAP MI J2EE server must be created as a scenario in Transaction GRMG (*generic request and message generator*). The scenario must then be imported into GRMG as an XML configuration file. Then, it can be activated.

Of course, it's important that organizational and process support exists for monitoring SAP MI. Only the discovery of disruptions and errors within a short period of time can trigger the implementation of the required countermeasures. All tasks and responsibilities of individual administrators involved in the monitoring process must be defined before an actual disruption occurs.

23   Database Server

This chapter describes IT security concepts for the Global Security Positioning System (GSPS) component, database server. It focuses on access security and the secure storage of business data.

23.1   Introduction and Functions

The *database server* is the central persistent storage area for all business data, customizing settings, data dictionary descriptions (DDIC), user master data, and so on for SAP Web AS systems. From a technical viewpoint, the database can be implemented in one of two ways. In the first option, it can be implemented on a central database server. Each SAP Web AS system would be connected to the central database server and receive its own database instance. In the second option, each SAP Web AS system would have its own database on its own database instance.

The advantage of a central database instance is an ability to centralize management of the database more easily. Easier management includes design, backup, and monitoring functions. This approach also allows for a physical separation of SAP Web AS and the database, which corresponds to a separation of application logic and data storage. This approach can raise the level of security, because access to the database server from the Internet must cross various demilitarized zones (DMZs).

The SAP environment can use database systems from the following manufacturers:

▶ IBM DB2

▶ Informix

▶ MaxDB

▶ Oracle

▶ Microsoft SQL Server

This book cannot examine the security aspects of each manufacturer's database system. Instead, it will examine basic security principles.

23.2   Risks and Controls

The methodology introduced in Chapter 2 for risk analysis will now be applied in a simpler form to the database server to determine the primary, critical security risks and the required controls (see Table 23.1). The sections that follow will provide more specification of the controls and illustrate them with examples.

No.	Classification	Description
1.	Risk potential	Access to database resources has not been restricted.
		Access rights to important database resources for UNIX operating system users have not been restricted.
	Impact	The lack of limited access rights (especially for the UNIX operating system) to important database resources can bypass access limitations within the database management system. Such a situation can compromise the integrity of the database. Unauthorized access that manipulates tables is also possible.
	Risk without controls	Extremely high
	Control(s)	Restriction of access rights to database resources under UNIX.
	Risk with control(s)	Normal
	Section	23.3
2.	Risk potential	No password change.
		The passwords for default database users (technical users) used for impersonal access to the database were not changed or not set.
	Impact	If the default passwords are not changed, the database management system, OBDC, and JDBC can be used to establish a connection to the database. Because default database users usually have administrator rights and must have them in SAP systems, users can view and modify tables and objects without authorization.
	Risk without controls	Extremely high
	Control(s)	The passwords of default database users must be changed in all cases. The password selected must be sufficiently complex, i.e., to prevent possible brute force attacks. If possible, use an operating system user (such as <sapsid>) to select authentication integrated with the operating system.
	Risk with control(s)	Normal
	Section	23.3
3.	Risk potential	Unnecessary entries for database users.
		The database management system (DBMS) has entries for extraneous database users (such as demo users).

Table 23.1 Risks and Controls for the Database Server

No.	Classification	Description
	Impact	An attacker can use extraneous database users to compromise the entire database. By exploiting this vulnerability in the system, an attacker can obtain broader rights and thereby view and manipulate tables in the database without authorization.
	Risk without controls	High
	Control(s)	Remove the superfluous database user entries in the DBMS.
	Risk with control(s)	Normal
	Section	23.4.2
4.	Risk potential	Unprotected DBMS. Access to the DBMS is inadequately secured. For example, the Oracle Listener is configured to allow logons to the database from every computer in a less trustworthy network segment.
	Impact	Insecure access to the database can compromise tables and the business data they store.
	Risk without controls	High
	Control(s)	Restriction of access to database management and use of firewalls to secure access to the database server from a less trustworthy network segment.
	Risk with control(s)	Normal
	Section	23.4.3
5.	Risk potential	Missing database backup concept. No strategy or concept to back up and archive the database. Legal requirements (for example, from the GoBS) might be disregarded.
	Impact	The lack of a database backup concept can lead to a partial or complete loss of all business data. Disregarding legal requirements can lead to fines.
	Risk without controls	Extremely high
	Control(s)	Design and setup of a database backup concept.
	Risk with control(s)	Normal
	Section	23.4.4

Table 23.1 Risks and Controls for the Database Server (cont.)

No.	Classification	Description
6.	Risk potential	Missing upgrade concept.
		No design of a regular upgrade concept for the database to implement the most recent security patches.
	Impact	Security weaknesses are corrected too late with the appropriate patch. A potential attacker can exploit this vulnerability. Ultimately, the database can be compromised.
	Risk without controls	High
	Control(s)	Design and implementation of an upgrade concept for the database.
	Risk with control(s)	Normal
	Section	23.4.5

Table 23.1 Risks and Controls for the Database Server (cont.)

23.3 Application Security

You must be very restrictive when setting access rights to files of database resources, especially where UNIX is concerned. The following sections display the settings for two common database systems, DB2 and Oracle.

For DB2 on UNIX, the access rights to database-relevant resources must be set as shown in Table 23.2: <dbsid> stands for the database ID. User db2<dbsid> is the technical user who installed the database, which runs at operating-system level. This user belongs to UNIX group SYSADM_GROUP.

Directory or file	Access rights in octal form	Owner	Group
/db2/db2<dbsid>	755	db2<dbsid>	SYSADM_GROUP
/db2/<DBSID>/db2dump	755	db2<dbsid>	SYSADM_GROUP
/db2/<DBSID>/log_dir	755	db2<dbsid>	SYSADM_GROUP
/db2/<SAPSID>/sapdata*	755	db2<dbsid>	SYSADM_GROUP
/db2/<SAPSID>/sapdata*/container	600	db2<dbsid>	SYSADM_GROUP
/db2/<DBSID>/saptemp1	755	db2<dbsid>	SYSADM_GROUP

Table 23.2 Access Rights for DB2 Directories and Files Under UNIX

For Oracle on UNIX, the access rights to database-relevant resources must be set as shown in Table 23.3. User ora<dbsid> is the technical user who installed the database, which runs at operating-system level. This user belongs to UNIX group dba and is also referred to as a database instance user.

Directory or file	Access rights in octal form	Owner	Group	Comment
/oracle/<DBSID>/sapdata*	755	ora<dbsid>	dba	
/oracle/<DBSID>/sapdata*/*	755	ora<dbsid>	dba	
/oracle/<DBSID>/sapdata*/*/*	640	ora<dbsid>	dba	Data files
/oracle/<DBSID>/oraarch	755	ora<dbsid>	dba	
/oracle/<DBSID>/oraarch	640	ora<dbsid>	dba	Archive files
/oracle/<DBSID>/saparch	755	ora<dbsid>	dba	
/oracle/<DBSID>/sapreorg	755	ora<dbsid>	dba	
/oracle/<DBSID>/sapbackup	755	ora<dbsid>	dba	
/oracle/<DBSID>/dbs	755	ora<dbsid>	dba	
/oracle/<DBSID>/sapcheck	755	ora<dbsid>	dba	
/oracle/<DBSID>/sapstat	755	ora<dbsid>	dba	
/oracle/<DBSID>/saptrace	755	ora<dbsid>	dba	
/oracle/<DBSID>/saptrace/*	755	ora<dbsid>	dba	
/oracle/<DBSID>/saptrace/*/*	640	ora<dbsid>	dba	
/oracle/<DBSID>/origlog*	755	ora<dbsid>	dba	Redo log directories
/oracle/<DBSID>/origlog*/*	640	ora<dbsid>	dba	Redo log files
/oracle/<DBSID>/mirrlog*	755	ora<dbsid>	dba	Redo log directories
/oracle/<DBSID>/mirrlog*/*	640	ora<dbsid>	dba	Redo log files

Table 23.3 Access Rights for Oracle Directories and Files Under UNIX

23.4 Technical Security

23.4.1 Changing Default Passwords

Passwords have default settings once the database server has been installed. Every database administrator is generally aware of the passwords, which can be looked up easily on the Internet. That's why they must be changed after the installation. The following criteria should be applied when changing the passwords to achieve the necessary level of complexity:

- ▶ Length of at least eight characters
- ▶ At least one special character
- ▶ At least one letter
- ▶ At least one number

The following tables list the important database users for the database systems used primarily with SAP: DB2, Oracle, and SQL Server. The password should be changed for each system. Table 23.4 lists the important technical database users for DB2.

Name	Type	Method to change the password	Description
db2<dbsid>	UNIX and database	UNIX command `passwd`	Database instance user
<sapsid>adm	UNIX and database	DB2 program `dscdb6up`	The SAP system administrator with authorization to start and stop the database.
sapr3 or sap<sapsid>	UNIX and database	DB2 program `dscdb6up`	This user is the owner of all database objects of an SAP system. The SAP system connects to the database with this user.

Table 23.4 Important Database Users for DB2

Table 23.5 lists the important technical database users for Oracle.

Name	Type	Method to change the password	Description
<sapsid>adm	UNIX	UNIX command `passwd`	The SAP system administrator with authorization to start and stop the database.
ora<dbsid>	UNIX	UNIX command `passwd`	Database instance user
SYS (internal)	Database user	BRCONNECT (as of release 6.10), SQL-PLUS chdpass	Database administrator

Table 23.5 Important Database Users for Oracle

Name	Type	Method to change the password	Description
SYSTEM	Database user	BRCONNECT (as of release 6.10), SQL-PLUS chdpass	Database administrator
SAPR3/SAP<SAP SID>	Database user (SAP system)	BRCONNECT (as of release 6.10), or the OPS$ mechanism (chdpass)	This user is the owner of all database objects of an SAP system. The SAP system connects.to the database with this user.

Table 23.5 Important Database Users for Oracle (cont.)

Another important feature of the Oracle database is the OPS$ mechanism, which functions as follows.

The SAP system authenticates itself to the Oracle database with database user SAPR3 or SAP<SID>: the user's password is stored in Table SAPUSER. Authentication does not occur directly. In the first step, the SAP system authenticates itself with user OPS$<UNIX_system_user>. Consider this example: OPS$<SAPSID> adm, where this user represents a UNIX system user and is identified in the database as external. In the second step, the password for user SAPR3 or SAP<SAPSID> is read from Table SAPUSER. The third step consists of the login using database user SAPR3 or SAP<SAPSID>.

The advantage of this procedure is that it does not need to exchange a password over an unencrypted communications connection because the external user (OPS$<UNIX_system_user) has already authenticated itself to the operating system.

Table 23.6 lists the important technical database users for SQL Server.

Name	Type	Method to change the password	Description
sa	Windows and database	Windows operating system command	Database administrator
<sapsid>	Windows and database	Windows operating system	This user is the owner of all database objects of an SAP system. The SAP system connects to the database with this user.

Table 23.6 Important Database Users for SQL Server

Name	Type	Method to change the password	Description
<sapsid>adm	Windows and database	Windows operating system	The SAP system administrator with authorization to start and stop the database.
SAPService <SAPSID>	Windows and database	Windows operating system	Maintenance user

Table 23.6 Important Database Users for SQL Server (cont.)

Prior to authenticating on the SQL Server, you should switch to a mixed logon mode of *SQL Server* and *Windows authentication* before logging on to the SQL server database.

23.4.2 Removing Unnecessary Database Users

Extraneous database users like demo users, or those users employed for development, must be deleted. Otherwise, such users can be exploited for unauthorized access. Also, if the database server is to operate for an SAP system, no other application should run at the same time as the database server. For each SAP system, a different database user should also be used for the connection.

23.4.3 Limiting Database Access

Access to the database server, for example, with SQL*NET commands in the case of Oracle, or with other database management systems from the office communications network of the organization, must be limited. For Oracle systems, the limitation can occur with file *sqlnet.ora*. This file can specify the IP addresses of the management consoles from which access should be possible.

A firewall is another way of restricting access to the database server. The firewall rules should be specified so that only SAP systems and the management consoles obtain access to the database server.

The databases use the following default ports:

▶ **SQL Server**
TCP/IP Port 1433

▶ **Oracle Listener**
TCP/IP Port 1527

▶ **DB2**
TCP/IP Port 4402

23.4.4 Design and Implementation of a Database Backup Concept

By now, the existence of a database backup concept should be a standard operating procedure (SOP). Nonetheless, the following sections briefly describe this necessary measure.

Various strategies exist for a database backup concept. It's generally simpler to implement a concept for a centrally used database server for all SAP systems, because only one, centrally controlled database has to be managed instead of several, distributed database servers. Accordingly, the database server can also be backed up centrally.

The backup can involve a simple design, such as a daily backup run to a tape drive. A complete backup occurs at regular intervals; incremental backups of changes occur later. However, this design requires the shutting down of system operations during the backups, which many companies cannot handle.

A more advanced design synchronizes the database with a parallel database. In this case, all updates to the database are simultaneously executed in a mirrored database. The advantage of this design is that work can continue uninterrupted—with the mirrored database immediately—should the primary database fail. No time-consuming reconstruction of the database is required and production does not need to grind to a halt.

Long-term archiving must be regulated by legal requirements. For example, companies must follow the requirements of the Generally Accepted Accounting Principles in the United States (USGAAP). Consider the following excerpt:

> Generally, data performing voucher functions must be retained for six years; data and other necessary records performing journal or account functions for 10 years. The system documentation on the IT-supported accounting system is one of the operating procedures and other organization documents referred to in Section 257 (1) Commercial Code and Section 147 (1) Tax Code, and must generally be maintained for 10 years. Parts of the system documentation performing voucher functions only (such as the documentation on IT-supported voucher generation, from which postings result) generally must be retained for six years. The system documentation can be maintained on microfiche, microfilm, or other data storage media. The retention periods for system documentation begin at the end of the calendar year in which data related to accounting was recorded, generated, or processed using the respective system.

23.4.5 Design and Implementation of an Upgrade Concept

Because they provide central persistence of all business data, database systems require a particularly high level of security protection. They must therefore be upgraded to the latest versions as soon as possible. A patch or upgrade must be implemented as soon as a manufacturer discovers new vulnerabilities and provides the appropriate patch or upgrade. *Patching* must be an essential component of security management for SAP Web AS systems. Implementation of new patches must adhere to the requirements of the standard change management processes. Before they can be implemented, patches must also undergo a quality assurance process with the required tests. In an emergency, this process must be accelerated.

24 SAP Web Dispatcher

This chapter describes IT security concepts for the Global Security Positioning System (GSPS) component, SAP Web Dispatcher. It focuses on the security functions provided by SAP Web Dispatcher.

24.1 Introduction and Functions

SAP Web Dispatcher is installed at the first access point (similar to a reverse proxy) for incoming HTTP(S) requests in Internet scenarios of a web application, such as Business Server Pages (BSPs), Web Dynpro for ABAP, Java, or a Java Server Pages (JSPs) of an SAP Web AS system. It serves primarily as a load distributor to distribute incoming requests equally on the SAP Web AS systems if the SAP Web AS system is a cluster. However, SAP Web Dispatcher can also handle smaller security functions like URL filtering, as well as serve as a scheduling point for Secure Sockets Layer (SSL). This feature can ensure network-side security for confidential applications, such as business applications that run on SAP Web AS. But, you must not confuse SAP Web Dispatcher with a complete application level gateway that offers a much higher level of security against Internet attacks, such as cross-site scripting, cookie poisoning, and so on.

24.2 Risks and Controls

Because SAP Web Dispatcher is not a security solution, the following description of risks and controls refers to the security functions that SAP Web Dispatcher provides. We'll now apply the methodology for risk analysis, which we introduced in Chapter 2, in a simpler form to SAP Web Dispatcher to determine the primary, critical security risks and the required controls (see Table 24.1). The sections that follow provide a greater specification of the controls and illustrate them with examples.

No.	Classification	Description
1.	Risk potential	Direct access to SAP Web AS from the Internet.
		Access from the Internet to applications provided by SAP Web AS (a BSP application, for instance) can occur directly.
	Impact	Direct access to SAP Web AS from the Internet can increase the potential risk of compromising the server. Such a case can result in unauthorized viewing of a file, the loss of data, or triggering unauthorized transactions.

Table 24.1 Risks and Controls for SAP Web Dispatcher

No.	Classification	Description
	Risk without controls	Extremely high
	Control(s)	Use of SAP Web Dispatcher as a reverse proxy solution.
	Risk with control(s)	Medium
	Section	24.4.1
2.	Risk potential	Access to unprotected HTTP services (URLs). HTTP services needed only for the intranet are active on SAP Web AS. Only internal employees of the organization should be able to access these services.
	Impact	External attackers can exploit the HTTP services and completely compromise the integrity of, or take over, SAP Web AS.
	Risk without controls	Extremely high
	Control(s)	Configuration of SAP Web Dispatcher with URL filtering functionality that blocks specific HTTP services from the Internet.
	Risk with control(s)	Medium
	Section	24.4.2
3.	Risk potential	Unencrypted Internet connection. Communication between the web browser and SAP Web Dispatcher is unencrypted.
	Impact	Unencrypted communication can allow viewing of passwords or other confidential business information. The information can be used for a later attack on the SAP application.
	Risk without controls	Extremely high
	Control(s)	Configuration of the web browser with an SSL-encrypted communications connection from the Internet to SAP Web Dispatcher.
	Risk with control(s)	Normal
	Section	24.4.3
4.	Risk potential	No monitoring of SAP Web Dispatcher. SAP Web Dispatcher and its functions are not being monitored.
	Impact	The SAP application cannot be accessed. This situation can (depending on the type of application) result in lost revenue for the organization.

Table 24.1 Risks and Controls for SAP Web Dispatcher (cont.)

No.	Classification	Description
	Risk without controls	High
	Control(s)	Configuration and monitoring of the SAP Web Dispatcher functionality.
	Risk with control(s)	Normal
	Section	24.4.4

Table 24.1 Risks and Controls for SAP Web Dispatcher (cont.)

24.3 Application Security

SAP Web Dispatcher does not require special consideration of application security, because it handles only technical security aspects. SAP Web Dispatcher is installed as a service (Windows) or daemon (UNIX) on a server. No access authorization concept exists for this service. Access must be limited at the operating-system level.

24.4 Technical Security

24.4.1 Use of SAP Web Dispatcher as a Reverse Proxy

As noted, SAP Web Dispatcher can be used as a reverse proxy. See Chapter 19 for information on this type of function. It does not offer any filter or security functions on OSI level 7. SAP Web Dispatcher functions as a central request point for all incoming HTTP(S) requests from the Internet, as shown in Figure 24.1. Its central function is that of a load distributor. It receives load information on the individual instances, and Internet processes from the message server of the central instance of the SAP Web AS system, and uses it to distribute the load. It stores the status information in its own memory so that follow-up requests from a given client end up on the same instance of SAP Web AS. This feature is particularly important for applications that absolutely require status information. The HTTP(S) requests are redirected to the Internet Communication Managers (ICM) of the individual SAP system instances.

SAP Web Dispatcher is installed separately on an additional server. It runs there as a service in Windows operating systems and as a daemon in UNIX operating systems.

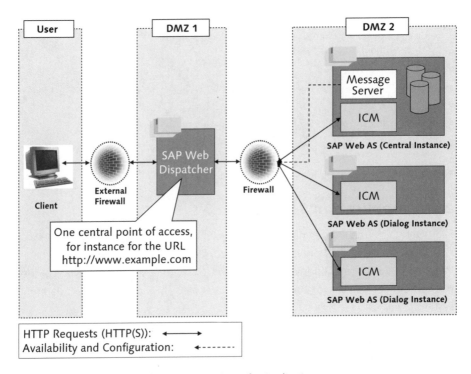

Figure 24.1 SAP Web Dispatcher as Reverse Proxy for Applications

From the viewpoint of technical security, SAP Web Dispatcher technically separates the network and implements the DMZ concept. Because SAP Web AS systems cannot be accessed directly from the Internet, they can be placed in a trustworthy network segment (DMZ 2).

All communications connections (between the Internet and SAP Web Dispatcher, between SAP Web Dispatcher and the message server, and between SAP Web Dispatcher and the ICM of the SAP Web AS system instances) can be completely switched to encrypted SSL communication. They can also be set for *mutual authentication*: authentication at the technical level based on X.509 certificates. See Section 24.4.3 for more details.

The configuration file *sapwebdisp.pfl* is used to configure SAP Web Dispatcher. The file contains all required configuration parameters, which are read when SAP Web Dispatcher is started.

At a minimum, a sample configuration file would appear as it does in Listing 24.1.

```
# SAPSYSTEMNAME of SAP Web Dispatcher must be set
# so that the default profile can be read.
# Otherwise, a warning will be displayed in the console.
```

```
SAPSYSTEMNAME = BIN
# SAPSYSTEM (instance number of SAP Web Dispatcher) must
# be set so that the shared memory
# areas can be created.
# The number must differ from other SAP instances on the
# computer
SAPSYSTEM = 10
# Description of the message server
# Name of the computer that the message server is running on
rdisp/mshost = binmain
# Port and protocol SAP Web Dispatcher uses
# to get the required load information
ms/server_port_0 = PROT=HTTP,PORT 8081
# Description of the access points for SAP Web Dispatcher.
# In this case, http requests can be accepted at port 80.
# HTTPS requests are accepted at port 443
# and redirected right to the
# SAP systems.
icm/server_port_0 = PROT=HTTP,PORT=80
icm/server_port_1 = PROT=ROUTER,PORT=443
```

Listing 24.1 Sample Configuration File for SAP Web Dispatcher

SAP Web Dispatcher is started using operating system commands. In Windows, startup can be automated by setting up a Windows service. Under UNIX, startup can be automated using the configuration as a daemon.

24.4.2 Configuration of SAP Web Dispatcher as a URL Filter

SAP Web Dispatcher can be configured as a URL filter. In this case, specific HTTP services (URLs) provided on the SAP Web AS systems can be made inaccessible. Such URLs can include those in the Internet Connection Framework (ICF) of SAP Web AS that might have to remain accessible only for internal access. These URLs can be deactivated using Transaction SICF (see Chapter 8). SAP Web Dispatcher can use the URL filter to block access to these from the Internet.

Here, the file *ptabfile* must be installed on the SAP Web Dispatcher server. The location of the file is defined in the SAP Web Dispatcher configuration file with the following parameter:

```
wdisp\permission_table = <ptabfile>
```

The file *ptabfile* is the absolute or relative path of the appropriate file. The name of the file can be chosen at will. The following example (see Listing 24.2) shows you a possible definition of an access restriction for a URL with the file:

```
# Sample SAP Web Dispatcher file for a
# Permission_Table
P    /sap/bc/test.cgi
D    *.cgi
P    /sap/bc/cachetest
P    /sap/bc/public/*
P    /sap/bc/ping
D    *
```

Listing 24.2 Sample File for URL Access Control with SAP Web Dispatcher

This file is set up so that—from the very start—it searches for an applicable rule. As soon as the rule is found, the search is terminated. You can enter one of three parameters in the first column:

▶ **P**
Permitted

▶ **D**
Denied

▶ **S**
Accessible only with secure protocol HTTPS

The sample file allows a call of the CGI program *test.cgi* only, and not of any other CGI programs. You can enter a *wildcard* (*) at the beginning or end of the URL definition. If the position of the first two lines were reversed, no CGI program could be called. The first line would prohibit calling a CGI program—even if the second line would allow it. This situation results because the search is terminated after the first applicable rule. Entry of "D   *" at the end of the file means that only the URLs expressly allowed can be called and no others.

The following list contains important security parameters in the context of URL security. They can be set in the SAP Web Dispatcher configuration file:

▶ **wdisp\max_permitted_uri_len**
Indicates the maximum permitted length of a URL in letters. (Integer, default: 2,048)

▶ **wdisp\max_permission_table_size**
Indicates the maximum number of URL entries in the Permission_Table. (Integer, default: 300)

▶ `wdisp\max_permission_table_entry_size`
Indicates the maximum length of a URL entry in the Permission_Table. (Integer, default: 256)

24.4.3 SSL Configuration

SAP Web Dispatcher supports all possible combinations of SSL communications connections. Figure 24.2 illustrates the combinations. As the figure indicates, all combinations are possible. The parameter `icm/server_port_<xx>` with option `Port` determines whether SAP Web Dispatcher accepts SSL (HTTPS) requests.

The parameter can accept the following values:

▶ HTTP
SAP Web Dispatcher accepts HTTP requests on the port (see Figure 24.2: cases 1 and 2).

▶ HTTPS
SAP Web Dispatcher accepts HTTPS requests on the port. It decrypts the request before redirecting it to an application server (see Figure 24.2: cases 3 and 4).

▶ ROUTER
SAP Web Dispatcher receives HTTPS and redirects the request without decrypting it (see Figure 24.2: case 5).

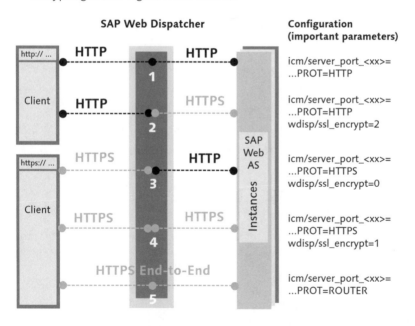

Figure 24.2 Possible SSL Combinations with SAP Web Dispatcher

The parameter `wdisp/ssl_encrypt` determines if SAP Web Dispatcher (re)encrypts the request using SSL before it redirects it (see Figure 24.2). The parameter can accept the following values:

- ▶ 0

  An HTTPS request is scheduled in SAP Web Dispatcher and is redirected without encryption.

- ▶ 1

  An HTTPS request is scheduled in SAP Web Dispatcher and is redirected with encryption.

- ▶ 2

  An HTTP request is scheduled in SAP Web Dispatcher and is redirected with encryption.

The parameter `wdisp/ssl_auth` determines if SAP Web Dispatcher and the SAP Web AS system must undergo mutual authentication. If the parameter is set to "1," mutual authentication is executed. In this case, however, the parameter `wdisp/ssl_host = <Common Name of SAP Web Dispatcher>` must also be set. To establish the SSL connection to SAP Web Dispatcher in cases 2 and 4, the "<Common Name>" of the SAP Web AS systems must also be specified. This <Common Name> must correspond to the <Common Name> for the certificate issued for the SAP Web AS systems. The names can be viewed using Transaction STRUST.

SAP Web Dispatcher must be equipped with the ability to encrypt if the HTTPS connection is scheduled in it. The ability to encrypt is accomplished with the following steps

1. Installation of the SAP cryptographic library on the server that runs SAP Web Dispatcher

2. Definition of the SLL parameter given above

3. Creation of the *personal security environment* (PSE) including generation of a certificate request for SAP Web Dispatcher, for website *http://www.sample. com*, for example.

4. Signature of the certificate request by a Certificate Authority (CA).

5. Import of the signed certificate into the PSE.

6. Generation of access credentials for SAP Web Dispatcher on its PSE so that the certificate can be read at runtime.

7. Reboot of SAP Web Dispatcher.

After these configuration steps have been performed, SAP Web Dispatcher can be addressed from the Internet with secure protocol HTTPS.

24.4.4 Monitoring

SAP Web Dispatcher can be monitored with a web browser–based monitoring program, or using the command line program *icmon*. The web-based interface for administration and monitoring of SAP Web Dispatcher is started with the web browser. The functionality and setup are comparable to those of the Internet Communication Manager (ICM) in SAP Web AS, set with Transaction SMICM. The browser-based administration interface is started with *http://<Web Dispatcher_ Host>:<Web Dispatcher_port>/sap/wdisp/admin/default. html*.

The following preconditions for administration with the web browser must be met:

▶ The most recent version of SAP Web Dispatcher is installed in a directory.

▶ Packet *icmadmin.SAR* is unpacked in its own directory.

▶ The value `icm/HTTP/admin`, (`icm/HTTP/admin_0=PREFIX=/sap/wdisp/ admin,DOCROOT=./admin`, for example) is maintained in the profile of SAP Web Dispatcher.

A file for authentication of the administrators exists (*icmauth.txt*). The file is automatically generated when starting SAP Web Dispatcher with the `–bootstrap` option.

▶ SAP Web Dispatcher was configured for SSL, because the password is also transmitted to the monitoring console during log-on access with the web browser.

After the administration interface has been installed, the most important functions of SAP Web Dispatcher can be monitored. Unfortunately, a connection to the Computing Center Management System (CCMS) of the SAP Web AS system is not currently possible to achieve central monitoring.

25 SAProuter

This chapter describes IT security concepts for the Global Security Positioning System (GSPS) component, SAProuter. It focuses on the description of the security functions provided by SAProuter.

25.1 Introduction and Functions

SAProuter is an application level proxy that has been specifically developed for the SAP protocols DIAG and RFC. It grants only specific SAP GUI users in specific network segments access to an SAP Web Application System (Web AS) system. For this reason, SAProuter acts as a restrictive router between SAP GUI and SAP Web AS. It can also restrict the communication between two SAP Web AS systems.

The security function of SAProuter can be used only to its full extent, if the direct connection between a SAP GUI and an SAP Web AS system is cut off via a network segmentation. You must ensure that the connection between a SAP GUI and an SAP Web AS can be established only by the SAProuter that receives the request from the client and forwards it to the relevant SAP Web AS system.

25.2 Risks and Controls

Because SAProuter is, itself, a security solution, the risks and controls described below refer to the security functions provided by SAProuter. In this section, we'll use a simplified version of the proposed risk analysis methodology, which was described in Chapter 2, to identify the main security risks and the necessary controls (see Table 25.1). The controls are described in more detail in the subsequent sections and illustrated on the basis of examples.

No.	Classification	Description
1.	Risk potential	Direct access to an SAP Web AS system using the DIAG or RFC protocol.
		The protocols DIAG (SAP GUI) and RFC enable direct access from a non-trustworthy network to an SAP Web AS system.
		This eliminates the proposed network segmentation from being established and divided into trustworthy and less trustworthy areas.

Table 25.1 Risk for SAProuter

No.	Classification	Description
	Impact	The direct access to the SAP Web AS system from a non-trustworthy network segment increases the potential risks that can ultimately compromise the integrity of the system. In that case, unauthorized accesses to the system are possible. Ultimately, unauthorized financial transactions can be triggered.
	Risk without controls	High
	Control(s)	Use of SAProuter as an application level proxy for the SAP protocols DIAG and RFC.
	Risk with control(s)	Normal
	Section	25.4

Table 25.1 Risk for SAProuter (cont.)

25.3 Application Security

We don't need to consider any application security aspects for SAProuter, because this SAP component is exclusively responsible for technical security.

25.4 Technical Security

To ensure that the security routing function of SAProuter functions properly, you must terminate the direct communication between the SAP GUI clients and the SAP Web AS systems with a restrictive network router or a firewall. You must design the firewall rules in such a way that SAP GUI clients can access only the SAProuter that forwards the requests to the relevant SAP Web AS systems using the DIAG and RFC protocols. The SAProuter checks the origin of the requests. This check is performed on the basis of the defined routing rules. Figure 25.1 illustrates this relationship.

The configuration file *SAProuttab* is used for configuring the routing rules for SAProuter. This configuration file contains a list of entries of the following type (see also Figure 25.1):

```
[D|P|S]{#before,#after} <Source IP> <Target IP> <Port> {password}
```

Each line contains the identification code [D|P|S] that is used for describing the access right. D stands for *Deny connection*, P stands for *Permit connection*, while S stands for *Permit only SAP Protocols*.

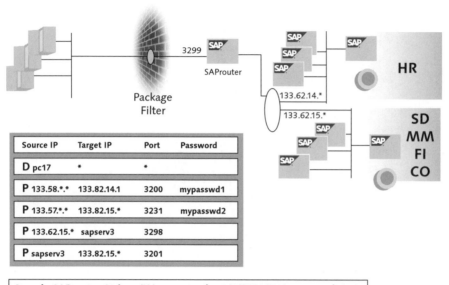

Source IP	Target IP	Port	Password
D pc17	*	*	
P 133.58.*.*	133.82.14.1	3200	mypasswd1
P 133.57.*.*	133.82.15.*	3231	mypasswd2
P 133.62.15.*	sapserv3	3298	
P sapserv3	133.82.15.*	3201	

Sample SAProuter String: /H/saprouter_host/S/3299/W/mypasswd1/H/

Figure 25.1 Network Configuration and Sample Configuration File for SAProuter

The source IP addresses of the SAP GUI clients for which the connections are to be permitted or denied must be entered in the ⟨Source-IP⟩. The ⟨Target-IP⟩ must be provided with the target addresses of the SAP Web AS systems that the SAP GUI client wants to have access to. The ⟨Port⟩ value must contain the network TCP/IP port used by the message server of the SAP Web AS system for receiving requests. Optionally, you can specify a {password} that must also be sent by the SAP GUI client so that the connection is permitted.

SAProuters can also be cascaded. The {# before} and {# after} parameters can be used to specify how many upstream or downstream SAProuters are permitted.

The SAProuter string must be entered in SAP GUI so that the SAP GUI client can establish the connection through the SAProuter. That string tells SAP GUI through which SAProuter the connection to an SAP Web AS system can be established. Figure 25.1 also contains an example of such a string.

26 SAP Internet Transaction Server

This chapter describes IT security concepts for the Global Security Posi-
tioning System (GSPS) component, SAP Internet Transaction Server.
It focuses on authentication and communication security functions.

26.1 Introduction and Functions

SAP Internet Transaction Server (SAP ITS) is the link between SAP Web AS and SAP
GUI for HTML (web browser). It is used to format dynpro-based applications
(transactions based on ABAP) in HTML, so they can be controlled using a web
browser. SAP ITS was developed to expedite the connecting of dynpro applications based on ABAP to the Internet. Although SAP provides specific programming techniques for Internet-based applications, such as Business Server Pages
(BSPs), Java Server Pages (JSPs), or Web Dynpro applications for ABAP and Java,
the importance of SAP ITS hasn't diminished in recent years—the reason being
that the majority of SAP applications are still transactional ABAP applications,
which can be used as web applications only with the help of SAP ITS. SAP ITS
transforms the ABAP transactions that have been started on the SAP Web AS into
HTML format in order to display them in SAP GUI for HTML.

SAP ITS consists of the following two components: *Web Interface Gate* (short
name: WGate) and *Application Interface Gate* (short name: AGate). WGate is an
extension for a web server that translates the HTTP requests it receives from a
web browser into a format that is understood by AGate.

The following web browsers are supported:

▶ Microsoft Internet Information Server (IIS) including the required Information
Server Application Programming Interface (ISAPI) by SAP

▶ Netscape Enterprise Server (NES) including the required Network Server Application Programming Interface (NSAPI) by SAP

▶ Apache Web Server—Apache including the required Web Server Application
Programming Interface (WSAPI) by SAP

AGate then converts the request into a DIAG call (or into an RFC call) and forwards it to the SAP Web AS. The requested transaction, which must exist as an
Internet Application Component (IAC) in the Internet Connection Framework
(ICF) is then called and executed. For this reason, the AGate is the actual gateway
in SAP Web AS.

The response is sent from SAP Web AS to the Agate, where it is converted into an HTML page. That page is transferred through the WGate to the web browser, from where it can be forwarded in HTML format to the requesting web browser. For SAP Web AS, SAP ITS appears to be a regular SAP GUI, because the request is sent to the SAP Web AS via the DIAG protocol. The complete SAP ITS architecture is illustrated in Figure 26.1.

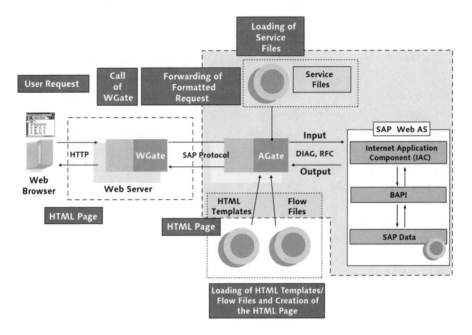

Figure 26.1 Technical Architecture of SAP ITS

Figure 26.1 displays the logical process flow of the web-based user request up to the SAP Web AS. The following protocols are used:

▶ HTTP between web browser and web server/WGate

▶ SAP-proprietary protocol, similar to the DIAG protocol, between WGate and AGate

▶ DIAG protocol and RFC protocol between AGate and SAP Web AS

The configuration illustrated in Figure 26.1 is a *dual-host configuration* in which WGate and AGate are installed separately on two different servers. However, it is also possible to install WGate and AGate together with the web server to be used on a single machine. This type of configuration is referred to as a *single-host configuration*. Nevertheless, for security reasons the dual-host configuration is preferable, as we'll see later in this chapter.

All services provided by SAP ITS, such as the SAP GUI for HTML access to an SAP Web AS, which is frequently referred to as WebGUI, or the administration console for SAP ITS, and so on, are defined via parameters in service files in the AGate file system. Parameters that are applied to all services are stored in the file *global.srvc*. Specific parameters such as those for the SAP GUI for HTML access are defined in separate files, in this case in *webgui.srvc*; a separate file must be created for each additional service.

The AGate contains other, equally important files, namely the HTML templates and flow files. The HTML template files contain predefined structures that are necessary to complete the individual transactions that are called. The flow files contain information for defining the request flow.

All the aforementioned descriptions refer only to Release 6.20 of the SAP ITS. In the interim, SAP ITS has been integrated in the latest release of SAP Web AS 6.40. In this context, the WGate functions have been replaced by an integration into the Internet Communication Manager (ICM) of SAP Web AS 6.40. The AGate runtime environment has been included into the ICF of SAP Web AS 6.40. However, SAP still provides support for the standalone version of SAP ITS 6.20. And, due to the widespread use of that version, we'll also include it in our descriptions here. The security measures required for the new integrated SAP ITS are described in Chapter 8. They're identical to the security measures that are required for BSP applications.

26.2   Risks and Controls

The methodology for risk analysis, which was introduced in Chapter 2, will now be applied in a simpler form to SAP ITS in order to determine the primary, critical security risks and the required controls (see Table 26.1). In subsequent sections, we'll describe the controls in more detail and provide examples.

No.	Classification	Description
1.	Risk potential	No access rights for service files have been defined.
		The rights for accessing the service files (*global.srvc* and so on) at the operating-system level of the AGate server have either been incorrectly defined or not defined at all.
	Impact	The missing or incorrectly defined access rights for service files enables unauthorized employees or external attackers to modify the configuration of the SAP ITS. This provokes further attempts to compromise the SAP Web AS. Ultimately, unauthorized financial transactions can be triggered.

Table 26.1 Risks and Controls for SAP ITS

No.	Classification	Description
	Risk without controls	Extremely high
	Control(s)	Definition of access rights for the service files for user groups at operating-system level.
	Risk with control(s)	Normal
	Section	26.3.1
2.	Risk potential	Lack of an administration concept for SAP ITS. There is no administration concept in place for SAP ITS. Even OS administrators can access the SAP ITS configuration.
	Impact	The lack of an administration concept enables third parties to compromise the configuration of the SAP ITS. This can lead to unauthorized accesses to the SAP Web AS. Ultimately, unauthorized financial transactions can be triggered.
	Risk without controls	High
	Control(s)	Implementation of an administration concept for SAP ITS.
	Risk with control(s)	Normal
	Section	26.3.2
3.	Risk potential	SAP ITS is configured as a single host. The components of SAP ITS, the web server, WGate, and AGate are installed on one server. The network is not segmented into trustworthy and less trustworthy network zones or demilitarized zones (DMZs).
	Impact	The AGate server that stores the service files can be accessed directly from the Internet. Possible misconfigurations—such as incorrectly defined access rights for the files—enable unauthorized parties to perform further successful attacks even on the backend SAP Web AS.
	Risk without controls	High
	Control(s)	Implementation of a network segmentation concept and subdividing the SAP ITS components into corresponding DMZ network areas.
	Risk with control(s)	Normal
	Section	26.4.1

Table 26.1 Risks and Controls for SAP ITS (cont.)

No.	Classification	Description
4.	Risk potential	No encryption of communication channels. The communications connections between the web browser and WGate, WGate and AGate, and between AGate and SAP Web AS are not encrypted.
	Impact	When accessing the SAP Web AS through the SAP ITS, authentication data—like user IDs and passwords—is transferred (the access through the SAP ITS involves the same authentication process for a user as the SAP GUI access). Because this data is not encrypted properly, it can be eavesdropped and then used for an unauthorized logon. This eavesdropping of data can have very deleterious results for the company.
	Risk without controls	Extremely high
	Control(s)	Encryption of all communication paths between the web browser, WGate, and AGate up to the SAP Web AS.
	Risk with control(s)	Normal
	Section	26.4.2
5.	Risk potential	The selected passwords are too simple. The passwords selected for authenticating to SAP Web AS through SAP ITS are too simple. This weakens the entire authentication process.
	Impact	Passwords that are too obvious make it easier for attackers to get access to SAP Web AS. The possible effects of this can be extremely negative for the company.
	Risk without controls	High
	Control(s)	Implementation of a stronger authentication process based on X.509 certificates for SAP Web AS users. The certificates can be managed by a company-specific PKI.
	Risk with control(s)	Normal
	Section	26.4.3
6.	Risk potential	Too many passwords are being used. The users of SAP Web AS applications must memorize a separate password for each individual application. For this reason, they either choose structured passwords, or write down the individual system access data on a piece of paper that they keep somewhere near their PC.

Table 26.1 Risks and Controls for SAP ITS (cont.)

No.	Classification	Description
	Impact	Passwords that are too obvious make it easier for attackers to get access to SAP Web AS. It will be even easier for them, if they can use the passwords that have been written down on the piece of paper. The possible effects of this can be extremely negative for the company.
	Risk without controls	High
	Control(s)	Implementation of a Single-Sign-On (SSO) process using the *Pluggable Authentication Service* (PAS) that's available for SAP ITS. This service enables the integration of the authentication with an external authentication service such as the Windows domain.
	Risk with control(s)	Normal
	Section	26.4.4

Table 26.1 Risks and Controls for SAP ITS (cont.)

26.3 Application Security

26.3.1 Defining Access Rights for Service Files

As we mentioned in the introduction to this chapter, the service files, HTML templates, and the flow files are stored on the AGate server in a directory structure of the operating system. Those files must be protected against unauthorized access. For this reason, the access rights for the files must be defined correctly.

The rights are set during the installation process for the SAP ITS. The following security levels are available:

▶ **ITS Administration Group only**
This is the highest level of security. Only the SAP ITS administration group can modify all files. All other OS administrators are granted read-only access.

▶ **ITS Administration Group and ITS Users**
This is a medium level of security. In addition to the ITS administration group, which still keeps its full access rights, ITS users are granted partial write access to service files. These users are ITS developers who are defined as a group in the operating system. All other OS administrators are granted read-only access.

▶ **Everyone**
This is the lowest level of security. In this case, all OS administrators are granted write access to all files of the SAP ITS. This level should only be applied to internal sandbox systems that don't provide access to security-critical applications.

Table 26.2 provides an overview of the available security levels.

Security level	OS user group	Access rights	Assessment
ITS Administration Group only (high)	ITS administration	Read and write access to all ITS files	This configuration must be used for production systems or for production-related QA systems.
	All others	Read access to all ITS files	
ITS Administration Group and ITS Users (medium)	ITS administration	Read and write access to all ITS files	This configuration should be used for development systems.
	ITS Users (developers)	Read access to all ITS files and write access to specifically selected service files and HTML templates that must be edited by a team of developers.	
	All others	Read-only access to all ITS files	
Everyone (low)	All	Read and write access to all ITS files	This option should only be used for non-production-related sandbox systems on the intranet.

Table 26.2 Access Rights for SAP ITS Files

26.3.2 Administration Concept

The SAP ITS is administrated through a dedicated web application. This administration console must be specified as a service and, as all other services, defined in the file *admin.srvc*. The service can be called via the following sample URL, provided the sample website (URL of the web server) has been configured as *http://www.example.com*:

http://www.example.com:1080/scripts/wgate/admin!

By default, the administration service is called through port 1080. Accordingly, in an Internet usage scenario, this port must be blocked in the external firewall.

The default super administrator is called "itsadmin." This name cannot be changed. The super administrator has full authorization for the SAP ITS administration. It represents the only account that is authorized to create new administrators for the SAP ITS. For that reason, it is imperative that the default password for the super administrator be changed immediately after the installation is completed. You should choose a complex password. No more than two administrators, a main administrator and an assistant, should know the details for the itsadmin account. If possible, you should ensure that access to the itsadmin account is restricted by applying the four eyes principle. Technically, this is currently not supported and must therefore be implemented at the organizational level.

The "itsadmin account" is authorized to create new administrators. The newly created administrators are also granted full access to the ITS files and configurations; however, they cannot create any new administrator accounts. But those administrators do have an important authorization—the starting and stopping of the SAP instance. Furthermore, because they can restrict the administration right at the SAP instance, the assignment of an administration account should be very restrictive.

In addition, a read-only administration account can be set up for support desk employees who are responsible for performing error searches. Such a read-only administration account enables them to view the SAP ITS files and to check the operational status of the SAP ITS. The read access can also be restricted at the level of SAP ITS instances.

The entire SAP ITS administration assignment occurs at operating-system level, for example, for a Windows server, this assignment occurs in the Windows registry. The exact definition is described in the SAP ITS manuals.

26.4 Technical Security

26.4.1 Installing a DMZ Network Segmentation

Due to the existing logical separation of WGate and AGate, a DMZ concept can be easily set up (see Figure 26.2). The WGate, which is directly connected to the web server as an ISAPI (in the case of Microsoft IIS), is placed in DMZ 1. Internet access must be configured so that only the web server including WGate can be addressed via TCP/IP port 80 or 443 (if HTTPS is configured). All other ports must be blocked in the external firewall.

The communication between WGate and AGate must also be restricted with the internal firewall to such an extent that a communication is only possible between those two servers. Typically, you must configure TCP/IP port 3900 for this (i.e., for the first AGate; for AGate clusters, 3901 must be used for the next one, then 3902, and so on).

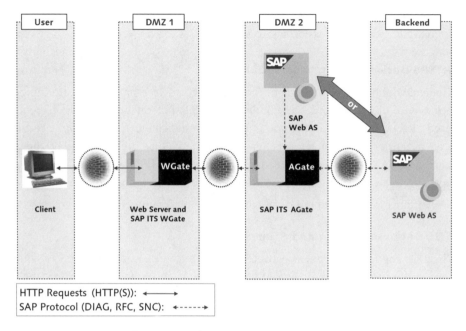

Figure 26.2 DMZ Network Concept with SAP ITS

You can implement another security layer by establishing an additional firewall separation between AGate and SAP Web AS. In that case, the communication can be restricted even further to a permitted communications connection between AGate and SAP Web AS. We recommend this option if the backend application has a high need for protection.

Another option is, of course, to connect the AGate directly with the SAP Web AS within the same network zone (for example, DMZ 2). That SAP Web AS can then establish a communication with critical backend applications via RFC connections. In that way, you can implement a very detailed structure of permitted communications connections. Moreover, at the network level, you can set up a cascading protection if you so choose.

26.4.2 Encrypting Communications Connections

As indicated in Figure 26.2, you can encrypt all communications connections between the client and WGate, WGate and AGate, and between AGate and SAP Web AS. This enables you to meet two additional security requirements: You can establish a protection against unauthorized access to the data being transferred, as well as an additional mutual authentication at the technical level between WGate and AGate and between AGate and SAP Web AS. The increased stringency of the authentication process is attained by using the digital certificates that are required for encryption according to the X.509 standard.

HTTPS Between Client and WGate

The encryption between the client (i.e., the web browser) and the WGate can be achieved by using HTTPS. The configuration depends on the web server being used. If you use Microsoft IIS, you must request a digital certificate from a certificate authority (CA), which must then be imported. Once the certificate has been imported, the communications can be switched to HTTPS for the WGate service with just a few clicks of the mouse. You can also configure the WGate service for using HTTPS only.

SNC Between WGate and AGate

The SNC connection between WGate and AGate can be established in the same way as the connection between AGate and SAP Web AS. In the following, we'll describe this in more detail. To establish Secure Network Communications (SNC), you must first replace the default SAP Security Library (SAPSECULIB) with the SAP Cryptographic Library (SAPCRYPTOLIB) in all SAP ITS components, that is, in WGate, AGate, and on the SAP Web AS. The communications connections can be encrypted only by using the cryptographic programs contained in that library. Here, you must consider whether you want to use the *Personal Security Environment* (PSE) to assign a certificate to each ITS component (i.e., WGate and AGate), or if you want to assign a separate certificate to each component. The advantage of using a PSE and therefore only one certificate is that the configuration is less complex and the trust relationship between the ITS components is automatically established. The disadvantage of such a solution is that if the WGate is compromised by an external attack, the trust relationship can be exploited so that the attack can be extended to the backend application. We therefore recommend that you assign a separate PSE to each component and establish a mutual trust relationship by exchanging the certificates among the ITS components. In only this way can you establish a shared, technical authentication between the components.

SNC Between AGate and SAP Web AS

To establish an SNC connection between AGate and the SAP Web AS, you must perform the following steps on the SAP Web AS:

1. Install the SAP Cryptographic Library and the license key. Typically, the SAP Cryptographic Library is copied into the executing directory while the license key is copied into the instance directory. Then, you must set the profile param-

eters `sec/libsapsecu` and `ssf/ssfapi_lib` to the installation directory of the executing directory.

2. Start the Trust Manager (Transaction STRUST) to set up the PSE for SNC. In the Trust Manager, you must request a digital certificate with a **Distinguished Name** for the SAP Web AS. Once the CA has signed the certificate, you can import it using the Transaction STRUST. This step ensures that the SAP Web AS is assigned a unique digital identity (**Distinguished Name**) for the SNC connection.

3. Establish the trust relationship with AGate using the Trust Manager. For this purpose, the public certificate must be imported in the Trust Manager under SNC PSE in the directory for trustworthy certificates.

4. Specify the AGate that is granted access to the SAP Web AS in Table SNCSYSACL. You can do this by using Transaction SM30 (table maintenance) or Transaction SNC0 or Report RSUSR300. The AGate must be defined as an external system with its entire **Distinguished Name**, with a prefixed letter "p": `CN=my_agate, O=my_company, C=us`.

Perform the following steps in the AGate using the web-based administration tool for SAP ITS:

1. Install the SAP Cryptographic Library. This can be done directly in the administration tool.

2. Set up an SNC PSE using the administration tool. We recommend that you create a separate PSE for the AGate. The access to that PSE is protected by an additional Personal Identification Number (PIN).

3. Save the PSE name in the server registry. This can also be done directly in the administration tool.

4. Import the public certificate of the SAP Web AS (which you must first export there using Transaction STRUST) using the function **Advanced PKI Operations · Import trusted certificate**. In this way, you can establish a trust relationship with the SAP Web AS.

5. Then you must maintain the SNC name of the SAP Web AS in the **SAP Connection Maintenance** of the administration tool.

6. Restart the AGate at operating-system level.

The SNC connection can be used once the AGate has been restarted. If any problems arise, you can delete the contents of the `sncNameR3` parameter, which results in a deactivation of the SNC connection.

26.4.3 Setting Up a Certificate-Based Authentication Process

Users who log on to the backend application of an SAP Web AS system via the SAP ITS can do so via their user ID and password, which is similar to the logon procedure via SAP GUI, or by using a digital certificate based on the X.509 standard. In the latter case, however, they will inevitably have to set up an HTTPS connection between the web browser and the web server, including the WGate, which forces a client authentication (mutual authentication). Furthermore, it is advisable that all communications connections—up to and including SAP Web AS using SNC—be encrypted.

The mechanism is shown in Figure 26.3. In this context it is important that the user possesses a digital certificate issued by a trustworthy CA that is either stored as software in the web browser or on a hardware component such as a smart card. An example of a software-based solution is *Secude* by iT Sec Swiss, while Kobil Systems offers a solution for a smart card-based procedure.

To enable a certificate-based strong authentication via the SAP ITS, you must set the SAP ITS parameter ~clientCert to the value "1" using the web-based administration tool. Moreover, you must ensure that the **Distinguished Name** is synchronized with the SAP user ID, which is stored in the SAP Web AS system. For example, the user ID could be "Alice". This synchronization must be done in Table USREXTID, which can either be managed via the table maintenance (Transaction SM30), or by using Report RSUSREXTID, if many users are involved. Once the entries have been activated, the certificate-based user authentication can be used.

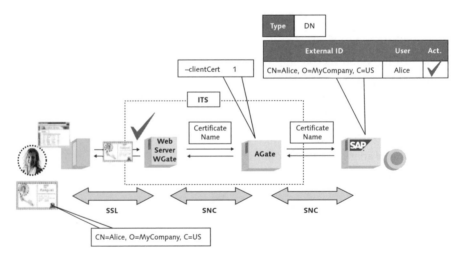

Figure 26.3 Certificate-Based Logon via SAP ITS

To use this option in an enterprise scenario, you should consider using a public key infrastructure (PKI), because the digital certificates must be securely managed. A PKI is most efficient in an interaction with an identity and access management solution, such as *eTrust Identity Manager* from Computer Associates, *Control/SA* from BMC, or DirX from Siemens, because those systems are then responsible for distributing the certificates. In that case, all the identities that are included in the SAP Web AS system network are managed centrally.

26.4.4 Setting Up a Pluggable Authentication Service

Another option to consider when you want to authenticate users is integrating the SAP ITS authentication mechanism with an external authentication service such as the Windows Kerberos authentication. To do that, you can use the *Pluggable Authentication Service* (PAS). As shown in Figure 26.4, here, the system trusts an external authentication instance during the authentication process. In this way, an additional Single-Sign-On (SSO) mechanism is used for distributed SAP applications, because the authentication process is always controlled by the SAP ITS.

The user authentication process functions as follows:

1. The user calls the PAS by entering the corresponding URL.
2. The user enters his or her credentials for the PAS (for example, a Windows user ID and password).
3. The Pluggable Authentication Service verifies the user ID and the password. If the details are correct, the user is transferred to the SAP Web AS system, which issues an SAP logon ticket (see Chapters 8 and 19).
4. The SAP Web AS system runs a comparison between the external user credentials and the SAP user ID. If the user is also stored as an SAP user, the corresponding SAP system issues an SAP logon ticket, the validity of which is confirmed by a digital signature using the system PSE. The SAP logon ticket is returned as a cookie to the user's web browser.
5. The AGate redirects the user to the SAP Web AS system, to which the user had originally requested access.

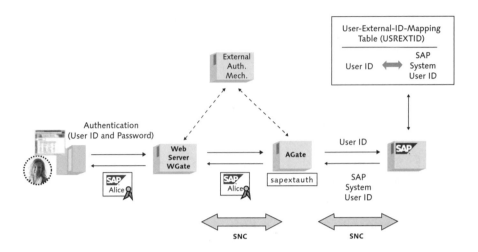

Figure 26.4 PAS Using SAP ITS

The benefit of this process is that the user doesn't need to log on to any other SAP Web AS systems. Nevertheless, you should ensure that all communications connections are encrypted; otherwise, potential attackers could be enabled to sniff the SAP logon ticket and hijack the already authenticated logon.

PAS is available for Windows operating systems (Windows NT, 2000, and XP). Additional PAS modules are available for an LDAP bind and X-509 certification services. You can set up PAS for the WGate or the AGate. You must perform the following steps:

1. Install the PAS module, for example, for Windows (*ntauth.sar*), in the SAP ITS installation directories, *services* and *templates*.

2. Set the parameters as follows:

   ▶ **~xgateway sapextauth**
   activates external authentication.

   ▶ **~extauthtype ⟨NTLM, NTPassword, LDAP, X509, HTTP, DLL⟩**
   defines the type of external authentication service.

   ▶ **~extid_type ⟨NT⟩, ⟨LD⟩, ⟨UN⟩ oder ⟨user-defined⟩**
   defines which user ID is to be returned by the external service, for example, NT ID, or SAP user ID, if UN is set.

   ▶ **~mysapcomgetsso2cookie 1**
   defines the acceptance of the SAP logon ticket.

   ▶ **~dont_recreate_ticket 1**
   indicates that the SAP logon ticket is not reissued.

- ► `~redirectHost <host_name>`
  name of the SAP system to which the user is redirected after a successful authentication.

- ► `~redirectPath <Path>`
  defines the path to which the user is redirected.

- ► `~redirectQS <host_name>`
  defines the logon parameters for the SAP system to which the user is redirected, for example, "client".

- ► `~redirectHttps 1`
  defines that HTTPS is used for the redirection.

- ► `~login_to_upcase 1`
  specifies that the entries in Table USREXTID are maintained using only uppercase letters.

3. Maintain the comparison table for external user IDs and SAP user IDs in Table USREXTID of the SAP Web AS system that issues the SAP logon ticket. To do this, use Transaction SM30 or Report RSUSREXTID.

Once you have set these parameters and made all the necessary settings, you can use SAP ITS to perform an external, delegated authentication. You should note that it is important to ensure that the SAP user IDs are consistently maintained in all accessible SAP Web AS systems; otherwise, the mechanism won't work.

27 SAP GUI

This chapter describes IT security concepts for the Global Security Positioning System (GSPS) component, SAP GUI. It focuses on the authentication and Single Sign-On functions, and also provides a description of the Secure, Storage, and Forward (SSF) function.

27.1 Introduction and Functions

SAP GUI is the default frontend for ABAP-based dynpro applications. It is available in three different variants: *SAP GUI for Windows*, *SAP GUI for Java*, and *SAP GUI for HTML*. Since the latter is actually a web browser that connects to SAP Web AS via SAP ITS (see Chapter 28), we only mention it here so as to include all variants. SAP GUI for Java is the version that's available for UNIX platforms. But, the most popular SAP GUI is SAP GUI for Windows, which is often referred to as WebGUI. Furthermore, because Windows is the most commonly used operating system, SAP GUI for Windows is the most widespread SAP client. For the sake of being succinct, we'll use the name WebGUI from hereon in this chapter.

WebGUI establishes a connection to the SAP Web AS using the proprietary SAP protocol, DIAG. In doing so, it first connects to the SAP Web AS message server, which forwards the request through the dispatcher to an available dialog process of SAP Web AS.

WebGUI's advantages over other web-based applications include its faster performance and its ability to map all dynpro functions, some of which are not available in SAP GUI for HTML. Furthermore, as is standard in most client/server applications, it performs a plausibility check (i.e., a verification of the client-side entries according to the specified entry format, for example, for dates) without requiring a roundtrip to the server. The main disadvantage of using the WebGUI is that it must be distributed by a software distribution mechanism to the relevant devices (desktop PCs) before it can be used. Moreover, the DIAG protocol limits the options to use the WebGUI in Internet scenarios. This would only be possible by using a virtual private network dial-up connection to the company network.

Regarding its functionality, the WebGUI is very powerful, which is why we have devoted this chapter to describing the IT security aspects associated with it.

27.2 Risks and Controls

In this section, we'll use a simplified version of the proposed risk analysis methodology described in Chapter 2 to identify the main security risks and the necessary controls (see Table 27.1). The controls are described in more detail in the subsequent sections and illustrated on the basis of examples.

No.	Classification	Description
1.	Risk potential	Non-compliance with legal requirements.
		Due to legal requirements such as the Electronic Signatures in Global and National Commerce Act (E-Sign), documents are transferred unsigned in a business process. Especially in the pharmaceutical industry, application documents for the approval of a new drug must have a digital signature.
	Impact	The lack of digital signatures and of the frequently necessary encryption enables unauthorized parties to modify the quantities of orders for orders that have been placed in electronic business processes without the confirmation of the ship-to party. The resulting incorrect deliveries can cause high financial burdens for the company. Regarding the drug approval, it would mean that the approval occurs too late, which would lead to a loss of revenue.
	Risk without controls	High
	Control(s)	The SSF interface (*Secure Storage and Forward*) integrated in the WebGUI can be used to trigger the signature function for documents.
	Risk with control(s)	Normal
	Section	27.3
2.	Risk potential	Passwords that are too numerous and too simple.
		The SAP Web AS users must memorize a separate password for each SAP Web AS and non-SAP application. Therefore, they either choose structured passwords, or write down the individual system access data on a piece of paper that they keep somewhere near their PC.
	Impact	Passwords that are too simple make it easier for attackers to get access to SAP Web AS. It will be even easier for them, if they can use the passwords that have been written down on the piece of paper. The possible effects can be extremely negative for the company.
	Risk without controls	Extremely high

Table 27.1 Risks and Controls for the WebGUI

No.	Classification	Description
	Control(s)	Implementation of a Single Sign-On (SSO) process using the Secure Network Communications (SNC) interface of the Web-GUI for integrating the WebGUI authentication into the Windows or UNIX environment respectively. In that case, the user logs on only once to the operating system and is then granted access to SAP Web AS due to the integrated authentication mechanism.
	Risk with control(s)	Normal
	Section	27.4.1
3.	Risk potential	Passwords that are too numerous and too simple.
		The SAP Web AS users must memorize a separate password for each SAP Web AS and non-SAP application. Therefore, they either choose structured passwords or write down the individual system access data on a piece of paper that they keep somewhere near their PC.
	Impact	Passwords that are too simple make it easier for attackers to get access to SAP Web AS. It will be even easier for them, if they can use the passwords that have been written down on the piece of paper. The possible effects can be extremely negative for the company.
	Risk without controls	Extremely high
	Control(s)	Implementation of a powerful SSO process using the SNC interface of the WebGUI on the basis of digital certificates. This ensures that each user must use a digital certificate to log on to the relevant SAP Web AS. The certificate must be issued by a trustworthy performance key indicator (PKI) and must be stored or made available in a secure storage location (or smart card) on the user's desktop PC. This situation can be attained via a personal security environment (PSE).
	Risk with control(s)	Normal
	Section	27.4.2
4.	Risk potential	Missing access control.
		Unauthorized users such as external employees use their Web-GUI installation to obtain access to an SAP Web AS of the company for which they have no authorization, for example, mySAP ERP HCM.
	Impact	Because access to the network is unprotected, a potential hacker can address the SAP Web AS and obtain access with a brute-force attack.

Table 27.1 Risks and Controls for the WebGUI (cont.)

No.	Classification	Description
	Risk without controls	High
	Control(s)	Restriction of SAP Web AS access using SAProuter for WebGUI-based access.
	Risk with control(s)	Normal
	Section	27.4.3

Table 27.1 Risks and Controls for the WebGUI (cont.)

27.3 Application Security

Since Release 4.6A, SAP has provided a *Secure, Storage, and Forward* function (SSF) that can be used to sign and encrypt electronically stored documents.

27.3.1 Types of Signatures

The SSF function can be customized in accordance with the relevant legal requirements. The following scenarios are possible:

▶ **User signature with person-specific certificate**

In this case, the user has a person-specific certificate, which is used to generate the signature for a document in the WebGUI. This is only possible for Windows-based systems. The certificate is issued by a trustworthy certificate authority (CA), and the associated private signature key can be stored as software on the hard disk, or on a smart card or another hardware-based storage medium. If the signature is supposed to comply with the Electronic Signatures in Global and National Commerce Act (E-Sign), the certificate must be issued by an authorized certification service provider. In addition, it must be stored on a secure hardware storage medium such as a smart card. When the certifcate is issued, the user must be personally present to provide proof of his or her identity, for example, by showing a passport. Only then can the certificate be called a "qualified certificate." Otherwise, it is referred to as an "advanced digital certificate."

If the signature is used among partner companies, the partners can specify the certificate requirements themselves. To use the person-specific signature efficiently, a separate *public key infrastructure* (PKI) must be used.

This signature process represents the highest security standard. But it is absolutely necessary that the document to be signed is actually displayed to the signatory in the WebGUI so that he can sign it with his private signature key.

▶ **User signature with server certificate**

This type of signature uses the server certificate or the signature key of the SAP Web AS instead of the person-specific certificate. The document to be signed is displayed to the user in the WebGUI and the user must provide proof of his or her identity by using the SAP user password so that SAP Web AS signs the document on behalf of the user. During the signing process, the signature key of the SAP Web AS is complemented with the user name of the signatory.

This process does not comply with the requirements established by the Electronic Signatures in Global and National Commerce Act (E-Sign), but it can be used in the approval procedure for drugs that is applied by the FDA (*Food and Drug Association*) in the United States.

The advantage of this signing process is that no separate PKI is required because it uses the server certificate; however, the disadvantage is that this type of process cannot be used for the interaction with the portal, because the user must provide proof of his or her identity to the backend application, which is where the actual signature process occurs.

▶ **Server signature**

As the name implies, this process uses the signature key of the server. There is no interaction with the user. For this reason, this process is applied primarily when the backend applications are in batch mode, for example, when mass signatures are required. It specifically focuses on protecting documents against unauthorized modification, when the documents are forwarded to business partners. In that case, the business partners can agree on using this type of protection. The process is also used specifically in the SAP Exchange Infrastructure (SAP XI) area.

▶ **Server signature linked to a natural person**

This type of signature uses the certificate of a natural person (for example, of an authorized signatory) instead of a server certificate. Using a machine-readable system such as a smart card reader, the certificate can also be used in batch-mode operation for mass signatures. In this case, the use of several person-specific certificates is also possible. This solution complies with the requirements set by the Electronic Signatures in Global and National Commerce Act (E-Sign), if the smart card reader is located in a secure environment.

The use of a PKI is not mandatory in this scenario; however, the certificates on the smart card must be issued by an accredited certification authority.

27.3.2 Supported Electronic Document Formats

The following electronically saved document formats are supported by the SSF functions provided by SAP:

▶ **PKCS#7**
PKCS#7 stands for *Public Key Cryptography Standard (version 7)*. This standard was defined by RSA Security and it specifies the secure exchange of documents through the Internet. PKCS#7 is used to "wrap" the actual document in a new binary format and to assign a signature to it. SAP provides a signature for this format for both the ABAP and the J2EE stack.

▶ **XML**
XML is fast becoming the leading standard for information exchange. It is also used for the exchange of documents; for example, the document is converted into an XML format and stored with a signature in a corresponding XML structure. The conversion is carried out using an XSL (*Extensible Stylesheet Language*) definition. The advantage of XML is that this format can be further processed by any web browser. SAP currently supports this format only for the J2EE stack of SAP Web AS.

▶ **S/MIME**
S/MIME is the standard for signing email. SAP currently supports this format only for the J2EE stack.

27.3.3 Technical Implementation of the SSF Functions

The SSF library for the ABAP stack is used in applications that have been written in ABAP. It supports the functions for generating and verifying digital signatures (PKCS#7), as well as those functions that are used for encrypting and decrypting documents.

The functions that are used for encrypting and decrypting are provided through the following programming interfaces:

▶ SSF-Sign generation of digital signatures

▶ SSF-Verify validity check of digital signatures

▶ SSF-Envelope encryption of documents

▶ SSF-Develop decryption of documents

To make these functions available, SSF requires an external security product. The standard product provided with the SAP system (SAP Web AS) is the SAP Security Library (SAPSECULIB). However, this library supports only digital signatures and no cryptographic hardware such as smart cards, tokens, and cryptoboards.

Besides SAPSECULIB, you can also use SAPCRYPTOLIB, which you can download from SAP Service Marketplace (*http://service.sap.com*).

SAPSECULIB supports the DSA algorithm (digital signature algorithm), whereas SAPCRYPTOLIB supports both the DSA and the RSA algorithms. To decide which algorithm you must use in your signature process depends on the certificate authority (CA) that issues the certificate. Most CAs use the RSA algorithm. For SAPCRYPTOLIB, you should note that it is subject to country-specific export regulations.[1]

For the support of document encryption and decryption at the frontend (i.e., WebGUI), and for generating digital signatures using cryptographic hardware, an external security product provided by a certified partner is required. Such security products operate the SSF interface of the SAP system and are certified by SAP for this purpose. The list of certified partner products currently includes the following:

▶ *Entrust/PKI* by Entrust

▶ *Secude securedoc* by iT Sec Swiss

▶ *PrisArc* by Prisma Gesellschaft für Projektmanagement und Infosysteme

▶ *KeyOne Toolkits for SAP R/3* by Safelayer Secure

▶ *SafeSignOn* by Softforum

▶ *SafeGuard Sign&Crypt 3.0* by Utimaco Safeware

The details of all these solutions would exceed the scope of this book and therefore will not be discussed here. You should therefore check the SAP websites regularly to see whether new providers have been added to this list.

The Java SSF Library supports all Java applications. SAP has provided this library since the release of SAP J2EE Server 6.30. It is based on the IAIK Toolkit developed by Graz University of Technology in Graz, Austria. This SSF library also supports the generation and verification of digital signatures. For document encryption and decryption, the IAIK Toolkit must be installed, which you can download from SAP Service Marketplace. For this reason, no external security product provided by an SAP partner is needed, nor does SAP provide a certification program for the Java SSF Library. PKCS#12 and the Java Keystore are used for storing the keys, which means that currently digital signatures can only be created without using any cryptographic hardware. In contrast to the library provided for the ABAP stack, the Java library can also generate XML and S/MIME signatures, in addition to the PKCS#7 signature.

---

1   SAP Note 39175 contains further information on this subject.

A central interface—ISsfData—is available for the Java version, which contains all basic methods such as `sign`, `verify`, `encrypt`, and `decrypt`. This interface is implemented for the different classes (SsfDataPKCS7, SsfDataSMIME, Ssf-DataXML) that provide specific methods for each document format. An SSF profile containing the private key and the certification path is required for signing and decrypting documents. An SSF PAB (`Public Address Book`) containing a list of trustworthy root certificates is required for verifying and encrypting documents.

The SSF profile is a parameter used by SSF functions that require the private key. For a digital signature, this would correspond with the function **SSF_Sign**, which is used to generate a digital signature. The SSF profile is either the name of a file or a smart card that specifies the public key information such as the private key and the certification path. The exact form of the profile depends on the security product that is used.

The `Private Address Book` is a parameter used by SSF functions that require a list of trustworthy certificates. For a digital signature, this would correspond with the function SSF_Verify, which is used to verify the digital signature. Depending on the security product that is used, the `Private Address Book` can be stored in different ways in the system. Microsoft Keystore is used for Signature Control, whereas Keystore Service is used for the SAP J2EE Engine.

As noted above, a display component for the document to be signed is required specifically for the person-specific signature, and also for the user-specific signature with the server certificate. This signature display component is available specifically for WebGUI (only for Windows-based versions as of Release 6.40) and for programs that are based on business server pages (BSPs). It is referred to as *Signature Control* and provides the following functions for programmers:

▶ **SSFS_Call_Control**
Launches Signature Control

▶ **SSFS_Get_Signature**
Retrieves the signature value from the Control component

▶ **SSFS_Server_Verify**
Verifies the digital signature by the application server

The document to be signed is displayed in plain text, HTML, XML, or PDF format in the Signature Control. The signature verification process occurs as follows:

A signed document contains the signature value and the digital certificate of the signatory. During the verification of the digital signature, cryptographic algorithms are applied to the document and the signature value. If the verification is successful, the document will not have been modified and will have been signed using the private key that belongs to the signatory. Another step must then verify whether the certificate of the signatory is valid and whether it was issued by a trustworthy certificate authority (CA). This is done using the `Private Address Book`.

Then it must be checked whether the certificate has been revoked by the CA, for example, because the smart card was lost. The CAs provide a list of revoked or invalid certificates (Certificate Revocation List, CRL). You can either download the CRLs directly from the CAs' websites—within a specified validity period, which needs to be configured accordingly—or, you can use the *Online Certificate Status Protocol* (OCSP), which is based on HTTP. This new standard is faster, easier to handle, and more reliable than using the CRLs. The application sends a request to a server application, the *OCSP responder*, which keeps current status information on the following three responses: "valid," "invalid," or "unknown."

Generally, OCSP services must be purchased. The use of qualified certificates is an exception in this context. Most of the accredited trust centers provide this service free of charge for qualified certificates, because, for example, the German Electronic Signature Act prohibits the use of CRLs.

27.3.4 Saving Digitally Signed Documents

To sign a process step, and therefore a document with a digital signature, means that the signature must be saved. The application used and the legal framework to be applied determine the way in which the signature is saved. If the signature process must comply with the the German Electronic Signature Act, for example, the generic document must be saved to a non-rewritable medium, such as an optical archive.

If the document is modified in subsequent process steps, it must be possible to access the original version of the document at any time. Long-time archiving is another important aspect. If you are legally obligated to archive the signed document for a longer period of time, you must sign the documents with a new qualified digital signature prior to the expiration date of the usage period for the algorithms, or prior to the expiration of a five-year limit. The previous qualified digital signatures must be included in the new signatures, and therefore be preserved so that they cannot be alleged of being counterfeit should that occur at a later stage. A qualified timestamp is required for new qualified digital signatures to prevent them from being used and then predated to a time when the security value of the previous digital signature had decreased to such an extent that the creation of counterfeits was possible.

You don't have to generate the new digital signature and the qualified time stamp separately for each electronically signed document. Instead, the documents can be signed with one new digital signature.

If the signature process is not subject to any legal requirements, the signature or the signed document could be stored in a database table, an archive, or in a file. SAP NetWeaver provides SAP ArchiveLink, the SAP Archive Development Kit (ADK), and SAP Knowledge Warehouse (SAP KW) for archiving documents.

The standard version of SAP KW supports the use of a batch process to save data as of Release 8.0. A revision-proof storage of the data is supported. Because the required functions for process-controlled archiving are not yet available in the standard version, we won't discuss the archiving process for SAP KW here.

SAP ArchiveLink is a document management interface to external storage and archiving systems, as well as a service for SAP applications to store and retrieve documents in a revision-proof process according to different methods. The SAP ADK is a data-archiving subset used for archiving database tables. At this stage, it must be decided whether the signed data should be stored in a revision-proof form. Both SAP ArchiveLink and the SAP ADK can communicate with external storage systems such as an optical archive. If the data is not supposed to be archived as revision-proof, the SAP Content Server that is based on the database technology can be used as a storage system.

Both tools provide transactions for accessing the archive. The decision in favor of either the SAP ADK or SAP ArchiveLink depends on the type of signed data used. If the signed data is stored in a database table, the ADK must be used; otherwise (e.g., for PDF files, Word files, and so on), you can use SAP ArchiveLink.

27.3.5   Installing the SSF Functions

To be able to use the SSF functions, you must first install them. That is the case whenever a partner product is used on client computers that run WebGUI, and on the relevant SAP Web AS backend systems, which are also supposed to use the SSF functions. Because the installation procedure itself depends on the respective partner product used, we cannot discuss this process in detail here.

27.4   Technical Security

27.4.1   SSO for the WebGUI by Integration into the OS Authentication Process

You can also create a Single Sign-On (SSO) solution on the basis of the traditional WebGUI. To do that, you must use the SNC (*Secure Network Communication*) interface that is available in the WebGUI, or the *Generic Security Application Programming Interface* (GSS-API) that can be used to integrate external partner authentication methods (e.g., Windows NTLM or Kerberos). The partner products must be implemented in the WebGUI and in the SAP Web AS systems for which SSO is to be used. In that case, the authentication occurs outside of the SAP system, for example, in the Windows domain. The successful external authentication is then confirmed to the WebGUI via the interface and then forwarded to the connected SAP Web AS. The SAP Web AS trusts this external authentication through the SNC mechanism and performs a comparison between an external user ID, which is located on the operating system and has been forwarded by the WebGUI, and the SAP user ID stored in the system. If the user IDs are identical, a unique one-to-one relationship exists and the user can log on to the SAP Web AS. The assignments of external user IDs to SAP user IDs are stored in Table USREXTID, which must be maintained using Transaction SM30. However, this type of authentication is restricted to users of the Windows domain.

There are out-of-the-box solutions available for Windows NTLM and Kerberos. For this purpose, the two libraries *gssntlm.dll* and *gsskrb5.dll* are available. The exact installation and integration depend on the respective partner products and therefore cannot be discussed in greater detail here.

27.4.2   SSO for the WebGUI by Using Digital Certificates

It is also possible to integrate the WebGUI with certificate-based external authentication procedures. Compared to the external authentication in the operating system on the basis of a user ID and a password, this method is more secure, because it involves a powerful authentication process based on digital certificates (X.509).

But, this method requires the implementation of a process for managing person-specific certificates, which can only be attained by using a *public key infrastructure* (PKI). The reason for this is that each employee must be assigned a unique certificate, which must be withdrawn when an employee leaves the company. Moreover, it should be possible to call the certificate from any work center within the company, because usually the work centers aren't related to specific persons.

However, if they are, server-based certificate storage locations can be used. In this case, the certificate is imported to the relevant desktop PC, when a user logs on to the respective server using an additional PIN. Another alternative is the use of smart cards (for example, a company badge) for storing the certificates, which is currently one of the most secure and most convenient solutions.

To implement a certificate-based authentication through the WebGUI to a network of SAP Web AS systems that use SSO, you must integrate an external partner product via the SNC interface (GSS-API). The integration must be carried out for the WebGUI and for all SAP Web AS systems. The following list contains several partner products that can be used in this context: *SECUDE signon&secure* by iT Sec Swiss, *Entrust/PKI* by Entrust, *Kobil eSecure* by Kobil Systems, and *eTrust SSO* by Computer Associates. You can view the complete list at *http://service.sap.com/ security* (**Security Partners** link).

In the following sections, we'll briefly describe the most important steps involved in setting up an SSO solution based on the WebGUI with digital certificates:

1. In the first step, you must define a naming convention for the SNC name of the user (**Distinguished Name** in the X.509 certificate). Make sure the name is unique. It is advisable to adhere to the following convention with CN=Common Name with a unique use ID, OU=Organization Unit (e.g., department or division), O=Organization (name of the company), and C=Country (country in which the company is located). Example:

   CN=SMITH1,OU=SALES,O=SAMPLECOMPANY,C=US

2. Installation of the chosen partner product in all SAP Web AS systems that use SSO. Because this step depends on the partner product, we cannot discuss it further here.

3. Configuration of the important SNC parameters in the SAP Web AS systems. This includes the following parameters:

   ▶ **snc/enable**
   Activate SNC on the application server

   ▶ **snc/user_maint**
   Transaction SU01, maintain SNC name

   ▶ **snc/gssapi_lib**
   Path and file name of the shared GSS-API V2 library (the partner product library)

   ▶ **snc/identity/as**
   SNC name of the application server (SAP Web AS is also assigned an SNC according to the schema defined above.)

- ▶ `snc/data_protection/min`
  A minimum level of security is required for SNC connections (e.g., activation of strong authentication only, or additional activation of data privacy protection)

- ▶ `snc/accept_insecure_gui`
  Accept logon attempts by the WebGUI that are not protected by SNC on an SNC-protected application server.

- ▶ `snc/force_login_screen`
  Display logon screen for each SNC-protected logon.

4. Maintenance of the access control list (ACL) in each SAP Web AS system involved. This can be done using Transaction SU01, or directly in the maintenance of Table USRACL using Transaction SM30. The maintenance of the ACL ensures that each existing user in the SAP Web AS system, who is defined with a user ID, is assigned a corresponding SNC name (see Step 1). That way, a unique assignment is guaranteed. Only if this entry exists can an authentication be ultimately performed on the basis of the certificate name.

In general, the use of certificate-based SSO methods is recommended, even though it requires that a PKI be established first, as well as some additional implementation work. In the long run, it is a worthwhile investment because it eliminates the often-distributed identity management and the related high administration costs, while ensuring a much higher level of security. An authentication solution based on digital certificates is highly recommended, especially in this age of increasing integration of additional business partners and the growing importance placed on a secure management of your identities and access rights.

27.4.3 Restricting Access to an SAP Web AS Using SAProuter

The access to an SAP Web AS can be restricted for the WebGUI using SAProuter. The reason for this is to grant only specific WebGUI clients access to specific SAP applications on specific SAP Web AS systems (see also Chapter 25).

28 Web Browser

This chapter describes IT security concepts for the Global Security Positioning System (GSPS) component, web browser. It focuses on the description of a secure configuration of the web browser.

28.1 Introduction and Functions

The development of the *Hypertext Markup Language* (HTML), which is transferred between a client and a server using the standardized transfer protocol HTTP (*Hypertext Transfer Protocol*), laid the foundation for the triumphant success of the web browser as the standard frontend for the client application. The advanced development of the HTML language and the addition of other programming languages like Java, JavaScript, and so on, enabled the development of interactive client/server programs (and even multiple-layer applications with frontend, presentation layer, business logic layer, and data storage layer). The standardized frontend in the form of a *web browser* and the standardization of the protocols added further to the success of this technology, which was also supported by the Internet and the associated global network of servers.

SAP has recognized this trend as well and initially supported the technology with its SAP Internet Transaction Server (ITS) and SAP GUI for HTML (WebGUI). Since then, SAP has added many other programming technologies to its portfolio, such as Java Server Pages (JSPs), Business Server Pages (BSPs), and Web Dynpro for ABAP and Java that exclusively use the web browser as their frontend. The benefit of a web-browser-based frontend—which in SAP terminology is referred to as SAP GUI for HTML—is that it allows for a standardized use on the Internet. Moreover, the architecture no longer requires any software distribution mechanism that distributes the required client software to the relevant desktops. Another boost in efficiency for individual users comes with the option to bundle applications in SAP Enterprise Portal (SAP EP), which acts as a central point of entry.

And yet, the standardized and widely used implementation of this technology bears certain security risks that will be addressed in the following sections. In doing so, we'll describe the potential risks, independently of the type of web browser being used (Internet Explorer, Mozilla, Netscape Navigator, Firefox, Opera, and so on).

28.2   Risks and Controls

In this section, we'll use a simplified version of the proposed risk analysis methodology described in Chapter 2 to identify the main security risks and the necessary controls for the web browser (see Table 28.1). The controls are described in more detail in the subsequent sections and illustrated on the basis of examples.

No.	Classification	Description
1.	Risk potential	Missing protection against malware (malicious software or viruses). Inadequate anti-virus software is installed on the desktop PC, or is not updated on a regular basis.
	Impact	The missing protection, especially against Trojan horses and other malware, enables the unauthorized installation of such destructive programs on the desktop PC when downloading content from the Internet. This situation allows attackers to obtain information that can be used for additional exploits, for example, for performing unauthorized business transactions. Those unauthorized business transactions can result in high financial losses.
	Risk without controls	High
	Control(s)	Implementation and, above all, updating of the anti-virus software on the desktop PC.
	Risk with control(s)	Normal
	Section	28.4.1
2.	Risk potential	Lack of a personal firewall on the desktop PC. No personal firewall is installed on the desktop PC.
	Impact	Unauthorized attackers can exploit the open network protocols of the device (especially Netbios) to connect to the company network and access business data, especially when using mobile devices that use dial-up procedures, which are offered by telecommunications providers. Or they can use mobile devices to log the HTTP communication. That way, transactions that are activated through the web browser can be manipulated by unauthorized parties.
	Risk without controls	High
	Control(s)	Implementation of a personal firewall on the desktop PC to suppress accesses to the PC while being connected to public networks.

Table 28.1 Risks and Controls for the Web Browser

No.	Classification	Description
	Risk with control(s)	Normal
	Section	28.4.2
3.	Risk potential	The security settings in the web browser are too broad. The security settings (or security levels) in the web browser are too broad and enable the execution of malware on the desktop PC.
	Impact	Since the security settings in the web browser are not sufficiently restrictive, malware can be executed on the desktop PC. This can ultimately lead to an unauthorized execution of financial transactions.
	Risk without controls	High
	Control(s)	The security settings of the web browser must be more restrictive. The permission to execute ActiveX controls, in particular, should be regarded as very critical. The execution of Java applets and even JavaScript should also be permitted to signed versions. When encrypted HTTPS connections are established, the validity of the server certificate must be checked.
	Risk with control(s)	Normal
	Section	28.4.3

Table 28.1 Risks and Controls for the Web Browser (cont.)

28.3 Application Security

There is no specific authorization concept available for the web browser or SAP GUI for HTML. It can only be attained via the operating system and the use of access control lists (ACL).

28.4 Technical Security

28.4.1 Anti-Virus Software and Its Update for the Desktop PC

It's common knowledge that an anti-virus solution must be set up specifically for desktop PCs. And the best way to do that is to use a server-based solution that is automatically updated on a regular basis. Since many companies provide these types of solutions, we won't delve into further detail here regarding their implementation.

28.4.2 Using a Personal Firewall on the Desktop PC

Personal firewalls are less frequently used on desktop PCs than are anti-virus solutions. Such a firewall is referred to as a "personal" firewall, because it is installed on the desktop PC; in other words, it's installed on a user's personal device, instead of separating two server networking segments, which is what firewalls usually do.

The use of mobile devices to establish a connection to the company network through public networks, in particular, represents an increased danger for the laptop computer. The reason is that many services such as Netbios for mapping drives, and so on, are usually activated on the laptop computer and can be accessed from outside, that is, via the public network, if no firewall is in place. That way, an attacker could try to map the hard drive of the laptop computer and therefore gain access to data or install malware. The consequences of such an attack would, of course, be disastrous.

For this reason, a personal firewall should be set up in devices that frequently connect through public networks to the company LAN. The personal firewall should be configured in such a way that critical protocols like Netbios cannot be accessed from outside. FTP and Telnet connections should also be disabled. The best solutions are those that use a central server to configure the firewalls on the devices, which notify the central instance of critical events. The central reporting component can then react to critical events and adjust the firewall configuration. Internet Security Systems offers such a solution.

28.4.3 Security Settings for the Web Browser

Unfortunately, the security settings for the web browser always represent a compromise between the highest possible level of security and the program functionality. Today most applications use client-side active content (based on JavaScript, Java applets, and ActiveX controls), which is a security risk in itself, because it enables the execution of malware on the desktop PC through the web browser. Moreover, many software publishers, including SAP, haven't abandoned JavaScript functions entirely, since that would severely restrict the functionality of an application. That is also the reason why JavaScript cannot be deactivated. However, you should only permit those scripts that have been signed by the manufacturer. For all other scripts, you should ensure that the settings are made in such a way that the user is prompted to confirm the execution of the scripts.

The execution of ActiveX controls should be restricted to signed scripts only as ActiveX controls explicitly permit access to the operating system. The same holds true for .NET-relevant components, which should also be permitted only when they have been signed.

In addition, the system should always prompt a user to confirm the downloading of files or programs from the Internet. The security setting **Check for Revocation**, which verifies the validity of a certificate, should also be used to verify server certificates.

In general, you should ensure that you use the latest patch level of your web browser to make your web browser more secure and less vulnerable to potential attacks. The manufacturers of all known web browsers provide corresponding news sites on the web for this very purpose.

29 Mobile Devices

This chapter describes IT security concepts for the Global Security Positioning System (GSPS) component, mobile devices. The security of replicating applications and data are the primary considerations.

29.1 Introduction and Functions

The function of *mobile devices* has already been described in the context of SAP Mobile Infrastructure (SAP MI) (see Chapter 22). Mobile devices provide the user interface for the mobile user.

They represent a particularly high risk potential for the company, because business information is often stored locally on these devices, which are all too frequently stolen. Originally, most of the mobile devices were designed for private use, so it is still not uncommon to end up with devices that don't have authentication procedures.

For this reason, a comprehensive security concept must be designed and implemented specifically for mobile devices, because they can be used to access company resources directly through the Internet via virtual private network (VPN) connections, which is the case if SAP MI is used.

29.2 Risks and Controls

The methodology introduced in Chapter 2 for risk analysis will now be applied in a simpler form to the mobile devices to determine the primary, critical security risks and the required controls (see Table 29.1). The controls are described in more detail in the subsequent sections and illustrated on the basis of examples.

No.	Classification	Description
1.	**Risk potential**	Inadequate multiple-user concept.
		The multiple-user concept for the mobile device is inadequate. Applications that don't allow for a multiple-user concept, because an authorization control is impossible, are implemented on the mobile device.
	Impact	Other users of the mobile device can perform unauthorized backend transactions.
	Risk without controls	Extremely high

Table 29.1 Risks and Controls for Mobile Devices

No.	Classification	Description
	Control(s)	Only those applications that permit the required authorization control should be implemented on the mobile device.
	Risk with control(s)	Normal
	Section	29.3
2.	Risk potential	Lack of an authentication mechanism. Because simple mobile devices are often designed for private use, such as PDAs for instance, they seldom provide a means in which to authenticate a user.
	Impact	Other unauthorized users can use the mobile device without any prior authentication, and can therefore trigger unauthorized transactions in the connected backend applications or view confidential information that is stored on the device.
	Risk without controls	Extremely high
	Control(s)	Implementation of an authentication mechanism for the mobile device. The mechanism should be strong, that is, it could use biometrical or certificates-based processes (e.g., smart card).
	Risk with control(s)	Normal
	Section	29.4.1
3.	Risk potential	Unencrypted hard disk or storage medium. The hard disk or storage medium of the mobile device is unencrypted.
	Impact	In the event of theft or loss of the mobile device, the confidential business data stored on it can be viewed easily. Moreover, the stored passwords can be accessed by unauthorized persons who can use them for an unauthorized logon to the backend applications. This enables them to carry out unauthorized transactions.
	Risk without controls	Extremely high
	Control(s)	Implementation of an encryption process for the mobile device.
	Risk with control(s)	Normal
	Section	29.4.2
4.	Risk potential	No anti-virus protection. No anti-virus protection has been set up on the mobile device.
	Impact	Viruses can infect the mobile device when connecting to the Internet and thereby completely disable its functionality. All business data stored on the device can be destroyed. All data that hasn't been synchronized with the backend applications will be lost.

Table 29.1 Risks and Controls for Mobile Devices (cont.)

No.	Classification	Description
	Risk without controls	High
	Control(s)	Installation of an anti-virus software on the mobile device.
	Risk with control(s)	Normal
	Section	29.4.3
5.	Risk potential	Open connection ports. No personal firewall is installed for the mobile device that can be used to restrict the access to the SAP MI client at the protocol and port levels.
	Impact	The web server that is available in the SAP MI client can be addressed from outside. This enables unauthorized parties to browse through important directories. Passwords that are stored in local directories can also fall easily into the hands of unauthorized persons. The passwords can be used to launch an attack on the backend applications from another mobile device.
	Risk without controls	High
	Control(s)	Installation of a personal firewall on the mobile device to restrict external access to the device.
	Risk with control(s)	Normal
	Section	29.4.4
6.	Risk potential	Missing backup concept. The data on the mobile devices is not backed up on a regular basis.
	Impact	All business data that is stored on the mobile device and hasn't been synchronized with the backend applications will be lost. This can lead to inconsistencies in the datasets, for example, if goods receipts are incorrectly posted.
	Risk without controls	High
	Control(s)	Design and implementation of a backup concept for the mobile devices.
	Risk with control(s)	Normal
	Section	29.4.5
7.	Risk potential	Access rights for important system files are not restricted. The access rights for system files that contain password information are not restricted to authorized users or technical users.

Table 29.1 Risks and Controls for Mobile Devices (cont.)

No.	Classification	Description
	Impact	Passwords can be spied on. This enables unauthorized parties to log on to the backend applications. Unauthorized transactions can be triggered and confidential business information can be viewed.
	Risk without controls	High
	Control(s)	Restriction of access rights for important system files at the operating-system level.
	Risk with control(s)	Normal
	Section	29.4.6
8.	Risk potential	Users lack the awareness for security. The user of the mobile device lacks an adequate awareness for security and installs, for example, his or her own software, which has not been verified. Another example of users' lack of security awareness is their having an inadequate theft protection of the device, and so on.
	Impact	The mobile device and tha data that is stored on it can be compromised by unauthorized third parties.
	Risk without controls	Extremely high
	Control(s)	Implementation of a policy and training the user on the correct use of the mobile device.
	Risk with control(s)	Normal
	Section	29.4.7

Table 29.1 Risks and Controls for Mobile Devices (cont.)

29.3 Application Security

If mobile devices are used for mobile business scenarios on the basis of SAP MI, the distribution of mobile applications to the devices must be carried out exclusively via the SAP MI synchronization mechanism. Otherwise, the user can install mobile applications that don't allow for a multi-user concept—which includes an adequate authorization concept—or simply disturb the system stability of the mobile device. Applications that haven't been tested can create vulnerabilities, which can, in turn, be exploited by potential attackers.

For this reason, the operating system must be configured in such a way that a user cannot install any applications on the mobile device. The manufacturers of mobile devices provide different options to do that, but we won't describe them in detail here, as that would exceed the scope of this book.

29.4 Technical Security

29.4.1 Using Mobile Devices with Authentication Mechanism

When using mobile devices for business scenarios based on SAP MI, it is important that the devices provide authentication mechanisms. You should consider this feature when purchasing the devices.

There are many different authentication mechanisms available, so we'll only briefly describe the most common authentication mechanisms here:

► **User name and password**
This is the standard specifically for the use of mobile notebooks based on Windows operating systems.

► **Biometric fingerprint**
This type of authentication is used particularly for personal digital assistants (PDAs) from HP. They initialize the system that the user scans, for example, with his thumb, ensuring that he can only use the device if the PDA recognizes his thumbprint at the next system startup. However, the scanners that are currently being used are not yet sufficiently reliable, which makes the entire authentication mechanism rather unreliable.

► **Pictograms**
Instead of using typical passwords that consist of letters, numbers, and so on, the pictogram procedure uses small pictures that the user has to enter for authentication purposes. During the initialization procedure for this method, the user must memorize a small number of pictures (five pictures, for example), which he must later recognize when prompted to choose those five pictures from among a large number of randomly compiled pictures.

► **Signature**
PDAs that require the use of a stylus allow for an authentication based on signatures. In that case, the user must identify himself or herself with a signature prior to using the device.

► **Smart card**
In this case, users authenticate themselves via a smart card that stores a corresponding certificate. The device then checks the correctness of the certificate. This method is recommended, because it involves a "two-factor authentication" based on the following questions: "What does the user possess? (smart card)," and "What is the user's secret? (PIN)"

Since these mechanisms depend largely on the corresponding manufacturers, we cannot discuss them in greater detail here. It is essential that you check the reliability of the authentication mechanism prior to selecting a mobile device for a specific business scenario.

29.4.2 Implementing an Encryption Method for Storage Media

Because a large quantity of business data must be stored on a hard disk or other storage medium, particularly when using a mobile device based on SAP MI, we recommend that you implement an encryption mechanism for storing data in a persistence storage medium. Depending on the type of device, many third-party vendors provide corresponding options.

The following vendors provide cryptographic encryption methods for hard disks and storage media: Secude, Applian Technologies, Asynchrony.com, Certicom Corporation, Cranite Systems, Developer One, Inc., Handango, Inc., Pointsec Mobile Technologies, SoftWinter, Trust Digital LLC, and Utimaco Safeware AG.

29.4.3 Implementing Anti-Virus Protection

As you do with stationary PCs, you should also implement an anti-virus protection mechanism for mobile devices. Again, many third-party vendors provide the necessary anti-virus solutions even for small mobile devices. The most important of these vendors are Computer Associates, F-Secure, Handango, Inc., McAfee, SOFTWIN, and Symantec.

29.4.4 Installing a Personal Firewall

If possible, you should also set up a personal firewall on the mobile device, the reason being that a web server is required particularly for the SAP MI client, which is implemented on the mobile device. The web server is required to display the HTML pages for the mobile device and to establish the synchronization with the SAP MI server.

The web server is a Tomcat web server, which typically uses TCP/IP port 4444 to connect to the SAP MI server. Because the synchronization mechanism is always triggered by the mobile device, we suggest that you close all inbound ports, if the device is used exclusively for mobile purposes. Consequently, the only outbound port is then port 4444, which is used for synchronizing with the SAP MI server.

The *RealSecure Desktop Protector* by Internet Security Systems is a frequently used personal firewall solution.

29.4.5   Implementing a Backup Concept

As mobile devices are often exposed to severe environmental conditions, such as changing temperatures, transport shocks, and so on, the storage media can be damaged. For this reason, the data that is stored on mobile storage media must be backed up daily.

If the mobile device is used exclusively for mobile SAP applications, the backup occurs via the synchronization mechanism (*smart synchronization*) for business data with the SAP MI server. This type of synchronization can be automated using the `timed sync` parameter. Depending on the business scenario, the use of such an automated synchronization method is recommended. During the synchronization process, the required software-related components are also installed on the mobile device so that they don't need to be backed up in a separate procedure. The configuration of each mobile device is stored on the SAP MI server.

For all other business data that is stored on the mobile device, a separate backup concept provided by third parties must be established.

29.4.6   Setting Up Access Rights for Important System Files

The SAP MI client should be implemented on the mobile device as a service that runs under a specific technical user (typically SYSADM). Only this user should be granted access to the installation directory of the SAP MI client. All other users should be excluded by defining access control lists (ACLs).

29.4.7   Fostering a User's Security Awareness

A security policy should be established that clearly illustrates the critical security situation—inherent with mobile business processes—to each mobile device user. The policy should list the rules of conduct that must be applied when using mobile business applications.

In case of theft, it is vital that the responsible administrators be informed of the situation immediately, so that the synchronization access to the SAP MI server can be locked at once.

The Authors

Mario Linkies works as a consultant whose primary focus is IT security, in particular, providing comprehensive strategic consulting with regard to risk and control management, authorization concepts, change management, data protection, and legal compliance. Mario has over 15 years' experience in the areas of SAP and security. As the Director of the Security Department for both SAP Systems Integration (SAP SI) and SAP Global Focus Group Risk Management & IT Security at SAP Consulting, he provides internal SAP consulting services, supports national and international clients in different industries, and continuously fosters awareness for security topics in numerous initiatives. Mario is one of the initiators of the SAP Global Security Alliance.

After completing his financing and banking studies at Humboldt University in Berlin, Germany, he worked for Shell Chemicals Europe and Deloitte in Canada. Mario Linkies is married, has a daughter, Nomiko Taima, and resides in both Canada and Germany.

Dr. Frank Off is Assistant Director of SAP Global Focus Group Risk Management & IT Security at SAP Consulting. The focus group is a virtual global consulting group that sets the directives for best-practices solutions within the SAP consulting organization. His consulting activities focus on the definition and implementation of a comprehensive SAP security strategy. Dr. Off's responsibilities also include designing technical solutions for identity and access management and trust management, and finding secure authentication solutions based on SAP NetWeaver and partner products.

Prior to joining SAP Consulting Germany, he worked for several years as a management consultant for IT security management at Accenture GmbH in Kronberg/Taunus, Germany. Dr. Off holds a degree in aerospace technology at the University of Stuttgart, Germany. He received a doctor's degree in process engineering with a concentration on technically applied information sciences at the Swiss Federal Institute of Technology in Zurich, Switzerland. While holding his first job at DaimlerChrysler AG in Stuttgart, Germany, he finished his post-graduate studies in business administration. Dr. Off has been married for eight years, and has two children, ages four and one-and-a-half years old. His free time is rare and is therefore dedicated to his only true pursuit—spending time with his family.

Index

Migrating Your SAP Data

www.sap-press.com

Michael Willinger, Johann Gradl

Migrating Your SAP Data

This completely revised and updated edition of our bestseller is a comprehensive practical companion for ensuring rapid and cost-effective migration projects. It illustrates the basic principles of migration, discusses preparatory measures for a project, and shows you how to migrate your data using the methods offered by your SAP system economically, rapidly, and without the need for programming. The new edition is up-to-date for ECC 6.0 and provides you with the latest available information on eCATT and SAP Accelerated Data Migration. An ideal companion for administrators and technical consultants, this book also serves as a helpful resource for power users in specialized departments.

**The benchmark work
for release 4.0**

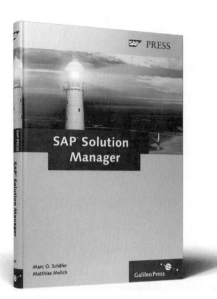

500 pp.,2006, 69,95 Euro / US$ 69,95
ISBN 978-1-59229-091-8

SAP Solution Manager

www.sap-press.com

M.O. Schäfer, M. Melich

SAP Solution Manager

This unique book helps administrators and IT
managers to quickly understand the full functionality
of SAP Solution Manager, release 4.0. Readers get a
thorough introduction in the areas of Implementation and Operations, especially in the scenarios
Project Management, Service Desk, Change Request
Management, and the brand new function
Diagnostics (root cause analysis).
The integration capabilities with third-party tools
from the areas of Help Desk and Modelling, as well
as the relation between the functionality and ITIL
Application Management are also dealt with in
detail.

**Revised new edition,
completely up-to-date
for SAP ERP 6.0**

**New functions and
technologies: Archive Routing,
Transaction TAANA, XML-based
archiving, and many more**

405 pp., 2. edition 2007, 69,95 Euro / US$ 69,95
ISBN 978-1-59229-116-8

Archiving Your SAP Data

www.sap-press.com

Helmut Stefani

Archiving Your SAP Data

This much anticipated, completely revised edition of our
bestseller is up-to-date for SAP ERP 6.0, and provides you
with valuable knowledge to master data archiving with SAP.
Fully updated, this new edition includes two all-new
chapters on XML-based data archiving and archiving in SAP
ERP HCM and contains detailed descriptions of all the new
functions and technologies such as Archive Routing and the
TAANA transaction. Readers uncover all the underlying
technologies and quickly familiarize themselves with all
activities of data archiving—archivability checks, the
archiving process, storage of archive files, and display of
archived data. The book focuses on the requirements of
system and database administrators as well as project
collaborators who are responsible for implementing data
archiving in an SAP customer project.

**Learn how to use
SAP NetWeaver MDM to
design, implement and
maintain your Enterprise Data
Management system**

**Discover master data basics
and explore SAP's powerful
MDM tools**

584 pp., 2008, 69,95 Euro / US$ 69.95
ISBN 978-1-59229-115-1

Enterprise Data Management with SAP NetWeaver MDM

www.sap-press.com

Andrew LeBlanc

Enterprise Data Management with SAP NetWeaver MDM

Build Foundations for Continual Improvements
with SAP MDM

Master data is your company's DNA, and effective
master data management demands extensive preparation. This book is the key to developing and
implementing your own comprehensive SAP MDM
strategy. Readers get all the essential prerequisites
for building a successful and sustainable MDM
strategy. Fully up-to-date for SAP MDM 5.5 SP04,
this comprehensive book contains all the resources
needed to set your own MDM strategy.

Input and output processing
basics, validation, BDoc modelling,
groupware integration, data
exchange, and more

Optimization measures for
queues, mass data processing,
distribution model, and
Replication & Realignment

407 pp., 2007, 69,95 Euro / US$ 69.95
ISBN 978-1-59229-121-2

SAP CRM Middleware Optimization Guide

www.sap-press.com

Juliane Bode, Stephan Golze, Thomas Schröder

SAP CRM Middleware Optimization Guide

This book, based on the experience of SAP Active Global Support, helps you proactively avoid problems with CRM Middleware — whether they be performance losses or even complete system freezes. You'll learn the basics of data processing in the Middleware (input processing— validation — output processing) and get concrete administration advice for troubleshooting. Plus, uncover a vast array of optimization options for all critical parts of the Middleware, as well as practical instruction on how to avoid performance bottlenecks and on how to handle those bottlenecks once they've occurred. Based on CRM Release 5.0, this book is also highly useful for the older Release 4.0. Wherever possible, the authors provide you with sneak previews on the upcoming release 6.0 as well.

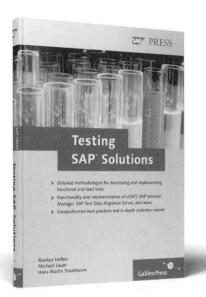

MDM technology, architecture, and solution landscape

Detailed technical description of all three usage scenarios

Includes highly-detailed, proven guidance from real-life customer examples

331 pp., 2007, 69,95 Euro / US$ 69,95
ISBN 978-1-59229-131-1

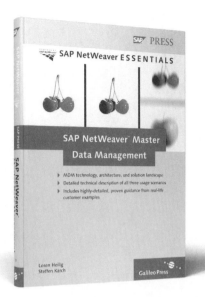

SAP NetWeaver
Master Data Management
www.sap-press.com

Loren Heilig, Steffen Karch, Oliver Böttcher, Christiane Hofmann, Roland Pfennig

SAP NetWeaver Master Data Management

This book provides system architects, administrators, and IT managers with a description of the structure and usage scenarios of SAP NetWeaver MDM. It uses three comprehensive real-life examples to give you practical insights into the consolidation, harmonization, and central management of master data. Plus, more than 120 pages are dedicated to an MDM compendium, complete with detailed information on individual components, data extraction, options for integration with SAP NetWeaver XI, SAP NetWeaver BI, and the SAP Portal (including user management), as well as on workflows and the Java API.

**Complete technical details
for upgrading to
SAP NetWeaver AS 7.00**

**In-depth coverage of all upgrade
tools and upgrade phases**

**Includes double-stack upgrades
and the combined upgrade &
Unicode conversion**

586 pp., 2007, 2. edition,
79,95 Euro / US$ 79,95
ISBN 978-1-59229-144-1

SAP NetWeaver Application Server Upgrade Guide

www.sap-press.com

Bert Vanstechelman, Mark Mergaerts, Dirk Matthys

SAP NetWeaver Application Server Upgrade Guide

This comprehensive guide covers the regular as well as the new »double-stack« upgrades. It describes a complete project, explains project management questions, provides technical background information (also on the upgrade of other systems like CRM, Portal, XI, and BI), and then walks you through the project steps — from A to Z.
The authors cover the entire process in detailed step-by-step instructions, plus how to plan the upgrade project and the impact on the system landscape during your SAP upgrade.

Understand the principles of administration and development

Gain insights on KM, collaboration, unification, application management, and the transport system

462 pp., 2008, 69,95 Euro / US$ 69.95
ISBN 978-1-59229-145-8

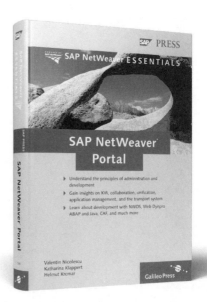

SAP NetWeaver Portal

www.sap-press.com

Valentin Nicolescu, Katharina Klappert, Helmut Krcmar

SAP NetWeaver Portal

This book introduces IT managers, portal administrators and consultants to the structure and application areas of SAP NetWeaver Portal (Release 7.0). A main focus is to describe key portal functions and the underlying architecture — all from the technical viewpoint. Topics covered include role management, authentication mechanisms, knowledge and content management, developing and administrating applications, application and system integration, as well as many more. Readers gain a solid technical grounding in all the relevant aspects of the SAP NetWeaver Portal, and the skills needed to effectively implement them in practice.